GORDON BROWN

Blind Eye to Murder

Klaus Barbie: Butcher of Lyons

The Paperclip Conspiracy

Maxwell: The Outsider

Red Web

Tiny Rowland: A Rebel Tycoon

Heroes of World War II

The Perfect English Spy: Sir Dick White

Maxwell: The Final Verdict

Blood Money: The Swiss, the Nazis and the Looted Billions

Nazi Gold

Branson

The Paymaster: Geoffrey Robinson, Maxwell and New Labour

Fayed: The Unauthorized Biography

Broken Dreams: Vanity, Greed and the Souring of British Football

GORDON BROWN

TOM BOWER

HarperCollins*Publishers*

HarperCollins*Publishers*
77–85 Fulham Palace Road,
Hammersmith, London W6 8JB
www.harpercollins.co.uk

Published by HarperCollins*Publishers* 2004

1

A catalogue record for this book is
available from the British Library

ISBN 0 00 717540 X

Set in Meridien by
Rowland Phototypesetting Ltd,
Bury St Edmunds, Suffolk

Printed and bound in Great Britain by
Clays Ltd, St Ives plc

To Sophie, with love

CONTENTS

ILLUSTRATIONS

Gordon Brown's father the Reverend John Brown, and his brothers John and Andrew. *(Wattie Cheung/Camera Press London)*

Brown during his student days at Edinburgh University. *(SCLP/Camera Press London)*

Princess Margarita of Romania.

Marion Caldwell. *(Big Pictures)*

Sheena McDonald. *(Mike Forster/Solo Syndication)*

Fife MPs at Carnegie Hall, Dunfermline, in 1987: Dick Douglas, Lewis Moonie, Gordon Brown and Henry McLeish. *(The Courier, Dundee © D.C. Thomson Co. Ltd)*

Neil Kinnock identified Brown very early as a future Labour leader, but Cherie Blair opposed his ambitions. *(Alisdair Macdonald/Mirrorpix)*

John Smith was a friend and colleague, but by 1992 Brown was disenchanted by his inflexibility. *(Daily Telegraph)*

Brown's partnership with Tony Blair suffered after the party supported Blair against him. *(Edward Webb/Independent)*

Brown with Mo Mowlam. *(Crispin Rodwell/Reuters)*

Brown and Peter Mandelson. *(Adam Butler/PA Photos)*

Brown's collaboration with Mandelson, Alastair Campbell and Blair transformed Labour into an extraordinary political success. *(Tom Stoddart/IPG/Katz Pictures)*

Geoffrey Robinson. *(Andrew Hasson/Camera Press London)*

Ed Balls, the 'deputy chancellor'. *(Peter Jordan/PA Photos)*

Brown's raffish spokesman Charlie Whelan. *(Michael Crabtree/PA Photos)*

Sue Nye and her husband Gavyn Davies. *(James Peltekian/ Solo Syndication)*

Cartoon by Charles Griffin. *(Centre for the Study of Cartoons and Caricature, University of Kent)*

Brown and Terry Burns, permanent secretary at the Treasury. *(Lucy Husband/PA Photos)*

Brown and Eddie George, governor of the Bank of England. *(Peter MacDiarmid/Reuters)*

Chris Smith. *(PA Photos)*

Robin Cook. *(Ian Hodgson/Reuters/Corbis)*

Brown with deputy leader John Prescott. *(Alisdair Macdonald/Mirrorpix)*

Nick Brown. *(John Stillwell/PA Photos)*

Brown insisted on the appointment of Harriet Harman as secretary of state for social security, with Frank Field as her deputy. *(Reuters)*

Tony Blair, Margaret Beckett and George Bain, chairman of the Low Pay Commission. *(Paul Hackett/Reuters/PA Photos)*

After considerable pressure, Brown finally agreed to a staged photograph with Sarah Macaulay on 15 March 1998, five years after their first date. *(Chris Ball/News of the World/NI Syndication)*

The next day, just before presenting his budget, Brown was photographed at the birthday party of Sue Nye's son. *(Adam Butler/PA Photos)*

In July 1998, after successfully resisting Blair's attempt to dismiss Geoffrey Robinson, Brown posed for a photo with Stephen Byers, Patricia Hewitt, Dawn Primarolo and Robinson. *(Neil Munns/PA Photos)*

Following Peter Mandelson's appointment as trade and industry secretary, Brown posed with Alistair Darling,

Mandelson and Byers to suggest the restoration of relations. *(Adam Butler/PA Photos)*

Increasingly, Brown relied on Sarah Macaulay to manage his domestic life. *(Ian Waldie/Reuters/Corbis)*

Newly-married Ed Balls and Yvette Cooper in Eastbourne. *(Andrew Hasson/Camera Press London)*

Brown with David Blunkett, Robin Cook, Margaret Beckett and Frank Dobson during the 1997 election campaign. *(Matthew Polak/Corbis)*

Shriti Vadera, Brown's transport adviser. *(Alex Lentati/Solo Syndication)*

Sir Alastair Morton, the first executive chairman of the Strategic Rail Authority. *(Neil Munns/PA Photos)*

Derek Wanless, appointed to investigate the NHS. *(Johnny Green/PA Photos)*

Labour's 2001 election campaign was marred by poor relations between Brown and Blair. *(Sean Dempsey/PA Photos)*

Gordon and Sarah Brown's wedding on 3 August 2000 was, until the last moment, a closely guarded secret, and then became a media event. *(George Wilkie/Rex Features)*

The birth of the Browns' first child Jennifer ended in tragedy in January 2002. *(ROTA/Camera Press London)*

Gordon and Sarah Brown with their son John in October 2003. *(Jeremy Stockton/Getty Images)*

Brown and Richard Branson. *(Chris Young/PA Photos)*

Charles Clarke. *(Chris Young/PA Photos)*

John Reid. *(Matthew Fearn/PA Photos)*

Peter Hain. *(Chris Young/PA Photos)*

Tony Blair's rousing speech at the 2003 Labour party conference received rapturous applause – except from Brown. *(Russell Boyce/Reuters/Corbis)*

Cartoon by Ken Mahood. *(Solo Syndication)*

Gordon Brown presents his seventh budget on 17 March 2004. *(Stefan Rousseau/PA Photos)*

INTRODUCTION

Their laughter was raucous. Seated in the Club section of the British Airways aircraft, the ten men were bonded by their love of football and their anticipation of a laddish weekend in Rome. Five months after the general election, the new Chancellor of the Exchequer was laughing with his intimate gang. There was much to celebrate.

On Saturday, 11 October 1997, England was playing Italy in a qualifying match for the World Cup. The valuable tickets for the game had been obtained for the group by Geoffrey Robinson, the paymaster general, as a favour to Gordon Brown, who was seated in the front of the jet. The prospect of football, beer and banter in Rome appealed to the former schoolboy footballer. The game was a male's world, an emotionally satisfying conclave excluding women. The weekend would also be an opportunity to develop relationships with journalists, whose sympathetic reports about his successes would enhance his reputation and help his dream to become Britain's prime minister. Brown, the host of many noisy parties during and after his student days in Edinburgh, enjoyed the mixture of politics and sport.

The invitations to the journalists had been issued by Charlie Whelan, the chancellor's sparky press spokesman, who was seated near Brown. Over the previous years Whelan had regularly offered friendly journalists tickets to special football matches and issued invitations to memorable parties before

international fixtures in Robinson's flat at the Grosvenor
House Hotel in Park Lane. 'Oh, Geoffrey,' quipped Brown as
they flew over Tuscany, 'your villa is down there. We should
have a campaign: one villa one vote.' The reference to the
villa controversially loaned to Tony Blair and his family during
the summer triggered more laughter. Brown had been in good
form ever since they assembled at Heathrow. 'What's the difference,' he had asked as they waited for the plane, 'between
Jim Farry [the chief executive of the Scottish Football Associ-
ation] and Saddam Hussein? One is an evil dictator who will
stop at nothing, and the other is the leader of Iraq.' The banter
was joined by Ed Balls, the chancellor's personable and intelligent adviser, and the fourth of the quartet – Brown, Robinson,
Balls and Whelan. Balls's eminence in the Treasury was
resented only by the envious and the defeated. The thirty-
year-old was the intellectual guide of the chancellor's conversion from a traditional socialist to the mastermind of New
Labour's appeal to the middle classes. Since Labour's landslide
victory Balls had become guru, gatekeeper and 'deputy chancellor' in the Treasury.

The four had unashamedly fashioned their capture of the
Treasury as storm troopers assailing a conservative bastion,
revolutionaries expelling the old guard. Over more than a
decade Gordon Brown had plotted and agonised to achieve
that coup. Disputes and distress had marred the route to
11 Downing Street, and five months after his victory the new,
unconventional inhabitants of Whitehall incited malicious
gossip about the introduction of bull market tactics into
Westminster politics, prompting Blairites to accuse Brown of
behaving like a Mafia godfather, an accusation he resented.

The only unease among the six journalists was caused by
their Club class tickets, each costing £742. Geoffrey Robinson
had privately settled the account, leaving a suspicion that the
journalists would not be pressed to repay. His guests briefly

considered the millionaire's motives. Robinson's ebullience made the trip feel like one of those louche jamborees organised by public relations companies for anxious clients. His fortune, earned in suspicious circumstances and concealed in offshore banks, had financed Brown's private office before the election. For any politician to be associated with Robinson provoked questions. The journalists judged that the chancellor was not suspicious about the motives of their host, whose generosity had relieved the Scotsman's social isolation in London. Nevertheless, before the jet landed, some resolved that regardless of Charlie Whelan's inevitable scoffs, their fares would be reimbursed, with a request for a receipt.

The laughter halted. Gordon Brown, dressed in his customary dark suit, white shirt and red tie, fumed, 'Do you know they've sold the Scotland match against Latvia to Channel 5, and only half of Scotland has Channel 5?' The admirer of Jock Stein had travelled to see Scotland play in Spain during the 1982 World Cup, and was dogged by a grievance about the day's other qualifying match. The gripe erupted again after the landing at Rome airport.

The privileges of political office had been snatched by the chancellor's party. On the instructions of Sir Thomas Richardson, the British ambassador, the embassy's economic secretary, Rob Fenn, welcomed the group at the airport. But rather than drive direct to the embassy, Brown asked Fenn whether he knew anyone in Rome who subscribed to Channel 5. 'I've got to see the Scotland–Latvia match,' he said. After frantic telephone calls, Peter Waterworth, a first secretary, was unearthed. 'His mother gave him a Sky subscription for his birthday,' reported Fenn with relief. 'Channel 5 comes with the card.' 'Well done,' gushed Brown. Robinson beamed. A brief diplomatic chore over lunchtime had been arranged with Carlo Azeglio Chamoi, the Italian finance minister, to justify the trip. After that, the pleasure could start.

'Latvia, we love you,' chanted a group of England fans, spotting Brown step from the ambassador's car in the centre of Rome. Brown smiled back. Public recognition elated the congenitally clandestine bachelor. Football's tribalism was a bond, and he assumed that Waterworth, a Manchester United fan from Belfast, would welcome a Scottish fan in his living room. 'Hello, I'm Gordon Brown,' smiled the chancellor as Cathy Waterworth opened the door. 'I'm so grateful that you'll have us,' he said, leading thirteen people into the flat before his putative hosts could have second thoughts. Geoffrey Robinson immediately assumed the role of waiter, ferrying bottles of Peroni beer from the fridge at the far end of the flat to the chancellor, already hunched up close to the television, revealing the handicap of his single eye. Preoccupied, Brown uttered only a few comments throughout the match. At half-time he disappeared to be interviewed by a journalist for Monday's newspaper. Robinson used the opportunity to look at Waterworth's oil paintings. 'My father's the artist,' explained the host. 'Would you me sell that one?' asked the paymaster general. The doorbell rang. A journalist returned with a bunch of flowers for Cathy. When the second half started, Robinson resumed his duties as waiter, and as Scotland's 2–0 victory seemed assured, the atmosphere became light-hearted. 'Great,' announced Brown at the end. After more jokes, he bade farewell. He looked forward to the live match later that night.

The next stop was the British embassy. 'I wonder how much we'd get if we flogged this lot,' chortled Whelan in his south London accent as they walked into the marbled, ornately furnished building. The chancellor smiled at the joke directed at Robin Cook, the foreign secretary, one of Labour's tribe whom Brown, during his fraught journey up the party's hierarchy, had grown to loathe. They were joined by Stuart Higgins, the editor of the *Sun*, Tony Banks, the minister for sport, and Jack Cunningham, the minister of agriculture.

Neither of the politicians was a 'Brownite', and their politeness towards the chancellor was noticeably diplomatic. Standing in the corner was Sir Nigel Wicks, the Treasury's second
permanent secretary. 'Are you going to the match?' Wicks
was asked. 'No,' he replied hesitantly. 'Why?' 'Prudence.'
'What?' 'I'm here on business, and I would not want my
presence in Rome to be misinterpreted.' The Treasury, some
speculated, had contrived the visit to the Italian finance minister as a fig leaf to justify the junket. The final guest, the genial
former Manchester United star Bobby Charlton, was uniquely
guaranteed Brown's affection.

Relationships were important to Gordon Brown. His un-
swerving loyalty to family and friends had marked him as a
clan chieftain. The admiration and love he attracted was contrasted with his ferocious hatred of others. 'Peter Mandelson is
in Rome,' the ambassador told Brown while the champagne
was poured. 'But he returned to London rather than watch
the match.' The chancellor's relief was unconcealed. His
fraught relationship with his former friend was a source of
widespread gossip.

The brief visit to the embassy mirrored the conflicts of interest, personalities and policies swirling around every nuance
of the chancellor's hectic life. Just as renowned as his intelligence, education and shrewdness were his vendettas. 'Never
hate your enemies,' said Michael Corleone, the son of Mario
Puzo's Godfather. 'It affects your judgement.' Gordon Brown
ignored that advice, but did embrace Corleone's confession
to his lawyer: 'I don't feel I have to wipe everybody out, Tom.
Just my enemies.' Surrounded by his intimates, the Godfather
expected loyalty and obedience towards himself. Those who
thwarted his ambitions were despised and occasionally
destroyed. His justification was faultless: his beloved party and
his ambition required submission to his agenda. In return for
his trust, his 'family' honoured his requirements.

Driving in a minibus from the embassy past the Colosseum, the home of bloody gladiatorial contests, towards Rome's Olympic stadium for the football match, the chancellor might have reflected upon the ancient building's symbolism. Two thousand years earlier, only the fittest survived, and even at the moment of glory, the bloodied victor could be ravaged by the spectators' dissatisfaction. His party's antics back home resembled ancient Rome's lack of generosity. The pernicious undercurrents in Westminster often turned friend into foe. Over the years, Gordon Brown had accumulated many enemies. To win the ultimate prize required a new strategy. Inviting the journalists to Rome was another step to win favour for his inheritance of the premiership.

At the stadium, Brown was seated with Carlo Azeglio Chamoi. The match was enjoyable but by the end at 10.45 p.m., both were disappointed by the goalless draw. Gazing down from the directors' box, Brown watched as Italy's supporters and some of the 16,000 England fans began fighting. With drawn batons the police were charging the Britons. Patiently, Brown waited for two hours in the minibus until the six journalists could leave the stadium. Robinson had fretted that his reservation at Harry's Bar for a lobster and champagne dinner would be cancelled, but the famous restaurant loyally waited for the party, as did the soprano hired to sing for them. The bill for the enjoyable dinner was paid by Robinson.

After the group's return to London, the trip attracted some curiosity. For a time the presence of the journalists with the chancellor was suppressed by some newspapers, and when, seven weeks later, Geoffrey Robinson became embroiled in a scandal about his financial dependence on an offshore tax haven, some of those journalists who had accepted his hospitality were inclined to vouch for his probity. Consumed by self-righteousness, Gordon Brown disparaged those criticising his paymaster, and steadfastly resisted any public admission of Robinson's wrongdoing. Concessions, he knew, signalled weakness. Thanks to Brown's support, Robinson would survive the first accusations of sleaze. But the lifebelt caused many to puzzle about the chancellor's psychology. His defiance was forged, some suggested, during his Scottish childhood in order to camouflage his spiritual torment. Others speculated why one character simultaneously aroused extremes of sympathy and outrage. Gordon Brown himself volunteered few clues. Incapable of self-analysis, he zealously sought to prevent outsiders from penetrating the origins of and reasons for his emotions. An unmentioned spirituality certainly lurked among the foundations of his life. The possibility of entering the priesthood had never featured among his ambitions, yet the conflict between good and evil had dominated his formative years. The mystery was his journey from his childhood credo of God and love to the less forgiving characteristics that would dominate his adulthood. His ostensible compassion for humanity confused the search for clues about that transition yet bequeathed the riddle: Gordon Brown, saint or sinner?

ONE

Ghosts and Dreams

The stench of linseed oil and coal drifting up the hill obliterated the salty odour of the cold sea waves crashing just four
hundred yards from his family's large stone house. Two linoleum factories were part of Kirkcaldy's lifeblood, just as the
small town's financial survival relied upon the local coalmines. Both were dying industries, threatening new unemployment in the neighbourhood. The men of Fife profess
to be self-contained, but are vulnerable to their environment.
Kirkcaldy's stench, grime and decay shaped Gordon Brown's
attitude towards the world.

Kirkcaldy in the 1950s could have been a thousand miles
from Edinburgh, although the elegant capital lay just across
the Firth of Forth. Gordon Brown's home town was shabby,
and the townspeople were not a particularly united community. John Brown, his father, the minister at St Brycedale
Presbyterian church, struggled unsuccessfully to retain his
congregation. Some had permanently renounced the Church,
while others had moved to the suburbs, abandoning the less
fortunate in the town. Outsiders would have discovered nothing exceptional about John Brown's ministry in Kirkcaldy's
largest church. His status was principally attractive to those
at the bottom of the heap, who called regularly at Brown's
rectory – or manse – for help. The preacher of the virtues of

1

charity was willing to feed the hungry, give money to those
pleading poverty, and tend the sick. Some would smile that
John Brown was an unworldly soft touch, giving to the undeserving, but his generosity contrasted favourably with Fife's
local leaders. There was little to commend about the council-
lors' failure to build an adequate sea wall to protect the town
from the spring tides of 1957 and 1958. During the floods,
young Gordon Brown helped his father and his two brothers
distribute blankets and food to the victims, proud that his
father became renowned as a dedicated, social priest. 'Father,'
he later said, 'was a generous person and made us aware of
poverty and illness.' The dozens of regular callers at the house
pleading for help persuaded Brown of the virtues of Christian
socialism, meaning service to the community and helping
people realise their potential. Living in a manse, he related,
'You find out quickly about life and death and the meaning
of poverty, injustice and unemployment.' The result was a
schoolboy bursting to assuage his moral indignation.

Friends and critics of Gordon Brown still seek to explain the
brooding, passionate and perplexing politician by the phrase 'a
son of the manse'. To non-believers, unaware of daily life in
a Scottish priest's home, the five words are practically meaningless. Only an eyewitness to the infusion of Scotland's culture by Presbyterianism's uncompromising righteousness
can understand the mystery of the faith. Life in the manse
bequeathed an osmotic understanding of the Bible. Under his
father's aegis, Gordon Brown mastered intellectual discipline
and a critique of conventional beliefs. In a Presbyterian house-
hold, the term 'morality' was dismissed as an English concept,
shunned in favour of emphasising 'right' and 'wrong'. Even
the expression 'socialism' was rejected in favour of 'egalitarianism'. At its purest, Presbyterianism is a questioning
tradition, encouraging a lack of certainty, with a consequent
insecurity among true believers brought up to believe in

perpetual self-improvement. 'Lord, I believe,' is the pertinent prayer. 'Help Thou my unbelief.' Moulded by his father's creed, not least because he admired and loved the modest man, the young Gordon Brown was taught to be respectful towards strangers. 'My father was,' he recalled, 'more of a social Christian than a fundamentalist ... I was very impressed with my father. First, for speaking without notes in front of so many people in that vast church. But mostly, I have learned a great deal from what my father managed to do for other people. He taught me to treat everyone equally and that is something I have not forgotten.'

In his sermons, quoting not only the scriptures but also poets, politicians and Greek and Latin philosophers, the Reverend John Brown urged 'the importance of the inner world – what kind of world have we chosen for our inner self? Does it live in the midst of the noblest thoughts and aspirations?' He cautioned his congregation and sons against 'those who hasten across the sea to change their sky but not their mind'. Happiness, he preached, is not a matter of miles but of mental attitude, not of distance but of direction. 'The question which each of us must ask, if we are not as happy as we would wish to be, is this: Are we making the most of the opportunities that are ours?' The young Gordon Brown was urged to understand the challenge to improve his own destiny. 'So let us not trifle,' preached his father, condemning wasted time and opportunities, 'because we think we have plenty of time ahead of us. We do not know what time we have. We cannot be sure about the length of life ... Therefore use your time wisely. Live as those who are answerable for every moment and every hour.'

John Brown's ancestry was as modest as his lifestyle. In the eighteenth and nineteenth centuries the Browns were tenant farmers, first at Inchgall Mill near Dunfermline, and later at Brigghills farm near Lochgelly, in the midst of the Fife coalfields. Ebenezer Brown, Gordon Brown's grandfather, the fourth of eight children, became a farmer at Peatieshill in New Gilston, and on 26 October 1914 Gordon's father was born in the farmhouse. Eventually Ebenezer gave up farming and became a shepherd, encouraging his only child to excel at school and to break out of the mould. At eighteen, John Brown's efforts were rewarded by a place at St Andrews University to read divinity. After graduating in 1935, he studied for an MA in theology until 1938. Unfit for military service, he spent the war as a minister in the Govan area, along the Clyde, living among the slums and destitution of the factory and shipyard workers. Only the heartless could emerge from that poverty without some anger about society's inequalities.

Soon after the war John Brown met Jessie Elizabeth Souter, the daughter of a builder and ironmonger in Insch, west Aberdeenshire. She was four years younger than him. Until 1940 Jessie had worked for the family business. She then joined the WRAF, working first on the Isle of Man and then in Whitehall. They married in Govan in July 1947. Their first child, John, was born in 1948. James Gordon, their second son, was born in Glasgow on 20 February 1951. Three years later John Brown was appointed the minister at the St Brycedale church. Kirkcaldy was then an unknown backwater, except to historians. In the eighteenth century Adam Smith, arguably one of the world's greatest economists and the architect of free trade, the foundation of Britain's prosperity, lived in the town. A monument to the enemy of socialism was erected exactly opposite St Brycedale church. The juxtaposition was pertinent to Gordon Brown's life. Not until forty years after his birth did he begin to sympathise with his fellow townsman's philosophy. By then his reputation as an irascible intellectual was frustrating his ambitions. His inner conflict, pitting his quest for power against his scholarship, his mastery of machine politics in conflict with the protection of his privacy, had been infused by the influence of his beloved father.

'Ill pairted', the principal doctrine bequeathed by the tee-total father to his sons in the manse, condemned the unfair distribution of wealth in the world and stirred up his family's obligation to seek greater equality, not least by good works and charity. The collapse of the textile and coal industries, casting hundreds in the town onto the dole, imbued a gut distaste for capitalist society in Gordon Brown, not least because his father taught that work was a moral duty. 'Being brought up as the son of a minister,' he recalled, 'made me aware of community responsibilities that any decent society ought to accept. And strong communities remain the essential bedrock for individual prosperity.' Unspoken was the Scottish belief in superiority over the English, and the Presbyterian's sense of pre-eminent differences with Anglicans – both compensations for surviving as a minority.

Helped by Elizabeth Brown's inheritance of some small legacies, the Browns were middle class. Their financial advantages over the local miners and factory workers spurred the father to encourage his children to conduct their lives with a sense of mission, duty and benign austerity. Any personal ambition was to be concealed, because the individual, in John Brown's world, was of little interest, and personal glory was, history showed, short-lived. Rather than bask in the prestige accorded to his office, he preached that his children should be more concerned by the legacy they bequeathed to society. The son of the manse was expected to suppress his ego. That exhortation, repeated constantly throughout his childhood (he attended his father's church twice on Sundays), imposed upon Gordon Brown a lifelong obligation to answer to his father's ghost.

Any austerity was, however, tempered by love. Elizabeth Brown was not as strong an influence as her husband, but

she was a true friend. 'She was always supportive,' Brown
insisted, 'even when I made mistakes.' At the age of thirty-
seven, he was to say: 'I don't think either of my parents
pushed me. It was a very free and open family. There were
no huge pressures.' His comment was either self-delusion or
obfuscation. Quite emphatically, from his youngest years,
Brown was under exceptional pressure to excel, and infused
with an obsession to work hard, to disappoint no one and to
win. 'What is started, must be finished,' was a constant par-
ental admonition to the Brown brothers. Failure was inconceivable. From the pulpit the Reverend John Brown preached
that many of the young 'are failing to think life through and
are living carelessly and irresponsibly'. They forgot, he said,
that regardless of any remarkable achievements on earth,
'after death we must appear before the judgement seat of
Christ'. He admonished 'the multitudes' who gave 'little
thought of accountability for their conduct and way of life'.
Gordon Brown was warned about a day of reckoning: 'With
many, judgement begins and ends with themselves and they
reckon not on any judgement from elsewhere. Such live to
please themselves and not to please others, even God.' John
Brown urged his congregation to look forward to His com-
mendation: 'Well done, good and faithful servant, enter into
the joy of thy Lord.'

Gordon Brown's blessing, or possibly misfortune, was his
stardom. From his earliest years he was praised as outstanding,
destined to outclass his contemporaries. Like all Scots children, he was embraced by the country's excellent system
of state education. At Kirkcaldy West, a primary school close
to the linoleum factory, he was taught the three 'R's by
repetition, writing with pencils on slate boards, with a wet
rag to wipe off his daily work. He devoured books and, thanks
to an aunt, a music teacher, appreciated classic literature.
The teachers instantly recognised his unusual intelligence,

reporting that he was a year ahead of other pupils in maths and reading, as was one other boy, Murray Elder, who would remain his friend in Scottish Labour politics and Westminster until the present day. At the age of ten, Brown and Elder were enrolled at Kirkcaldy High School, the town's grammar school, in an educational experiment to fast-stream the town's brightest schoolchildren by intensive learning.

The High School was a genuine social mixture. The children of dustmen, miners and millionaires were educated together, ignoring their social differences. But the searing recollections of the parents of the poorer children about the days before the creation of the NHS made a lasting impression on Brown. Their elders spoke of the poor abandoning treatment in hospitals when their money was spent, and asking doctors about the cost of visits and medicine before deciding whether their finances were adequate for them to receive treatment.

Ferociously clever, although not the cleverest in the class, Brown never appeared as a swot. Rather he was known as 'gregarious and jolly', and the quickest to provoke laughter with a snappy, funny line. 'The banter and wisecracking that would go on between the boys was great,' recalled a former class friend. Brown's passion was sport. He excelled at tennis, rowing, sprinting, rugby and especially football. Around the time he heard the radio commentary of Scotland's 9–3 humiliation by England in 1961, he resolved to become a professional footballer. On Saturdays, he was seen at the ground of Raith Rovers, the local football team, selling programmes with John, his elder brother, to earn pocket money before cheering the local side. Combining work and pleasure was his father's doctrine. The most notable result was the newspaper Gordon produced in his pre-teens with his brother and sold for charity. John was the editor while Gordon wrote the sports reports, and later added commentaries about domestic politics. In successive weeks in 1964 he welcomed Harold Wilson's

election, interviewed an American space pioneer, described
the persecution of Jews and supported Israel's existence, and
explained the background to crises in the Middle East and
Southern Rhodesia. Justifying the new state of Israel was a
particular theme encouraged by his father. Brown revealed
himself not as precocious, but as a sensible and informed
youth. His love of history and politics was partially influenced
by 'Tammy' Dunn, the school's left-wing history teacher,
although his historical hero in the fourth form was Robert Peel,
the nineteenth-century Tory prime minister praised for placing
principle before party. In a competition organised by the Scottish *Daily Express* to write an essay anticipating Britain in the
year 2000, Brown won a £200 prize. He predicted that Scotland's inequalities would eventually be removed: 'The inheritance of a respect for every individual's freedom and identity,'
he wrote, 'and the age-long quality of caring, both transmitted
through our national religion, law and educational system
and evident in the lives of countless generations of our people,
makes Scotland ideal for pioneering the society which tran-
scends political systems.' Forty years later he remained faithful
to what he called those 'absolutely basic' visions and values.

In 1963 Brown witnessed real politics for the first time.
Aged eleven, he followed the election campaign in Kinross
and Perthshire of Sir Alec Douglas-Home, the prime minister.
Ill-health had forced Harold Macmillan to resign, and his successor Earl Home had revoked his peerage to lead the Conservatives in the House of Commons. After a day following the
politician across the constituency, the impression of a politician
making the same speech at every venue, recalled Brown, was
'awful'. He was particularly struck by Home's response to a
question of whether he would buy a house in the constituency. No, replied Home, he owned too many houses already.

At fourteen Brown took his 'O' levels, and under the fast-
track experiment was scheduled one year later to take five

Highers, a near equivalent of 'A' levels. He was a year ahead
of his age group. His reputation was of an outstanding student
and sportsman, particularly a footballer, whose conversation,
magnetising his class friends, made him the centre of attention. Despite his popularity in the mixed school, he stood back
from the girls. At the popular dances organised by his older
brother in the church hall, Gordon did not bop, and disliked
the waltz and quick-step lessons. No one recalled him ever
speaking about girls. Even during a hilarious school trip to
Gothenburg, his behaviour was impeccable. Some believed
that the arrival every week of his father as school chaplain to
preach to the children inhibited him. As predicted, at fifteen,
he scored top marks in his Highers and qualified for university.
He had survived the intensity of the 'E' experiment, but was
troubled by the casualties among other 'guinea pigs' who,
having collapsed under the pressure, were depressed by having failed to gain a place at university and being deprived of
an opportunity to try again. Sensitive to the raw inequalities
of life, uncushioned in Scotland's bleak heartlands, he sought
a philosophy which promised change.

At that age most teenagers rebel against their parents'
values, but Brown, inspired by his close family life, accepted
his father's traditionalist recipe for reform. In their unequivo-
cal judgements of society, the Presbyterians' solution was to
empower the state to castigate the rich and to help the poor.
In Kirkcaldy, Adam Smith's philosophy for curing society's ills
by self-reliance and free enterprise was heresy. The socialist
paradise promised by Harold Wilson, embracing the 'white
heat of technology', redistribution of wealth and economic
planning, was Gordon Brown's ideal.

One irony of Brown's registration at Edinburgh University
in 1967 to read history would have been lost on the sixteen-
year-old. The university was a bastion of privilege, isolated
from Scotland's class-ridden society. Dressed in a tweed jacket,

grey flannels, white shirt and tie, Brown arrived with Kenn
McLeod and other working-class achievers from Kirkcaldy
High. While McLeod and the sons of miners and factory
workers had neither the money nor the background to
become involved in the horseplay of student life, Brown was
introduced to the power brokers by his elder brother John.

'This is my brother Gordon,' John told Jonathan Wills, the
editor of the student newspaper. 'He's sixteen and wants to
work here. He's boring but very clever.' Brown was in heaven.
The student newspaper was a cauldron of the university's
political and social activity. Within the editorial rooms he
could witness heated debate and crude power-broking.
Inspired by the worldwide student revolt then taking place,
Jonathan Wills had begun a campaign to become the university's first student rector. Free of the inhibitions imposed by his
small home town, Brown indulged himself amid like-minded
social equals. The liberation and the dream were short-lived.

Six months earlier, during a rugby match between the
school and the old boys, he had emerged from the bottom of
a scrum suffering impaired vision. Instinctively private, he did
not complain or visit a doctor. The problem did not disappear.
In a football match during the first weeks at university he
headed the ball and his sight worsened. This time he consulted
a doctor, who identified detached retinas in both eyes. The
six-month delay in treatment had increased the damage, and
there was a danger of blindness in the right eye. In the first
of four operations over two years at the Edinburgh Royal
Infirmary, surgeons sought to reattach the retinas. Brown was
ordered to lie immobile for six months in a dark hospital ward,
knowing that among the drastic consequences was the certain
end of his ambition to become a professional footballer. Whatever the outcome of the operation, playing contact sports
would be forbidden. During those months of darkness, with
the combination of loneliness and fear described by him as 'a

living torture', unable to read and hoping that he would not be permanently blind, Brown's psychology changed. Sensitive to his plight and preoccupied by his ambitions, he became impatient with life's trivialities, and resolved in future not to waste time or to suffer fools. 'I felt such a fraud,' he later said, 'lying in bed for hours on end when there was nothing wrong with me except that I couldn't see.' Irritated by medicine's limitations, his infirmity became a blow to his self-confidence, compounding the insecurity which would bedevil his life and inspire reconsideration of his faith. In a later interview, Brown mentioned his trepidation about the predestination preached by Calvinists. 'The idea that it doesn't matter what you do, that you could be predetermined for damnation' was unappealing, he explained. He disliked the concept of 'no credit for human endeavour since all decisions are made by God. It's a very black religion in that sense.' By contrast, his teetotal father's practice of good works and charity was infinitely preferable; but doubts had also arisen about that. The Presbyterian ethic – that the afterlife was not so attractive – was also unappealing. Rather than embracing religion as support for his torment, his certainty about God and the scriptures had weakened. Neither in public nor in private would he ever express thanks to God or refer to Christianity as an influence, guide or support for his life.

He rejected the paraphrase of a poem often recited by John Brown at the sickbed:

> He gives the conquest to the weak,
> Supports the fainting heart,
> And courage in the evil hour
> His heavenly aids impart.

Rather, he was influenced by a pertinent sermon of his father's summarising the lesson of anguish and salvation:

'Blindness is surely one of life's sorest handicaps . . . For them vistas of loveliness are shut off and bring no joy and gladness.' John Brown's sympathy for the blind switched to rhetorical criticism of the sighted: 'Is it not the case that many of us – yes, most of us – even though we have our seeing faculties, walk blindly through life? We notice so little when we could see so much, passing by the wonders of creation without giving them a thought . . . Perhaps more people suffer from blindness than we realise . . . Through an over-concentration on trivialities, they have lost sight of the things that really matter.'

Any trace of his son's dilettantism was expunged. After six months in hospital, there was relief that one eye was saved. The left, dead eye permanently changed Brown's appearance. His smile no longer triggered the normal facial muscles, gradually creating a slightly dour expression. At the time he spoke of the operation as a success, but he would tell a friend years later, 'The operation was botched. Everyone can make mistakes.'

In spring 1968 he courageously resumed his studies and re-engaged in university life. The seventeen-year-old self-consciously hid any suggestion of impairment and the psychological consequences of six months' darkness. Compared to the shy fresher introduced by his brother to Jonathan Wills as a potential contributor to the student newspaper, Brown now displayed more self-confidence than previously. Propelled by a single-minded lust for success, in one way he resembled Willy Loman in Arthur Miller's play *Death of a Salesman*: 'He had the only dream you can have – to come out number-one man.' In effect, Brown sought control over others. Within weeks, most students at the university were conscious of an exceptional undergraduate in their midst.

The contrast between the outstanding student diligently pursuing his degree and the near squalor of his first home in the Grassmarket, just behind Edinburgh Castle, and later his

second, larger home in Marchmont Road, entered the university's folklore. At first the rooms at 48 Marchmont Road were
shared with six or seven other students as a statutory tenant,
but after fifteen years he would buy them for a bargain price.
With some pride Brown would confirm his chronic untidiness,
retelling a story of a policeman reporting a burglary at his
flat. 'I have never seen such mindless vandalism in thirty
years in the force,' said the police officer of the chaos. Brown
surveyed the scene. 'It looks quite normal to me,' he replied.
Those sharing his flat tolerated not only the anarchy but also
one unusual tenant who one afternoon caught a burglar
entering through the skylight. Instead of calling the police she
invited the intruder to stay, for an affair lasting several weeks.
Her room was subsequently occupied by Andrew, Gordon's
younger brother, a keen party host. Those who ever voiced
a suspicion that Andrew was riding on his elder brother's
achievements were promptly cautioned. 'Please don't hurt
me by criticising Andrew,' Brown once told Owen Dudley
Edwards, his university tutor. 'Criticise me, but not Andrew.'

Politics was his passion, and his political stance was set in
concrete. He joined the Labour Party in 1969, and while growing his hair long, ignored the fashionable far left, refusing to
join the Campaign for Nuclear Disarmament (CND) or to join
the movement for greater Scottish independence following
the discovery of oil in the North Sea. He was never seen
smoking pot or uncontrollably drunk, even as the host of his
frequent parties. The dozens who regularly crowded into the
flat to drink beer and eat dry cubes of cheese at the end of
toothpicks, influenced by the turbulence in England during
the sixties, fashioned themselves 'The Set', convinced that
they were destined to change the world, and particularly
Scotland. No one could accuse Brown of conducting himself
like Adam Morris, the ambitious undergraduate played by
Tom Conti in the successful 1970s television dramatisation of

Frederic Raphael's novel *The Glittering Prizes*. But the more
self-important of his elegant friends – like Wilf Stevenson,
who hosted dinner parties – and those who joined Brown at
the cinema, theatre and particularly the Abbotsford pub just
south of Princes Street, regarded themselves even if inaccurately as Edinburgh's equivalent of the Bloomsbury set, noisily
quoting artists, writers and politicians. Even during his
absence from those meetings, Brown's ghost was present.
'People liked being around him,' recalled Madeline Arnot, a
guest at his flat. 'Everyone liked talking to him. He was at
the centre of everything.' While 'The Set' cast themselves
in an unspoken competition as society's future movers and
shakers, the city's working class – as remote from the students
as the Eskimos – classed the boisterous elite as a gaggle of
Hooray Henrys. By any measure, they were neither a golden
nor a doomed generation.

The routine presence at these parties in 1970 of Princess
Margarita of Romania, the eldest daughter of the exiled king,
enhanced that image. Good-looking, charming and intelligent, Margarita had been introduced to Brown by John
Smythe, one of the six people sharing his flat. Heads turned, it
was said, whenever Margarita, of French, Greek and Romanian
parentage, with a pedigree derived from the Habsburgs,
Romanovs and Hohenzollerns, entered a room. The modest
student of sociology and politics, who spoke English with a
middle-class accent, hid her real background. Her family's
small home was near Lake Geneva, but thanks to her friendships with the king and queen of Spain, the exiled king of
Greece, and Europe's minor royalty, she was accustomed to
living in mansions and palaces across the continent. Since
their backgrounds were so different, Brown's attraction to the
'Red Princess', as she became known, puzzled many. Some of
Brown's flatmates, who like him were becoming increasingly
politically active, were irritated by the gilt-edged invitations

arriving through the letterbox just as their flat was becoming the centre of a revolution. He offered no explanation when she moved into his bedroom. His silence reflected his Scottish respect for her privacy and, more importantly, his belief that intimacies were not public property. Friends, however, understood the attraction. Margarita's looks and character were exceptional and, more important, compared to Katie, the English county girl whom Brown had been dating, she was unusually supportive. Unlike British girls, Margarita was accustomed to women offering compassion and encouragement to their men, which precisely matched Brown's requirements. She provided maternal care, acting like a mother hen, worrying about the health of his remaining eye, deciding what he should eat (usually tuna and lettuce sandwiches), wear (the same tweed and flannels), and occasionally do. 'He's too busy to wash up,' Margarita told their flatmates after the jolly communal breakfasts. Dressed in a pink nightdress, she insisted that Gordon's life's work was too important to be distracted by domesticities. Her pedigree had given her experience and toleration beyond her years. Her enjoyment of making decisions on his behalf appealed to a man who disliked annoying friends and who was reluctant to cause upset. But the princess would also roar in his face if his Presbyterian obduracy became irksome, deflating the pompous Fife boy.

Those who would subsequently criticise Brown for favouring intense hard work at the cost of human relationships would not have recognised him during those early months of the relationship. Margarita's misfortune was that her boyfriend's prevalent feminine influences were his mother and the absence of a sister. His loyalty to the ultraconventional woman of the manse required some disguise of his lifestyle. During a visit to the flat in Edinburgh, Elizabeth Brown found some items of female underwear in the bathroom. 'I don't know how they got there,' exclaimed

Brown with embarrassment. 'They must have come by mistake from the laundry.' In turn, his mother would be untroubled by his bachelorhood until, she confided to a friend,
he met someone whom she could approve. Out of a sense of
duty towards his parents, he agreed to a mixture of concealment and denial. Margarita faced other hurdles. Despite her
unsnobbish charm, she found difficulty in supplanting the
male culture of Brown's circle. Sport was intrinsic to Brown's
life. Regularly he met a large group of friends, including many
from his school, on the terraces at Murrayfield for rugby inter-
nationals or at club grounds for local football and rugby
matches. Margarita was not invited. She was also excluded
from his daily discussions and plots with his student allies
about politics. In his second year at university he was elected
chairman of the Labour Club, was the editor of the student
newspaper, and was regularly sitting at the same desk in the
university library, working so hard without coffee breaks that
Madeline Arnot, who became a Cambridge don, later thanked
him for her good degree. 'I followed him as a role model,'
she later volunteered. Others followed Brown, albeit still a
teenager, as a political leader.

In 1970, aged nineteen, disappointed like so many to have
missed out on the student revolt witnessed in other cities such
as Paris, he spotted an opportunity to assert student power
in his own kingdom. The issue was whether the investments
owned by Edinburgh University included shares in South Afri-
can companies, a taboo for those seeking to destroy apartheid.
The vice-chancellor Sir Michael Swann, a respected member
of the Tory establishment and thus an easy man for Brown
to dislike, stated publicly that the university did not invest in
'companies known to be active in the support of apartheid',
but documents leaked to Brown by a disgruntled university
administrator showed that in fact the university owned shares
in many companies active in South Africa, including the

mining company de Beers, which had been accused of unacceptable employment practices. Working from the student newspaper office, Brown composed a special news sheet exposing the university's deception, electrifying the university's community.

By accident rather than design, Brown found that midway through his studies he was leading a revolution, without realising the possible repercussions. Edinburgh's establishment was a tight clique. Every lunchtime there was a procession of the city's great and good from the university, financial institutions and government offices to the New Club. Their midday discussions during those days did not focus on censuring Swann for his deception, but expressed their apoplexy about the challenge to their authority by an upstart student posing as a symbol of integrity against a foreign impostor. In the long term the confrontation harmed Brown, but in the midst of the dispute his disarming manner towards the ruling class shone as a virtue.

By contrast to many of the 'revolutionary' students protesting in the 1960s across Britain and other parts of Europe and North America, Brown's politics were reasoned and principled. He adhered to Labour's traditional values. Unlike many students, he did not succumb to the emotional appeals of the Govan shipbuilders during their confrontation with Edward Heath's government in 1971 over the closure of their yard; in fact he predicted the shipworkers' ultimate failure. In an article for the student newspaper he criticised the 'alternative society seekers, Trotskyite students and liberal documentary makers' who had visited the Upper Clyde shipyards: 'The trendies are looking in vain for their kind of revolution. While they may plan the final end of capitalism, the mass meetings, the George Square demos and the fighting talk of the stewards should not belie the real campaign on the Clyde; for this is a work-in not for workers' control, but an attempt to save jobs, and not a demand for the abolition of private ownership.' His analysis was probably correct, but his political inexperience blinded him to the machinations between the trade unions and the government. To his surprise, in 1972 Heath capitulated and agreed to invest in the doomed yard. Many aspiring politicians learnt from Heath's humiliation, including Margaret Thatcher. Brown learnt the lesson twenty years later. His ragged journey to that eventual wisdom, understanding the art of political strategy and intrigue, started soon after he achieved a first class degree in history in 1972. Some would say that his was the best first ever awarded by the university.

Aged just twenty, he embarked upon a doctorate about the Labour Party in Scotland which gradually developed over the following decade of research and writing into 'The Labour Party and Political Change in Scotland 1918–29'. Originally he intended to explain the two-hundred-year development of labour from the seventeenth century to the emergence from the trade unions of the Labour Party in the twentieth century. His eventual thesis, less ambitiously, described Labour's struggle to establish itself as the alternative to the Conservatives. In the course of his research he became entranced by the romanticism of Scotland's heroic socialist pioneers – Keir Hardie, Robert Smillie, John Maclean, Willie Gallacher, John Wheatley – striving against capitalism to build the perfect society. In particular he alighted on James Maxton, a Presbyterian orator with spellbinding powers, preaching about socialism's Promised Land. Maxton, the son of a Presbyterian headmaster closely involved in the Church, was MP for the Bridgeton seat in Glasgow from 1922 until his death in 1946. 'He was a politician,' wrote the great historian A.J.P. Taylor , 'who had every quality – passion, sincerity, unstinted devotion, personal charm, a power of oratory – every quality save one – the gift of knowing how to succeed.' In Brown's words, Maxton, a crusading rather than a career politician, 'had sought to make socialism the common sense of his age'. His Christian desire to promote human happiness and equality bore similarities to the sermons of the Reverend John Brown. During those years researching his PhD, Brown sought to learn from Maxton's mistakes: the consequence of splits within a party and the occasional advantage in politics of being feared rather than loved. Scotland, he understood, produced two types of socialist – the romantic and the pragmatic. The ideal was to be the pragmatic inspired by the romantic. His test-bed was the campaign to embarrass Sir Michael Swann.

In November 1972 Brown proposed that he should be elected as rector of the university, a ceremonial office usually awarded to honour establishment personalities. A precedent had been set the previous year with the election of Jonathan Wills, the editor of the student newspaper. To Swann's relief Wills had resigned, but to his irritation Brown launched his first successful election campaign, a rousing operation supported by 'Brown Sugars', miniskirt-clad students posing as dolly girls. No one of that era would ever label Brown a puritanical Scot with a humourless, wooden face and a grating habit of repetitiously uttering identical slogans. On the contrary, he was regarded as an amusing, sincere idealist with a 'little boy lost' approach who articulately galvanised supporters to translate his ambitions into a convincing victory over Swann's candidate.

With the new rector's election came the right to chair meetings of the University Court, the ultimate authority. Excitedly, Brown exercised this power, with the intention of agitating against the university's administrators and governors. The battle lines were drawn in a row that engulfed the campus. Outraged by the usurper, Swann sought to remove Brown as chairman. Brown responded with an appeal to the Court of Session, Edinburgh's High Court, for a judgement against the vice-chancellor. Brown won. Swann tried one more legal ruse, but was outgunned when the Duke of Edinburgh, the university's chancellor, influenced the University Court in Brown's favour. Brown had appealed to Prince Philip for help through Margarita – his goddaughter.

The experience, Brown later acknowledged, was a baptism of fire. Delighting in the scandal, he sought to avoid pitfalls and to succeed by exhaustive preparation. Every event was treated as a serious occasion. His speeches could be made more effective, he learnt, by rehearsing them to his flatmates and asking them to suggest jokes. He advanced his arguments by carefully placing pertinent stories in newspapers. Patiently, he sat through tedious meetings with a pleasant, laid-back manner, displaying a high boredom threshold until he had worn down his opposition. Glorious successes were followed by miserable setbacks, but through it all the rector discovered the mechanics of power-broking and mobilising support. 'It was quite a revelation to me to see that politics was less about ideals and more about manoeuvres,' he reflected twenty years later. His cruder assessment was: 'The experience persuaded me that the Establishment could be taken on.' Both conclusions conceal a deep injury. At the end of his three-year rectorship Brown had changed the University Court, but was nevertheless ambivalent about an achievement which was so blatantly irrelevant to the outside world. The cost was the accumulation of many vengeful enemies who frustrated his attempts, despite his qualifications, to be appointed a permanent lecturer at the university. In later years he would condemn those who rejected his promotion from his part-time lectureship as plotters rather than fair judges of his abilities. 'They forced me out,' he complained in a surprised voice, ignoring all the trouble he had caused. Student politics had roused his appetite for parliamentary politics but would provide barely any preparation for his struggle to win the Labour Party's nomination for a Westminster constituency.

Among the Scottish Labour Party's many divisions was one between the graduates of Glasgow University and those of other universities. Brown suffered a double deficiency. His humiliation of Edinburgh's establishment denied him one source of support, while Glasgow's clique, which included John Smith, Derry Irvine, Donald Dewar and Helen Liddell, shunned him as unworthy to join a group convinced of its right to govern the country. In the last months of 1973 many of those activists were searching for nominations to parliamentary constituencies in time for the next general election.

Edward Heath called an election for February 1974 in an attempt to turn the nation against the coalminers, who were engaged in a strike which the Conservatives interpreted as politically motivated. Dwindling coal supplies forced Heath to impose power cuts and to reduce British industry to a three-day week. That crisis hit particularly hard in Scotland, the home of many miners led by either communist or left-wing trade union officials. The miners' cause was emotional as well as political. The communities whose menfolk dug coal in appalling conditions were part of the backbone of the country's working-class culture, and their suffering evoked widespread sympathy. There was every reason for Brown to forge relationships with Mick McGahey, the engaging communist miners' leader, and Lawrence Daly, a committed national official and a Labour Party member. Both particularly welcomed support from ambitious activists. Their endorsement, Brown knew, would help his chances of nomination as a Labour parliamentary candidate.

Another qualification for nomination was to have worked as a footsoldier for an existing candidate. Brown volunteered to help Robin Cook, a tutor at the Workers' Education Offices Association and a leading member of Edinburgh council who was standing as the Labour candidate for Edinburgh Central. Their relationship, forged at the university, was built

upon Cook's acknowledged seniority. There was good reason
for Brown to respect Cook, the son of a headmaster and grandson of a miner blacklisted for his activities during the General
Strike of 1926. Cook, six years older than Brown, displayed
forensic intelligence and remarkable debating skills. He had
also secured Brown a teaching post at the WEA after
Edinburgh University rejected his application.

Every night during the election campaign Brown recruited
twenty friends, including his tenants, to knock on the doors
of a working-class area in Edinburgh Central, a marginal
constituency, urging support for the Labour candidate. On
28 February 1974, thanks to an unusually high swing, Cook
won the seat with a small majority which many credited to
Brown's efforts. Yet, returning from the election night celebrations, Brown, Margarita and their friends expressed their
surprise that Cook had not shown more gratitude for their
hard work. Too often he had drunk whisky alone at one end
of the Abbotsford's bar while they drank beer at the other.

In the country as a whole Edward Heath won more votes
than Labour, but not an overall majority of seats, and
resigned. Few doubted that Harold Wilson, after forming a
minority government, would call another election in the
autumn. That was Brown's opportunity. Edinburgh South, a
marginal Conservative seat, was ideal territory. Securing the
nomination required cut-throat tactics to elbow aside other
applicants. 'I was almost a candidate,' he said years later. 'I
was invited by people to stand, but it just didn't work out.
It would probably have been better had I done that.' The
impression is of a man facing a critical test of courage and
bloody-mindedness who meekly withdrew. In reality, he
faced a selection conference against the favoured candidate,
Martin O'Neill, a friend from the student movement, and
was beaten. In the election of October 1974 O'Neill lost the
seat by 3,226 votes, leaving Brown ruefully to reflect that

more aggressive campaigning might have tipped the balance.

Labour's overall majority in the new parliament was three seats. Recognising that the government, with the Liberals' help, could survive for some years, Brown reconciled himself to establishing his own life while he waited for the next opportunity. For the first months he suffered a personal crisis. He entered hospital for an operation on his right eye, uncertain whether he would emerge completely blind. Other than Margarita, few were aware of his true feelings. Some of those sharing his house say that he emerged from hospital crying, and unexpectedly began smoking twenty cigarettes a day. Some suspected that his hectic schedule of teaching at the WEA, researching his PhD, writing a book on James Maxton based on the politician's private papers, and his Labour Party activities placed him under unusual pressure. Others accepted his explanation that his tears were for the Labour Party.

The party's internal affairs had become ugly. North Sea oil had increased the demand for Scotland's independence, and in the October election the Scottish Nationalists had won seven seats, campaigning on the slogan 'It's Scotland's oil'. The shock of the SNP's success, and the crisis in Scotland's shipyards, coalmines and manufacturing industries, posed a threat in Labour's heartlands. Labour's Scottish leaders decided to end their dialogue with the Nationalists. In that battle, there would be no help from Harold Wilson and the party's headquarters in London. Brown joined the campaign, attempting to discredit the Nationalists' call for independence by compiling an account of socialist policies to rebuild Scotland.

The 'Red Paper on Scotland' was proposed by Brown as twenty individual essays bound in a slim 180-page volume. Among those invited to contribute were journalists including Tom Nairn, the playwright John McGrath, lecturer in politics John Foster, and two MPs, Jim Sillars and Robin Cook. After eighteen essays had been commissioned, Brown decided his idea was too good to waste. At parties, meetings and in pubs, he invited eighteen other contributions about Scotland's economy and politics, devolution, the ownership of the country's land and oil. 'We'll have to increase the price from £1.20 to £1.80,' his flatmate John Forsythe, who was responsible for the publication through the Edinburgh University board, announced. 'Or could we reduce the number of commissions?' 'No,' replied Brown, 'and it's got to be £1.20.'

Unwilling to offend any contributors, he fled to the Meadow Bar to meet Owen Dudley Edwards, his genial tutor. 'A great bubbly baby,' was how Dudley Edwards described Brown. 'One of the sweetest people I know, with a wonderful smile. He knows how to say "Thank you," and his body language is reproachful if someone declines his request.' 'All right,' Brown announced to Forsythe on his return from the pub. '£1.80, but no reduction in the contributions.' The book's print was reduced to the minuscule size of a Biblical dictionary's footnotes, but it was still a success, heading the Scottish bestseller list for two weeks, although few readers can have ploughed through all the tiny script.

In microscopic print, Brown's well-written introduction, 'The Socialist Challenge', criticised the puerile debate indulged in by the country's politicians, who ignored 'Scotland's real problems – our economy and unacceptable level of unemployment, chronic inequalities of wealth and power and inadequate social services'. He offered a rigid solution to the contradiction of managing a capitalist economy while providing the requirements of society, rejecting 'incentives and local entrepreneurship', and supporting state planning to orchestrate a national economic revival. He advocated more nationalisation of Britain's industry, a planned economy and the destruction of the ruling classes. Scottish socialists, he wrote, could not support independence, but should control more of their own lives. Because capitalism had failed, and the private ownership of industry was hindering 'the further unfolding of the social forces of production', Brown's cure was neo-Marxism. Young Labour activists were now hailing Brown as a celebrity. His dramatic appearance and good oratory, enhanced by his immersion in the history and tradition of Scottish Labour, won admirers for his vision of 'Ethical Social-ism'. He could have been destroyed by his early success, but his upbringing reined in any temptation to boast. Privately, he nevertheless hoped that his achievement would ease the path to a nomination for a safe parliamentary seat.

Securing that nomination depended upon a successful apprenticeship. The party recognised Brown's ability but wanted evidence of more than a commitment to the com-munity and worship of the Bible, Burns and Keir Hardie. To prove his understanding of liberating working people, he was required to intone the religious code of the Scottish Labour movement – 'socialism' and 'social justice' – with suitable references to the fundamental morality established during the Scottish movement's history. By 1976 he had established those ideological credentials, regurgitating endless facts to prove that Harold Wilson's government and its technological revolution would create thousands of new businessmen and enterprises, revolutionising the nation's wealth. As a party loyalist he qualified for nomination; but among many of Labour's older generation his image grated. While the party faithful admired the impassioned man, some griped that he was too fast, too clever, and too interested in courting popu-larity. The picture of a disorganised twenty-three-year-old, wearing a dirty Burberry coat, carrying a plastic bag stuffed with newspaper clippings, pamphlets and notes, flitting between speeches and committee meetings, invariably late because he had forgotten his watch, hardly appealed to work-ing-class stalwarts. They joked that while holding the plastic

bag under his arm, the information seeped into Brown's brain
by osmosis through a sensor in his armpit.

Occasionally Brown returned to Marchmont Road close to
tears. At political meetings he was shouted down by critics
angry that he had acknowledged the SNP, a ghost the Labour
Party preferred to ignore. The policies pursued by Harold
Wilson's Labour government antagonised many in Scotland,
and Brown was among the casualties, blamed for deviation
from true socialism. Some members of the Scottish Executive,
especially Jimmy Allison, the party's organiser, treated him
roughly. In 1974 the party had opposed devolution, but subsequently, after receiving a report from the 'Devolution Committee' chaired by Brown, it supported partial home rule. The
disagreements excited anger. 'The older people hated him,'
Henry Drucker, a writer and friend, recalled. John Forsythe
listened to his long-haired friend's lament that the representatives of the working class criticised him as soft, self-indulgent
and a dilettante. Brown was frustrated that those he consulted
for advice were not as clever as himself, and could not offer
better insights into Labour's problems in Scotland. His family
life had not equipped him to deal with calculated ruthlessness.
Any achievement would have to be the result of unglamorous
hard graft.

Eventually his perseverance was rewarded. In 1976 he was
nominated as the prospective candidate for Edinburgh South,
a Conservative seat. Considering the growing antagonism
towards the Labour government his election to the Commons
was doubtful, but the breakthrough was critical. After a good
speech in favour of devolution at the Scottish party's conference in 1977 Brown was elected to Labour's Scottish Executive. Full of excitement, he telephoned Donald Dewar, a
solicitor and an MP since 1966 with whom he watched football matches, to share his excitement. The older politician
instinctively replied, 'I can assure you it will be awful.' John

Smith, the thirty-nine-year-old minister responsible for devolution in Westminster, was more supportive. Brown had been flattered to be invited to Smith's home shortly after Smith's appointment as a cabinet minister, and had been surprised to find that Smith was more interested in listening than in talking. Smith, Brown would appreciate, 'genuinely believed people were equal'. Like Donald Dewar, John Smith became another 'friend and mentor'. Brown was content to have established himself close to the party's possible future leaders.

His election to the party's executive coincided with the earlier appointment of Helen Liddell, a bus driver's daughter who would later be known as 'Stalin's Granny', as the Scottish party's general secretary, and George Robertson as chairman. His encounters with both did not improve his popularity. As BBC Scotland's economics correspondent, Liddell had a high public profile, and was an attractive face for Labour. Her appointment did not interrupt her frequent appearances on television news. Self-promotion, carped her critics, seemed more important to Liddell than engaging in the grind of party work and leadership. Her supporters countered that her value was in forging good relations with people. That was no consolation for Brown. Generally he did not handle women well, and he particularly lacked affection for Liddell. At executive meetings he was humiliated as she launched criticisms of him, especially of the 'Red Paper on Scotland', whose neo-Marxism she regarded as a threat to the party, regularly beginning with the phrase 'The national leadership says . . .' Those seemingly innocuous words could be fatal to Brown's ambitions. His energy and politics were creating rivals and occasionally enemies, just as his need for friends and benevolent advisers had become greatest.

In 1978 his impatience to become an MP was damaging his relationship with Margarita. Repeatedly, planned visits to the cinema and parties were abandoned as he responded to a

telephone call and rushed to yet another meeting. In desperation, one night she had telephoned Owen Dudley Edwards
with a ruse, asking, 'Can you come down? Gordon wants
you.' Dudley Edwards arrived to discover that Brown was still
drinking in a pub with two friends. Leaving Margarita alone
had caused him no concern. The three friends eventually
returned, slightly merry. Normally Brown's companions
would crash out on the floor while he flopped in an armchair
to read a serious book. But on this occasion, while Margarita
loudly reproached him, he picked her up and laughingly
carried her to their bedroom. 'You can see how in love they
are,' sang Dudley Edwards.

In an attempt to restore their faltering relationship, Margarita
organised a weekend trip to a country cottage, and disconnected the telephone. Brown exploded in a rage. Relationships with women were sideshows in his life. He had become
disturbed by the uneasy contrast of living with a sophisticated
woman who enjoyed good food and elegant clothes, and the
plight of Scottish workers, striking in large numbers across
the country. While the party was immersed in strife as it tried
to resolve the turmoil, Margarita seemed merely to tolerate
Scottish provincialism, being principally concerned about the
arrangements to visit her family in Geneva and her royal
friends in their palatial homes across Europe. After five years,
she also wanted evidence that the relationship had a future.
Regardless of his affection, Brown was uncertain whether he
could commit himself to a woman who was not a socialist,
or could risk appearing with a princess before a constituency
committee.

This crossroads in his personal life coincided with a remarkable political opportunity. Alexander Wilson, the Labour MP
for Hamilton, a town south of Glasgow, died, and the constituency was looking for a candidate for the by-election on
31 May 1978. Hamilton had many attractions for Brown. The

seat was a Labour stronghold, several senior party members
had offered him their support, and his parents had moved to
a church in the town. The obstacles were the other aspiring
candidates. Alf Young, a journalist, was among them, although his chance of success was nil. Brown telephoned
Young and asked whether he would stand aside. Young
politely refused, adding that George Robertson, the Scottish
party's former chairman, who was supported by a major trade
union, appeared certain of success. Brown aggressively challenged Young's obstinacy, but failed to persuade him to surrender. A decisive voice, Brown knew, would be Jimmy
Allison's, the party's organiser and a mini-Godfather. 'It's
tight,' said Allison, who knew the area well, 'but you can win
if you fight.' Crucially, Allison pledged his support if Brown
mounted a challenge. There might be blood, warned Allison,
but that was acceptable among brothers. Even George
Robertson, the favourite, acknowledged that there would be
'a big fight' if Brown stood, and the outcome would be
uncertain.

'I don't know,' Brown told Allison a few days later. 'I think
I should be loyal to the people in Edinburgh South. I don't
want to be seen as a carpetbagger and offend the good people
who have helped me.' Allison dismissed that as an irrelevance.
Brown grunted and agreed to contact the party activists in
Hamilton. But they, Allison heard, were unimpressed by his
eagerness to avoid a fight with Robertson. Brown spoke about
not being disloyal to the electors of Edinburgh South, but in
truth he lacked the courage to work the system with a killer
instinct. His caution was unexpected. Six years earlier he
had confidently challenged Michael Swann. Outsiders were
puzzled why the same determination now seemed to be lacking. They failed to understand Brown's insecurity. He was still
shocked by the consequences of his university protest for his
academic career. His judgement, he believed, had been faulty.

While he could confidently repudiate intellectual arguments, he lacked the resilience to withstand emotional pressure. He needed reassurance, but he had no one he could rely on. Some of his friends would dispute that he lacked courage. Others would say he feared failure. His consolation was hard work. Diligence, he believed, merited reward, and without hard work there should be no reward. That credo may be commendable for normal life, but not for ambitious politicians. Brown withdrew. Without a serious challenger, Robertson was nominated, and won the by-election by a margin of more than 6,000 votes. If Brown had arrived in Westminster in 1978, his own life, and possibly the Labour Party's, would have been markedly different.

Similar indecisiveness plagued Brown's relationship with Margarita. For weeks he hardly spent any time in Marchmont Road. James Callaghan had succeeded Harold Wilson as Labour prime minister, and increasingly Brown was preoccupied by the erosion of Callaghan's authority – the government's dependence on other parties at Westminster for a parliamentary majority had become unreliable – and the slide towards industrial chaos. In Scotland the party's problems were compounded by disagreement about devolution. A referendum was to be held in March 1979, and the party was divided.

Excluded from those preoccupations, Margarita decided to end the relationship and leave Marchmont Road. 'I never stopped loving him,' she said in 1992, 'but one day it didn't seem right any more. It was politics, politics, politics, and I needed nurturing.' Brown's friends would say that he terminated the relationship. 'She took it badly,' they said, 'that she was less important than meetings.' But in truth Margarita simply was fed up, and walked out. A few weeks later she met Jim Keddie, a handsome fireman, with whom she started an affair that would last for six years. During the first months

Brown telephoned her frequently to arrange meetings, but despite his entreaties that she return, she refused. Over a long session of drinks with Owen Dudley Edwards, Brown repeatedly said, 'It's the greatest mistake of my life. I should have married Margarita.' If he had been elected to Westminster in 1974 or 1978 they might have married, but the uncertainty created irreconcilable pressures. Jim Keddie was convinced that Brown remained haunted by Margarita. Although Margarita never mentioned any regret about leaving Brown, for several months after her departure she would turn up without Keddie at parties in Marchmont Road, or would see Brown at dinner parties held by Wilf Stevenson, a man convinced of his own glorious destiny. Keddie sensed that she hoped the relationship might be rekindled, but there was no reunion. 'It just hasn't happened,' Brown would say thereafter about love and marriage. In the space of a few months he had lost the chance of both an early arrival in Westminster and marriage to a woman he loved. Whether he was influenced by his research into James Maxton's life, with all its failures and disappointments, to avoid similar distress himself is possible, but he had failed to overcome his caution and indecisiveness.

Beyond a tight circle of friends, Brown concealed his emotions and re-immersed himself in politics. For an aspiring realist, the prognosis could not have been worse. The trade unions were organising constant strikes, public services were disintegrating and inflation was soaring. The 'winter of discontent' began. Rubbish lay uncollected on the streets, the dead remained unburied and hospital porters refused to push the sick into operating theatres. The middle classes and many working-class Labour voters switched to the Conservatives to save them from what they felt had become a socialist hell. The opinion polls predicted Margaret Thatcher's victory whenever James Callaghan dared to call the election. Brown's prospects in Edinburgh South looked dismal, but once again he was offered an attractive alternative.

Martin O'Neill, who would himself be elected to parliament in 1979, called Brown with an offer. O'Neill was chairman of the Labour Party in Leith, and he explained, 'There isn't a strong candidate here, and you could win a safe seat.' Brown hesitated. 'I don't know,' he replied. 'I don't think I can let the people in Edinburgh down.' He expressed his fear of bad publicity after his failure to stand in Hamilton, and the probability of being tarred as an opportunist. The impression again was of indecision and fear of a competition whose outcome was, despite O'Neill's assurances, uncertain. He sought refuge in hard work.

The first battle was to persuade the Scottish people to support devolution in the forthcoming referendum. Without uttering any overtly nationalist sentiments, he campaigned in favour of the 'yes' vote, speaking at dozens of meetings. Despite campaigning in the midst of widespread strikes, Brown believed he could deliver victory. Scotland, he argued, did not share England's disenchantment with the Callaghan government. Fighting against the odds brought the best out of him. During one debate against Tam Dalyell in York Place, Edinburgh, Brown arrived after a last-minute invitation. 'He stood up to me better than anyone else,' Dalyell told a friend afterwards. 'I was pretty formidable, but he had thought about it better than anyone I had met.' Among his other opponents was Robin Cook, praised by some but damned by more, especially the former Labour MP Jim Sillars, who would later join the SNP: 'Cook believed that he was intellectually superior to God.' Dalyell watched the two sparring with each other. 'They were two strong young men who knew that one of them would get in the way.'

On election day, 1 March 1979, Scotland's airports were closed and there were food shortages. Productivity had fallen since 1974, annual wage increases were about 15 per cent and inflation was 15.5 per cent. The 'yes' and 'no' votes were evenly divided, but under the rules of the referendum the 'yes' vote could only be successful if it received not just a simple majority, but a majority of all those who were entitled to vote. Brown, like many in his party, deluded himself about the reasons for failure. Scotland's new oil wealth had encouraged the belief that while England was dying, their country was being revitalised. Scottish voters, Brown failed to understand, were disenchanted by Labour. He was nevertheless optimistic about victory in the general election, which was finally called for May 1979.

Energetically he began campaigning in Edinburgh South against Michael Ancram, the Conservative candidate. His speeches were notable for their use of repetition as an oratorical strategy, and for their tidal wave of minutiae. Watching Brown's campaign, Alf Young spotted its flaws: 'He was always surrounded by a blitz of paper and a million bullet points. He exuded the belief that everything could be reduced to micro-targets and micro-meddling.' His campaign ignored the widespread disgust with the strikers, and specifically rejected any increased control over trade unions, especially over picketing and unofficial strikes. Despite dozens of friends and supporters, including Margarita, working on his behalf, Brown was defeated by 2,460 votes. Later, in the party headquarters with a group including Robin Cook and Nigel Griffiths, a local activist, he confessed his devastation. Politically, Margaret Thatcher's victory with a majority of forty-three seats was shattering. Brown was baffled by the national mood and the unexpected end of the Labour era.

The following morning, while television pictures showed Thatcher standing on the steps of 10 Downing Street quoting Francis of Assisi, Brown was slumped in a tattered armchair in Marchmont Road, surrounded by the debris of his campaign,

contemplating his life until the next election. He had made a
terrible mistake in refusing Martin O'Neill's offer of a safe
seat. No one congratulated him for fighting and losing. He
would continue lecturing at the Glasgow College of Technology and the WEA, and would secure a junior researcher's
job on *Ways and Means*, a political programme produced by
Scottish Television. After some complaints about the lack of
political balance in his contributions he was moved to *What's
Your Problem?*, a weekly consumer programme exposing rip-
offs by shops and local authorities. His productions were
renowned less for their artistic qualities than for the efforts
he took to rectify ills.

His new companion was a feisty former student at Edinburgh University, Sheena McDonald, born in Dunfermline,
Fife. A brief introduction at one of his university parties by
his brother Andrew had been remembered when they met
again while working at Scottish Television. Dark, intelligent and fun, McDonald bore some physical resemblance to
Margarita, but their characters differed sharply. She was an
ambitious journalist, and prized her personal independence.
Unlike Margarita, she had no intention of marrying Brown,
although they had much in common. Like Brown, she was a
child of the manse; her father was a former moderator of the
General Assembly of the Church of Scotland.

Brown's attitude towards women had become entrenched.
He knew he was attractive. He was well built – 'fit, with good
legs' as one admirer recalled – but he denied to himself any
need to share his life with a woman, or to trust anyone beyond
his immediate confidants: his two brothers, Wilf Stevenson
and Murray Elder. At the end of a day he was content to go
home, endlessly watch games of football on television and
listen to recordings by Jessye Norman or Frank Sinatra. He
was neither interested in a woman's life nor prepared to
divulge his own secrets. Confessing to any doubts or exposing

his weaknesses was anathema. Nothing would be allowed to undermine his determination to portray himself as supremely self-confident. His relationship with Sheena McDonald, like his job, was temporary while he found a safe seat. The obstacles to that, however, appeared to be multiplying.

The Labour Party in England was convulsed by defeat. In the leadership elections after Jim Callaghan resigned, the left-wing Michael Foot defeated Denis Healey by 139 votes to 129. The parliamentary Labour Party had patently misread the electoral result. Rather than distancing themselves from the wild antics of the militant trade unions, a majority of Labour MPs sought to encourage them. The growing split in the English party between sympathisers of the neo-Marxist Militant Tendency and the traditional socialists only partially infected the Scottish party, but Brown's comrades nevertheless were embroiled in bitter disagreements about personalities and ideology. 'Anyone who can survive that viciousness,' sighed Jimmy Allison, 'can survive anything.' In that battle Brown represented the traditional Tribunites on the party's executive, the ethical socialist rather than the Marxist. He faced hard-liners including George Galloway, the son of Irish immigrants, and Bill Speirs, a future general secretary of the Scottish TUC. For hours every week they battled about the transfer of power to left-wing activists, and whether Tony Benn and the left's caucus should be supported despite Benn's refusal to accept collective responsibility. Resisting any dalliance with those outside the mainstream, Brown argued against factionalism and declined invitations by Galloway and Speirs to join their group in the pub after meetings. He would insist that he was engaged in intellectual rather than malicious, personalised debates, and preferred to talk with the trade unionists. Both Galloway and Speirs, he believed, were blocking his promotion and influence. They would deny any subterfuge, although neither was particularly fond of Brown.

In Galloway's opinion he was an egghead, a brainy backroom boy and a workaholic policy wonk, but not an intellectual. Galloway believed him to be ambitiously manoeuvring to build relationships for his own personal advancement, rather than trying to build a better society. 'He's chosen not to be a comrade,' agreed Speirs.

Their disagreements mirrored the sectarian division within the Scottish Labour Party. Galloway, a Catholic from the west coast, did not warm to Brown's east coast Presbyterianism. He was scathing about Brown's silences at the late-night meetings held by Alex Murray, a famed Scottish trade unionist in Ayrshire, at which Brown refrained from engaging in the debates. He was also irritated that Brown, despite being steeped in the history of the Labour movement, appeared to be motivated by instinctive beliefs rather than philosophy. Not an original thinker, concluded Galloway, nor a man who had suffered grinding poverty. As Galloway fondly repeated, the divisions within the Scottish Labour Party ran deep, and as with all divisions within a family, the disagreements were aggravated by personality differences. Brown's idiosyncrasies could be particularly aggravating. While chairing the party's Scottish Council, he would pull bits of paper out of his bulging plastic bag, say, 'See, this is how we deliver,' and list twenty points.

The disagreements intensified in 1980. In England, the Militant Tendency and the Bennites were emasculating the Labour Party. In Scotland, by contrast, the party was divided over unilateral disarmament and withdrawal from NATO, but remained united as a coherent group, despite outbursts of ill-discipline. The rows irritated Brown. At a meeting on 14 November 1981 he was disturbed that Galloway, representing the hard left, berated Michael Foot for not supporting Tony Benn against Denis Healey in the election for deputy leader. Brown had attached himself to the soft-left, Neil Kinnock tendency, advocating a 'moral crusade' to rebuild

Labour's appeal to voters. His personal response to the warfare was 'One Person, One Vote', a lacklustre pamphlet attacking the trade unions' undemocratic use of the block vote to wield influence. All his other ideas had been rejected by the electorate. His support for John Silkin, a forlorn London lawyer, as deputy leader confirmed his own isolation from the realities in London. With a general election expected within two years, he still faced huge hurdles if he was to find a safe parliamentary seat. New hopes rested on his election in 1982 as the Scottish party's vice-chairman and on a journalistic scoop – publishing an internal document of Britoil, an oil company operating in the North Sea which was on the verge of privatisation. The 'strictly confidential' document showed that the company's profits would not grow for five years. The scoop, he hoped, would discourage private investors from buying Britoil shares from the government, but he was to be disappointed by the response. Despite his high profile and his loyal efforts for the party, he still sensed that he suffered handicaps. He sought advice from Jimmy Allison. 'Get your nose in with the unions,' Allison advised, adding that he would need to neutralise the opposition of the communists, who possessed sufficient influence in the Scottish Labour Party to veto any aspirant.

The most approachable trade unionist was Jimmy McIntyre, a popular leader of the Transport and General Workers' Union (TGWU). McIntyre was concerned that in television interviews, compared to their employers, his members made fools of themselves. Brown agreed to organise a media course for Scottish shop stewards, using role playing – 'You're on strike, what do you tell media?' In return, he expected McIntyre to help him gain selection for a safe seat. He also sought advice from Robin Cook. At a meal in a Chinese restaurant in Soho arranged by Murray Elder, Brown asked Cook for help. 'I am sure you will do very well, Gordon,' Cook replied. Brown

repeated his request and, he told his authorised biographer
Paul Routledge, received the same non-committal reply. They
did however agree to co-author a book. *Scotland: The Real
Divide*, a collection of essays about poverty, would be published the following year.

The pace of Brown's life remained frenetic. His relationship
with Sheena McDonald had ended and he was seeing Marion
Caldwell, a dark, good-looking lawyer born in Glasgow. They
had met in 1981. Since neither wanted to sacrifice their professional career, there was an understanding that they would
meet whenever he was minded. Their relationship was not
exclusive. At the same time, Brown was also meeting Carol
Craig, a publicist who would live with the journalist Alf
Young. Off-hand relationships precisely matched Brown's
requirements. He was thirty years old. He had waited six
years for a parliamentary seat. His impatience was explosive.
Margaret Thatcher's unpopularity, he calculated, would
secure a Labour victory at the next election.

Over the previous months he had forged relationships in
his native Fife. Helped by Tom Donald, a local journalist, and
Jimmy McIntyre, he had taught politics at weekend schools
for trade unionists and participated in their discussions, even
mouthing support for Bennite co-operatives and nationalisation. 'I don't want any more pudding heads as MPs,' McIntyre
had reassuringly told Brown. 'We don't need any more ill-
disciplined big drinkers in the Commons. We need clever,
media-savvy types.' Brown was his man. 'Spend every
evening at meetings,' McIntyre advised him. That advice was
endorsed by Alec Falconer, the TGWU's shop steward at the
Rosyth shipyards. When the opportunity arose, Brown was
promised, the clan would beat off his rival contestants.

Having secured the support of the trade union officials,
Brown needed to win over two kingmakers. First, Hugh Wyper,
a leader of the local Communist Party, was approached.

George Galloway says that he was consulted by Wyper and, despite his reservations, urged that the communists support Brown because the trade unions needed his brainpower. Wyper gave his approval. Second was Alec Kitson, the deputy general secretary of the TGWU at its headquarters in London and a communist sympathiser, albeit a member of the Labour Party. He agreed that Brown was a suitable candidate. Having secured that support, Brown waited for an opportunity.

In 1983 Dunfermline East, a safe Labour seat near Edinburgh, was looking for a candidate. Known locally as 'Little Moscow', the old coalmining area had been represented from 1935 to 1950 by Willie Gallacher, a communist MP. Both the communists and the TGWU agreed that Brown, the Scottish Labour Party chairman that year, was ideal. All other challengers were rebuffed and the selection was predetermined. Nervously, Brown travelled with Jonathan Wills from Edinburgh to make his speech to the party committee in Cowdenbeath. David Stoddart, the constituency agent, was primed to favour Brown. Like any prospective candidate, Brown promised the committee, if selected, to be active, to care for the constituency's children, pensioners and the poor, and to fight for the destruction of the hated Tory regime. Soon after his speech, the machine delivered him the guaranteed seat in Westminster.

That summer, during the Edinburgh Festival, John Reid, who was then working for Neil Kinnock, was drinking in a pub with Roy Hattersley, a member of the Labour shadow cabinet. 'You should meet Gordon Brown,' Reid told Hattersley. 'He's a young man who's bound to be leader of the party one day.' Hattersley, a traditional socialist, made a note of this newcomer who shared his dislike of the Bennite extremists but supported public control of the economy and a planned economy. He and Brown also shared a disgust that Roy Jenkins, the idol of many in the party, had won a parliamentary seat at a

by-election in Glasgow Hillhead in 1982 for the new SDP, a
breakaway party led by the 'gang of four' former Labour cabinet ministers – Jenkins, Shirley Williams, David Owen and
Bill Rodgers.

Brown had immersed himself in the politics of that by-
election while employed as a researcher for a television documentary. He regarded Jenkins as a traitor, and could not
understand why the split had occurred. Like many party activists, he remained oblivious to the public's anger about strikes
by public sector workers. He was convinced that the increase
in unemployment under Margaret Thatcher to more than
three million and her cuts in public spending would persuade
the voters to return to Labour. He discounted the Tories'
appeal to the middle classes, the fact that inflation had fallen
from 20 per cent to 4 per cent, and their pledge to control
the unions by introducing secret ballots before strikes and
removing the protection of union funds from civil litigation.
The evidence of his political blindness was displayed in
Scotland: The Real Divide, the book he co-authored with Robin
Cook. Both damned Thatcher's analysis of Britain's economic
weaknesses, and extolled the virtues of Clement Attlee's post-
war legacy.

In common with many party stalwarts, Brown regarded
Attlee's nationalisation of industry, the creation of the NHS
and his education reforms as a historic benchmark. He ignored
the food rationing, industrial stagnation and economic incompetence which eroded Labour's popularity before the 1950
and 1951 general elections, excluding the party from office
for thirteen years. In Brown's judgement, Attlee's glory was
the destruction of the barriers to equality and social justice.
Those landmark successes, he lamented, were being reversed
by the Thatcherite assumption that inequality was permanent.
To restore Attlee's legacy, he urged the redistribution of
wealth. The top 10 per cent of the population, who, he

claimed, owned '80 per cent of our wealth and 30 per cent of our income even after tax', should suffer higher taxes while the disadvantaged received a guaranteed minimum wage, higher state benefits and more public spending. He opposed the proposed privatisation of the utilities, British Telecom and British Airways. Enterprise, in Brown's opinion, meant state initiatives or personal work as approved and aided by the government. Prices, incomes and wages, he believed, should be fixed by statute. He supported subsidies to dying industries and opposed legislation to end overmanning and restrictive practices in the docks and industry. He mocked the chancellor Nigel Lawson's 'Medium Term Financial Strategy', which intended to abandon short-termism and create a climate for long-term economic growth without inflation. Until the socialist society was built, Brown confidently predicted in his new book, 'the era of automatic growth is not only over but unlikely to return in the near future'.

Brown was proud of the book, and looked forward to the launch organised by Bill Campbell, a university friend and the publisher, at a press conference in Edinburgh. As usual, Brown was late. Cook, the local MP, did not wait for him, but launched into a speech suggesting to the audience that he was the sole author. Rushing into the room, Brown discovered that Cook had stolen the limelight. His fury towards Cook that day, some would say, caused the permanent breach between the two. That is unlikely. The grudge was older than that. Cook's insensitivity was just the latest instance of his ungenerous nature. Besides their many disagreements at Edinburgh University and in committee meetings, not least over devolution, Brown was angry that Cook had refused to endorse his campaign for chairmanship of the Scottish Labour Party or to help him find a parliamentary seat. The image of Cook drinking whisky alone at the Abbotsford bar was that of a man who was simply disliked. Brown suspected, probably correctly, that Cook was unwilling to help a potential rival, and his fury never abated.

The general election was called for 9 June 1983. Britain's recent military victory in the Falkland Islands overshadowed the domestic recession. The sharp rise in unemployment, from one million to three million, caused by the Tory squeeze on manufacturing and the public services encouraged Labour to hope for support from disillusioned Tory supporters. But Labour's Achilles heel was its manifesto. Michael Foot's promise of renationalisation, the reintroduction of controls and the withdrawal of Britain from the EU, damned by shadow cabinet member Gerald Kaufman as 'the longest suicide note in history', destroyed the party's electoral chances.

Brown, however, had good reason for elation. He won his seat by a 11,301 majority, gaining 51.5 per cent of the vote. His ambition to enter parliament was finally realised. After delivering a rousing acceptance speech at Lochgelly town hall he was driven to the home of David Stoddart, his agent. Grouped around the television, he and his supporters watched the results from around the country. Jonathan Wills, Brown's old friend, arrived shortly after. 'Gordon, well done,' shouted Wills as he entered the dark room, expecting a jubilant celebration party. 'There's a beer over there,' snapped Brown. 'Sit down and shut up.' Wills obeyed. 'I've never seen anyone as depressed in my life,' he said later.

Gloom came easily to Brown. Some blamed his Presbyterian puritanism, but others identified a more profound trait. His misery reflected his remoteness. He had not understood the electoral plight of socialism. He was perplexed that his hatred for the Tories was not shared by everyone. The Scottish socialist was isolated from the mainstream of English political thought. To his credit, he resolved before travelling to Westminster to avoid the 'Scottish trap', making a deliberate effort not to be identified as predominantly concerned with Scottish issues. He would be a national rather than a regional politician. The star of Kirkcaldy and Edinburgh University expected to shine as a star in the capital.

TWO

Metamorphosis

Gordon Brown's first impression of Westminster was of Bedlam. Bellowing, triumphant Tories boasting a 144 majority pushed past the dejected remnants of the Labour Party. Dressed in sharp suits, gleaming shirts and polished shoes, the swaggering representatives of the establishment reinforced Brown's belief in society's inequities and his commitment to the disadvantaged. His election victory had brought clarity into his life. There was a noticeable self-assuredness during his first days in the Palace of Westminster. His intellect and surviving a decade of political turmoil in Scotland protected him from the nervous breakdown affecting others in the party. While they behaved feverishly, he sensibly focused on establishing his presence with political journalists, positioning himself as a Tribunite, and supporting Neil Kinnock against Roy Hattersley in the leadership election. He preferred the Welshman's left-wing, anti-European policies. Like most of his tribe, he was resolved to reimpose socialism. Even the collapse of the socialist experiment in France just eighteen months after President Mitterrand's election was not absorbed as a portent.

Luck, fate and effortless success had barely influenced Brown's career so far. Everything he had accomplished had been earned by diligence and unpleasant experience. After the election there would be profits, losses and mixed blessings.

Among the last were the arrangements for his office, which were certainly fateful and, in the long term, unhelpful.

The small, windowless office he was assigned in the heart of the building could barely contain two desks and filing cabinets. Discomfort did not bother Brown, nor was he anything more than a little bemused by the choice of his co-occupant, Tony Blair, another newly elected MP. Subsequently, some would say that the coupling was not mere coincidence, but was the manoeuvre of a skilful matchmaker in the whips' office brokering the notion that the two novices epitomised the party's future hopes. That is unlikely. The two new young MPs were markedly different, although bonds would eventually develop.

Tony Blair had never abandoned the fringes of the Labour Party adopted as a long-haired rock guitarist at Oxford. Uneducated about political theory, he had shown little interest in politics, pursuing an unremarkable career at the Bar. His affability, eagerness and flattery of Brown's political mastery appealed to the Scotsman who already bore the scars of political battles. Together they could laugh. Blair was a good mimic, and Brown's sarcasm was witty. Brown was generous: as a television producer he had perfected the art of scripting his interviewees' opinions into snappy, pertinent soundbites. Blair received the benefit of that black art, also learning how to write eye-catching press releases, compose structured public speeches and cultivate the techniques of self-presentation. Taught to encourage the best in people, Blair deferred with courtesy to the confident grammar-school boy. Brown and Blair, in that order, became affectionately known around Westminster as 'the twins' or 'the blood brothers'.

Weeks after the election, over a drink in a Glasgow pub with Doug Henderson, then a regional organiser for the GMWU, Brown spoke about his experiences and about some of the other new MPs. Henderson had known Brown for ten

years, discussing politics on platforms around Scotland and
against each other on *The Lion's Share*, a local television programme. 'That Blair fellow,' said Brown, 'he's quite clever.'

Although Brown was instinctively more left-wing than
Blair, he benefited from the proximity of a sympathetic soulmate. During their frequent conversations, not least later
during their journeys abroad, they discovered a mutual frustration about the party's direction and a common bewilderment about the solution. But in his maiden speech on 27 July
1983, Brown revealed no ideological dilemmas. His theme
was the plight of his unemployed constituents. In an engaging
delivery, he described 'a new arithmetic of depression and
despair' – the 'tragic toll' of mass unemployment: 'The chance
of a labourer getting a job in my constituency is 150 to 1
against. There is only one vacancy in the local careers office
for nearly five hundred teenagers who have recently left
school.' He criticised the government for not only causing
unemployment in the crumbling coal, linoleum and textile
industries, but for penalising the helpless victims of those
closures. There was heartfelt grief in his description of those in
the desolate communities expecting redundancy and fearing
permanent financial hardship. Ignoring their plight, he continued, the government proposed to reduce benefits while
taunting the unemployed that new jobs were available, if only
they looked. The government's task, he said, was to create
those new jobs: 'The House was told in 1948 that the welfare
state was created to take the shame out of need. Is that principle to be overthrown by an ever-increasing set of government assaults on the poor that are devoid of all logic, bereft
of all morality and vindictive even beyond monetarism?'
Brown was pleased by the murmurs of approval his ardour
evoked. In his opinion, only state intervention and the imposition of a minimum wage could help those at the bottom of
the social ladder. The conviction socialist derided the notion

that free markets and self enterprise were preferable to planning by Whitehall.

On the Conservative side there was respect for the feisty newcomer, but also some derision. Brown ignored the Tory riposte that Labour was responsible for unemployment in Fife. Jim Callaghan's government had plunged the country into chaos, and now this young Scotsman was proposing to reintroduce the same discredited politics. Labour's cure for 'the sick man of Europe' was similar to the Marxist dogma then crippling the communist countries of eastern Europe. Brown might win smiles by ridiculing the notion of the unemployed becoming self-reliant, if only by buying a ladder, bucket and cloth and offering themselves as window cleaners; he might arouse titters of laughter by taunting the Tories that 'Up your ladder' appeared to have replaced Norman Tebbit's 'On your bike' speech; but the nation had now voted twice in succession against the legacy of Attlee, Wilson and Callaghan.

Brown was undeterred. To him, self-improvement was as repulsive as the government's plan to persuade the young unemployed to accept lower wages or face a cut in their benefits if an offer of training was refused. 'Essentially,' he told the Commons, quoting confidential government documents leaked to him by a sympathiser, 'the papers say that the DHSS are to inculcate good working habits in the unemployed. What the government would be better doing is bringing new jobs to the area.'

Penalising the personal behaviour of the working classes through taxation had been attacked in 1937 by Ernest Bevin, Attlee's future foreign minister who was then leader of the TGWU. For Bevin and all socialists, the worst aspect of such retribution was the means tests to assess whether the poor should receive assistance from the state. The degradation of the inspections to assess poverty, argued Bevin, inhibited the poor both from saving and from seeking work. Forty-seven

years later, Brown repeated the same arguments as an attack
on the Conservative government's review of universal payments of benefits to all, irrespective of wealth. In his opinion,
even to consider targeting payments exclusively towards the
poor was heresy. Means tests, he believed, were inhuman
because they 'would deter the claims of those most in need'.
In his excitement he criticised the right-wing Adam Smith
Institute on BBC TV's *Panorama* on 10 December 1984 for, as
he claimed, recommending the end of child benefit and the
abolition of the welfare state. Sixteen months later, after
difficult negotiations, the BBC apologised for broadcasting
Brown's erroneous statement. Brown was embarrassed. He
prided himself on quoting carefully researched facts, and took
exception to any accusation of mistakes or worse, distortion.

In London, his life beyond politics was limited. He shared
a flat in the Barbican with Andrew, his younger brother, who
was also employed as his personal assistant. He worked relent-
lessly, rarely appearing in the Commons bars or tea rooms to
cultivate friendships. On Friday afternoons, long after most
MPs had returned to their constituencies and homes, he sat
alone in his cramped office, the floor covered in press releases,
books and newspapers, speaking on the telephone. On Saturdays in Edinburgh he was occasionally seen with Marion Caldwell at parties, but he preferred that she remained out of
sight. He liked drinking with his friends in pubs and especially
working men's clubs. There was a sincere fraternity in having
a pint with workers who shared his love of the Labour Party
and its heroes. He fumed against the reduction of grants to
the Rosyth naval shipyard in his constituency, deriding proposals to privatise it and publishing a pamphlet attacking the
arms trade and proposing that the yard should be converted
for civilian use. He also opposed the closure of any coalmines,
although they were often uneconomic, and caused many of
those who worked in them to suffer fatal illnesses. On every

social and economic argument he supported the hard, socialist solution. A test of those sentiments arose during the miners' strike in March 1984.

Few doubted that Arthur Scargill, the National Union of Mineworkers' leader, was intent on repeating the miners' triumph against Edward Heath in 1974. He wanted to prove his power to protect miners' livelihoods and to embarrass a Conservative government. In 1981 he had humiliated Thatcher by threatening a strike if the government closed down uneconomic mines. Having assessed that the stocks of coal were low, Thatcher retreated. But two years later the government had quietly accumulated sufficient coal stocks to withstand a strike of at least six months. As anticipated, on 1 March 1984 Scargill declared a strike in Yorkshire. Knowing that he would lose a national ballot, he organised strikes in militant localities across the country without organising proper votes. Flying pickets intimidated other miners to strike. The television pictures of fierce clashes between trade unionists and the police, resulting in thousands of injuries and arrests, raised the stakes. If Scargill won, the Thatcher government would be as vulnerable as Heath's had been. Her advantages were preparation and sharp disagreements among the miners. The outcome was not inevitable.

Regardless of Arthur Scargill's shortcomings, the miners' plight became a human tragedy. Neil Kinnock refused to condemn the strikers, while Gordon Brown openly supported them, protesting against the government's 'vindictive cuts' and refusal to pay benefits to their families. Instead of condemning the violence, he pleaded with the police and government to release imprisoned miners, and never publicly criticised Scargill despite the strike's questionable legitimacy and the lack of support from workers in the power, steel and transport industries. On the picket lines he openly praised the miners despite being irked to be standing with their wives in the cold and rain, organising their communities' survival, while some strikers were drinking in their clubs. At Christmas a trickle of English miners returned to work, isolating the militants. In March 1985, after one year, the strike collapsed. Brown, however, had never wavered. He earned the miners' gratitude, accepting in appreciation gifts of miners' lamps and certificates.

Like most in the Labour movement, he did not fully understand the implications of the miners' defeat. He thundered against the reduction of regional aid and the gradual loss of manufacturing jobs, and demanded that the government create new jobs, but he was bogged down in an ideological wasteland. Labour had reached a nadir, and was unelectable until the extremists in the party were expelled. Neil Kinnock had many weaknesses, but among his strengths was the courage in November 1984 to confront the militants in order to save the party from fratricide. Unlike many Labour MPs, Brown did not openly join that struggle. He did not travel through England supporting the fight against Tony Benn and the Militant Tendency, nor did he overtly attack the militants. Rather, he preferred to return directly to Scotland from London. Nevertheless, he was among the members of the new intake offered a chance to break the extremists' stranglehold. Neil Kinnock told Roy Hattersley, 'I want Tony Blair in the Treasury team.' To avoid the impression of outright favouritism, Hattersley suggested that Kinnock appoint two new MPs, and that Brown also be promoted to speak on employment and social security. Labour needed his abilities, said Hattersley. Kinnock had met Brown during the devolution debates in Scotland. Although they had disagreed, he appreciated the young Scotsman's efforts to prevent a party split. Soon after the 1983 election Donald Dewar had proposed that Brown should join the Scottish team, but Kinnock had resisted, saying he should cut his teeth first. By the time Hattersley made his suggestion, Kinnock felt Brown deserved promotion. But while Blair accepted the offer and was appointed spokesman on the City and finance, Brown refused. 'I wasn't ready,' he later explained. 'It's crazy that Gordon rejected the offer,' Blair complained to Hattersley. 'The problem is that Gordon is so honest,' replied the bemused deputy leader.

Brown's refusal was not wholly altruistic. He had, he believed, too much to lose by accepting a junior post, not least a delay to the completion of his biography of James Maxton. If he had written the book a decade earlier, his analysis of Maxton's life would have lacked his personal experience of political struggle. In his heart Brown idolised his hero's idealism for social responsibility, education and the abolition of poverty. But in his head he understood how Maxton had undermined his ambitions for a better society by refusing to compromise to obtain power. 'The party whose cause he championed for forty years could, with justice,' Brown wrote, 'be accused of committing political suicide for the sake of ideological purity.'

In spring 1985, as the biography neared completion, Labour moved ahead in the opinion polls and the opposition parties won important victories in the local elections. Electorally, Labour's devotion to traditional socialism appeared justified. Despite the defeat of the miners, the government had been shaken by the botched privatisation of British Leyland, rising inflation and high unemployment. Brown was writing a regular weekly column for the *Daily Record*, the Scottish version of the *Daily Mirror*, providing money to pay his researchers and access to a wide audience. Through his many contacts he sought confidential information to embarrass the government in the Commons and in the newspaper. Once it was seen that he handled leaks properly and could be trusted, he expected a regular supply.

In May 1985 he secured a confidential government review proposing to encourage the young unemployed to find jobs by reducing their social benefits. This, he raged, was 'a raid on the poor'. In July he attacked the government for employing undercover agents to investigate young mothers claiming benefits for single households while secretly cohabiting. Those investigations, he claimed, punished the poor. Brown's pride lay in his probity. Lawyers at the *Daily Record* were disturbed by the threat of a libel writ following an item in his column about the sale of council houses in East Kilbride. The newspaper wanted to settle, but Brown refused. He was, the newspaper's lawyers remarked, 'obsessive to be perceived as utterly truthful'. He discreetly warned the complainants, 'If you want to carry on and do business in the future when we're in government, you should drop the libel action.' The complaint was withdrawn, and eventually Brown's allegations were confirmed. Since Robert Maxwell had bought the Mirror Group in July 1984 Brown had refused invitations to his parties, albeit without revealing his reasons. Nevertheless, he was content to take Maxwell's money and promote his own profile.

The change of the political atmosphere in 1985 persuaded Brown to accept a front bench appointment. The invitation in November to work with the shadow spokesman for trade and industry by specialising in regional affairs was issued from John Smith's office. Initially the two men forged an easy relationship, convincing themselves that the omens for electoral success were good. Thatcher's position looked vulnerable, especially in Scotland, after a huge increase in rates. As the value of sterling fell following a drop in the price of oil, Labour was convinced that capitalism was in crisis. The mini-earthquake caused by 'Big Bang', the deregulation of the stock market in October 1986, confirmed their belief that capitalism was besmirched. The sight of bankers and brokers selling their companies for huge sums to foreign invaders aroused disdain about Thatcherism and free markets. Brown did not anticipate the social revolution sparked by the disappearance of the City's traditional classes, or the rise of a meritocracy who would be unimpressed by his campaign to renationalise the privatised industries. Others close to him did understand however. In conversations with Gavyn Davies, then an economist at Goldman Sachs, the American merchant bank, and husband of Neil Kinnock's assistant Sue Nye, John Eatwell, a Cambridge economist who was advising Kinnock, and especially Peter Mandelson, the party's new director of press and public relations, he heard the first arguments in favour of a reconsideration of Labour's policies.

Peter Mandelson, the grandson of Herbert Morrison, a prominent minister in Atlee's government, and a former television producer, was attractive to Brown. He appreciated Mandelson's vision for the party to 'modernise', although neither fully understood the obstacles to Labour's re-election. Both were encouraged by a new self-confidence at the party conference in 1986 in Blackpool, not least by the first defeat of the extremists. Under Mandelson's influence, Labour was distancing itself from the Attlee legacy to attract the middle classes. The red flag, the party's traditional symbol, was replaced by a red rose, to suggest the abandonment of a strident socialist agenda, especially confiscatory taxes, although the party's actual policies contradicted the impression. Brown returned to Scotland to fight the 1987 election pledging to abandon Britain's independent nuclear capacity, close America's military bases, halt the sale of council houses and repeal the Tory laws limiting trade union power.

Labour's certainty that the Tories would not win a third consecutive election should have been shaken in the new year. The economy improved – growth increased to 4.8 per cent – and despite violent picketing outside News International's new headquarters in Wapping, Labour refused to condemn the trade unions outright. Three million were

unemployed, but the opinion polls swung back in the Tories'
favour, showing Labour at 29 per cent, the SDP-Liberal
Alliance at 26 per cent and the Conservatives at 43 per cent.

In the early days of the election campaign at the end of
May 1987, Brown and his party leaders were nevertheless
optimistic. Mandelson's coup of a glossy election broadcast by
Hugh Hudson of Neil Kinnock and his wife walking hand-in-
hand in visually stunning photography roused the party's
spirits. Kinnock's popularity rose sixteen points overnight.
The reports from Conservative Central Office of arguments
among Tory leaders gratified Labour's planners, convinced
of their strength on health and education. Labour's undoing
started in the last week of the campaign. In a television interview, Kinnock was asked what would happen if Russia
invaded Britain, unprotected by a nuclear bomb. He replied
that guerrilla bands fighting from the hills would resist the
invader. That strategy found few sympathisers in the Midland
conurbations, London and the south-east. Portrayed as a leftist
loony, Kinnock was also vulnerable on taxation. Roy Hattersley and John Smith had pledged to reverse privatisation
and restore most social benefits. The cost of that, the Tories
claimed, would increase income tax to 56 pence in the pound.
At first Kinnock insisted that only those earning over £25,000
a year would face higher taxes, but under persistent questioning he admitted that those earning over £15,000 would pay
'a few extra pence'. The newspaper headlines 'Labour Tax
Fiasco' frightened the middle classes. Thatcher's accusation
that with Labour 'financial prudence goes out of the window'
struck a mortal blow.

Campaigning in Scotland, Brown was distanced from these
misfortunes. The swing to Labour in his area suggested that
there would be a rout of Tory seats. He did not believe the
national opinion polls, and was heartened on election night
by a BBC *Newsnight* exit poll predicting huge Tory losses and

a 'hung' parliament. His smile disappeared long before his personal result came in. The Tories lost in Scotland but would be returned with an overall 101-seat majority. Brown won his seat with an increased majority of 19,589, practically 50 per cent of the votes cast. His personal pleasure was suffocated by the national result. 'He was shaken by the defeat,' reported a close friend the next morning. 'He thought Labour would win nationally as it had in Scotland.' Ten years later, Brown would claim to Paul Routledge that at the time of the 1987 election he had blamed Labour's plans for high taxation for having 'put a cap on people's aspirations'. In reality he appears not to have contemplated lower taxation until long afterwards.

In the autopsy of the defeat, the dissatisfaction with the party's deputy leader Roy Hattersley was widespread. John Smith, popular, funny and fast at the dispatch box with a joke or a mocking aside, was expected to inherit the shadow chancellorship despite his poor grasp of economics. He encouraged Brown to stand for election to the shadow cabinet, impressed by the young man's loyalty, hard work and use of leaked documents to discomfort the government. Brown was pleasantly unintoxicated by his status, arriving at meetings like an overgrown student with bundles of ragged papers spilling onto the floor. He was also noticeably devoid of the argumentative stubbornness that would emerge later. Smith's endorsement was critical to Brown's campaign in the election. Helped by Nick Brown, a northern England trade union officer also elected to parliament in 1983, he came eleventh out of forty runners, an unexpected success. John Smith was duly appointed shadow chancellor and Brown shadow chief secretary to the Treasury, the youngest member of Neil Kinnock's new team. 'He's going to be the leader of the Labour Party one day,' Kinnock told Tom Sawyer, a member of the party's National Executive Committee. Kinnock regarded Brown as a kindred spirit against John Smith, of whom he was wary, although he judged both Scots to be reliable. The Scottish MPs were a group of experienced politicians, held together despite personal differences by a tribal brotherhood based upon ability. United by their hatred of Thatcher and not scarred by Militant, their principal shortcoming was provincialism. Everything was interpreted from a Scottish point of view, and as a result their contribution to the inquest into the causes of the unexpected election defeat was muddled.

Kinnock ordered a review of the party's whole ideology. Labour, he acknowledged, was unelectable without the support of the middle classes. The review of the economic policies was entrusted to Bryan Gould, a New Zealander and the shadow spokesman for trade and industry. Gould, an organiser of the recent election campaign and a member of Labour's left wing, believed that traditional socialism remained the party's anchor. Brown no longer agreed, and refused to participate in Gould's work. His unease had emerged after forensic discussions about the party's policies with Doug Henderson, John Smith and Murray Elder – all Scotsmen who would spend one week every August hill-walking and mountaineering in Scotland with their families. 'Brown wanted a break from the past,' reflected Gould sourly. 'His idea was to be more congenial towards the City.' Gould, more senior than Brown, was unwilling to accommodate Brown's ill-defined opinions, and was encouraged to pursue his course by Peter Mandelson, whose patronage had promoted Gould's importance in the media. 'Peter gave me a very comforting feeling,' Gould acknowledged, 'introducing good contacts and placing my name in very good contexts.'

The stock market crash on 19 October 1987, 'Black Monday', confirmed Gould's conviction about 'capitalism's irreversible crisis'. Ideologically, Brown could offer no solution to Labour's unpopularity in the polls or suggest an alternative to Thatcherism, apart from announcing that Gould's intention

to re-impose economic controls would guarantee electoral disaster. 'Bryan's being unhelpful,' Brown was told some weeks
later by John Eatwell. 'His report to the party conference will
recommend the renationalisation of some privatised companies.' Brown agreed that Gould's proposals, the springboard
for his ambitions to be party leader, were reckless. He combined with Blair to urge Mandelson to abandon Gould. While
Mandelson pondered, Brown and Blair took it upon themselves to frustrate the review.

Busy preparing to dispatch his final report later that day to
the printers, Bryan Gould was surprised when Gordon Brown,
Tony Blair and John Eatwell entered his office in the Norman
Shaw building unannounced. 'We want all references to
nationalisation and renationalisation taken out of the report,'
announced Brown. 'You're too late,' replied Gould angrily.
'You refused to sit on the committee and do any work, and
now you want to interfere. No way. Go away! All of you!'
Gould stared particularly at Blair. His presence was inexplic-
able, since he, as shadow spokesman for employment, was
not even eligible for membership of the committee. The report
was dispatched and printed. Gould's victory, however, was
bittersweet. At the end of 1987 a series of unfavourable references to him appeared in newspapers. He suspected that he
knew the identity of the source, but his repeated attempts
to reach Peter Mandelson were unsuccessful. Eventually he
elicited an unexpected response. 'You should get to know
Gordon,' said Mandelson. 'He wants to be a friend of yours.'
Gould realised that he was being abandoned. Mandelson's
seduction – the offer of friendship, with its concomitant
demand for emotional commitment – had been aborted. Even
worse, Mandelson had switched. He was now briefing against
Gould and promoting Brown and Blair. 'It's an ideological
war,' Gould realised, but was nevertheless relieved when his
report, 'The Productive and Competitive Economy', was

approved by the party executive on 25 May 1988. Unintentionally, he had prompted the conception of an emotional,
triangular relationship between Mandelson, Brown and Blair.

Peter Mandelson had become persuaded that Gordon
Brown was the party's future. Compared with so many
Labour politicians, Brown was immensely attractive. Unaware
of his lurking volcanic aloofness, Mandelson regarded Brown
as a sensitive, handsome, entertaining professional tainted
only by impatience and intensity. Among other MPs he was
regarded as unselfish, willing to help those in difficulty, extending personal kindnesses even to those with whom he
disagreed if they had won his respect as an intellectual equal,
and arguing from knowledge rather than purely prejudice.
Watching him at receptions, as he glad-handed and back-
slapped the faithful with apparent conviction, and without
betraying his dislike of the performance, few would have
recognised the brooding workaholic who invariably arrived
late at a restaurant for dinner with friends and, after gobbling
down his steak and chips or a plate of spaghetti, would rush
back to his rooms to either type a speech or read a book.

Brown's combination of intellect, sophistication, ambition
and popularism appealed to Mandelson. Standing on the steps
of the party's headquarters in Walworth Road, he told Andy
McSmith, a Labour press officer, 'Gordon will one day be the
party's leader.' Mandelson's prediction surprised McSmith.
Brown was still largely unknown. Mandelson acknowledged
that obstacle, but had repeatedly promised Brown that it
would be overcome. During their frequent meetings Brown
constantly complained, 'I'm not getting enough mention in
the papers. My name's only in a couple of them.' Mandelson
reassured him that his hard work would be rewarded. Both
were grappling with the party's ideology, and belatedly welcomed the opportunities of the 1987 defeat. With the support
of the party's left wing and the endorsement of Neil Kinnock,

Brown believed he would eventually succeed the Welshman as the party's leader. He dismissed the chances of his rivals, except possibly John Smith, who was handicapped by his poor relationship with Kinnock. Brown's quandary was how to develop an alternative to Thatcherism. Marooned among orthodox Scottish socialists, he was still estranged from the consequences of 'Big Bang'.

Nigel Lawson's boom had visible fault-lines, but Thatcherism appeared irreversible. Relying on people and markets rather than Whitehall civil servants to manage the economy was attractive to electors. Mandelson, alert to the new ideas, understood the dilemma. 'I think you should go to Gordon,' he told Michael Wills, a television producer at LWT's *Weekend World* who drafted policy documents and speeches for him. 'Help him become prime minister.'

Interested in the failings of British industry, Wills had just completed a series of documentaries revealing the limitations and frustrations of British managers. In particular he had been struck by an interview with a supplier of car components who volunteered that he had resisted borrowing money from the banks in order to build a new production line to manufacture gearboxes for Honda. His reason was depressing. In the early 1980s he had borrowed for a similar venture, but interest rates had soared and he had been financially crippled. Ever since, he had decided to remain small and safe by not borrowing. He spoke eloquently and authoritatively about the Conservative government's failure to help industry. This was fertile ground for Labour to exploit, Wills told Brown. Wills introduced Brown to the experts consulted by *Weekend World*, with whom he discussed the essence of Thatcherism and its American counterpart, Reaganism. Reluctantly, he began to recognise the strength of some Tory policies and the disadvantage of Labour's adherence to Attlee's consensus. There was reason to acknowledge that the growth of Europe's and

America's successful economies was not the result of state intervention. Listening and brooding, he agonised over how to balance incentives to entrepreneurs, the restriction of public spending and the financing of social justice. 'We need a fairer Britain,' he repeated as he learnt to sympathise with the market economy. 'We've got to work from first principles towards policies,' he told his confidants, irritated by Kinnock's ignorance of economics and John Smith's resistance to change. Under Smith as shadow chancellor, Labour's economic policies remained rigidly anti-market, against joining the ERM and in favour of controlling exchange rates. 'We must persuade the rich of the need for fairness,' Smith had said, apparently without realising the inherent contradiction. Wealth creators, by definition, are not social philanthropists, but ruthlessly ambitious to earn money for themselves.

Three successive election defeats had convinced Brown that simply damning the Tories' sympathy for the rich would not reverse Labour's political decline. The party needed new ideas. That summer he spent three weeks in Harvard's library, studying industrial policy and discussing the cause of America's economic success with local academics. He returned to Westminster emboldened by his intellectual rejuvenation. His task was to find a compromise between old Labour's philosophies and Thatcherism. There were many false starts. Essentially, he was searching for ideas to help him write a new Labour epic that could rank with Anthony Crosland's *Future of Socialism*, a 500-page analysis of how to create an egalitarian, socialist Britain, published in 1956. Throughout, Brown asserted with evangelical sincerity that social Christianity could provide greater fairness and prosperity through a more efficient economy, all in the cause of socialism.

Nigel Lawson's budget in 1988 was another ideological challenge. Treasury statistics showed that the reduction in the top rate of tax – from 83 per cent under Labour in 1979 to 60 per cent nine years later – had actually increased the amount of money received by the Treasury, as the rich had less reason to evade and avoid taxes. In his penultimate budget, Lawson announced that the top rate of tax would be reduced from 60 per cent to 40 per cent, and the basic rate cut to 25 per cent from 33 per cent. The Labour benches erupted in uncontrolled protest. The Commons was suspended for ten minutes. Brown joined in the protest. He rejected Lawson's argument that encouraging enterprise would benefit the poor. Too many millionaires, he raged, were enriching themselves from tax loopholes, not least from share options. Lawson's budget allowed company directors to buy shares at 1984 prices and take the profits in 1988, paying capital gains tax of 30 per cent rather than 60 per cent. 'Britain is fast becoming a paradise for top-rate tax dodgers,' Brown protested, demanding that the 'share option millionaires' should be penalised. Instead of rewarding the rich, the government should invest in education and training. Brown was echoing the mantra voiced by Harold Wilson twenty years earlier, although six years of Wilson's government had ended, at best, in economic paralysis. His unoriginal accusations did not dent Lawson's claim to have achieved a hat trick – higher spending on public services, lower tax rates and a budget surplus.

Overshadowing Lawson's self-congratulation was the rising value of sterling and his bitter row with Thatcher about whether Britain should join the Exchange Rate Mechanism (ERM). The growing strain between Lawson and Thatcher, and the prospect of rising inflation and an implosion of the boom, encouraged Brown's belief that the government's economic policy was doomed. Neil Kinnock's misfortune was that his alternative policies were unattractive to Labour's far left. Their representative, Tony Benn, launched a bid for the leadership, and the old internecine war erupted once again. Benn's bid was trounced at the 1988 autumn party conference

in Blackpool, but all the percentage points gained from the
Tories shown by the opinion polls evaporated. Labour remained a party of protest, and not an alternative government.

At the end of the party conference Brown returned to Edinburgh with John Smith. Over the previous week the shadow
chancellor had as usual enjoyed himself, living up to his reputation at many parties as a heavy drinker, and smoking cigars
after big meals. On reaching home he felt unwell, and was
examined in a hospital. While getting dressed afterwards, he
suffered a heart attack. Smith's misfortune was Brown's
opportunity. For twenty years he had prepared himself for
the spotlight, and now his chance had arisen at the most
favourable moment as, during Smith's convalescence, he took
his place on Labour's front bench. Nigel Lawson's strategy
appeared to be crumbling. The Tories were becoming the victims of their own mistakes. There were widespread protests
in Scotland against the new poll tax, inflation was climbing
above 4 per cent, interest rates were rising towards 14 per
cent, unemployment was stuck at three million and, with a
worsening balance of payments, there was a run on sterling.
Lawson's boast about his 'sound management of the economy' was an easy target.

'This is a boom based on credit,' mocked Brown, eager to
prove his skills during the debate on the autumn financial
statement on 1 November 1988. Standing at the dispatch box
in a crowded chamber, glancing at a speech printed out in
huge letters to compensate for his poor eyesight, Brown
relished the occasion. Countless speeches in dank Scottish
assembly halls had primed his self-confident, exquisitely
timed flourishes, mixing statistics and oratory while displaying
his mastery of the dialectic, the rapier of eloquent Marxists.
He deployed artful mockery to rile an arrogant chancellor for
allowing consumption to spiral out of control and for making
consistently wrong forecasts. 'Most of us would say,' scoffed

Brown at his crestfallen target, 'that the proper answer is to keep the forecasts and discard the chancellor.' Each cutting jibe, accompanied by whoops of derision from the Labour benches, rattled Lawson's pomposity. The chancellor had not anticipated the humiliation or the lukewarm support from the Tory benches. His pained expression was Brown's reward. The result, Brown would later say, was 'an unequal dialogue between a chancellor who had not yet made up his mind when to retire and a prime minister who had not yet made up her mind when to sack him'. During those magical minutes, Labour MPs felt a surge of hope. Here, perhaps, was the new hero they had sought so desperately. Brown sat down to roars of approval.

Walking through the arched corridors of Westminster later that afternoon, he was suitably modest, feeling an inner calm about his good fortune. In just two days, Labour MPs would vote for the shadow cabinet. The combination of his Commons performance with his astute handling of a series of leaks had earned him an irreproachable reputation. Once again, he sought the help of Nick Brown to lobby for votes. The result, late on 6 November, was electrifying. As he rushed from Committee Room 14, Brown was laughing. He was top of the poll. Following him out of the room, Tony Blair was seen telephoning his wife Cherie to report his own first appearance on the list, his reward for humiliating Lord Young, the secretary of state for trade and industry, about the government's misconduct of supervising Barlow Clowes, an investment company which collapsed as a result of dishonesty. The next morning's newspapers praised Brown as 'high flying' and 'a horse for early investment'. One sage wrote, 'He appears to possess the ultimate political quality of luck.' A few, aggressively briefed by Mandelson, speculated that Brown had become a future contender for the party's leadership. Willie Whitelaw, the Tory elder statesman and former home secretary, said that both Brown and Blair were 'improved and becoming a little dangerous'. Another observer noted that even at that moment Brown appeared affected by self-doubt: 'He is very ambitious, but he seems to lack the nerve to go right to the very top.' Brown's image among the agnostics was not of a leader but of the Scottish engineer on the ocean liner, toiling away below decks in the engine room, polishing the pistons and removing the grease.

An opportunity to shed that reputation was again provided by Lawson. After journalists briefed by the chancellor reported that he intended to target the poor and pensioners with benefits while withholding the money from the rich, Lawson complained that he had been misquoted. The furore allowed Brown to parade his Christian conscience. 'The government's real objective,' he taunted the tarnished chancellor in the Commons, 'is to move from a regime of universal benefits to a regime of universal means testing, jeopardising for millions of pensioners security in ill-health and dignity in old age.' Means testing pensions, said Brown, was 'the most serious government assault so far mounted on the basic principles of Britain's post-war welfare state'. His reputation harmed by scathing headlines whose implication – 'Veteran Chancellor Bloodied by Upstart' – was clear, Lawson's misfortunes resulted in rich kudos for Brown. The Commons was the perfect platform from which to parade his loathing for complacent Tories feigning to help the poor. They were men, he sniped, who cared for power and money rather than principle. Lawson and Nicholas Ridley, the secretary of state for the environment and High Thatcherite minor aristocrat, ranked among the worst. Ridley's aspiration was to deregulate, to withdraw subsidies, and to delight in not pulling the levers of power. Ridley sneered at Brown's 'supply-side socialism'. Standing in the crowded chamber, Brown reacted with genuine anger to the chain-smoking minister who appeared to care more about his ashtray than his departmental in-tray. Above all, Brown reviled Thatcher's affection for photo-opportunities: one day she was seen promoting science, the next day campaigning against litter, then advancing the cause of women and later urging the regeneration of the inner cities. 'Today a photo-opportunity,' he wrote, ridiculing the 'Maggie Acts' headlines, 'tomorrow a new issue, the last one all but forgotten. The government's main new investment in these vital concerns has been in its own publicity.' His incandescence at the rising cost of official advertising, from £20 million to £100 million, seemed genuine. Four years later he would adopt the same tactics as virtuous ploys to help win an election.

Brown's pertinent strength in 1988 was his patent sincerity. Like a machine-gun, around the clock, seven days a week, he worked to capture the headlines, firing off press releases on every subject, with newsworthy coups offering leaks of confidential Whitehall information. One day he publicised a government memorandum about civil servants not encouraging grants for high-technology research; another day he produced secret government statistics showing that the poorest four million homes were worse off than they had been ten years earlier; another day he trumpeted a report by Peter Levene, the personal adviser to Michael Heseltine at the ministry of defence, recommending that, to save money, Royal Navy ships should be refitted by private contractors. Levene's discovery that the efficiency of the naval dockyards could not be assessed because their accounting systems were 'entirely meaningless' was derided by Brown's assertion, to cheers, that 'this is the most devious government we've had this century'.

Success fuelled his passion: at 7.30 on Boxing Day morning he telephoned Alistair Darling, a lawyer and Scottish activist. 'Have you seen the story in today's *Daily Telegraph*?' he asked. 'No,' replied Darling. 'I'm still asleep.' Deprived of a personal family life, Brown had become preoccupied by politics. Gradually, his passion distorted his perspective on life. Some accused him of hyperactivity, of becoming over-exposed as a rent-a-quote politician, robotically spouting One True Faith. He confessed his awareness that 'rising can turn into falling pretty quickly', and blamed his irrepressible desire to lead Labour away from its past and towards new policies. His fervour would brook no opposition, especially from other members of his party.

Among the most difficult were his fellow Scots. His old foe George Galloway and John Reid, previously a sociable partner, had become argumentative and occasionally unreasonable. Reid and his group, Brown suspected, were quintessentially sectarian west Scotland left-wing hardmen, meeting as a caucus before general meetings to agree their arguments and votes. 'He's a music hall artist,' Brown said of one agitator whom he castigated as 'a prisoner of his upbringing', perhaps failing to recognise that he too was a hostage to his own past.

Among the shackles of that past was the feud with Robin Cook. 'It's chemical between those two,' John Smith told friends, concerned about the sour relationship. Cook was himself renowned as a good hater and not a team player. 'A bombastic pain when I first met him,' was Jimmy Allison's judgement about a man accused of flip-flopping on major policies – the euro, nuclear weapons and Britain's relationship with the United States. While Cook spoke impromptu on those issues, alternating between vehement opposition and support, Brown avoided extremes, courteously delivering written speeches based upon intellectual reasoning, only rarely being wrong-footed. His success increased Cook's tetchiness. In turn, Brown became convinced that Cook, as he told friends, was 'trying to destroy me'. No one regarded this apparent paranoia as serious, but there was a less attractive personality beginning to emerge. Success and publicity had transformed Brown into a man with an unqualified belief in himself, convinced that he was the best socialist, the best thinker, the best persuader, the best media performer and the best at everything else. The political truth was gradually defined as what suited Gordon Brown at that moment, and socialism was defined as those ideas that best served his interests. If his black-and-white judgement about Cook was challenged, a grim mood enveloped a man now increasingly consumed by hatreds. Only occasionally could he restrain his monochrome ambition.

To help John Smith's recovery, Brown accompanied him in regular ascents of Scotland's mountains over 3,000 feet in height – known as Munro-bagging – occasionally with Chris Smith, the MP for Islington, and Martin O'Neill. Those walks inspired Brown to write a pamphlet, 'Where is the Greed?: Margaret Thatcher and the Betrayal of Britain's Future'. At heart, the pamphlet revealed an old-fashioned Christian socialist concerned to alleviate suffering, seeking a modern way to vent his spleen against the Thatcherite conviction that state interference was a principal cause of society's faults. Only the state, he claimed, could redress the growth of poverty and inequality since 1979. Eager to win the next election, the 'new realist' despaired about the past decade of Labour history and the danger of following John Maxton into oblivion. His solution, using new words to promote old ideas, was a rehashed attack on 'free market dogma'.

John Smith sympathised, but was alarmed by his friend's hyperactivity. During his convalescence he regularly telephoned Roy Hattersley, the deputy leader, and asked, 'What's Gordon up to?' 'Nothing,' replied Hattersley, 'but being loyal.' To certify his reassurance, Hattersley invited Brown to lunch the week before Smith's return. 'What job would you like to do?' he asked. 'I think I'll remain as shadow chief secretary,' replied Brown, 'to help John back to health.' Brown's

restlessness for change and personal success did not appear
to endanger Smith.

In early summer 1989, Margaret Thatcher became personally vulnerable. The poll tax had provoked violent protests,
and her antagonism towards the ERM was dividing her from
Nigel Lawson and Geoffrey Howe, the foreign secretary. To
reinforce her position, Howe was demoted to leader of the
House and Sir Alan Walters, an enemy of Lawson, was recalled as her personal economic adviser, based in 10 Downing
Street. Lawson was incandescent. The disarray among the
Tory leadership was oxygen for an accomplished political
debater blessed with sharp wit, and Brown deployed his invec-
tive in a masterful Commons performance. 'Many lonely, sad
and embattled people,' he said, mocking Lawson across the
dispatch box, 'labour under the delusion that their thoughts
are being influenced by the Moonies next door . . . I assure
the right honourable gentleman that he is not paranoid. They
really are out to get him.' Lawson sat stony-faced as Labour
MPs jeered, 'Go on, smile,' and roared their approval as Brown
recited the wretched statistics about inflation at 6 per cent,
interest rates at 15 per cent and a growing trade deficit which
undermined the chancellor's reputation. No Labour politician
wanted to hear that unemployment had fallen to 1.7 million
and that manufacturing output had increased every year
between 1983 to 1989 by an average of 4.75 per cent. Brown
feigned deafness to Lawson's assertion that Britain's managers
had finally been liberated to earn profits because of real competition, the destruction of protectionism and the strangu-
lation of the trade unions' restrictive practices. Devotion to
socialism, retorted Lawson, was restricted to Albania, Cuba
and Walworth Road. Not so, replied Brown spurred on by a
party cheered by their discovery of a potential leader; there
was socialism in Sweden, France and Spain. And soon, they
hoped, in Britain. Lawson's misery fuelled his opponent's

morale. As the chamber emptied, the crowd followed Brown and John Smith to the Commons bar. Endless hands smacked the dark-suited back of the man who fellow MPs were convinced was the star of the new generation, the future leader who would expunge the miserable memories of Wilson, Callaghan and Foot.

That evening, Brown was congratulated by Neil Kinnock. Confirming Brown's potential to inherit the leadership, the Welshman offered two pieces of advice: 'For credibility, you need to vote against the whip. And secondly, you've got to learn to fall in love faster and get married.' Brown laughed. He had introduced Kinnock to Marion Caldwell, but had no intention of proposing marriage, despite her fervour. 'Oh, there's lots of time for that,' he replied. Kinnock's advice may not have been followed, but an unlikely source would possibly be more influential.

Just before the summer recess, Brown was travelling with Michael Howard, the secretary of state for employment, on a train from Swansea to London. Howard recognised Brown as a fellow intellectual. Flushed by the Conservatives' continuing supremacy despite their difficulties, Howard settled back in his seat and presented a detailed critique of Labour's unresolved electoral weaknesses. The party, he said, would never win another election until it ceased alienating the 'margins'. Brown listened silently as Howard lectured him about appealing to voters' personal interests in taxation, schools and health. To overcome middle-class antagonism, concluded Howard, Labour needed to address the details of those individual issues rather than blankly preach socialism. On arrival in London, the opponents bade each other farewell. In later years Howard would wonder whether his free advice had helped Labour finally to defeat his own party.

Brown was certainly anxious to learn during that summer. Americans had become his inspiration. The previous year he had met Bill Clinton in Baden-Baden, in Germany. Clinton was touring the world to meet other politicians before declaring his bid for the presidency. His big idea to roll back 'Reaganomics', with its greed and debts, was to introduce a 'New Covenant', reasserting the existence of a 'society' in America and declaring that citizenship involved responsibilities as well as rights. Brown found Clinton engaging, although intellectually muddled. There was nevertheless scope for a partnership between Clinton's advisers and Labour's 'modernisers', including Peter Mandelson and Geoff Mulgan, a policy adviser. One year later, Brown would spend the summer in Cape Cod, reading through a suitcase of books on which the airline had levied an excess weight charge, and seeking out Democrats to hear about their new ideas.

He returned to Westminster anticipating excitement, but not the earthquake of 26 October 1989. Margaret Thatcher's refusal to join the ERM and her protection of Alan Walters had humiliated Nigel Lawson. Insensitive to the danger, she allowed Lawson to resign, and then dismissed Walters. The prime minister's relationship with Walters was an easy target for Brown's derision: 'It was the most damaging appointment of an adviser by a head of government since – I was going to say, since Caligula's horse, but at least the horse stayed in Rome and worked full-time.' Turning to the choice of John Major to replace Lawson as chancellor, Brown jeered, to the unrestrained acclaim of the Labour backbenches, 'He has had the right training for the job over the past few weeks when he was foreign secretary – private humiliation, public repudiation and instant promotion.' In the shadow cabinet elections in autumn 1989 he again topped the poll, and was appointed shadow spokesman for trade and industry.

For the modernisers, especially Blair and Mandelson, Brown embodied their best hopes for Labour's eventual success. Suggestions that he was a candidate for the leadership inevitably roused his personal enemies and political critics on the left to question the essence of the man. The sceptics sensed a lack of ruthlessness, judged his charm as weakness, and doubted his willingness to grasp the jugular in order to advance his cause. Perhaps, they speculated, he lacked a game plan eventually to win the leadership. Their doubts were reinforced by Brown's notorious disorganisation, persistently arriving late for, or completely missing, meetings. He was known to be irked by the practical details of life. Frequently he arranged a meeting in a restaurant but forgot to book a table, or even found the doors locked. His sometimes uneasy relationship to reality led to gossip concerning his uncertain commitment to others. His obsessive privacy, suggesting a fear of embarrassing revelations, also fuelled rumours, while his provincial rough edges suggested foreignness to the metropolitan media. 'I think most Scots are pretty reserved about their ambitions or personal lives. I think I am,' he told an interviewer in 1989 who asked why he so rarely smiled. His friendship with Nigel Griffiths, a confirmed bachelor and the MP for Edinburgh South since 1987 who worked devotedly for him, excited unjustified gossip, not least after Owen Dudley Edwards said the two were like 'Christopher Robin and Pooh Bear in an enchanted place in the forest'.

Outside Edinburgh, few were aware of 'Dramcarling', Brown's new double-fronted red-brick house in North Queensferry, set on a hill above the road with a garden rolling down towards the Firth of Forth and with a view of Edinburgh Castle on a clear day. He had after many years found his dream. The house epitomised his love of Scotland – its poetry and scenery. The interior reflected another trait, having been neither redecorated nor refurnished. The dirty sofas from the shambolic top floor of his Edwardian house in Marchmont Road were dropped into the rooms overlooking the garden, and a familiar pile of books, government reports and newspapers began accumulating across the floors, around the battered typewriters and discarded word processors, towards the ramshackle kitchen. The man without taste hated domesticity.

During the decade Brown knew Marion Caldwell, his attitude towards women and relationships aroused bewilderment. Although he spent holidays with Caldwell in America, she remained in her own home in Edinburgh. He regularly disappeared for substantial periods, arriving at her doorstep when it suited him and failing to excuse himself if he was absent. Relationships with women in Brown's life tended to be one-way affairs. Nurturing them was unimportant; affection was only perfunctorily acknowledged and reciprocated. Caldwell was among those women who were fascinated by his magnetism – the Alpha Male – and who pandered to his demand for immediate attention whenever requested. He happily allowed her to develop her career in Scotland. She was welcomed to the North Queensferry house at weekends, to sit quietly while he wrote endless articles, speeches and pamphlets. On Saturday nights he often refused to go out, preferring to watch *Match of the Day*. He expected Caldwell demurely to enjoy his pleasures, grateful that she was unable to visit London during the week. Sharing a flat in Kennington with his brother Andrew, he liked partying among high-achieving Scots in London. Although some have described a blissful romance with Caldwell in Scotland, Brown was interested in other women in the south. Some witnessed him pursuing Maya Even, a pretty Canadian presenter of the BBC's *Money Programme*, while others recall him considering forging a relationship with Anna Ford after a dinner party at her home in Chiswick. The discretion of witnesses and the absence of chitchat protected Brown, who was classed by one Conservative newspaper as 'single, reticent, good humoured and charming'.

Divergence of opinion about a politician's character is not

unusual, but in Brown's case it became particularly pertinent as he and John Smith reached a Rubicon. Economics, they agreed, had become a more serious business in politics. In any future election manifesto, Labour would need to provide statistics to establish its financial responsibility and to substantiate its challenge to Thatcherite orthodoxy. Any promises would require proof of proper costing. 'Competence' was the buzz word both bandied. To expunge the memory of Harold Wilson's devaluation of sterling in November 1967 and the humiliation of Denis Healey begging for help from the International Monetary Fund in October 1976, it was best, they agreed, to support Britain's entry into the Exchange Rate Mechanism. Labour's support for the ERM would convince the electorate of the party's commitment to non-inflationary policies. Smith and Brown approached Neil Kinnock for his support. Kinnock, who was equally worried about Labour's image as irresponsible economic managers, was persuaded by the other two that the party needed to become conventional about spending and inflation, and against devaluation. Supporting the ERM, he was told, would prove Labour's responsibility. At the same time, the party should also abandon its undertaking to withdraw from the European Union and even pledge to revalue the pound if the Tories devalued.

During those weeks, Brown did not ask himself how he, an anti-monetarist, could support the identical policy as Nigel Lawson, a monetarist. The more important conundrum was preventing new divisions in his own party. Inevitably, there would be arguments and casualties. Once Kinnock had committed Labour to Europe, the anti-Europeans would fight back, especially Bryan Gould, the aspiring left-wing leader of the party who was still promoting renationalisation and devaluation. The only solution to Gould's opposition, Brown and Smith might have agreed with Samuel Brittan of the *Financial Times*, was to 'put him on a slow boat to China'.

Brown's method was more subtle. By stealth, Gould's influence was to be obliterated.

At the shadow cabinet meeting on 16 November 1989, John Smith described his proposed embracing of the ERM. By not joining, Brown added, Britain's prosperity had been damaged. As predicted, Gould protested, outrightly opposing a policy switch. Kinnock did not respond. 'It's like fighting a marshmallow,' Gould realised. 'No one is willing to take me on.' At the end of that day Gould blamed Mandelson for his humiliation, but in retrospect he understood his mistake. Gordon Brown, not Mandelson, had been planning his downfall, but Brown's opposition had been so 'subterranean' that Gould had wrongly identified his enemy. He was being sidelined by Brown on the grounds of personal dislike and political disagreement. Lacking a powerbase within the party, Gould could not outwit a machine politician with fifteen years' experience in Scotland of settling grudges without overtly plunging the dagger. 'I'm being destroyed by stealth,' Gould complained. 'I've never been confronted with the reasons for my demotion.'

Brown misunderstood the ERM. At a subsequent meeting of the Parliamentary Labour Party (PLP) to discuss the system, he told MPs that by linking the value of sterling to that of other currencies, Britain would be applying socialist planning to the economy rather than relying on market forces. In crude terms, he was convinced that the ERM would disarm, even punish speculators. 'We can fight speculators if we join the ERM,' he told the PLP, revealing his ignorance of the mysteries of markets. He failed to understand that speculators profit from fixed exchange rates, and that membership of the ERM would prevent Britain from unilaterally changing its interest rates. 'This is the economics of the madhouse,' thought Gould as he listened to Brown's arguments. Brown and Smith, he realised, genuinely believed that the ERM was 'a new magical device which would insulate their decisions about the currency against reality'. Brown was deluded that a handful of central bankers could beat the money markets.

To improve his understanding of economics and improve his relationship with the media, Brown recruited three advisers – Geoff Mulgan, Ed Richards and Neal Lawson. Mulgan, the senior adviser, had already established a relationship with Bill Clinton's staff in order to learn how Labour might change its image and policies to appeal to the middle classes. Richards and Lawson were young and inexperienced, but satisfied Brown's need for help both to mount a sustained attack against Thatcherism and to promote himself within the party.

Margaret Thatcher's encouragement of greed, according to Brown, had splintered British society. In a seminal article published in the *Guardian* on 21 September 1990, he expounded his loathing for 'an ageing leader' who sounded too old to care and who was, like Mao, determined to stay on at any price. His accusations were harsh. The result of her 'dream of unrelieved competition to produce improvement', Brown wrote, accompanied by the 'nightmare of any support by the state', had been that 'the rich have done better, the poor worse'. He railed against Thatcher's 'unfettered market', her 'promoting self-improvement of the poor' and the 'weaning [of the poor] from welfare'. He attacked the proposed privatisation of prisons, air traffic control and London Transport as sinful, cursed by 'the enthusiasms of an extremist tendency too young to care'. The Thatcherites' pretensions and wild assertions were, he wrote, merely a smokescreen to 'promote self-indulgence among the very rich'.

In a similar vein he toured Labour associations, occasionally helped by Douglas Alexander, a young Scottish lawyer crafting his speeches, damning the 'markets [which] cannot educate' and urging investment in British technology to fill the country's 'innovation gap' and 'training gap'. His campaign was not universally applauded by his colleagues. He was accused of being an effective critic, delivering coruscating diatribes against Thatcherism, but providing few new ideas for a cure. He spoke fluently, full of certainties, simultaneously as a moderniser and a traditionalist, but seemed uncertain about the consequences of his proposals. His reputation rested on his industry, but the party's intellectuals wanted a heavy-weight, left-wing analysis of Thatcherism. They questioned whether Brown was merely a Labour loyalist, promising the creation of 'economic powerhouses' to create jobs and an end of unemployment, or an original thinker. His journalistic, broad-brush approach to politics, rarely arguing about socialist philosophy, was proof for his critics of frivolity. 'He has a moral revulsion against the government,' wrote Paul Addison, 'but you felt he would only offer a more decent form of Thatcherism in its place. It's no longer really a socialist solution.'

Brown hated any criticism, and these attacks were particularly serious. His reaction was noticeable. The formerly witty, approachable man was gradually assuming the posture of a burdened statesman. To prove his suitability for power and to protect himself from making mistakes, he adopted a new gravitas in order to help establish Labour's reputation for competence. Journalists travelling with him noticed how his good humour evaporated when a camera appeared, and despite his friendship with an interviewer, a sheet of plate glass would suddenly seem to separate the two. Anxious to micro-manage his appearances, Brown adopted a habit of robotic repetition. One memorable example of his repeated attempts to manipulate the agenda occurred during an interview with David Frost. In reply to an enquiry, Brown said, 'That isn't the question.' Frost retorted, 'Yes it is, because I just asked it.' The mystery for his new audience was whether Gordon Brown would emerge as an undisputed leader thanks to some hitherto unseen magic, or whether the enigma merely masked blandness.

His opportunity to disarm the cynics came on 5 October 1990, the last day of the Labour Party conference in Blackpool. After many bitter arguments, Margaret Thatcher had reluctantly announced that Britain would join the ERM, at the rate of £1 for DM 2.95. Critics immediately predicted disaster, believing that the pound was overvalued. The prime minister was beleaguered. By contrast, Smith and Brown appeared serene. Labour's lead in the polls had soared to double figures, and the party leadership, convinced of the country's weariness with Thatcher, believed that electoral victory was inevitable. The question was whether Labour would support the government's application to join the ERM at the high exchange rate. Most people were unaware that a year earlier, John Smith had quietly announced his support. At 4 p.m. on the last day of the conference, Roy Hattersley called Smith. 'What's our policy on ERM?' he asked. 'No alternative but to support the government,' said Smith.

Five years earlier the party, including Blair and Brown, had supported a policy of withdrawal from the European Union. Brown had played a significant part in transforming Labour into a more electable party, as had Blair. Charles Clarke, Neil Kinnock's chief of staff, had asked John Monks, then deputy general secretary of the TUC, to meet the two MPs as examples of the party's encouraging future prospects. In Monks's opinion, Blair had proven his abilities in 1988 by astutely negotiating an agreement with the unions to acknowledge that the new Conservative laws ending the closed shop (which compelled workers to belong to a union) would not be revoked by a Labour government. That success had, in Monks's opinion, catapulted Blair up to Brown's level.

Although the two were close, their differences were marked. Blair took a metropolitan view of politics, eager to lobby for the support of the rich and to criticise the trade unions. By comparison, Brown refused to attack the trade unions, and remained antagonistic towards capitalism. The similarity between the two was that both felt 'modernisation' was necessary to win an election. While Brown's journey had been a struggle through a mass of research and intellectual reasoning, Blair acted largely by instinct. One marked difference was in their attitude towards John Smith. Brown was committed to his mentor, but in Blair's opinion Smith was tainted by his toleration of cronyism and corruption among local party activists employed by the council in his Monklands constituency. Similarly, Blair had little confidence in Kinnock. By the end of 1990, Brown's mood about the party's leadership was edging closer to Blair's. The countdown to the test of his character began on 28 November 1990. The outcome would depend upon his courage.

Eight days after failing to win sufficient votes in the first ballot of Conservative MPs in a leadership vote brought about by Michael Heseltine's challenge following Geoffrey Howe's devastating resignation speech, Margaret Thatcher resigned as prime minister. John Major's election as the new leader revived the Tories' fortunes in the opinion polls. Labour fell 5 per cent behind the Conservatives. Overnight, Brown's unease about Labour's election chances increased. The task of persuading the electorate of Labour's financial competence fell to him and John Smith. Smith proposed launching an offensive in the City, which had been rapidly denuded of Tory grandees following 'Big Bang', which transformed not only the City but Britain as a whole.

Over the next two years, Smith and Brown frequently visited financial institutions in a 'prawn cocktail circuit' in an attempt to attract supporters. They were successful among the American, Australian and continental bankers who lacked tribal prejudice against old Labour. But British stalwarts like

Lord King, Rocco Forte, Lord Delfont, Stanley Kalms, Alan Sugar and Clive Thompson were incontrovertibly grateful to Thatcher's revolution. Few were convinced that Smith and Brown actually liked the City's denizens, or understood the complexities of bank capital. Brown appeared not to have lost his conviction that ministers and civil servants could manage industry better than the entrepreneurs. His references to the Guinness and Barlow Clowes scandals cast him as a mudslinger, unaware that the development of the City as the world's third-largest trading centre would destroy the amateurs he loathed.

Brown was scathing about such criticism. Honesty, he said, was more important than undeserved wealth. His 'vision for the new world' to replace the Tories' 'bleak, gigantic market-place of self-seekers, each in lonely competition with each other' was 'a community of opportunity'. The rottenness of Thatcherism was epitomised by the appointment of fourteen former Conservative ministers as directors of companies they had helped to privatise. Those appointments suggested more than greed. 'Privatisation,' Brown said tersely about the new millionaires, 'began with selling the family silver. It is now ending in the farce of golden parachutes for departing cabinet ministers.' The recipients of 'jobs for the boys' included Norman Fowler, the former transport minister who joined National Freight, a company privatised by his department; Norman Tebbit, the ex-industry secretary who became a director of the newly privatised British Telecom; Peter Walker, formerly energy secretary and now a director of British Gas; and Lord Young, another former industry secretary who, after overseeing the privatisation of Cable and Wireless, was appointed a director of the company.

Those apparent conflicts of interest were to Brown as repellent as the huge profits earned by the newly privatised utilities and the unprecedented pay increases which their directors

awarded themselves. His cure was a reaffirmation of the
virtues of public ownership, a national investment bank,
legislation to ban 'unjustified rises in company directors' pay'
and a ban on 'huge perks'. Labour insiders including Charles
Clarke noticed Brown's cautious retreat from 'modernisation'
as he once again opposed the privatisation of state monopolies. Nothing was said, however, because his attacks
helped bring John Major's honeymoon to a quick end. Electors voiced their disenchantment about perceived corruption,
the faltering economy and bickering ministers. Major, who
irritably described Brown as 'a master of the personal insult'
and 'a dismal Jimmy, always jumping onto bad news and
ignoring anything good', appeared vulnerable.

Rattling the prime minister emboldened Brown. He had
won a reputation as a serial embarrassment to the government
by regularly revealing confidential information supplied by
disgruntled civil servants; his latest had exposed the government's refusal to increase consumers' rights against the privatised utilities. By spring 1991 he consistently appeared the
outstanding member of the shadow cabinet, ranking among
Labour's giants. The perceptive interpreted his speeches as
reflecting his serious disenchantment with the party's leadership. To Kinnock's irritation, he was mentioned as the leader-
in-waiting. Dissatisfaction was particularly prevalent among
Scottish MPs fearful of a fourth election defeat.

Although the opinion polls had swung back in Labour's
favour, a weariness was infecting the party, and there was
uncertainty about whether Kinnock could win an election
victory. With Blair's encouragement, his personal assistant
Anji Hunter and Peter Mandelson were touring Labour constituencies to identify kindred spirits who supported radical
change despite intimidation and threats of deselection. The
roots of the New Labour project, forging a brotherhood of
survivors before the outbreak of renewed conflagration,

started just one year before a general election which Kinnock
anticipated winning. The birth of this magic circle, born from
despair and cemented by bonds of close friendship, was
gradual. In Mandelson's version, he was uncertain whether
Labour could ever win an election with a Celtic leader. Over
lunch with a sympathetic journalist in 1991, shortly after
his selection as the parliamentary candidate for Hartlepool,
Mandelson mused, 'It's time we had an English leader.' He
was already veering towards Blair. 'People listening to the
BBC's broadcasts of Blair's speeches,' continued Mandelson,
'say here is the next leader of the Labour Party.' He would
later deny having turned away from Brown so early.

Brown was more concerned by the substance than the
image. Despite his visits to the City, John Smith favoured the
old-style socialist command economy rather than an equal
partnership between the government and capitalists. Brown's
conversations at his regular dinners with Doug Henderson,
Martin O'Neill and Nick Brown revolved around replacing
Smith's obsolescent ideology with a new agenda. 'You're
promising things you can't deliver,' O'Neill told Brown. 'It's
the same trap as the seventies.' Usually, Brown did not comment. Despite the Glasgow versus Edinburgh friction, he
shared the same Christian socialist values as Smith. Both
favoured community values rather than satisfying the aspirations of the enfranchised ex-working classes. Like Smith's,
Brown's world revolved around Scotland's party machine and
the plight of Kirkcaldy and similar Scottish communities –
uneconomic coalmines, decrepit linoleum factories and
Harold Wilson's failed investments in technology – and what
he called 'the causes of poverty which are unemployment
and a welfare state that isn't working'.

To avoid criticism from the trade unions, Brown resisted
questioning Smith's agenda even among friends, although he
knew he would have to break away from that view. During

1991 he confided to Peter Mandelson that Smith would be unsuitable as chancellor if Labour won the 1992 election. Smith, he believed, was too dogmatic and simplistic on economic matters. Mandelson and Brown agreed that electoral success depended upon committing the party to as little as possible. Contrived obfuscation was the ideal strategy. The obstacles were Smith, who was antagonistic towards such tactics, and Kinnock, who was reluctant to endorse Brown's proposals to prove Labour's economic competence.

The disputes between the three – Kinnock, Smith and Brown – Kinnock complained, were loud and long. They agreed not to revoke the Conservatives' trade union legislation or to advocate a return to 83 per cent tax rates; but they were firmly committed to the redistribution of wealth. Would it be inviting electoral suicide, they wondered, to mention tax increases and a commitment to full employment in the manifesto? Watching John Smith ploddingly composing the tax plans for the shadow budget depressed Brown. Despite his sparkling performances in the House of Commons, Smith lacked originality. The more he insisted that the manifesto would pledge to levy 'fair taxes', the angrier Brown became. Smith spoke of 'one more heave' to prevent a fourth Tory victory, a term condemned by Brown as self-revealingly crude and destined to end in a similar fiasco to 1987. Brown believed that only he foresaw the imminent disaster. He alone was certain of the proper route to victory. In response, Smith castigated him for offering no new ideas.

Quietly, Brown began consulting trade unionists, key party activists and sympathetic MPs about the possibility of an alternative to Smith as party leader if Labour was defeated at the general election. He calculated the permutations to see whether he might beat Smith, or at least achieve a sufficient vote to mark his future inheritance. The more Smith insisted on the manifesto overtly pledging higher taxes, the more resolutely Brown sought out dissidents. His unhappiness climaxed during one stormy meeting. Kinnock had agreed with Smith to pledge tax increases in the manifesto. Brown disagreed vociferously, and questioned Smith's principles. Did Smith actually understand economics? Brown found his bonhomie irritating, and suspected his regular attendance at church was deceptive. Brown's dislike of what he saw as the bigotry of western Scotland – the area of John Smith, John Reid and Helen Liddell – swelled. In the back of his mind lurked new doubts about Smith's tolerance of corruption in his local party. The murkiness in Monklands seemed to reflect Smith's self-limiting terms of reference towards house prices, wages and human motives. All his attitudes were shaped by his experience in Scotland. His caricature of middle England was the expensive, eccentric neighbourhood of Hampstead in north-west London, and he did not understand the real middle England's reaction to the prospect of higher taxation. Nor did Kinnock. As for John Reid, Brown was disdainful of a man he characterised as an untrustworthy, indiscreet, alcoholic thug.

Despite his disparagement of John Smith's insularity, Brown himself was uneasy with England's growing multiculturalism. The essence of his Scottishness – his integrity, grittiness and clannishness – were familiar characteristics in the English shires, but not across the urban sprawls. Proud of his background, he felt only contempt for the criticism of him by London's media classes and those Labour MPs who disliked his refusal to peel away his Scottish skin. Like Smith, Brown knew little about middle England's mood beyond the windows of the northbound express train from King's Cross to Scotland on Friday nights. Neither man had much affection for England's neat villages, picturesque market towns and manicured countryside. To Brown London was a workplace, not a cultural home. He was rarely seen in the capital's theatres or concert halls, in contrast to his attendances at the Usher Hall in Edinburgh. Scots, he was happy to remind others, are an internal people, well known to each other but distant from outsiders.

The gap between the two cultures irritated Mo Mowlam, Brown's deputy as shadow DTI spokesman. In 1991 he criticised her slapdash approach and coarseness, sparking her dislike of the northern cabal around him. After one dinner in an Indian restaurant with Brown, Henry McLeish, Nigel Griffiths, Doug Henderson and Nick Brown, she told friends the experience was so appalling that she believed Brown was unfit to become the party's leader. His companions were hardly impressive praetorian guards. Unlike Winston Churchill, Brown did not like dominating first-rate minds. The esprit de corps his loyalists engendered magnified his character traits.

In a rare attempt to humanise his image and attract support, he agreed to co-operate with Fiona Millar, a young Labour supporter employed by the *Sunday Express*, on a newspaper profile. The overt reason was Brown's candidacy to be the party's next leader. Naturally, he told Millar that he was 'cool towards the notion'. He did however admit that his personality and policies irritated many Labour MPs. 'It's the old story,' he confessed, 'that your opponents are across from you in the House of Commons and your enemies are next to you. There are a number of people who resent me, but all I have done is get on with my job, and I don't think anyone would accuse me of not being a team player.' The profile's first public description of his home was not encouraging. The austerity of a new floral three-piece suite in the living room, and the undisguised sparseness of the other rooms with their bare walls and a solitary piano, a present from his mother, were not mitigated by his exclamation, 'Moving here has changed my life,' or the disclosure that he played golf and tennis, watched football and 'many films', and read detective novels.

Piles of books were scattered around the house, most of them about political theory and ideology. Only a few looked unread. The humanisation of Gordon Brown required something to fill the glaring gap – a woman in his life. Coyly, he explained, 'Marriage is something that hasn't happened yet. I've been too busy working, but everything is possible.' He admitted to a 'girlfriend who is a lawyer', but stipulated that Caldwell should not be named, to which Millar agreed. To compensate for that self-censorship, she conjured the colourful depiction of Brown as 'the thinking woman's crumpet', apparently known as 'the awayday favourite' by female staff on BBC's *Question Time* because he was their choice of companion when travelling outside London.

The interview, however, was a failure. Brown's resistance to introspection and reluctance to admit to any ambitions beyond politics left the reader baffled about the real man. There were no clues about his personal life, his ambition, his inner turmoil or even any mention of his unusual habit of always wearing dark blue suits, bought in bulk, and red ties. Unanswered was the question of whether Brown was merely a product of his era, or a man who might one day shape the nation's destiny. Some would say that he was not so much unwilling to reveal himself as incapable of self-analysis or even self-deprecation. Outside politics, he was unable to define himself. While there was no doubt that following his progress would be worthwhile, his destination was unresolved.

The only real consequence of the interview was to encourage Neil Kinnock to suspect plots. In the fevered atmosphere, he believed that Donald Dewar, with John Smith's support, was seeking to mount a coup against him in favour of Smith, an accusation Dewar's confidants laughingly derided. For his part, Smith was convinced that Brown was plotting against himself, and asked the GMB trade union leader John Edmonds to warn Brown off. Edmonds telephoned Mandelson at his

home in Hartlepool on a Friday night. 'I gather the mice
are playing,' he said. 'What are you talking about?' replied
Mandelson. 'People say you're plotting for Gordon and against
John.' Mandelson denied the allegation. Brown, Edmonds
continued, should cease manoeuvring to become the leader
after the 1992 election. In Edmonds's opinion, the party
would not skip a generation. John Smith was the party's candidate. Brown heard about the threat within minutes. Frustrated by Kinnock and irritated by Smith, he pondered
whether he should strike. His opportunity was short-lived.

Smith complained to Kinnock about Brown's 'precocious-
ness'. Kinnock appreciated Brown as a 'bright spark', and
since Smith was a year older than himself, half-favoured
Brown as the next leader; but Smith refused to countenance
the jump of a generation. Kinnock made no attempt to reconcile the two, except to bark, 'Grow up.' To reinforce his
position, Smith summoned Brown and demanded a personal
assurance that he would not stand in the next leadership
election. Instead of outrightly refusing to commit himself,
Brown mumbled some inconsequential platitudes. At the
crucial moment, calculating the compromises and betrayals
that would be necessary for success, he lacked the courage to
accept the challenge. 'You won't stand in my way after the
next election?' asked Smith directly. 'No,' Brown meekly
replied. He would tell his staff that he had refused to join any
plot because he feared that rumours of division could cost
Labour the election. The self-discipline of the machine politicians protected Kinnock from newspapers reporting disenchantment among the parliamentary party.

Gordon Brown had harmed his own cause. He emerged
from the foothills of a botched coup neurotic about the whispers. 'Who's saying things about me?' he asked Mandelson.
Doubts and distrust became embedded in his relationships. In
self-protection he began minutely controlling every aspect of

his life. At private meetings he became irascible, although in public his carefully written and rehearsed speeches, liberally sprinkled with original jokes, concealed his anxieties. His self-discipline suggested an assured future. At the 1991 party conference in Brighton he taunted the Tories about their grubby relationship with City 'fat cats': 'First a privatisation write-off, then a City sell-off – and then a Tory party pay-off.' The Conservatives, he mocked, depended on financial support from mysterious foreign billionaires, including a tainted Greek shipping owner. 'Most shamefully of all, [they take donations from] a Greek billionaire moving his money out of colonels into Majors.' The cheers temporarily reinforced his self-confidence.

Brown's contribution to the party's manifesto for the 1992 election – 'It's Time to Get Britain Working Again' and 'Looking to the Future' – reflected the next stage of his journey away from the Tribunites. He favoured regulation and competition rather than nationalisation, private business rather than state intervention, and supported seeking private venture capital on 'strictly commercial lines' for investment in public services. The flipside was his regurgitation of Harold Wilson's thirty-year-old mantra of the 'white heat of technology' in a 'new agenda for investment'. Using Wilsonian buzz words – technology, innovation, revolution, investment, modernisation – he castigated the Tories' 'trust in simplistic market answers', especially to create a skilled workforce.

Even Brown was frustrated by the lack of originality in relying on Wilsonian vocabulary. He blamed Neil Kinnock personally, and the coterie around him including Charles Clarke and Patricia Hewitt, who professed to understand 'modernisation' and 'the Project' but who in his opinion were an albatross around the neck of the party as it prepared for the election. His revenge was to take pleasure in irritating Clarke by arranging meetings with Kinnock without telling his chief of staff. The consequence was uncoupling during the

weeks before election day, 9 April 1992. Working from an
office near Waterloo station, Brown barely spoke to John
Smith, and fumed about the self-indulgence and lack of professionalism among the 'London losers', the wild and woolly
left in the London Labour Party who were organising the
hopeless campaign. He cursed the fact that Smith was approv-
ing policies without asking, 'Can we win with this?', and
speaking to Donald Dewar about policy while ignoring himself. He cursed the party's refusal to promote him as a spokesman on television, although he himself was partly to blame
for that. Unlike every other shadow minister, he refused to
appoint a liaison official at Walworth Road as a point of contact while he toured the country. Charles Clarke urged him
to do so, but was rebuffed. Geoff Mulgan, his senior aide,
never discussed Brown's personal campaign with David Ward,
Smith's campaign manager. 'You're not a team player,' Smith
raged at Brown. 'The problem is that you want to be the team
leader.'

Smith was right, but was too stubborn to understand the
reason. Convinced that tax increases were vote-winners,
he had arranged a dramatic unveiling of his proposals on the
Treasury's steps in Whitehall just days before the election. As
Smith stood in Whitehall surrounded by his smiling Treasury
team, Brown seethed. Two years later he would praise Smith's
passion for equality, but at that moment he knew the folly
of honesty. As they walked to their cars from the Treasury
steps, Brown sniped at Smith, 'You've lost us the election.'
Smith was visibly shocked, more by the disloyalty than by
the prediction. Even Kinnock, under pressure from Brown,
had confessed over dinner with friendly journalists at Luigi's
restaurant that Smith's shadow budget was 'wrong', and had
pledged to row back. Smith was unperturbed. A telephone
call on Monday, 6 April, three days before election day, from
Terry Burns, the Treasury's permanent secretary, reinforced

Smith's conviction. Burns invited Smith to visit the Treasury to discuss Labour's intentions if elected. There had been several previous conversations about Labour's plans, which included possible withdrawal from the ERM. As Smith confidently drove to Whitehall carrying some papers prepared by Brown, he was convinced of victory. Left behind, his assistant Helen Liddell said quietly, 'We've lost. Taxation has lost us the election.'

On advertising billboards across England, Smith's tax increases were exploited by the Conservatives as Labour's 'double whammy' of 'more taxes' and 'higher prices'. John Major, parading as the victor of the Gulf War, exploited Kinnock's waltz into the Tory trap of Labour's reputation for economic incompetence. Although in Labour's folklore the polls rose in their favour after Smith presented his shadow budget, nothing could save the party after Kinnock's disastrous performance at a premature victory rally in Sheffield. Middle England decided that Labour could not be trusted. Tax and his own personal image, Kinnock was told, had extinguished their chance of victory. Five years later Brown would say, 'I was always loyal to John Smith in public, but in private I had disagreements about the 1992 proposals.'

Just before election day, Tony Blair invited Robert Harris, an intelligent journalist and friend of Peter Mandelson, to lunch at L'Escargot in Soho. 'Do you think Labour will win?' asked Blair. 'Yes,' replied Harris. 'I don't think so,' said Blair. 'We're going to lose.' Labour had failed to break its dependence on the trade unions, and failed to understand the aspirations of hard-working English people of all classes. After the defeat, continued Blair, Gordon Brown would run against John Smith for the leadership, and Blair would stand for deputy. That scenario would require Brown to be courageous, and Blair appeared convinced that he would be. In fact Blair's conjecture was either naïve or provocative. Over the previous

twelve months, he knew, the trade unions had vetoed a challenge to Smith, and the parliamentary party was divided. He
was deftly promoting his own interests. Brown was close to
Smith, while Blair's impatience with the Glaswegian was well
known. Blair's influence in a shadow cabinet led by Smith
would be less than Brown's. A Brown coup was the best
option for Blair's future.

Watching from Scotland as the election result was announced for Basildon in Essex, Brown exploded in anger. The
sitting Tory MP had held on to a seat that Labour had to win
if it was to have any chance of gaining power. 'Basildon man',
cursed Brown, was 'selfish'. Labour's defeat was humiliating.
The Tory majority fell from 102 to twenty-one, but it was
their fourth succesive election victory. Although there was a
2 per cent swing to the Tories in his constituency, Brown
personally achieved a massive majority of 17,444. At that
desperate moment Brown could not understand why England's aspiring working class seemed to hate Scotland's passion for collectivism and government interference. Both he
and Blair were in despair.

THREE

Turbulence

The curtains of the Kinnocks' house in Ealing, west London, were tightly drawn on the bright morning of 10 April 1992. Inside, the occupants were crying. Neil Kinnock was shocked that Labour had not won the election. In the west of Scotland, John Smith was similarly distraught, but robustly rejected any responsibility for the defeat. On the banks of the River Forth, Gordon Brown was considering the consequences of Kinnock's resignation.

In his telephone conversations with close friends including Nigel Griffiths, Nick Brown, Martin O'Neill, Gavyn Davies and Doug Henderson, Brown alternated between bafflement and explosions of despair. Only Tony Blair aggressively argued in favour of Brown taking the risk of standing for the leadership. He invited Brown to meet at his home in Trimdon, in his Sedgefield constituency, with Nick Brown. As they walked in the countryside, Blair urged him to stand as the modernising candidate. Labour's English MPs, he said, would support him against Smith who they agreed was incapable of appealing to aspiring English people. Three times Brown had placed first in the elections for the shadow cabinet, and his continuing popularity guaranteed him a fourth victory in the autumn.

At this decisive moment, Brown was paralysed by his

91

emotions. The trade unions, he was told, favoured Smith; many MPs were against a divisive vote so soon after the party had been through hell to unite itself; and he had been assured that he would inherit the crown after Smith. In meetings over the following two days at Nick Brown's home in Heaton in Newcastle, and then at County Hall, Durham, with Mandelson, Brown repeated all those reasons for not challenging Smith. The judgement of the Scottish establishment, he told Blair, could not be ignored. All were united by a near-blood oath to the clan chief. The middle-class minister's son hated the thought of bloodshed. Listening to Brown, Blair was unimpressed by what he later dubbed a masquerade. In the opinion of those associated with 'The Project', Brown lacked courage to seize the opportunity and break the mould. He was a woolly *apparatchik*, eloquent about the party's ideal philosophy, but unable, like a star pupil politely waiting for the offer of a prize, to elbow his way brutally past those he despised. The conversations ended with Blair losing his temper. Brown, he said, lacked the resilience to withstand personal criticism from his peers, and feared failure. He was a coward. The scales, Blair would tell Anji Hunter, had fallen from his eyes. In the future he would be less deferential towards Brown, less obedient. 'He chickened out, taking the easy option,' judged Blair. Others were less critical. 'Gordon won kudos for not standing,' said Tam Dalyell.

Five years later, Brown presented his faint-heartedness as loyalty. 'I felt I owed a debt of gratitude to John Smith,' he told Paul Routledge. 'I felt I had to be loyal. It was for no other reason. I had worked with him for almost eight years on the front bench, and it was right for me to be loyal. I thought the Labour Party was more ready for change than people imagined, but I never thought for a minute of standing against John Smith.' He considered standing for the deputy leadership, but was turned down by Smith, who felt that

two Scotsmen would be electorally unattractive. In turn, Blair
rejected Smith's offer to be his deputy. Revealing his prejudices, Smith chose Margaret Beckett, a left-wing trade unionist certain to antagonise middle England. To minimise their
embarrassment and pose as 'agents of influence', both Brown
and Blair telephoned journalists to explain why they were
not standing for the deputy leadership. Few were convinced.

Brown, previously tipped as the leader-in-waiting, was
further deflated when, on 26 July 1992, the day after John
Smith's election victory, the *Sunday Times* devoted five pages
to a profile of Tony Blair as the party's next leader. Two days
later Charles Reiss, the London *Evening Standard*'s political
editor, published a percipient prediction under the headline
'Coming War Between Brown and Blair'. The whispers in
Westminster, reported Reiss, revealed a depth of unhappiness
among English Labour MPs about Smith's appearance as a
'smiling uncle'. Compared to Blair, who looked approachable
and urbane, the newly crowned leader was from the wrong
generation. Even the cautious and rhetorical Brown, he
wrote, offended some as old-fashioned. Some observers wondered whether the rivalry between Brown and Blair would
mirror the similar battle twenty years earlier between Roy
Jenkins and Tony Crosland, whose long friendship was cor-
roded by their acrimonious contest for the Labour leadership
during the 1970s. The speculation was short-lived. The party
was preoccupied by yet another autopsy about its failure to
overturn a Tory government responsible for a major recession.
The debate identified several culprits, including Gordon
Brown.

Shortly after his appointment as John Smith's shadow
chancellor, Brown hosted a drinks party in his office. In the
sombre atmosphere, Peter Mandelson, the newly elected MP
for Hartlepool, was openly rebellious. 'The party,' he said
loudly, 'has to modernise, and John Smith is not up to

it.' Mandelson's disloyalty caused no surprise. The dissent
was not directed towards Smith alone. Mandelson's audience knew that in other rooms Brown was under attack for
having approved Smith's discredited shadow budget. Brown's
silence was deemed to be incriminating. He dismissed the
criticism as irrelevant. In 1997 he would claim that his new
position as shadow chancellor had bestowed on him the
power to challenge Smith 'to change our whole economic
policy'. That was undoubtedly the Herculean challenge he
set himself in 1992, but at the time many doubted whether
he could overcome Smith's conservatism, and whether the
party could change sufficiently to avoid a fifth election
defeat.

The hunger for victory persuaded Brown finally to acknowledge the achievements of Thatcherism. He jettisoned any
affection for Neil Kinnock's 'Red Rose'. That misty-eyed,
superficial change of image had not neutralised the public's
perception that Labour would restrict options, dampen
ambitions and nationalise fitted kitchens. On the contrary,
Kinnock had reinforced 'Basildon man's' perception of Labour
as an enemy, keen to impose shackles on behalf of society.
Until the Attlee legacy was repudiated, the new shadow chancellor knew, Labour could not pose as a party offering people
opportunities. 'We've got to work from first principles towards
policies,' he again told his advisers including Michael Wills,
Geoff Mulgan and John Eatwell. The path back to power, he
accepted, was for Labour to appeal to the middle class by
changing its image and policies. The first obstacle was the
party members, including himself.

In July 1992 the party faithful were still cursing the 'culture
of contentment'. Gordon Brown hated 'Basildon man', the
motivated working-class aspirant whom he damned as 'a
selfish, indeed self-centred individual'. To win 'Basildon
man's' allegiance, he decided to conceal his disgust and pro-

mote the new credo that 'There is no clash between individual freedom and the advancement of the common good.' In the frenzy of his writing and speeches, he appeared to abandon his attachment to the idea of the state 'that all too easily assumes that where there is a public interest there must always be a centralised public bureaucracy'. The state itself, he acknowledged, could itself be a damaging vested interest. In his rush during the summer to compose a new ideology, there were inevitably contradictions. He abandoned pure socialism but espoused collectivism, arguing that individuals should group together for the common good. He abandoned state controls but wanted the markets to operate subject to such controls in the public interest. The new gospel was to revolutionise the Labour Party's image, but only partially its substance. Gordon Brown could not break away from his life's attachment to socialism. He urged the faithful not to despair, because 'The truth is that our natural constituency is the majority who benefit from a just society.'

In the new House of Commons, the Tories were soft targets. During the election campaign John Major had pledged, 'Vote Conservative on Thursday and the recovery will continue on Friday.' Instead, the recession had worsened. Unemployment was rising back towards three million, interest rates were increasing, property prices were falling, car workers were working short time, and the government was poised to announce massive spending cuts. Norman Lamont, the chancellor, was regularly lambasted for misleading the country that taxes would be cut, when in fact they were going up. Inexorably, an old-fashioned sterling crisis was about to explode. Devaluation from the exchange rate of DM 2.95 to the pound was the best cure, but Britain's membership of the ERM rendered that remedy unavailable. Lamont sought help from the German central bank, but was snubbed. Germany's economy was expanding while Britain's was shrinking.

Unusually, Lamont's crisis was also Brown's. He had supported entry into the ERM, and he rejected unilaterally
devaluing sterling.

The unfolding disaster fulfilled the predictions of Bryan
Gould and other Labour opponents of joining the ERM. Their
criticism was inflamed by Brown's aggressive dismissal of their
opinions. Robin Cook, supported by Peter Hain, Ken Livingstone and other anti-Europeans, wanted devaluation. Even
John Smith supported 'realignment'. 'Labour,' warned Smith,
'should know the dangers of fixed exchange rates. Harold
Wilson's greatest mistake was to hold sterling against the
dollar between 1964 and 1967.' Gordon Brown disagreed,
and insisted that Labour could never again be the party of
devaluation. The party, he warned, would lose credibility by
following such a policy. Tough on the new orthodoxy, he
was sticking to the ERM; forgetting the modernisation gospel
he had preached just days earlier, he promoted Old Labour
policies of cutting interest rates and greater government
investment. Using the identical lexicon as Harold Wilson
twenty-five years earlier, he regularly lashed out at the 'handful of shirt-sleeved speculators' and City whiz kids dictating
the lives of millions and the destinies of national economies.
The outbreak of warfare in the party became focused on
Brown, who appeared a confused ideologue.

In early September 1992 the economic crisis escalated. The
government's defence of the pound was faltering. Brown's
support for remaining in the ERM was emphatic. 'There are
those like Lady Thatcher who believe that Britain should
devalue,' he wrote in the *Sunday Express* on 6 September, 'and
turn its back on Europe and the exchange rate mechanism
with all the harsh consequences that would ensue.' Brown's
alternatives to devaluation were state subsidies and increased
taxes. Throughout that week, as the crisis intensified, he was
telephoned by journalists and asked why the pound should

not be devalued. 'I can't afford to think it's overvalued,' Brown replied, 'because it would seem as if Labour believed in devaluation.' Those who pushed him to promote Britain's exit from the ERM were met by a solid wall. He refused to consider the possibility that he was wrong. His inconsistency gave the impression that he did not understand economics. In 1997 he would tell Paul Routledge that he had anticipated the crisis. Considering his statements at the time, this appears to be untrue.

Late in the afternoon of Wednesday, 16 September 1992, Brown was in his office in 1 Parliament Street, overlooking the Treasury building. That morning he had still been convinced that the government would remain in the ERM, helped by Germany's revaluation of its own currency. He would be vindicated, he reassured John Smith, despite his critics including Ken Livingstone, who again had advocated devaluation. Around Brown were his advisers Neal Lawson, Michael Wills, Lord Eatwell and Geoff Mulgan. The tension was high. The constantly updated television news bulletins reporting Norman Lamont's battle to save sterling were unnerving. If Labour had won the election in April, Brown would have been the focus of the TV cameras outside the Treasury, and the target of baying Tory MPs inside the Commons. His plight was better than Lamont's, but the politician whose talent was to ridicule his opponents knew that he was vulnerable to mockery. He had allied himself to a policy which, to his amazement, was collapsing – and worse, he did not understand the reason.

At 7.30 p.m. everyone in Brown's office watched the television pictures of the chancellor emerging into the spotlights, brushing his hair, and confessing defeat. Britain, he announced, was withdrawing from the ERM and devaluing. In a surreal exercise, the viewers in Brown's office darted between the television and the window, gazing down at

Lamont in the distance to reassure themselves that the television pictures were reality.

After Lamont's announcement came to its abrupt conclusion, the atmosphere in the office was 'on a knife edge',
recalled one of those present. All eyes swivelled towards
Brown and then away. His shock was palpable. He had made
a fundamental mistake, and he was terrified. This was the
most testing moment of his political career. His refusal to seek
the nomination in Hamilton or to contest the party leadership
were failures of courage, but were not life-threatening. This
crisis endangered his entire future. At that moment he was
due to lead the attack against the Tories for a policy he himself
supported, and simultaneously he was under attack from the
left wing of his own party for ideological folly. No one was
certain whether he would cope with the explosion of emotion.
Under pressure, the ashen-faced Brown's behaviour was
extraordinary. Some eyewitnesses say they observed the
neurotic pessimism of the son of the manse. Others witnessing
the brooding volcano in that untidy office would mention the
inherent self-destruct button of the Scottish character.

But Brown did not self-destruct. He reasserted his self-
control, the tension eased, and he began designing a strategy
for his survival. Driven by his hatred for the Tories and his
searing ambition to become party leader, he contrived a con-
vincingly venomous denial of the past. 'We have to fight to
avoid going down with the government,' was the common
sentiment. His first decision was to reject an invitation to
appear on that evening's *Newsnight*. He knew he would have
to answer the charge that if Labour had won the election they
would have been hit by the same crisis, and would have
reacted identically to the Tories. The party, Brown decided,
had to avoid self-flagellation and pontificating about the 'current mess'. Instead, he would offer soundbites damning the
government.

As he faced the news cameras he propped a piece of paper in front of his eyes bearing the words, unseen by the viewers: 'Huge chasm'. His identical soundbites, emphasising this 'huge chasm' between the government and Labour, blamed everything on the Tories, and suggested that Labour had never endorsed the disastrous policy. 'We demanded interest cuts,' he repeated endlessly, although that was not a solution to the crisis. 'The government failed to listen to our warnings . . . The Tories are the party of devaluation . . . The Tories cannot be trusted on the economy.' The government's humiliation was transformed into a Labour success. 'I say to Norman Lamont: spend your energies pursuing the useful job of creating jobs for others rather than the futile goal of clinging to your own.' Of John Major he said: 'The recession started when he became Treasury secretary, worsened when he became chancellor and intensified when he took over as prime minister. Every time he changed jobs, thousands lost theirs.' Stubbornly, he repeated his rehearsed phrases and ignored supplementary questions. He may have turned the facts upside down, but the public was unconcerned. Their spleen was directed at the Tories. Labour's support for the policy was forgotten. Brown's calculated indifference to the truth did not impress the party cadres. The left, disgruntled by his modernisation agenda, was whispering against the now isolated shadow chancellor.

Two weeks later, Brown arrived at the 1992 party conference in Blackpool. The criticism had not relented. The opinion polls showed that Labour was still not trusted by voters on the economy. His fear had plunged him into a deep, black mood. He was convinced that Robin Cook and John Prescott were conspiring to expel him from the front bench, and that he was fighting for survival. Reconciling Brown with Cook, complained fellow shadow cabinet member Frank Dobson, the spokesman for employment, had become 'a lost cause'.

Brown's grudges exploded in private but were concealed from
the public. As he toured the corridors at the conference hall
he repeatedly told delegates he encountered, 'There is no way
that Labour could have kept its credibility if I'd come out in
favour of devaluation.' Because he had resisted the devaluation chorus, he continued, Labour had been immunised from
blame for the collapse of the pound. The Tories, he said,
should be cast as the party of devaluation. Repeatedly he told
his critics to blame the Tories for 'betraying Europe', twisting
the responsibility for the ERM crisis away from the real culprits, the Germans and the EU Commission who had refused
to support Britain. His conference speech was an old-
fashioned tirade: 'The City of London is Britain's biggest
casino, and the winners are celebrating over £500 million
won by cocky young men betting on a certainty.' He demanded curbs on currency speculators (whom he had earlier
predicted would be controlled by the ERM) and advocated
'managed exchange rates' as 'absolutely necessary'. The contradictions were glaring, but that was irrelevant. Despite his
faltering popularity, he was again first in that year's elections
for the shadow cabinet, with 165 votes.

Brown returned to London determined not to waver. Preoccupied by a zealous conviction of his virtue, he became
impenetrable and impregnable to the doubters. He was
dubbed a political glacier, but he pursued his duty. 'I must
come up with some big ideas,' he told friends. In 1906, 1945
and 1974, Labour had reinvented itself. In 1992 the party
again required a huge intellectual effort if it was to win credibility. Those pessimists preaching that Labour's support could
not break through the 35 per cent barrier, or that the party
had a declining base, were ignored. His tactics had provided
breathing space and an inspiration for a new crusade. He
immersed himself in rewriting Labour's policies to make the
party electable, in a style his supporters called 'radical popu-

list'. His latest political journey was calculated to convince electors that Labour was abandoning the economic policies on which it had fought the previous election.

Brown was resolved that Labour would never again pledge to raise taxes in an election campaign, but that was only the beginning. The image of Labour as the party of inflation, high spending and begging from the IMF had to be eradicated. No future Labour government, he decided, could finance failing industries or restore unlimited powers to the trade unions. He would pledge support for full employment, but refuse to support higher taxation or restore the earnings link to state pensions. He began speaking about the importance of developing Labour's response to the new shibboleths: globalis- ation, the financial markets and the 'knowledge economy'. Relying on competition in the market rather than imposing state controls, he slowly recognised, gave people greater opportunities; knowledge rather than capital had become the key to wealth, and he listened to those saying that the poor would be enriched by learning new skills rather than by the imposition of state control over wealth. The new gospel would present the party as a modernising agent for the economy, society and the constitution. Much of Thatcherism, Brown acknowledged, was irreversible.

His reward was more unpopularity. Senior colleagues including John Prescott, David Blunkett, Jack Straw, Robin Cook and Michael Meacher regarded his 'radical populism' as 'nauseating'. Brown, they believed, was 'harbouring danger- ously revisionist, pro-establishment ambitions for the party'. Although they did not share Bryan Gould's violent character- isation of him as a more fanatical monetarist than the Tories, they objected to any abandonment of socialism. Brown rebut- ted their criticisms. In the fashion of an evangelist, he behaved like the leader possessed of the truth and commanding his flock to follow. But to assuage his critics, he began perfecting the art of addressing different audiences with different messages. To please the left, he promoted himself as a true socialist. 'Labour,' he wrote in *Tribune*, 'rejects the notion that a free-market approach to currency markets will bring lasting benefits to the British economy . . . Never again must speculators control the policy of government. Action must now be taken to strengthen European co-operation to diminish the power and role of speculators.' Simultaneously, he was reinforcing loyalties among those friends who loathed the Tribunites. Supported by Blair and Mandelson, he confronted his critics. Robin Cook, the health spokesman, had predicted, 'Labour will never govern again unless it adopts proportional representation.' Cook was brushed aside by Brown with open scorn. Bryan Gould was damned as 'dangerous and reckless'. John Prescott was derided for criticising the modernisers' attempts to expunge the image of 'a party of the poor and the past' and to broaden Labour's appeal to the middle classes. Seemingly uninvolved in the steamy rows was John Smith. The party leader disliked any dilution of Labour's old ideologies. Just 'one more heave', he believed, would expel the Tories. Brown, Blair and Mandelson sought another route.

A possible way forward was revealed at a conference at Ditchley Park between the 'modernisers' and US presidential candidate Bill Clinton's advisers. Although he disliked Thatcher's indifference to social justice, Brown was impressed by Clinton's equal antagonism towards the idle poor and the idle rich. Everyone without a good excuse, said Clinton, should work. 'We want to offer a hand up, not a handout,' was his memorable piety. The growing success of Clinton's presidential campaign, thanks partly to his economic proposals, reinforced Brown's commitment to abandon Labour's traditional philosophy of universal benefits. Changing Labour's gods, he calculated, could only be done piecemeal, accompanied by pledges zealously to help the working poor and the underclasses. To stem the inevitable criticism that he was adopting Thatcherite policies, he planned successive diversions to restate his socialist credentials. He would criticise the very class whose support he was seeking – the capitalists who on the eve of the election he had condemned as 'doing well out of the recession' – and praise the performance of the Scandinavians, Germans and Japanese, although he knew comparatively little of their true economic predicament. Working up to fifteen hours a day, he analysed the party's weaknesses and concluded that its salvation required not just new ideas, but a new vocabulary describing a new party. Just as Margaret Thatcher had recruited Keith Joseph, Nicholas Ridley, Nigel Lawson and other intellectuals from the Chicago School to bury memories of the Heath government under new policies, Gordon Brown began, with Blair and Mandelson, to search for catalysts of a new party. For his personal quest, he needed new advisers.

His office had been reorganised under Sue Nye, an aggressive chain-smoker, formerly employed by Neil Kinnock, famous for asking 'Have you got a mint?' to disguise her habit. Although she might have been tainted by her association with the notorious pre-election rally at Sheffield, Nye was trusted as loyal, hard working and ruthless. Like Jessica Mitford, she decided by just a glance whether someone was acceptable or to be excluded. Her reasons for freezing out a person could be inscrutable, but her phrase 'If you're outside the family, you're radioactive' appealed to a man cultivating the authority of the clan chief.

Within the citadel, Brown needed a soulmate. His enquiries suggested that Ed Balls, a twenty-five-year-old Oxford graduate employed as a leader writer at the *Financial Times*, would be ideal. The Nottingham-born Balls, Brown heard, was a loyal Labour supporter but was disillusioned with John Smith. He had studied at Harvard under Larry Summers and Robert

Reich, both advisers to Bill Clinton, and was sparkling with ideas about monetarism, how to avoid boom and bust, never rejoining the ERM, giving independence to the Bank of England and revolutionising Britain's economy. Brown cold-called Balls to arrange a meeting. He was impressed. Balls's intellect and their mutual admiration of America helped to form an immediate bond. In an exchange of letters, they agreed that Labour's future success depended on winning the electorate's trust in the party's economic competence. Most importantly, Balls was prepared to undertake the grind to produce the fine economic detail that was beyond Brown's experience. The association with Balls and his future wife, Yvette Cooper, would change Brown's life.

In January 1993 Brown and Blair flew to Washington. Ed Balls had reinforced Brown's attraction to Bill Clinton's ideas, especially after Clinton's election victory the previous November. With Balls and Jonathan Powell, a diplomat at the British embassy, they listened to Larry Summers and Robert Reich explain Clinton's seduction of the American middle classes away from the Republicans, and his welfare-to-work programme. In a newspaper article after their return, Blair wrote enthusiastically about the exciting change in Washington. He praised the new vitality in the United States, and hailed the thousands of young people coming to Washington to build a new era. 'The Democrats' campaign was brilliantly planned,' Blair wrote. Labour, he suggested, should copy Clinton's policy, stressing 'the importance of individual opportunity; of community strengths'.

Brown also returned inspired to seize the middle ground from the Tories. He was attracted to Clinton's core proposition that governments had responsibilities to the whole community. That was not a new idea. Since 1988, Brown and others had discussed it with Clinton's staff. The Democrats' genius was their packaging. Labour, Brown felt, should avoid outrightly campaigning for egalitarianism. Rather than preaching 'total equality', the party should pledge 'equality of opportunity for all', with the assurance that 'everyone can fulfil his or her potential'. The new slogans would offer choice and social change. The critical promise would be to reduce unemployment in a 'partnership economy' without increasing taxes.

To position Labour as the party of low taxation, Brown developed new catchphrases despite the protests of the left: 'We do not tax for its own sake'; 'We do not spend for its own sake'; and 'We are not against wealth'. Simultaneously, he began to harp on the government's tax increases – albeit only 1 per cent since 1979 – which contradicted the Conservative election pledge to lower taxation. The Tories were crudely classified as liars: 'Either these ministers were incompetent on a scale which beggars belief, or . . . they set out to deceive the people of Britain on a massive and unprecedented scale.' The gauntlet was thrown down: 'There is no one left for this government to betray. They have no credibility. The electorate will never trust them again.' Endless repetition, Brown hoped, would produce rewards,

A journey to the Far East in 1993 reinforced his conviction to discard other Labour sacred cows. Britain, he realised, could not compete with China on the cost of production, but only on the quality of the products. To beat the Pacific Rim required a skilled British workforce. 'Capital', demonised over the previous century by socialists, was a worthless target, he decided. The buzz words of his new Labour creed were 'human capital' and 'knowledge corporations'. 'Their lessons must be applied here,' he wrote in countless newspaper articles about innovation in the Far East, developing the idea that 'the value of labour can be enhanced as the key to economic prosperity'.

To spread the message from his office in London, or over the weekend from his home in Edinburgh, he sought to dictate the news agenda with interviews and press releases, urging Peter Mandelson to hunt for every possible appearance on radio and television to place him in the spotlight. He preached the homily that 'in the modern economy we will earn by what we learn', and recommended that 'the system of personal taxation and benefits should favour those who upgrade their skills'. To improve those skills he proposed a University for Industry, bringing together universities, industry and broadcasters and using satellite communications to disseminate and constantly upgrade information.

The powerhouse for this change was to be the Treasury. 'I see the Treasury,' Brown wrote, 'as a department of national economic reconstruction to deal with the short-term problem of unemployment and the long-term national economic decline.' Revealing his own abandonment of socialism as a figleaf to give false comfort to the middle class, he ridiculed the Tories for relying on the free market and individual opportunity rather than government intervention to finance industry. 'I see the public sector as the engine of growth out of recession,' he wrote, re-emphasising his true beliefs. He spoke of levying a windfall tax on the excess profits of the privatised utilities – copying the Tories' windfall tax on banks – to finance a 'New Deal' on employment and, with another reminiscent whiff of Harold Wilson, he attacked the major banks for increasing their dividends.

This potpourri of socialism and Clintonism irritated John Smith. The leader disliked the modernisers' policies, and he ostracised Mandelson. Smith was not surprised when John Edmonds, the GMB union leader, called him personally to protest about Brown and Blair's visit to America. 'They're getting too much publicity,' complained Edmonds. 'This Project is mischief-making and about personal ambition.' Although a decade later Edmonds would acknowledge 'a lack of imagination among the trade unions in the early 1990s', he was gratified in 1993 by Smith's rejection of the modernisers' proposals for the next election campaign. Smith supported large government spending, and disliked Brown's refusal to commit Labour to use the proceeds from council house sales for more building. In meetings of the shadow cabinet, the leader remained silent when Brown's proposed windfall tax was criticised for being too small. 'We cannot meet those expectations,' Brown told Frank Dobson. Smith overruled Brown for being 'too conservative'.

In contrast, during their arguments, while Murray Elder, Smith's chief of staff, sat silently in the background, Smith growled, 'You're going too fast.' In private, Brown raged about Smith's unwillingness to support the modernisers while encouraging the traditional left. While in public Brown praised John Smith's 'egalitarianism' and 'concern for justice', emphasising Smith's concern as a Christian socialist for Labour's moral purpose, he detested Smith's blinkeredness. Smith ignored the Tories' private polls which showed that Labour was still regarded as 'dishonest and incoherent', and on the side of losers. Relying on the lowest common denominator for electoral appeal, Smith was sure, would prove successful. 'The Tories are destroying themselves,' he observed about the government's bitter battles over Europe. 'Labour can sleep-walk to victory.'

Brown found that his frustrating battle with John Smith to change Labour was losing him friends and allies. Visitors to his office reported that his Horatio-on-the-bridge act on the shadow spending ministers was causing him anguish. 'Gordon is torn and depressed about the irreconcilables,' John Monks observed. Trade union leaders whom Brown regarded as friends – Rodney Bickerstaffe, Bill Morris and John Monks – were surprised during their private meetings that the man casting himself as the future 'iron chancellor' forgot to smile while brusquely refusing to advocate higher public spending funded by higher taxes and borrowing. Brown's image was affecting his credibility. 'Gordon,' said one, 'is really not interested in people; he's only interested in people as economic agents, the ants in the anthill, and he wants ants to have a nice anthill.' The alienated Labourites did not disagree with Norman Lamont's successor as chancellor Kenneth Clarke when he jibed that Brown's regurgitation of lists, strategies, statistics and predictions of doom were self-defeating. 'He has as much policy content as the average telephone directory,' mocked Clarke languidly across the floor of the Commons, 'and if I may say so – it is a modest claim given the competition it faced – I thought the best parts of the hon. gentleman's speech came when he was quoting me.' Brown scowled. The dispenser of ridicule hated receiving similar treatment. Even John Smith's agreement to relaunch Labour on 9 February 1993 as the party of the individual and to abandon any commitment to renationalisation brought only temporary relief.

Brown's misfortune was that changing Labour's economic policy to attract the middle classes was more difficult than Tony Blair's task, as shadow home secretary, of altering the party's social policies. While Brown chased every news bulletin, Blair, also helped by Mandelson, concentrated on making limited appearances with 'warm and chatty' preludes to reflective answers suggesting the moral high ground. Blair's insistence on accepting interviews only on his own terms, and resistance to giving instant reactions to please the media's agenda, gave his rarer interviews a cachet, and gracefully neutralised his opponents.

Brown had become weary. A visit to Newbury in early 1993 to campaign in the by-election caused by the death of its sitting Tory MP, John Major's adviser Judith Chaplin, revealed the perils for self-publicists. The previously safe Tory seat was vulnerable. Norman Lamont had committed atrocious gaffes, not least his statement that high unemployment was 'a price

Gordon Brown's family, his father the Reverend John Brown, and his brothers John and Andrew, have been the greatest influence on his life and his best friends.

Brown learnt the arts of political propaganda, combat and survival during his student days at Edinburgh University, but the cost of his success and popularity was a raft of bitter enemies.

Gordon Brown's relationships with women – characterised by extraordinary secrecy – have sparked speculation and unhappiness. Princess Margarita of Romania (above, left) walked out after five years complaining of his obsession with politics; Marion Caldwell (above, right) was strung along for more than a decade; and Sheena McDonald (left) was upset by his unwillingness to commit himself.

Fife MPs at Carnegie Hall, Dunfermline, in 1987: Dick Douglas, Lewis Moonie, Gordon Brown and Henry McLeish.

Neil Kinnock identified Brown very early as a future Labour leader, but Cherie Blair, offended by Brown's behaviour, opposed his ambitions.

John Smith was a friend and colleague, but by 1992 Brown was disenchanted by his inflexibility.

The 'Hotel Group' forged Brown's alternative cabinet. Financed by Geoffrey Robinson (above, with his wife), Brown relied on the intellect of Ed Balls, 'the deputy chancellor' (below), on his raffish spokesman Charlie Whelan (opposite, above) to undermine his rivals, and on Sue Nye (seen opposite, below, with her husband Gavyn Davies) to organise his life.

"Look Gordon, you'll just have to accept the fact that the glass slipper fitted my foot and not yours."

well worth paying' to reduce inflation. The Tory candidate was an unappealing PR consultant. The seat should have been an easy trophy, but Brown's performance in front of the television cameras at Vodafone's headquarters, which were in the constituency, was unproductive. Confidently, he told journalists about the area's high unemployment. 'Rubbish,' exclaimed Chris Gent, Vodafone's managing director. 'Our company has grown by 25 per cent in the last year.' The Liberal Democrats won the by-election.

In March 1993 the London *Evening Standard* reported that while Brown was regarded with respect, Tony Blair was the frontrunner to succeed Smith. Brown was furious. On one occasion when Mark Seddon, the genial editor of *Tribune*, was interviewing Brown in his office, a member of Brown's staff announced, 'Tony's gone ahead without you,' referring to a meeting the two were to attend. Brown exploded, breaking a pencil in his fury.

The hostility towards Brown among his fellow MPs was growing. His monotone hectoring was criticised as all too revealing of an unworldly, unmarried forty-one-year-old mystified about the real world. His constant appearance in an identical uniform – blue suit, white shirt and red tie – regardless of the context bewildered those who judged people by such things. Brown's reputation was not helped by a story of a car journey through countryside when he allegedly said to his companion, 'Look, those cows have had their foals.' His new critics delighted in carping that he was 'a townie who didn't know where his fish and chips came from'. Others recited an eyewitness's account of Blair mentioning to Brown that he had once seen Marc Bolan perform. 'Where is he now?' asked Brown, preoccupied with drafting a statement. 'Dead,' replied Blair. Brown carried on writing, oblivious to the answer.

In fact he had become oblivious to everything other than his own truths. Like a man possessed, he steamrollered rather than reasoned with critics. Among his victims was Peter Hain, an ambitious left-winger brought up in South Africa whose circuitous route to the Labour Party via student protest, the Liberals and election as Tribune's secretary baffled many. Unwilling to accept Brown's economic prescription for an election victory, Hain wrote a pamphlet for the Tribune Group arguing for huge public spending, the abandonment of euro-monetarism and a return to full socialism. Labour, Hain complained, had never previously attacked the Tories for increasing taxes, yet Brown was appealing to richer voters by promising to lower direct taxation. 'Gordon has done a brilliant job in exposing Tory tax hikes,' said Hain, 'but voters need to be convinced that Labour can manage the economy more effectively. The modernisers have told us what we're against but not what we're for.' Hain did not grasp that the shadow chancellor had not abandoned socialism in favour of Thatcherism other than as an election ploy. He espoused measured concealment to defeat the Conservatives. Neutralising Hain should have been effortless, but Brown's methods compounded his predicament. Angry about its attack on himself, he sought to prevent Hain's pamphlet's publication. Hain was summoned to Brown's office and lambasted for thirty minutes. 'We believe markets must work in the public interest,' he was lectured. Brown did not understand markets and his list of do-gooding schemes – the University for Industry, a Global Environmental Task Force for young people – and his belief in 'the community and independence' did not impress Hain, who insisted that the publication of the pamphlet would go ahead. Convinced that even a single dissenting voice would damage the party, Brown tried to persuade other Tribune members to stop Hain, but without success. Next he sought Mandelson's help, warning about the pamphlet's potentially dire consequences. He failed again. With Robin Cook's support, Hain published his pamphlet. No one noticed its appearance. Brown began to lobby against Hain's re-election as Tribune's secretary.

The succession of rows instigated by Brown among Labour apparatchiks was costly. Repeatedly he lost his temper, screaming obscenities at those he damned as dishonourable or incompetent. Losing the sympathy of potential allies was undermining his status. His admonition that 'The policies are unpopular with the party but we have to stick with them,' combined with his refusal to smile while delivering his television soundbites, suggested a dour man. 'He loves mankind,' Voltaire is said to have written, 'therefore he does not need to love his neighbour.' To outsiders, Brown appeared a tough man, determined to carve out and control his empire; but in the privacy of his office, surrounded by the chaotic debris of books and papers, he violently chewed his fingernails and festered about his predicament. He was oblivious that his terseness, his seeming lack of human warmth, alienated others. Many could not identify with a rumpled, unusually driven man with limited small talk. Trying to understand his Jekyll and Hyde qualities tested the patience of too many. Brown's passion to transform Labour was understood, but the personal cost was not appreciated. A contemporary profile in the *Sunday Telegraph* described him, with his 'smouldering Celtic looks, dry humour and deep Scottish burr' as 'the natural heart-throb of the Labour Party'. That exaggeration was accompanied by the more accurate assessment that his qualities of laughter, wit and lightness 'shine in small company'. The mystery was why a man who could be warm and amusing among friends was so austere in public.

Any prospects of marriage had now receded. Brown's recent move from Kennington to a flat in Great Smith Street, Westminster, formerly owned by Robert Maxwell's company, had brought him physically even closer to his work. His relationship with Marion Caldwell had foundered, and at the instigation of a friend he was reunited with Sheena McDonald, who by then had become a well-known TV presenter about national politics. There was good reason for her to believe that as they had so much in common their friendship would develop into a permanent relationship, if not marriage. Fearing that any public appearance with Brown would compromise her independence as a journalist, she preferred the relationship to remain secret, which suited Brown, but did not help his image.

In early May 1993, in an attempt to recover the party's favour, Brown presented 'Labour's New Economic Approach', a policy paper proposing a radical assault on the free market and the City's vested interests. He had performed a half-reverse somersault from his new gospel. Labour, he promised, would attack bank charges, the business battalions, the fat cats, the monopolies and the shortages of choice, training and opportunity. To reinforce his credentials he launched a campaign against multi-millionaires residing in the UK but claiming to be domiciled overseas in order to avoid British taxation. 'The Tory Party,' he wrote, 'does not have the will to close the loophole, but Labour does.' The only 'modernisation' theme remaining was his rejection of the 'old battles' between the state and the private market. To the left, Brown appeared to have been trounced. Influenced by John Smith's supporters, *Tribune* celebrated the 'public hammering' of the modernisers and their 'pals' who, eighteen months after Kinnock's defeat, had failed to have 'Labour's future sewn up'. The 'sub-Thatcherite, euro-dreamland' and 'Clintonite supply-siders' had been defeated by 'Labourism'.

In July 1993, Brown and Blair were flummoxed. 'John's letting us hang out to dry,' Brown complained. In particular, Smith's negotiations to break trade union power within the party were proceeding with excruciating slowness. Introducing 'one man, one vote' (OMOV) to replace the unions' block vote was important if Labour was to capture the confidence of the middle classes. Smith, it appeared to Brown, was not supporting that change. Brown told Blair that Smith was even refusing to see him. 'Well,' replied Blair, 'just walk past his secretary, shout "I've got a meeting," and walk in.' That might work for Blair, Brown knew, but he lacked the audacity.

As Brown was tortured by Smith's obduracy, the weakness of his character emerged. While he could confidently withstand intellectual arguments, he lacked the resilience to cope with excessive emotional pressure. Unable to manage his rejection, Brown became depressed by the OMOV disagreement, and edged towards a nervous breakdown. 'We won't carry the party with that,' he repeated endlessly, fearful of risks and contemplating defeat. The contrast between Brown and Blair at this time was revealing. As Oliver Wendell Holmes, the US supreme court judge, commented about Franklin Roosevelt, 'A second-rate brain and a first-rate temperament is OK, because you can buy in first-rate brains.' Equally furious as Brown that Smith was not enthusiastically supporting modernisation, Blair coolly took risks to challenge Smith, and then considered retiring from politics. But his supporters urged him to be resolute. 'You've got to realise that you must stand as the next leader,' he was told while staying with friends in the country. 'But Gordon wants it so much more than me,' replied Blair. Until then, the two may have been known as 'the twins' or 'the blood brothers'. In summer 1993, the description 'Brown–Blair' shifted to 'Blair–Brown'.

Those gloating during that summer about the humbling of 'the king of soundbites' were premature. In the weeks before the party conference, after listening to the advice of Ed Balls, Gavyn Davies, Michael Wills and others, Brown regained his self-confidence and composed a seminal speech to re-establish the modernisers' gospel and purposely retreat from a commitment of wealth redistribution. Enthused by a slogan used by George Bush, he would replace 'tax and spend' with 'invest and grow'. The breakout on 28 July 1993 was a public renunciation of the 1992 manifesto. With gusto, Brown announced that Labour was not against wealth, and would jettison the commitment to levy a 50 per cent inheritance tax. He would no longer insist that managing exchange rates was 'absolutely necessary'. The counterattack was immediate. Angry trade union leaders and left-wingers telephoned journalists to condemn Brown's 'unfashionable' appeal to the wealthy. Brown retaliated in August. In inflammatory language, he pledged in 'The New Economic Agenda', a party pamphlet, to cut taxes and drop all specific spending plans. Labour, he reaffirmed, would never again 'tax for taxation's own sake'. 'From now on,' he wrote, 'Labour believes in creating the necessary wealth to fund the social benefits we demand.'

Without doubt he was inspired by his father's sermons about Christians triumphing over weakness, pain and misfortune not only courageously, but cheerfully. And, although not immune from misfortune and discouragement, he was urged to join those 'going forward with a smile . . . when all seems so dark . . . more than conquerors, helping us not just to scrape our way to victory but to gain victory very comfortably and successfully'. As the Reverend John Brown had exulted, 'Let no one go away saying: "I can't; I can't; it's not for me."' John Brown's inspirations were Winston Churchill and Ernest Bevin for being 'determined on set objectives'. He extolled his congregation, including his sons, 'Should not all of us, like these two statesmen, have set objectives which we are determined to attain?' That was Gordon Brown's Herculean task.

Over the following weeks, Brown was battered by the left.

On 26 September he arrived at a meeting of the National
Executive Committee prepared for a stormy confrontation.
Snide remarks about his competence were still being made
about a stunt in which he had posed with Harriet Harman in
front of a huge poster with the legend 'Tory Tax Bombshell'.
The event had misfired when he floundered about the size of
the proposed tax increases, with estimates ranging from £59
to £226. At the meeting, the anger towards him was worse
than Brown had anticipated. He was puzzled. As a child, he
had grown up understanding poverty. There were decaying
shipyards and coalmines down the road, worn boots shuffling
on the street and endless sermons from his father about the
deprived. He had worked passionately to help the poor, but
now, despite his commitment, he was being attacked. 'Don't
the bastards understand?' he shouted in the privacy of his
room. Then he surrendered. The Conservatives' tax re-
ductions during the 1980s, he said, had been indefensible, and
he supported higher taxes. The *Mirror*'s headline the following
morning – 'Brown Demands Higher Tax Rates for Wealthy' –
signalled his retreat, but during that day, 27 September 1993,
he began to reverse his recantation. The choice the party faced
was between John Prescott's 'traditional values in a modern
setting' and Brown's socially refined Thatcherism. Proud to
be a man of conviction without any doubts, he could be insensitive to the qualities of those who showed a hint of human
weakness.

The trade unions wanted a pledge from Brown to borrow
and spend £15 billion in order to reduce unemployment.
Brown became obdurate. The trade unions, he believed, were
the biggest single obstacle to Labour's election victory. Nye
Bevan, the giant of Labour's left, was quoted in Brown's
biography of James Maxton castigating Scottish rebels: 'I will
tell you what the epitaph on you Scottish dissenters will be
– pure but impotent. Yes, you will be pure all right. But

remember at the price of impotency. You will not influence the course of British politics by as much as a hair's breadth.' Brown would not repeat that mistake and damage Labour's election chances. Defiantly, he was prepared to bring the whole house down to crush the opposition. Unpopularity was the price for performing his duty. As he stepped into the corridor, he was asked, 'Does Labour still believe in the redistribution of wealth?' Impulsively, he replied, 'Yes.' Those were his principles. Later that night, reflecting upon his strategy for Labour's election victory, he said to those in the bars and corridors: 'I am not against wealth. I just want everyone to be richer.' Standing at other bars, Peter Hain and John Edmonds remorselessly disparaged Brown. 'We should not replace the Red Flag with the White Flag,' said Edmonds. Shedding Labour's traditional socialist image, agreed Hain, would destroy all hope of the party ever regaining power. Their animosity was personal.

Brown and Blair arrived at the 1993 party conference with Smith's reluctant agreement to curb the trade unions' control of the party and impose 'one man, one vote'. The union leaders were incensed. While they would expect Tony Blair to be anti-union, the transformation of Brown grated among the traditionalists. 'This is a phoney battle,' John Edmonds challenged Brown, 'to show Labour is not in thrall to the unions. This is all about Mandelson positioning you and Blair as acceptable, and is against John Smith.' The battle for OMOV, Edmonds believed, was a figleaf for Brown's sympathy with Thatcherism. 'You won't carry Labour support on these policies,' he told Brown. 'I don't believe in promising full employment any more,' Brown replied. 'It gives the impression of a government creating worthless jobs at great cost.' To hear that from Brown's mouth surprised the socialist.

That year's shadow cabinet elections, Brown knew, would be an uncomfortable test. The party man who had spent a lifetime attending committee meetings could no longer expect the unions' automatic support. Their antagonism caused him real pain. By contrast, Blair operated with a fresh and uncluttered style as shadow home secretary, showing affectionate curiosity about people. Unlike Brown, he had developed the technique of telling people what they wanted to hear, flattering potential critics and cultivating bores whom others would ignore. There was freshness to his soundbites, which were exquisitely delivered. 'Tough on crime, and tough on the causes of crime' had won plaudits which, as Brown never ceased to remind people, was a debt owed to him, who had conceived the slogan. But there was more to Blair than mere soundbites. His appeal was to the whole country rather than to a particular tribe or a class. His ambivalence – by refusing to feign sentimental links with the trade unions or to posture as a radical egalitarian – proved his chameleon appeal. Those qualities brought him limited favour in the elections to the shadow cabinet in autumn 1993. Robin Cook came top, Brown fell to fourth, while Blair was sixth.

Brown and Blair were driven back to London from the party conference by Derek Draper, Peter Mandelson's special adviser. Their conversation was dominated by their comparatively poor performances in the poll. Brown was worried about losing his seat on the shadow cabinet the following year. The solution, he suggested, was to employ a researcher to bolster their support. One week later Saul Billingsley was hired on a salary of £10,000, two thirds of which was paid by Brown, and one third by Blair. Blair's contribution was a calculated attempt to pacify Brown rather than confirmation of his own anxiety. Brown paid Billingsley from the income he earned from the *Daily Record*, but occasionally he ran out of money. 'Don't cash that cheque,' Sue Nye told Derek Draper on one occasion. 'Gordon is temporarily overdrawn.' Based in Brown's office in Millbank, Billingsley ana-

lysed each constituency's local issues. He sent fact sheets to
the constituencies showing the policies which Brown believed
would cure their particular problems, and with a message
from Brown. If there was an indication that a constituency
might be persuaded to shift in Brown's favour, Billingsley
would invite the local party leaders to meet Brown in Westminster. The tactic worked. Several constituency activists
praised Brown as 'active and committed', an important asset
in his fight against enemies like Peter Hain.

Hain had published another pamphlet demanding that £20
billion be spent on investment and training. This indiscipline
outraged the shadow chancellor. Hain, Brown decided, was
to be decapitated. With the help of Derek Foster, Labour's
chief whip, a large posse of born-again Tribunites marched
unannounced into the group's annual general meeting and
voted against Hain's re-election as general secretary. The coup
was smooth, and tax and spend was suppressed as an issue in
Labour's debates. Brown received little credit for neutralising
Hain; instead, he faced resentment.

Once again, to prove his credibility, his language against
the Tories became vehement. He accused them outright of
dishonesty: 'The Tories lied about taxation,' became a recurring theme. 'They're incapable in my view,' he said in a speech
on 1 December 1993, 'of telling the difference now between
truth and falsehood; incapable and unable to tell the truth,
or even recognise it.' Carefully honed phrases like 'thousands
of pensioners will have to choose between heating and eating'
failed to excite his party, although the opinion polls steadfastly
predicted a Labour election victory. To win trust, Brown constantly repeated, 'Unlike the Tories, there will be honest disclosure. We will be straight with the British people . . . There
will be no sleight of hand. What you see on taxes will be
what you get.' Opinion polls suggested that while the Tories
were unpopular with the public because of their tax increases,

Labour had still failed to convince them that they had a coherent economic strategy.

Over Christmas 1993, Brown pondered his fate. He had been the star pupil of Kirkcaldy, the star of Edinburgh University, and ever since his memorable maiden speech there had been expectations that one day he would be in Downing Street. Yet he appeared to be stymied. His jokes may have been memorable – 'John Major went to Pittsburgh and discovered he had no past. He came back to Britain and discovered he had no future' – but his critics questioned whether there was any more to him than cracking jokes and dissecting statistics. His sulks and his negative politics raised the questions of whether he was simply destructive or could ever inspire uncertain voters. Some of his personal traits were off-putting. He reluctantly posed for photographs in a pullover, and when asked to remove his tie replied, 'I never take off my tie.' He was also gauche, describing formal dinners as a waste of time. He lacked taste not only in art, furniture and wine, but also in food. He gobbled down whatever was offered without comment, suggesting an indifference to life's refinements. His impatience extended to parliament. 'During prime minister's questions,' he explained, 'I often have to sit in the chamber for an hour and may speak for only thirty seconds. The place is geared towards eloquence rather than the pursuit of excellence.' He was puzzled that some of his characteristics could irritate others.

Peter Mandelson offered help. Brown suffered, Mandelson calculated, from 'press mania'. His reliance on Ed Richards, an unremarkable apparatchik, had spawned a compulsion to seek appearances on news bulletins and current affairs programmes. Brown erupted in uncontrolled rages even if a rival Labour politician featured on a news bulletin at 5.15 on a Saturday afternoon. 'They're trying to do me down,' he shouted at Mandelson after watching one MP deliver a nine-second

soundbite. Everyone, he claimed, was trying to 'do him down'.
He was prepared to travel from Scotland to London early on a
Sunday morning to broadcast for a few fleeting seconds.

This hunger for influence was not accompanied by personal
vanity. Repeatedly, he refused the opportunity to watch the
playbacks of his party political broadcasts. Seemingly irked by
his own face, his unfashionable opinion about politics was that
the message rather than the image was important. Although
assured by Barry Delaney, the producer of Labour's political
broadcasts, that women found him attractive, he was ambivalent about American talkshow host Jay Leno's opinion that
'Politics is show biz for ugly people.'

Brown's mixture of frenzy and shyness prompted Peter
Mandelson to suggest in late 1993 that he hire Charlie Whelan
as his press spokesman. Mandelson had known Whelan since
the 1992 election, and had been impressed by his abilities at
the recent party conference while discussing OMOV. Brown
knew him from the regular Tuesday lunches hosted by Gavin
Laird, the general secretary of the AEUW. Laird had praised
Whelan, his spokesman, as having 'real flair'. Whelan's particular talent, reinforced by his natural energy and bonhomie,
was to spot opportunities for an AEUW representative to
speak on TV news programmes. While his officials appeared
in front of the cameras, rival trade unionists were ignored.
That expertise was precisely Brown's requirement.

Born in Peckham in 1955, Whelan would above all be
obedient and loyal to Brown's cause. 'Able but very lazy,'
was his headmaster's conclusion after the young Whelan
failed one examination. In the hope of solving the problem, his parents sent him to a fee-paying boarding school in
Surrey. He secured an unimpressive degree in politics at the
City of London Polytechnic. When he started his first job as
a foreign exchange dealer in the City, he spoke in a Home
Counties accent. One year later, employed as a researcher by

the AEUW, he spoke like a Cockney. Influenced by Jimmy Airlie, the forceful trade union leader renowned for his campaign to save the Upper Clyde shipbuilders, Whelan demonstrated his lack of political judgement when he joined the Communist Party in 1975. Whether he understood the reasons for the Party's dramatic decline since the Soviet invasions of Hungary in 1956 and Czechoslovakia in 1968 is uncertain. Probably the oppression of East Europeans was less important to him than loyalty to Jimmy Airlie. He only resigned from the Party in 1990, after the final collapse of communism.

The contrast between Charlie Whelan and Gordon Brown, the reserved, puritan non-smoker, could not have been greater – and that was the mutual attraction. During his fifteen years in the thuggish world of trade union politics Whelan had adopted a laddish style to promote his wheeler-dealer expertise. The clan chief spotted the chain-smoking, beer-drinking bruiser who shared a love of football as his man of business. Although Whelan was markedly unconscientious about detail, he would in some ways be an ideal soulmate. For his part, Whelan was flattered to be so close to the centre of attention. Whelan joined Ed Balls and Sue Nye within Brown's inner cabinet. He welcomed the responsibility of solving Brown's problems, delighted if the shadow chancellor telephoned six times in a day to seek consolation over an irritating news item. By then both had noticed that Peter Mandelson was less involved in Brown's daily activities. Eight years after his appointment, Whelan was asked whether he had felt any loyalty towards Mandelson. 'Yes,' he smirked, 'for about five minutes.' That retrospective sarcasm reflected Whelan's dislike for a man he called 'Trousers'.

On Monday, 9 May 1994, Roy Hattersley was chatting with John Smith in Westminster. Their conversation drifted towards the shadow chancellor. 'Gordon's doing very badly,' said Smith. 'He'd have no chance to be leader if there was an election now. Blair would get it.' There was no pleasure in Smith's judgement. He did not disguise his dislike for Brown's rival. 'But fortunately,' he added, 'there won't be an election tomorrow, so it will eventually be Gordon.' As if he had a premonition of his fate, Smith repeated this to David Ward, his chief of staff. Gordon Brown was unaware of Smith's opinion, but the disagreements between them had become insurmountable.

FOUR

Retreat

The telephone call soon after 9.30 on the morning of Thursday, 12 May 1994 was shattering. Saul Billingsley, Gordon Brown's assistant, reported that Murray Elder needed to speak to him very urgently. Brown was in his flat in Great Smith Street as he listened to his childhood friend's trembling voice. At 9.15, said Elder, John Smith had died after another heart attack. Brown was thunderstruck. His grief was genuine.

The night before, Brown and Smith had attended a fund-raising dinner at the Park Lane Hotel. The party had been jolly. Many rich men, former contributors to the Tories, had pledged their new loyalty to Labour. Success in politics, Smith knew, is the talent to exploit unexpected opportunities. John Smith's misfortune was Gordon Brown's chance.

During those first hours, Brown was not wholly in mourning. Instinctively, he considered his tactics. He had dedicated his life to becoming number one. The prospect of failure was intolerable. Those close friends whom he telephoned noticed that his voice was sombre but not distraught. Nothing, he urged his confidants, should be said or done. The son of the manse understood human suffering and respect for proprieties. Decency demanded delay, if he was to avoid accusations of opportunism. Sue Nye, Ed Balls and Charlie Whelan arrived. Their conversation was short, and they departed. In

the era before the widespread use of mobile telephones, communications would be slow.

Among Gordon Brown's telephone calls was one to Tony
Blair, who had just arrived at Dyce airport in Aberdeen to start
a campaign tour. So many words had already been exchanged
about John Smith that they got straight down to practicalities.
They agreed to meet later that day, after Blair had cut short
his journey and returned to London. Brown assumed that
Blair would wait until after they had met before making any
decisions.

After eleven o'clock, Peter Mandelson arrived in the flat.
Whatever his faults, Mandelson was a serious politician who
had dedicated himself to the party's election success. He was
also an astute judge of people's strengths and weaknesses.
Gordon Brown, he noted, did not regard Smith's death just
as a tragedy, but also as an opportunity which he was willing
to grasp. There were few words of mourning. Mandelson
spoke to Brown only about the succession. The Scotsman
was emphatic that he would stand. When Mandelson did not
comment, Brown misread his neutrality as support. Shortly
afterwards, Nick Brown joined them.

Sheena McDonald arrived at lunchtime. The three men's
discussions had reached stalemate. Mandelson was endlessly
on the telephone, Nick Brown was sitting silently on a chair,
while Gordon Brown paced quietly around the room listening
to Mandelson's conversations. McDonald departed, leaving
Brown to write an obituary for the next day's *Independent*
which would be notable for its hyperbole. John Smith, he
repeatedly emphasised, was witty and good company. His
premature death deprived 'the country as a whole of something irreplaceable', because Smith was 'uniquely equipped
. . . to bind this nation together and to heal the deep wounds
of the past fifteen years'. He lamented that Smith had been
standing 'at the brink of his greatest achievement', victory in

the next election. In truth, Brown knew, Smith was singularly ill-equipped for that challenge.

Sitting in a corner of the untidy living room following the media coverage of Smith's death in telephone conversations, Charlie Whelan's temper rose. Commentators were privately predicting that Blair was the favoured candidate for the leadership. More alarming was the early edition of the agenda-setting London *Evening Standard*. The newspaper's editor had heard about Smith's death from a doctor at the London hospital. Charles Reiss, the *Standard*'s political editor, baldly stated that Blair was the heir apparent in a 'dream ticket' with John Prescott as his deputy. Brown, by contrast, was dismissed as the son of John Smith, the new representative of Old Labour. By mid-afternoon, Brown was working behind closed doors in his Millbank office. Outside, Caroline Daniel, a new researcher, sensed an unusually tense atmosphere. Sue Nye was warning everyone not to speak to anyone on Blair's staff. 'It could all get heated,' she said. 'We need to ensure that everyone can be trusted.' This warning was odd, because two nights every week Anji Hunter, Blair's personal assistant, slept at Nye's home. During those visits they conveniently settled any outstanding differences between the politicians. Towards the end of the afternoon, after speaking with Nick Brown, Gordon Brown agreed that his closest confidants should gather at 6 p.m. in his office.

The six men who met that evening in Brown's corner office – Alistair Darling, Martin O'Neill, Doug Henderson, Nick Brown, Tom Clarke and Murray Elder – were all from Scotland and the north-east of England. Their purpose was to discuss how to bring about Brown's election as the new leader. The mood was businesslike. 'There's everything to play for,' announced Nick Brown. 'You've got an even chance to win.' Gordon Brown nodded. He acknowledged that Blair was his obvious rival, and did not mention any personal understanding between the two – either an agreement that Blair would stand aside for Brown, or that they would not campaign against each other.

Doug Henderson disturbed their composure. He had spent the day 'intelligence gathering' around Westminster and consulting his constituents. 'I've already spoken to my people in Newcastle,' he said, 'and you're not going to win there.' He then dropped a bombshell. 'I just don't think you can win. You're behind in the press stakes. We're half a lap behind. I didn't need a glass against my wall to hear Mandelson at work today.' 'What do you mean?' asked Brown. 'His room is next to mine,' explained Henderson. 'He's spent the whole day speaking to his favourites in Fleet Street promoting Blair.'

Brown's face fell. He was unsure whether Blair had approved Mandelson's activities, but Mandelson had for long been contemplating a coup against John Smith. Smith's death had possibly triggered a prepared plan. Brown never contemplated the possibility that Henderson might have been mistaken. Later, Derek Draper, Mandelson's assistant, would insist that Mandelson did not brief in Blair's favour for the first twenty-four hours.

The short silence was broken by Nick Brown. 'You've got to take him on,' he said in a pleading tone. 'You can win, and in any case you can't trust Blair. If you do a deal, it will be ignored and he'll welch on it.' Gordon Brown's childhood friend Murray Elder, a decent but uncombative man, cautioned him to 'wait and see'. Impaled more than Brown by fear of failure, Elder believed that the hurt of defeat would be worse than to take a risk. Charlie Whelan did not commit himself, although he would later say that Brown could have won if he had been better prepared.

Brown became gradually more grim-faced and silent. Someone opened the midday edition of the *Evening Standard*. A glowing profile of Blair by Sarah Baxter added to the misery in the room. 'I don't like talking about this on the same day as John died,' Brown unexpectedly announced. His friends nodded, although they might have been excused for thinking they had been doing nothing else since that morning. Brown looked up: 'I'm not going to make a decision until after John is buried.' In the folklore constructed over the next years about the events immediately following the death of John Smith, that first meeting in Brown's office was, like so many other details, erased from the record.

Tony Blair had flown back to London during the afternoon. He was met at Heathrow by his wife Cherie. Cherie didn't like Brown. She resented his brusqueness towards herself – the coolness and lack of respect he often showed to women. Even in the Blairs' own home, the temperature dropped whenever he appeared. As they travelled towards London, the Blairs agreed on their agenda. Tony Blair wanted the leadership, and key relationships had already been forged. Since 1992 he had established a network of supporting MPs across the north-east, and he knew that he could count on the majority of London's politicians, many of whom, like Chris Smith, were neighbours of his in Islington. Even some Scottish MPs, insulted over the years by Brown, had promised their support. Peter Mandelson, he believed, was also a firm supporter.

Months earlier, Mandelson had decided that Brown's abrasive style, provincialism and lack of populist appeal was not certain to win a general election. Not only was Brown seen as 'John Smith Mark 2', but in recent years the number of Celts among the party leadership had hampered Labour's appeal in England. There had been John Smith from Scotland, Neil Kinnock from Wales, and both Michael Foot and Jim Callaghan represented Welsh constituencies. Unlike Blair, Brown resisted giving interviews to *Cosmopolitan* magazine about his favourite cars, his record collection, his guitar and

his haircuts, nor could he dress casually for a loving pose with
a young family. Mandelson's opinions were shared by Donald
Dewar, the senior Scottish MP. Although they were friends,
Dewar doubted Brown's organisational skills. Dewar and
George Robertson would agree that Blair was the best candidate but, to avoid 'letting Gordon down', they would say
nothing. Over the following days Brown would be allowed
to find his own way to withdraw.

That evening Brown and his confidants left Millbank unaware of those allegiances and attitudes. The task of rounding
up Brown's supporters was delegated to Nick Brown, who
was ignorant of Gordon Brown's vulnerability in England. A
physical factor also limited his efforts. While Gordon Brown's
office was in Millbank, Blair had remained in Parliament
Street. Nick Brown would not know who was meeting Blair,
and did not realise that on that very evening Mandelson and
Blair were talking in the Commons. Mandelson's opinion was
critical. His decision on whether to support Brown or Blair
would determine which of the two modernisers possessed a
significant advantage. Gordon Brown was also handicapped
by his lack of an Anji Hunter, a 'gold star schmoozer' according
to her targets, who successfully persuaded the party's power
brokers to meet and like Blair. Brown relied on Sue Nye, loyal
but abrasive, who deterred rather than attracted.

At the end of the day Gordon Brown travelled to Islington,
to the home of Blair's brother Bill. The outstanding issue to
discuss was an agreement not to divide the modernisers' vote,
which would benefit John Prescott. Derek Draper drove Tony
Blair to his brother's house. 'You know,' Blair told Draper
during the journey, 'I told Gordon ages ago that he could not
be leader of the party without a wife and kids.' Inside the
house, Brown and Blair affirmed that they would not compete
against each other, but nothing more. Blair revealed that he
was under pressure to stand, an admission carefully contrived

to disarm Brown. Even as they met, the mood was swinging against the Scotsman. On *Newsnight*, Alastair Campbell, the assistant editor of the *Today* newspaper, openly supported Blair as the new leader. The *Evening Standard*'s last edition highlighted Sarah Baxter's article 'Why I Say Tony Blair Should be the Next Leader'. Broadcasters were naming Blair as the favourite. Brown returned to Westminster in a deflated mood.

Early on Friday morning he arrived at the Labour head-quarters at Millbank. On the coffee table at the entrance was a pile of newspapers clearly marked 'Do Not Remove'. Grabbing the papers, he brushed past the receptionists without a smile and rushed to his office. The newspapers were discouraging. Others had followed the *Evening Standard*'s prediction of Blair's success. A poll of Scottish MPs in the *Scotsman* showed that a majority opposed Brown. His friends would subsequently claim that the poll was fixed by Mandelson, but the tilt was certainly accurate. The comparisons unflatteringly mentioned Brown's lacklustre performances in the Commons and Blair's superior mental agility. English socialists, it was reported, had had enough of the Scots and the Welsh.

Those criticisms, Brown believed, would not determine the outcome of the leadership election. Under Labour's consti-tution, the votes of the MPs, the trade unions and the constitu-encies were of equal value, and the outcome was still uncertain. The question was whether he was prepared to fight. He still hoped to gain the backing of Peter Mandelson, whose unrivalled ability, proven over the past seven years, would enhance his candidacy. He could also rely on Charlie Whelan, whose voice was heard in a neighbouring room. Using two swear words where one would have been more than sufficient, Whelan was phoning journalists, urging them to understand that Brown would win the leadership. Nearby, Nick Brown, inexplicably wearing sunglasses, nodded his agreement although he had not yet contacted any allies in the trade unions or constituencies. Inside his office, Gordon Brown sat depressed.

Over the weekend he returned as usual to Scotland. His first call was on Elizabeth Smith, the former leader's widow. Helen Liddell, the party's former secretary, was outside the house waiting to give a television interview as he arrived. Tony Blair, Liddell noted, had not yet crossed the border to pay his respects.

The weekend's newspapers did not improve Brown's self-confidence. Their opinion polls showed that Blair was the favourite in the party and the country. Brown, it was implied, might withdraw on the basis of a prior agreement with Blair not to stand against each other. Brown called the party's pollster Philip Gould and asked who was the favourite to win. 'I said Tony without hesitation,' Gould recalled. 'Gordon asked me why, and I replied that Tony not only met the mood of the nation, he exemplified it. He would create for Britain a sense of change, of a new beginning, which Gordon could not do.' More irritating was Mandelson's appearance on Channel 4 News describing his ideal candidate as the person 'who would fully maximise support for the party in the country'.

Brown was stewing, and his mood worsened the following morning, Monday, 16 May, when a letter from Mandelson, setting out the position as he saw it, was delivered to Brown's office on the other side of the corridor. Brown, said Mandelson, was attracting sympathy from the lobby for his position, not least because of his unrivalled intellectual position, but he had a problem in not appearing to be the front-runner. The conclusion was painful. If Brown ran it would be a gift to the party's enemies, and he would be blamed by the media for creating the split. The remedy would be intensive briefings to sell himself, wrote Mandelson, but the regrettable consequence of that would be to weaken Blair's position. Even then, success could not be guaranteed. Ultimately, the card the media were playing for Blair was his 'southern appeal'.

Mandelson may have been stating the obvious in unpartisan words, but to Brown, coiled like a spring in his lust for power, the truth was intensely hurtful. He regarded the weekend's media analysis, the suggestion of an agreement between himself and Blair, and Mandelson's letter as calculated to undermine his chances. 'We've been betrayed,' he muttered to a friend. He also suspected that Mandelson was helping Blair, and encouraged *Tribune* to report the alliance. Blair was alarmed by that possibility and directed Anji Hunter and later Michael Meacher to telephone the editor Mark Seddon. 'It's simply not true,' Hunter exclaimed. The newspaper did not publish the accurate story.

Four days after John Smith's death, the message was 'Brown in mourning', but the reality was also of a politician fretting. Brown required a bandwagon if he was to win the prize. Mandelson's judgement was unfortunate but not necessarily decisive if Brown actively campaigned for support, seeking out and converting dissenters. Secluded in his office, he relied on an inner circle of MPs – Nick Brown, Doug Henderson, Andrew Smith, Nigel Griffiths and Eric Clarke, the former leader of the Scottish miners – for advice. He never paused to contemplate the possibility that outsiders might dislike a Scottish clique as much as he disdained the London establishment. Nor did he recognise how the personal weaknesses of his political advisers reflected poorly on himself. 'Tell me what you think,' Brown said to Henderson, who had been tramping around Westminster. 'I don't think you can win,' reported his ambassador, knowing that Brown's two brothers were urging him to stand.

While Brown hesitated, Blair, encouraged by a personal message from David Ward that Brown had not been John

Smith's favourite son, was actively seeking support. Chris Smith, David Blunkett, Adam Ingram, the MP for East Kilbride, and Frank Dobson each expressed their support. Brown was shocked. Dobson, he had thought, would favour his redistributive socialism. Instead, Dobson complained that rather than encourage consensus government, Brown would cluster his favourites around himself. 'He's an iceman,' was the hurtful quotation. Brown was perplexed that even his assumption of Neil Kinnock's endorsement was wrong. The former leader wondered aloud about Brown's suitability. He was a bowler, not a batsman, suggested Kinnock. Not surprisingly, Charles Clarke, Kinnock's chief of staff, was telling everyone that he had telephoned Blair immediately after Smith's death to urge him to run for the leadership. Presentation and personality rather than politics was the issue. The party was desperate for an election victory. Blair may have been too right-wing for many in the party, but he was likely to appeal to the English middle class.

John Smith's funeral service on Friday, 20 May at the Cluny parish church in Edinburgh was a gigantic gathering. Within the church were the kingmakers of the Labour Party who would decide Brown's fate. Smith's unexpected death gave him a moment to contemplate his own mortality in Burns's familiar couplet, 'Ev'n thou who mourn'st the daisy's fate, That fate is thine – no distant date'. Ever since his first eye operation, Brown had never doubted his race against time. Now, openly weeping, he knew he had been harmed by hesitation, but not, he still believed, fatally. He would begin to know the worst after the service.

At Blair's suggestion the two men had agreed to meet at the home of Nick Ryden, a schoolfriend of Blair's and a successful lawyer, in Polwarth, on the road to Edinburgh airport. Brown arrived at the house to discuss 'a family affair' over an Indian takeaway and a bottle of wine. Few understood his character better than Tony Blair. For eleven years they had consulted each other over speeches, tactics and strategy, travelling together, not least to Washington to be inspired by Clinton's victory. Blair knew that his friend might be a bruiser, but he was not an assassin. Brown had no lust to draw a fellow tribesman's blood. Blair planned to play a wild card that was calculated to destabilise Brown. In Ryden's home he suggested that Brown had wasted his opportunity to bid for the leadership in 1992, and that now it was Blair's turn. Blair knew that Brown had had no chance two years earlier, but his purpose was suited by the pretence that any sentimental understanding about Brown's precedence had been neutralised. There was little evidence of discomfort as he delivered his ultimatum: 'Whatever happens, I'm going to stand. You can do whatever you want.' Brown blinked. He did not attempt to outface Blair, nor did he agree to a deal. Forlornly, at 1.30 a.m. he ordered a taxi to return to North Queensferry. Not uncommonly, he had forgotten to carry any money. Ryden lent him £30 for the fare. Over the following hours, Blair was able to call on organisational talent and energy beyond Brown's imagination.

Brown's response was flat-footed. Unwilling or unable personally to lobby for support, he expected his hard work and ability to be rewarded by success. His behaviour during a meeting with John Edmonds revealed his attitude. Edmonds, like other trade unionists, was 'desperately seeking a candidate'. Blair was unacceptable, and Prescott 'would last only half a sentence'. Some union leaders, like Bill Morris, favoured Margaret Beckett, while others wanted Robin Cook. 'No,' replied Cook, 'my face doesn't fit. I'm not good-looking enough.' Lacking a base in Scotland, Cook enjoyed limited support in England, but did have the authority to influence MPs' votes for the leadership. The party was truly divided. Edmonds wanted to hear Brown's ideas first hand. Yet, to his surprise, during their conversation in Millbank Brown resisted his entreaties to make himself a more attractive candidate. He refused to endorse trade union rights, and added, 'We've got to be careful. We can't openly support full employment even if that's what I want.' Although he was campaigning to be leader, he never asked Edmonds if he could rely on his support, or presented himself as superior to Blair. His unwillingness to sully himself by campaigning triggered mistrust. Baffled by new rumours about Brown's sexuality, Edmonds departed 'not inclined' to give his support. 'He's too cautious,' he told his fellow trade unionists. Brown lacked magic.

'Because I'm not married,' Brown would complain, 'I'm seen as having nothing else in my life.' During the flight to John Smith's funeral Ed Balls and Geoff Mulgan had contemplated telling Brown that he should pose for the cameras with Sheena McDonald to prove his heterosexuality. But, anticipating Brown's angry reaction, they decided to remain silent. In that vacuum, the *Sun* newspaper was unsuccessfully trawling Britain for confirmation that Brown was a homosexual. The best 'evidence' the journalists could find, Brown heard, was the presence of one gay classmate in his school photograph. 'They're only offering £100 for information,' Brown sniffed. 'I thought I'd be worth more than that.' More worrying was the fact that fellow shadow cabinet members Mo Mowlam and Patricia Hewitt were reported as saying 'We need a family man.' Some mistakenly assumed that the two women were implying that Brown was a homosexual. In the search for the source of the rumours, suspicion fell on Mandelson. There was no strategy to counter the image of the solitary, unmarried man competing with Blair's telegenic 'trust me' looks as he posed with his three children and bubbly wife. Brown had done nothing to promote his natural wit and warmth. He railed against any suggestion of frivolity, and emphasised that the mind was the man. The consequence was the spread of false rumours, including a ludicrous story which Bryan Gould remembers doing the rounds of a front bench colleague walking into a darkened Westminster office one evening to discover Brown and Mandelson in a clinch. Although this was totally untrue, Brown's enemies circulated the mischief to undermine the candidate. 'My mother has to read this stuff,' complained Brown, hurt to his core. He had no stomach for a dirty fight.

The experience of unpopularity during the previous year had made him cautious. He feared the embarrassment of failure. He also lacked clarity. At the decisive moment, he appeared confused. An aide walking late at night along the corridor in Millbank heard grunts and groans from Brown's office. Suddenly a pair of trousers flew out of the door, then there was a crash. Brown was scrabbling through a bag, throwing socks and books onto the floor. 'I can't find my wallet,' he shouted. 'I need money for a cab fare to the airport.' His personal disorganisation prompted potential sympathisers to question his ability to lead the party.

Over the previous week Brown had been composing a speech to be delivered on Sunday, 22 May to the Welsh TUC at Swansea, a heartland of British socialism. He intended it to be a testament of his Utopia and a manifesto for the leadership. Even if he could not secure the votes of a majority of MPs, he hoped that those of the trade unions would secure him a majority. Around him he had gathered his closest confidants, Ed Balls, Colin Currie, a consultant in geriatric medicine and a friend from university, his brother Andrew and Charlie Whelan. All offered their help, sharing his anger against Blair as he hammered away on his computer, crafting a sermon filled with emotional phrases of hope for the New Jerusalem, appealing to every interest group to justify his refashioning of party policy.

The sermons of the Reverend John Brown, such powerful

influences on his son, were pertinent at this critical juncture.
'In congregation after congregation,' his father had preached,
'we find a reluctance to change methods and introduce anything new . . . Jesus warned us, "Do not cling to the past too
much." He is saying, "Your road is forward. My Church
should be a progressive movement, meeting the changing
situations in a spirit of adventure."' Although Gordon Brown
had adopted that lesson, he had ignored his father's sermon
about the advantages of encouragement. Considering the
plight of Paul, depressed by long imprisonment, John Brown
taught that even great men require praise: 'All need encouragement sometimes. Not least the outstanding in all walks of
life.' Christians, he said, 'should be first of all encouragers,
and if at any time they have to offer correction, they should
do it in as kindly and charitable way as possible'. He continued: 'How often initiative can be curbed by thoughtless
and harsh condemnation! And how often a word of encouragement spoken at the right moment can lead others to
greater heights of achievement! Have we not a duty to be
encouragers at all times – in the home, at work, and in every
line we follow?' That sermon tended to be ignored by his son.

Naturally, Gordon Brown would start with a tribute to John
Smith: 'The flame still burns, the work continues, the passion
for justice endures and the vision will never fade – the vision of
Labour in power, Labour using that power for . . . a life lived in
the service of others.' He drew inspiration from the Bible: 'To
everything there is a season and a time for every purpose. A
time to mourn and a time to renew. A time to reflect and a time
to move forward . . . For us now, more than ever before, this is
the time to unite. Together we have climbed too high for us
not to achieve the summit – it is near. Labour is the party
that, itself united, is ready to unite this country.'

At the core of the speech was his appeal to the 'values
handed down from one socialist generation to another'. In

language emulating his father's sermons, he thumped home his credo: 'When I see this gross disparity between the accumulated excess of wealth and power, and the gaping sorrows of the left-out millions, and when I see what the Tories have done to our social cohesion and our sense of community, I know that for Labour the hour has come.' He paused. He would naturally praise the unions and mock the Tories for their lies and corruption, and list their scandals to rally his supporters: Matrix Churchill, the Pergau Dam, the BMWs bought by overpaid NHS administrators, the millions squandered on red tape, 'compulsory workfare' and the need for a 'bonfire of the quangos'. He offered strategies for coal, full employment, a minimum wage and an end to the means testing of pensioners. As he banged on the keyboard, shouting for help to find material lost somewhere inside the computer, he sensed his power to draw in the brethren. He would work towards an impassioned plea to tilt the balance in his favour, or at least halt the tide towards Blair. He would preach about his 'vision of a new Britain for a new British century, humming with opportunities, alive with new possibilities and vibrant with a new dynamism and energy'. The eighteen pages, typed in a bizarre array of small, medium and block type, sometimes in short lines to pace his delivery, at other times in chunks, mirrored his untidy existence. The content reflected a man of remarkable concentration, but also one who was becoming desperate.

The news during Sunday was not good. Peter Mandelson was briefing *The Times* that while Brown would be appealing to Old Labour, Blair would be offering himself as the architect of a new Labour Party. John Monks and some other trade union leaders had publicly swung behind Blair and John Prescott. In their judgement Brown was either too close or too antagonistic to the unions, or too vulnerable to criticism. Brown was particularly unforgiving towards Monks for failing to rally his members to his cause. He had shuttled around the country, shaking countless hands at turgid meetings, to gather support for this day. For two years he had taken the flak for transforming Labour into an electable party. In return he received no thanks, only blame. He was unaware of which union leaders supported him. No one had approached them on his behalf for a declaration.

Friends telephoning that weekend could hear his gloom. 'Are you going to stand for the leader?' asked John Forsythe, his former flatmate from Edinburgh. 'No,' replied Brown, 'I've got an arrangement with Tony that he'll go first.' Forsythe, who had campaigned for Brown in the 1970s, was surprised. 'Decide if you really want it,' he said, 'because you may not have a second chance.' Brown grunted, but made no further comment. Another close friend telephoned and asked, 'What are you doing?' 'I'm thinking. I'm thinking,' Brown replied. 'I've done the arithmetic,' he confessed to Donald Dewar, 'and I won't get there.' Blair telephoned to ask for a sight of his Swansea speech. Brown refused.

The swell of excitement as he entered the Brangwyn Hall in Swansea that Sunday was intoxicating. Surrounded by hundreds of committed Welsh socialists, the salt of the earth, he felt at ease and at home. The spontaneous, rapturous applause for his eloquent speech gave him hope that the leadership was still possible. Friends, and especially his older brother John, urged him that night to reconsider his strengths. In a three-way race, the trade unions supporting Prescott would switch to him in the second ballot.

Brown travelled to London with some optimism, but mindful of those left-wing critics who had dubbed him a compromiser who had lost his old radicalism. The glimmer of hope was dashed by the arrival of Derek Draper, Mandelson's assistant, in his office. Draper found Brown furiously typing another speech he was to deliver in Luton. 'I'm very sorry,' said Draper. 'I've called twelve of my closest party contacts and they all want Tony.' Brown gripped a pencil tightly. 'Gordon, I know this is very hard for you, but I've spoken to dozens of people in the party and most of them, including those who admire you, think it should be Tony. It's not a reflection on you, it's just that they think Tony will play better in the South.' Ramming the pencil down onto his desk so hard that it broke, Brown replied, 'That's not what other people are telling me, Derek.' Mandelson's machinations would be neither forgiven nor forgotten.

Hurtfully, the newspapers over the following days gave unanimous support for Blair, confirming Draper's message. 'Blair has the looks, style and message that could appeal to many disenchanted Tory voters,' commented the *Sun*. 'Blair is the man the Conservatives most fear – a man of rare ability ... and he has an unblemished reputation for honesty and integrity,' echoed the *Daily Mail*. 'Labour would choose wisely if it elected Tony Blair as its new leader,' said the *Sunday Times*. The polls were similarly unpromising. An NOP poll on 25 May showed the trade unions favouring Blair. A BBC poll on 29 May reported that Brown had just 11 per cent of the party's support, compared to 47 per cent for Blair and 15 per cent for Prescott. On that poll, Brown would not even make the second ballot. There was no hope, Brown knew, but denying unfortunate truths was natural to him. The political historian understood how to gloss an inevitable defeat into an assertion of his own authority. He conjured a fantasy of posing as an equal to Blair.

In writing his Swansea speech, he had included a passage which portrayed a graceful withdrawal as the act of a team player rather than a prima donna. Unity, he had written, was Labour's strength, and he demanded that 'nothing – no personal ambition, no selfish endeavour, no sectional interest, no factional dispute, no cynical manoeuvring for position should stand in the way of this great public endeavour in which we carry the hopes of millions'. Seven days after that speech, his campaign was dead. He had no stomach for a fight. Like the manager of a defeated football team, he could not understand why the players had failed to understand the big picture. He was isolated, unable to reach people, and especially the English Establishment, in the same fashion as Blair. His own robust image of self-certainty was more than equalled by Blair's lack of self-doubt. His insecurity was swamped by Blair's overwhelming self-assurance. His rival's uncanny instinct outmatched his own methodical approach. He blamed his background and education for the deficiency in his self-confidence. In an unguarded moment, he confessed to a friend his misfortune in going to Edinburgh University rather than Oxford. 'If I'd gone to Oxford,' he said during an intimate conversation, 'I would have made a wide range of contacts.' A long silence followed that spontaneous confession. His desperation was self-evident. Being seen as a member of the Scottish mafia, he acknowledged, was harmful to his ambitions in London. Regardless of those still urging him to stand, he feared humiliation.

On Monday, 30 May, he summoned Nick Brown, Charlie Whelan and Murray Elder for dinner at Joe Allen's restaurant in Covent Garden. That day's opinion poll in the *Daily Telegraph* confirmed Blair's commanding lead. Accurately, however, the newspaper reported that Brown's supporters refused to surrender. Nick Brown led the resisters. One hundred and twenty MPs, said Nick Brown, supported Gordon outright, and there would be more. The trade unions, he felt, would turn, and Gordon would inherit John Prescott's supporters in the second ballot. There was prejudice, he added, against Blair's class and background. Brown mentioned Blair's broken promise not to stand against him. He and his supporters were angry, but the unassailable truth was poor poll ratings and the media's antagonism. Murray Elder reinforced his fears. 'Don't even try,' was his advice. Brown agreed. He would surrender, but only on strict conditions.

At about six o'clock in the evening of the following day, Tuesday, 31 May, Brown screwed up a piece of paper and threw it onto the floor of his office. An assistant picked it up after he left the room. In his large handwriting, Brown had scribbled 'Granita 7.30'. A meeting had been agreed with Blair at the Granita restaurant in Islington. Brown remained perplexed about the circumstances of his defeat. At 7.50 p.m. he, Whelan and Balls finished their drinks in the Atrium at Millbank.

As usual, Brown was late when he and Balls arrived at the Granita by taxi. Blair was sitting alone in the rear of the restaurant. They ordered drinks and food. After the first course, Balls left. Brown looked at the man about whom he later wistfully said, 'We always did everything together. We shared an office and went off on trips abroad together.' Quite clearly, he had underestimated his associate. His judgement would not improve. Beyond evaluating a man's intellect and his loyalty, Brown was immune to the nuances of another's character. He judged correctly, however, that Blair would be prepared to make some concessions in return for Brown's withdrawal from the contest. During their discussions over the previous two days, Blair had agreed that in a Labour government Brown would be chancellor, with responsibility for domestic, economic and social policies to pursue what was described as 'the fairness agenda'. Blair had limited interest in economic policy; it was a small sacrifice to him to allocate that area to Brown in the cause of defusing resentment and preventing a friend turning into an enemy. It would be suggested that Brown was 'a rare politician who undersells himself in public', but Blair recognised that the opposite was true, and applied the appropriate balm. Within an hour they agreed a text for Mandelson to brief the media. He would mention

Blair's agreement that Brown would have autonomy in domestic matters, in order to conceal his embarrassing defeat. The
six-paragraph note, unprecedented in British political history,
was typed on a single page. The following day Mandelson
faxed it to Brown for approval. The final draft read:

> The paramount consideration for Tony and Gordon
> throughout has been the best way for the party's interests
> to be served and for party unity to be maximised in order
> to win the election. A desire to unite the party is at the
> forefront of their thinking.
>
> Their soundings confirm that both have very strong sup-
> port in the party, with each having the support of around
> 80 MPs, with roughly equal numbers of shadow cabinet
> members backing each of them, and about the same
> number of MEPs and a lot of trade union leaderships appar-
> ently happy with either.
>
> The overwhelming bulk of this support is interchangeable
> between the two although opinion polls suggest that Tony
> has the edge. As Gordon has made clear in his statement,
> the leadership election should be conducted with only one
> purpose in mind, to ensure the election of a Labour govern-
> ment with everything done to achieve the greatest possible
> unity across the party. Gordon has taken, as he said he
> would, a decision which puts unity and teamwork above
> personal ambition.
>
> What makes this possible is the strong overlap of their
> approach to policy and their shared thinking on the key
> issues. Both recognise the importance of the partnership
> they have built up and of the Smith legacy of unifying the
> party and making use of all its talents.
>
> In his Wales and Luton speeches Gordon has spelled out
> the fairness agenda – social justice, employment opportuni-
> ties and skills – which he believes should be the centrepiece

of Labour's programme and Tony is in full agreement with
this and that the party's economic and social policies should
be further developed on this basis.

   Gordon is standing by the agreement not to campaign in
the leadership before June 9 but will be giving strong backing to Tony's campaign when this gets underway and in
the meantime no comment will be made until after the
European elections.

Brown read the draft carefully. In paragraph five he crossed
out the words that Blair was 'in full agreement with' the
fairness agenda, and scrawled 'has guaranteed this will be
pursued' in their place. Sue Nye faxed the page with the
amendment back to Mandelson. On the top of the paper Nye
had written, 'Peter Ring Me – Sue'. Mandelson called her and
told her that Blair would not accept Brown's addition of the
word 'guarantee'. Blair wanted to placate Brown, but did not
intend to put himself at his mercy. Anji Hunter did not know
about the document.

   By 10 p.m. the previous night Brown had returned from
Islington to Millbank. Whelan and Balls were waiting. He
invited both to walk to his nearby flat to open a bottle of champagne. Brown was bitterly disappointed. In the depressed
atmosphere, the events of the previous weeks were dissected
and endlessly reinterpreted. Presenting the best gloss on his
capitulation was critical to Brown's credibility. One exchange
with Blair was particularly pertinent. To console his friend,
Blair had mentioned that after he had had perhaps ten years
as Labour leader, Brown would get his turn. In Blair's mind
he wanted to achieve certain objectives, and unaware of the
hurdles in the way of effecting such changes, did not allot a
definite number of years to his leadership. The next general
election was expected in 1996, and parliaments ran for a
maximum of five years. To Blair those throwaway words of

comfort may have been unimportant, but that night in Great Smith Street Brown seized upon them as a liferaft. After twenty years in politics he understood sleights of hand, and at his side Charlie Whelan was becoming renowned as a master of 'stunts', particularly feeding false information to the gullible – also known as 'spin'.

Over the next ten years, whenever he was asked about his feud with Blair, Brown would retort that politics should not be trivialised by being reduced to personalities. The great issues, he would say impatiently, are about ideas and ideals, not relationships and images. He would disparage the mid-twentieth-century historian Lewis Namier, who believed that history was about manoeuvring by elites, rather than disputes about ideas and causes. He could not prove Namier historically wrong, but it suited his own character to pretend that his grudges and machinations were irrelevant to politics, whereas in truth they were at the core of what he did.

Late that night, Brown began telephoning his supporters. 'I'm not standing for the leadership,' he told a close journalist friend in Edinburgh. 'You must be off your leek,' replied his friend. 'I've been stitched up.' 'By Blair?' 'No, by Mandelson.' Brown then 'revealed' the 'agreement' that Blair would stand down after a second full term as prime minister. 'You're going to have to wait at least eight years,' protested his friend, 'and you don't know who else is going to come up and challenge you.' There was no reply to that truth, not least because there was no deal.

Over the following hours Brown telephoned nearly thirty people, mostly Scots, to deliver the same message about the deal. Murray Elder passed it on to Roy Hattersley: 'Gordon says he has a cast-iron assurance that Tony will go after two terms.' Hattersley was amused. 'It reminds me,' he replied, 'of Harold Wilson's story that every minister who was defeated in cabinet meetings would return to their department and boast of their victory.' By the time Brown called John Edmonds he had dropped the pretence. 'I've decided I can't win, so I'm pulling out.' 'I am not standing,' he abruptly told Doug Henderson in the morning. 'Make sure that Blair's people know.'

That day Brown was travelling with Ed Balls to Nottingham to campaign for the European elections. During the journey he composed a statement. 'Nothing was to be gained by me standing against my friend Tony Blair,' he wrote. 'I will encourage Tony Blair to stand and . . . I will give him my full support to become not only the Labour Party's next leader but the next prime minister of our country . . . I believe Tony Blair will lead us to election victory. I believe he can help us win in areas where we have never won before.'

That afternoon, Mandelson arranged for Brown and Blair to walk smiling below Big Ben for the television cameras. The *Mirror* agreed to publish a full-page article by Brown the following morning explaining why 'I'm standing aside for a united fight'. Personal ambitions, wrote Brown, were irrelevant compared to the overriding task of electing a Labour government. 'Looking at the situation in 1994,' he concluded, 'nothing was to be gained by me standing against my friend Tony Blair.' Labour's popularity in the opinion polls soared, and was not to fall for nearly a decade.

In the evening Brown sat in his Millbank office with friends to watch the television coverage of his decision. With his approval, a succession of supporting MPs appeared on the screen to testify that he was withdrawing to preserve party unity rather than from a fear of losing. At the end of the ITN report, political editor Michael Brunson stated that Brown's withdrawal was not an altruistic sacrifice for the party; he withdrew because he would have lost. Brown began to shout at the television. The shout became a scream. He lost all self-control. He rushed into his private office. Slamming the door,

he furiously kicked the furniture, ranting a string of obscenities. He was outraged by the truth. The antidote was to conjure
a fiction.

In public, there was nothing more to say. In private, the
poison began to spread. Blair naturally wanted to use the
database of sympathetic party activists, trade unionists and
MPs collected by Saul Billingsley for his election campaign.
Brown refused to make it available to him. After a ferocious
row he relented, and Billingsley arrived in Blair's office with
the valuable computer discs. Charlie Whelan was particularly
disconsolate, and by the end of the day he was whispering
about the 'great betrayal' which had 'cheated' Brown. The
finger was pointed at many people including John Reid, Doug
Henderson, Tony Blair and especially Peter Mandelson.

One unresolved matter was Blair's choice of deputy. Brown
supported Margaret Beckett, but Blair favoured John Prescott,
who would win trade union support. On Saturday night
Brown spotted Mandelson at a crowded party in Ed Balls's
flat in Dalston, east London. 'Stop pushing Prescott,' he told
him. The prospect of the inarticulate former waiter on cruise
liners speaking as the deputy prime minister horrified Brown.
'Don't tell me what to do,' replied Mandelson regally. 'We
agreed that I'd be consulted on these matters,' Brown shot
back. 'Well you weren't,' said Mandelson with a hint of
menace. Brown's voice rose, and a row erupted. Brown left
the party, upset by Mandelson's tirade.

These were defining moments for Brown's future relations
with the leaders of the party and the trade unions. 'Sleekit',
the Scots word for a moody grudge, was a frequently used
word. The injured Brown remembered his wounds long after
the physical scars had disappeared, and he would never forgive the perpetrators. James Callaghan's letter of commiseration noting 'I was sixty-five before I became party leader'
was poor consolation.

Blair's election as leader on 21 July 1994 with 57 per cent of the vote, against John Prescott (24 per cent) and Margaret Beckett (19 per cent), confirming a divided party, ignited Brown's speculation that perhaps he might have won the contest. Thereafter, Charlie Whelan undertook to stress the importance of 'the deal'. The arrangement he described over the following months was an old agreement between Brown and Blair that they would never compete against each other in a leadership election, and that Brown, as the more experienced politician, would be the candidate. As Blair's popularity grew after 1994, Brown never mentioned any deal about the succession agreed at the Granita, but he did admit to close friends that a family man had a better chance of winning a general election. He still had no intention of marrying, but he was vulnerable to suggestions.

FIVE

Seduction

Sarah Macaulay desperately wanted to help Gordon Brown. Over the previous eighteen months she had closely followed his career, regularly clipping newspaper articles about the man described as pathologically private. Breaking into his life, she knew, would be difficult, but the attractions in 1994 for both were considerable.

Macaulay had first come to Brown's attention two years earlier. In 1992 Spirit Design, her public relations agency, had produced the logo for a meeting of the '1,000 Club' in Westminster, comprising those who donated £1,000 a year to the Labour Party. Brown could not help noticing the striking woman's arrival in the hall. Not only did she enter markedly late, she had the dark, sophisticated looks he appreciated. Charlie Whelan also spotted Macaulay and introduced himself.

The daughter of a Scot, born on 31 October 1963, Macaulay had spent her childhood in east Africa until her parents separated and returned to Britain. She was educated at Camden School for Girls in north London, and had spent her summer holidays with her father in Fife, Brown's birthplace. After studying psychology at Bristol University, she worked for Wolff Olins, a left-wing public relations agency with a varied list of clients including publishers, pressure groups and trade unions. She gained a reputation for seeking out power brokers who had influence and were close to the spotlight.

In 1993, only four years after its creation, Spirit Design was destined for imminent dissolution. That misfortune propelled her towards a partnership with Julia Hobsbawm, an old schoolfriend and owner of a successful PR agency. Like Macaulay, Hobsbawm, the daughter of the famous Marxist historian Eric Hobsbawm, enjoyed good relations with the hierarchy of Labour's modernisers. Together they appeared to be a formidable team.

Among Hobsbawm Macaulay's clients was a trade union which in 1993 asked the company to organise a reception at the Dorchester for Bill Clinton. Charlie Whelan, by then a friend of Macaulay's, arrived with Brown, and the two were formally introduced. The attraction for Brown was immediate, and Macaulay's fascination with him was equally obvious. She began to visit Millbank regularly after February 1994, and with Sue Nye's help she would meet Brown and become acquainted with Labour's inner circle, including John Smith and Murray Elder. She arranged the publicity for the sponsors of the fundraising dinner at the Park Lane Hotel on 11 May 1994, the eve of John Smith's death.

In her office Macaulay read and cut out the newspaper articles covering his forlorn bid for the leadership. She noted in particular the reports comparing the dark bachelor's solitude with Blair's family life. Soon after, apparently by coincidence, they found themselves on the same flight from London to Edinburgh. During the journey Macaulay referred to their mutual interests – a love of Scotland and a zeal for Labour – and presented herself as a team player who could be useful to him. Engagingly, she appeared not to be a power junkie, but rather a Labour supporter who was prepared to stand in a powerful shadow. Their personalities were similar. Her friends described a shy, introverted person, cool even during relationships. Although she was assertive, her emotional restraint suggested diffidence. Her critics would say that, like many north London women she believed that good manners should be avoided, in order to prove that she was not a member of the despised middle class. To Brown's satisfaction, she initially suppressed her curiosity to know his whereabouts or to demand explanations for his long absences.

One obstacle to Macaulay snaring her man was Sheena McDonald. Brown had resumed their relationship in 1990, although its conduct, resembling his relationship with Marion Caldwell, was entirely on his terms. Over three years he disappeared for long periods, unexpectedly arriving at McDonald's home in Islington late at night and leaving at 6 a.m. Despite this behaviour he appeared to friends of McDonald's to be ferociously jealous, complaining in front of strangers about her social life and exploding angrily in public about her enjoying herself without his agreement. Everything, he demanded, was to be dropped for his sake. In his personal life, as in politics, he wanted total control. Those who witnessed his outbursts were surprised by his refusal to apologise for his rudeness and his demand for secrecy about the relationship. Even on foreign trips with McDonald he preferred to hide their relationship. Spotted by a woman friend during a visit to a Paris museum, dressed in Church's shoes and a cashmere pullover, the 'Full Man' fled rather than admit to be enjoying himself.

Sarah Macaulay also discovered that Brown was congenitally unwilling to commit himself. Their relationship could only be conducted on the usual terms of concealment in Soho House and other dark London bars. Regularly, while leaving Macaulay at home fretting about what to wear at their next meeting, he would go either to McDonald's house in Islington or the home of another woman. His relationship with McDonald was fraught. While he had not revealed his own affair with Sarah, he was outraged to discover that McDonald was herself seeing another man. His explosion of anger, in front of witnesses, that someone could encroach on his territory without his permission characterised his attitude that everyone was expected to show complete loyalty to him, while he himself was free to pursue his own interests. McDonald was surprised when she discovered his infidelity with Macaulay. During a BBC radio interview with Brown, she was noticeably hostile. 'What's going on here?' asked the producer. 'What do you expect when someone goes out with you and then drops you without even a goodbye?' she replied bitterly. 'Be professional,' the producer advised. 'How can you be professional,' she snapped, 'when you've been treated the way I've been?'

Brown suffered a similar problem with Tony Blair. The new party leader might have echoed Winston Churchill's reaction on becoming prime minister in 1940, which he described as 'a profound sense of relief. At last I had authority over the whole scene. I felt as if I were walking with destiny and all my past life had been but a preparation for this hour and this trial.' Blair set about imposing his own agenda to ensure victory at the next election. Uncaring about party history, he believed in leading from the centre, despite the complaints from malcontents on the left or from the trade unions. There was surprise in Brown's voice as he reported to friends, 'Tony's ditching socialism.' Brown had once written, 'If Labour's not about socialism, it's about nothing.' He was unprepared for Blair's radicalism. While Brown simply omitted mentioning socialism in order to make Labour electable, Blair really didn't believe in socialism. His overriding concern was to present an image of party unity to win the election, with the focus on himself. Brown was relegated to the shadows, a diminished figure, for failing to run for the leadership. His retaliation in private was to treat Blair as the junior of the two.

The seizure of the party by the 'modernisers' resembled the aftermath of the storming of the Winter Palace in 1917 by the Leninists. Improving upon the methods of the Militant Tendency ten years earlier, Blair imposed secrecy and iron self-discipline. Over the previous years his political family – Peter Mandelson, Anji Hunter, Philip Gould and Alastair Campbell – had forged close friendships. They worked as a tight team, not least to prevent leaks. Emulating the cell structure and tactics of the Leninists, they would pursue ideological change with unusual methods, including preliminary meetings to prepare their ground in order to win decisive votes. Stage management became their weapon against Old Labour and the Conservatives, preparing their spokesmen and delegates to adhere to the agreed opinion by employing speechwriters to compose telling soundbites and using Alastair Campbell to hone a single, righteous argument.

To win the general election, Brown would naturally endorse those tactics. He would not, however, allow Blair's cabal to dictate his domestic agenda. To protect his sovereignty, Brown depended upon his own clan. Besides Ed Balls and Charlie Whelan, he relied on Sue Nye and her husband Gavyn Davies. None of these possessed much political judgement, but all understood his requirement for obedience. His loyal kitchen cabinet neutralised his self-doubts and provided reassurance for his decisions. They pandered to his ambition to be the agent of radical change in the Treasury, as a rival powerhouse to 10 Downing Street. 'I want the Treasury under Labour,' he said, 'to be an engine of ideas, a catalyst for change and a force for economic dynamism.'

The outstanding problem was to repair his relations with Peter Mandelson. Both understood the need to restore a working relationship, but neither was willing to make sufficient concessions. The temperaments of the two men precluded a permanent truce. Brown never forgot a grudge, while Mandelson was incapable of giving the appearance of plain candour in order to suppress his compulsive self-righteousness. Brown's grinding pursuit of self-interest could easily destabilise his more emotional antagonist. That summer, Brown's resentment pursued Mandelson across the Atlantic. Still racked by the recriminations, screams and accusations, Mandelson hoped to repair his self-esteem in peace. But the recurring nightmare of Gordon Brown's anger prevented him from doing so. While Mandelson was travelling along the American east coast, Brown made repeated telephone calls from London and Edinburgh. Their conversations were fraught. Often shouting because he was using a primitive mobile phone, Mandelson reacted as if in the midst of a marital crisis. 'Of course I still love you, Gordon,' he shouted, only to shriek moments later, 'If you do that, I'll come and get you.' Their conversations ranged repeatedly over the same ground: loyalty, dependability and trust. 'I love you, but I can destroy you,' Mandelson frequently screamed, threatening to marshal his black arts against Brown. Any reconciliation in the autumn, Brown decided, would have to be on his terms.

During the summer, Blair and Brown agreed that that year's party conference would signal an abrupt break with the past. The party, they would declare, believed in capitalism, and sought to make it work better. They would openly abandon the assumption that higher spending and taxes would solve the economy's problems. There would also be an end to the conflict between the public and private sectors, with a rejection of state directives and nationalisation. Failed industries would not be subsidised, and like the Tories a Labour government would not seek to back 'winners'.

On 9 September 1994 the key modernisers met at Chewton Glen, a hotel in the New Forest, for a weekend conference. Blair's chairmanship was rigorous. Policy, he made clear, would not be discussed in the shadow cabinet. The only topics would be future events, speakers, interviews, the 'line' to be pushed and housekeeping. During one meeting, Brown mentioned several MPs who should be included in a future government. With a smile, Blair nodded. All those Brown had mentioned were his friends.

On the way back to his room that night, Brown said to Mandelson, 'You and I should agree everything beforehand and present it to Tony as a *fait accompli*.' 'No, that won't work,' Mandelson replied. Brown stopped dead. 'Why?' he asked. 'Because we must accept that Tony is the leader now.' Brown stared at the man with whom he had shared his political life in recent years. Despite all their time together, Mandelson clearly still did not understand his expectation of utter loyalty. 'Right, you've made your choice,' snarled Brown, then turned and walked away. From that moment onwards, he swore to himself, he would do everything in his power to destroy Mandelson, emotionally and politically. Everyone – politicians, journalists and friends – would henceforth be told to choose between the two of them. 'You can't be pro-Mandelson and prosper with me,' he would intimate. 'Gordon will never stop pursuing Peter,' Gavyn Davies told a friend, 'because he wants to destroy him. He fears that otherwise he'll be destroyed himself.' Naturally, Mandelson reported Brown's behaviour to Blair. 'You should have agreed,' said Blair.

Brown had been destabilised by his surrender to Blair. As a student of history, he was mindful that decisions which seemed sensible at the time could appear absurd in retrospect. In the public glare, one had only one chance. His new safety net against mistakes was brusquely to question advice with provocative, rhetorical questions to determine whether a particular course of action was safe and right. His conduct prompted some to wonder whether he lived in the real world, causing his popularity to decline further and his enemies to agitate for Robin Cook to be appointed shadow chancellor in his place.

Brown's uncertainty was reinforced by the strengthening economy – which was growing by 4 per cent per year – sharply falling unemployment, low inflation and a rise in exports. Only stagnant house prices and the Tories' own continuing civil war clouded reports of a booming economy and dashed any doubts about Labour's inevitable election victory. Nothing could be left to chance if the middle classes were to be persuaded to trust New Labour. The success or failure of Brown's attempts to seduce the business community would determine Labour's future as much as Blair's surprise initiative to revoke clause four of the party's constitution, which enshrined the principle of nationalisation. But Brown wanted something bigger – new ideas beyond the slogans about the 'fairness' agenda and the welfare system as a 'trampoline rather than a safety net'.

In the autumn of 1994 he turned to Professor Richard Layard, a respected economist specialising in labour problems at the London School of Economics. Layard had investigated the effects of a minimum wage on the low-paid, and had interested the Tories in his notion of a New Deal. In 1991, after five years' study into the causes of high unemployment, Layard had established that if the state paid benefits to the unemployed over a prolonged period, the result was long-term unemployment. As a solution, he proposed that the unemployed should be offered guaranteed work, and would risk losing their state benefits if they refused it. His ideas were adopted by Michael Heseltine and David Young, successive ministers at the DTI. Young's 'Action for Jobs' was hailed by Margaret Thatcher as 'the single most effective economic programme we launched in my term in office'. At the same time Layard met Blair, then Labour's employment spokesman. Blair agreed to sponsor on Labour's behalf a new

all-party Employment Institute, and introduced the professor
to Gordon Brown. But neither Neil Kinnock nor John Smith
was interested in Layard's idea of penalising the work-shy.
Worse, to Layard's consternation the institute's birth was
practically aborted in an internecine row initiated by John
Prescott. Impressively, Blair ignored Prescott and supported
Layard.

One idea particularly interested Brown. Layard argued that
training the unemployed would increase economic growth
and improve society. The notion was not new. Since the 1970s
governments had invented endless job-creation schemes, but
few genuinely new jobs were created, and even fewer people
remained permanently employed. That historic failure was
ignored by Brown, who was looking for a vehicle to redefine
socialism and relaunch his University for Industry, 'to use the
latest technology and bring learning straight to two million
workplaces and twenty-five million homes'. Another of
Layard's suggestions was that benefits should be paid through
the Inland Revenue to encourage work, an idea embraced by
Bill Clinton's administration as tax credits. Brown seized the
two ideas – tax credits and a New Deal – as vote-catching
slogans for a new relationship between individuals, the community and the state. The attractions were that tax credits
could be superficially excluded from public expenditure, it
was the employers who would bear the high cost of their
administration, and the recipients would be increasingly
dependent on the state, which appealed to Brown's commitment to social engineering,

Tax credits were an old idea. In 1964 the Labour government had rejected them because, as the great Lord Beveridge
had declared, they undermined incentives to work, inhibited
saving and were expensive; the Tories had introduced negative taxes in 1972, and admitted their failure; after 1979 the
Tories had reduced benefits in order to encourage work; and

in 1988 they had introduced family credits, a form of tax credit, but doubts had arisen over their effectiveness. Nigel Lawson was vulnerable to many criticisms, but his simplification of the tax system was an achievement. He rejected tax credits as over-complicated and an enticement to fraud. Brown dismissed all those objections. Rather than relieve the poor completely from paying taxes, he was attracted by the idea of mixing taxes and benefits to encourage the work ethic among them. He sounded like Margaret Thatcher in 1980, when she said, 'I learned from childhood the dignity which comes from work and, by contrast, the affront to self-esteem that comes from enforced idleness. For us, work was the only way of life we knew, and we were brought up to believe that it was not only a necessity but a virtue.' Brown's difference from Thatcher was his vision of a social wage determined by the government rather than the employer. He would redistribute wealth by stealth as public expenditure. Beguiled by the notion of the state masterminding a grand project, he delegated Ed Balls to research the detail.

Brown's support for Layard's theories aroused suspicions among the left. Tax credits sounded to them like means tests. Brown was unconcerned. In the months before the general election, assuaging the left was irrelevant. His preoccupation was to win the votes of former Conservatives by reducing the 'negative aspects' of Old Labour. His contrasting of New Labour's honesty and the Conservatives' degeneracy was slick. 'I want our government,' he said in a clever soundbite, 'to be remembered as wise spenders, not as big spenders.' Labour, he said, was against poverty, not against wealth. He avoided any commitment to wealth redistribution. Income tax, he pledged, would not rise under a Labour government. Among his confidants, Brown admitted the impossibility of pledging in public to reverse Nigel Lawson's tax cuts, although once in government, he confirmed, taxes would rise.

Brown's public declaration of intent suited his self-portrayal of supreme candour. There would, he promised, be 'no taxation without explanation. There will be no lies, no deceit, no irresponsible commitments . . . We must also deal with the disincentives to work caused by penal tax and benefit rates . . . Taxes must encourage long-term savings and investment.' Simultaneously, he damned the Tories for raising taxes to an all-time high. 'We must judge whether the Tories are honest,' he wrote. 'Ever since 1979, the Conservatives have given tax cuts with one hand and taken more away in tax increases with the other.' He accused the Tories of having done 'enormous damage to people's faith in politicians through making promises for one particular year or period that they can't deliver'.

Compared to the sleaze-ridden Conservatives, whose moral state was exemplified by the revelation on 20 October 1994 that MP Neil Hamilton had secretly taken cash payments from the Harrods owner Mohamed Fayed in return for asking questions in parliament, Brown presented himself as pure. He stormed against excessive golden handshakes and the huge salaries earned by directors of the 'you scratch my back, I'll scratch yours' club; he attacked Britain's 'undeserving rich bosses', the 'something-for-nothing elite' of the 'big bosses' gold rush'; and he pledged to curb tax havens and squeeze foreigners living in Britain but technically domiciled abroad in order to avoid taxes. 'The only tax that some people pay is the airport tax they pay as they come in and out of the country,' he said of this 'scandal'. There were endless targets, including Lord Archer for his suspicious purchase of Anglia shares; the 'quango culture' that paid Tories £10,000 a year for jobs and ex-cabinet ministers £100,000 a year for directorships in industries they helped to privatise; and the 'fat cat' utility bosses guilty of the 'daylight robbery' of consumers.

To Brown's surprise, his onslaught did not reconcile the

trade unions to New Labour. Union leaders were disenchanted by his unexpected inflexibility. 'I'm not going to cling to orthodoxies that because we did things twenty to forty years ago, we do them now,' he told a delegation from the TUC council. 'The public sector will get no special favours.' Modernisation of the NHS, he announced, would be a key test for a Labour government. His visitors were baffled. Brown wanted to terminate the new NHS trusts and restore centralised control, but without providing any extra money. None of them could believe that once in office Brown would not tax and spend, but he was emphatic: 'Middle- and lower-income Britain are paying very high taxes to pay essentially for economic failure. We would like to see the burden on middle- and lower-income Britain reduced.' 'It's election tactics, not orthodoxy,' the union leaders reassured each other.

Concerned that the revocation of clause four by 'New Labour' was depressing the traditionalists, Brown approached Tony Wright, an academic and Labour councillor in Birmingham, and told him that people needed to be persuaded that there was more to New Labour than dumping the clause. He asked Wright to 'instantly' produce a jointly authored book to be called *Values, Visions and Voices*, setting out his undiminished commitment to socialism. The detail, said Brown, was irrelevant. Wright agreed. The book would be published and quickly forgotten, but it served its purpose.

Towards the end of 1994, Brown began refining his plan to change British society. The Tory reforms of the welfare state – damned as the 'opt-out society' – offended his idea of 'community'. 'Once millions opt out of health, education, transport and even crime prevention,' he complained, 'there's no society left to opt out of.' His opportunity to seize control of the party's social policy was the presentation in October 1994 of an internal report by Gordon Borrie, an accomplished lawyer, and Patricia Hewitt, proposing the reform of the welfare state. The 'Commission on Social Justice' had been created after the 1992 election. Borrie's ideas on 'Strategies for National Renewal' embraced Brown's favourite theme: encouraging people into training and work, using the welfare state as a safety net for 'a springboard for economic opportunity'. The problem was partly presentational. Borrie used Old Labour's vocabulary about redistribution of wealth, equality and opposition to means testing. Another problem was the solutions: they were expensive and socialist. 'Labour,' Brown told the *Daily Telegraph* in an echo of a Tory phrase, 'must end life on benefits.' The report, he insisted, should be rejected.

In response, Tony Blair directed Chris Smith, the spokesman on social security, to produce a new policy on social security. Brown was not pleased. He did not like Smith. The Islington South MP, a metropolitan man, had supported Blair in the leadership contest, and now he was encroaching on Brown's territory. Quashing Smith would give him pleasure. A week after Smith's appointment, Brown announced without any consultation that a windfall tax would finance his New Deal for the unemployed, and that Labour would no longer allow the unemployed to permanently receive full benefits, a reversal of the party's established ideology. Smith's bewilderment was widely shared. The conflict coincided with the rebranding of both the party and Brown himself.

Defining New Labour for the general election preoccupied the modernisers. The unwritten agenda for the party's reincarnation was discussed under Brown's chairmanship in a committee which met regularly at 8.45 a.m. in Millbank. They required headlines rather than detailed policies. Speaking, writing and thinking at immense speed, Brown emitted a sense of urgency as he led the discussion about Labour's tactics to rebut negative newspaper stories, destabilise the Tories and influence the agenda of political reporting. Emphasising pragmatism to attract the vote of the 'aspirational voter', he wielded his influence over the regular participants including Alastair Campbell, Ed Balls, Charlie Whelan, the chief whip Donald Dewar, the party's chief press officer Dave Hill, Philip Gould, John Prescott's chief aide Jez Segar, and Ed Milliband, a new adviser. Depending on his mood and their latest argument, Peter Mandelson occasionally attended. Rebranding Labour was similar to rebranding Britain as 'Cool Britannia', an exercise undertaken by Demos, Geoff Mulgan's new think-tank. Although Brown loathed 'Cool Britannia' as a triumph of style over substance, he favoured the principle of rebranding, especially of himself.

To counter the criticism that he was 'a man who could brighten a room just by leaving it', he accepted Sarah Macaulay's advice to launch a charm offensive. The task was not easy. His image was of a shy workaholic, a pathologically private man 'raised on gloom', chewing his fingernails. His impatience, repetitiousness in interviews and brutal refusal to indulge fools had become legendary. His private tantrums, culminating once in a computer thrown onto the floor, were not offset by his charm. Encouraged by Macaulay, Whelan was told to concentrate on redefining Brown's media image as 'cool'. In interviews Brown was told to engage in small talk about films, football and novels. He was advised to avoid annoying *Daily Mail* readers. A comment in one newspaper profile that he read books in his bath provoked a ballistic reaction from Whelan. 'He'll look like a nerd. Take it out,' he screamed.

Whelan's hardest challenge was to encourage Brown to smile. Television interviews were the worst. Before the interview he was invariably friendly, but as soon as recording started he become stiff, anxious to divorce his personality from politics. Under Whelan's tuition he had tried to force a smile during recent television interviews. Obeying Whelan's precise instructions, he consciously stretched his facial muscles, elongated his lips and stuck his tongue into his cheek in an attempt simultaneously to speak and smile. The result – his jaw moved sideways in apparent disengagement from his face – prompted Whelan to yell at the television screen.

The results of a blitz of newspaper profiles initiated by Whelan in summer 1995 were hardly encouraging. Lynn Barber, a famed interviewer, noted, 'A year ago you never saw him smiling, but now he smiles for every camera.' One month later, the customary gloom had returned. Chrissy Iley described a 'rumpled and sad' face with an expression somewhere between serious and dour. Brown's dry, depersonalised language suggested a man who felt guilty about fun and self-indulgence. His continued bachelorhood was an enigma. Every probe into his emotions was rebutted.

Brown's relationship with Sarah Macaulay was finally revealed in the *Mail on Sunday* in April 1995, and instantly denied by Whelan. Three months later Brown was still unwilling to admit to a relationship which, he believed, would end like its predecessors. He agreed to interviews but refused to discuss his passions or his private life. He would confess that his personal life was changing, but refused to explain why he had never proposed marriage. The performance was not to protect Sarah Macaulay, but himself. By the end of the spate of interviews, his evasion was unravelling. 'The fact that I'm not married is just a fact that things didn't work out, or haven't so far,' he said in a *Daily Mail* interview, and added, 'Things will change.' The suggestion of normality was crushed by his tormented, pole-axed reaction to the unexceptional question 'Do you find it hard to fall in love?' After physically recovering, he replied, 'No, I don't think so at all ... I do have a relationship at the moment, but I don't think she'd appreciate me talking about it. I don't try to be secretive, but ... I think maybe my personal life's been changing quite a bit. I don't think talking about it in interviews particularly helps.'

In fact the opposite was true. Sarah Macaulay was desperate for their relationship to be acknowledged and her future settled. She had already established her value to him. Together they made a good team. She shared his indifference to money, and willingly concentrated on 'The Gordon Project', unswervingly sympathetic to his belief that the world was filled either with enemies or friends who were constantly required to pass tests to prove their trustworthiness. Endlessly she sat alone at home wondering whether he would telephone or arrive at her door, or would dress to go out only to be disappointed. She had quietly shown her love, but that was insufficient for Brown to commit himself in marriage. Instead, he forged an unusual relationship with Geoffrey Robinson, the fifty-seven-year-old Labour MP for Coventry North West. Robinson, the multi-millionaire son of a furniture salesman, offered more than undying friendship. He offered to finance Brown's dream of a rival centre of power to Tony Blair's.

Gordon Brown's attraction to Geoffrey Robinson was a decisive measure of his judgement. Unlike Brown, Robinson had devoted the best years of his life to the accumulation of money rather than the pursuit of politics. Amid a colourful lifestyle of champagne and girlfriends, Robinson had boasted in 1976, 'My ambition is to be Labour's first millionaire prime minister.' Labour insiders knew that while employed at British Leyland in the early 1970s Robinson had opened, but not declared to the Inland Revenue, a Swiss bank account. They also knew about his involuntary resignation as chief executive of Jaguar after suspicions were raised regarding his purchase of an expensive paint plant from an unqualified Italian acquaintance. Untroubled by the embarrassment, Robinson entered parliament after a by-election in 1975. By 1983 he had not prospered as an MP, and abandoned the House of

Commons for a decade to become rich. His part-time partner
was Joska Bourgeois, a Belgian divorcee and tax fugitive in
Switzerland. With her financial help he opened Transfer Technology, later known as TransTec, an engineering factory in
Birmingham. In suspicious circumstances over the years
TransTec obtained government grants and valuable patents
from universities without paying the royalties to the inven-
tors. The company also acted as an agent for a Swiss company,
but declared only losses in England while declaring profits in
Switzerland, a tax haven. Robinson justified his mysterious
profiteering as a cure for unemployment, but none of those
who lost money through their involvement with his
businesses could recall his personal contribution to that principle. He was judged to be a bumbler who understood little
about engineering, disliked detail and was vague about
finance and accounts.

In 1986, TransTec's profits were increasing. To expand
further, Robinson forged an alliance with Robert Maxwell, at
that time a role model for any Labour MP ambitious to become
a multi-millionaire. Maxwell offered Robinson the non-
executive chairmanship of Hollis, an engineering conglomer-
ate. By 1990, Hollis was sinking. Over the previous four
years the company's value had collapsed from £155 million
to minus £26 million. Hollis's financial records did not
fully reveal the catastrophe, but Robinson signed the
accounts, for which he charged and received from Maxwell
a fee of £200,000. His income from TransTec, Hollis and
Maxwell was not registered as required in the House of
Commons.

In 1991, TransTec was losing money. Through a secret
agreement with Maxwell, Robinson bought the best parts of
Hollis, reaping handsome profits at the expense of the shareholders. After Maxwell's death in November that year, Robinson's relationship with the shamed tycoon escaped public

notice. TransTec, valued at £104 million, was apparently booming and Robinson was personally worth well over £30 million, fuelling his publicised ambition to control a 'billion-pound high-tech company'. Two years later, his dream had soured. TransTec's profits sank, the shares were described as a 'disaster stock', and in 1994 Robinson was compelled to resign as an executive. He became the company's non-executive chairman, entrusting the management to others who proved to be disastrous, driving the company towards insolvency.

That same year, 1994, Joska Bourgeois's death offered Robinson extraordinary financial relief. As Bourgeois's executor he controlled her funds, and his inheritance was considerable. At least £9 million was secretly transferred from Switzerland to the Orion trust in Guernsey, a secret tax haven established for Robinson and his family. Subsequently, Robinson insisted that Bourgeois had arranged the trust without his knowledge, but he never provided evidence to support that assertion. More importantly, he never declared his interest in the secret trust.

One year later, Robinson re-emerged in the Commons. Unseen for nine years, no one challenged his self-presentation as an untainted, hugely successful industrial expert. 'I was New Labour before anyone thought of it,' he chortled. Robinson had been particularly attracted to Brown since the Scotsman's election to the Commons. 'I made way for Gordon Brown,' he would claim on his return. 'Gave the boy a chance. He was immensely grateful and he's never forgotten it. Yes, we had a secret pact.' Brown was unsure about that assertion, but in 1995 he eagerly accepted Robinson's patronage. Robinson's bonhomie, practicality and money fundamentally changed Brown's life. For the first time in London he could enjoy wealth and good company with political soulmates. Most importantly, Robinson offered to finance the realisation of Brown's dream – to become the greatest Labour chancellor in history.

Before 1994, Robinson had given £200,000 to John Smith's Political Economy Unit. Smith's office had also been financed by the Labour Finance and Industry Group (LFIG), a trust created to involve businesses with Labour. The same group, under Lord Haskel, a businessman, had provided a blind trust for Brown, but LFIG's money was insufficient to finance his new ambitions. Robinson offered not only money and introductions to City power brokers, but also ideas. In particular, he suggested that in preparing for government Brown should recruit London's best brains to produce workable schemes to present to the civil servants after the election for immediate implementation. That sensible idea, combined with a mutual interest in football, cemented Robinson's relationship with Brown's Treasury group.

Over the following months the relationship between Brown and Robinson intensified. With Brown's encouragement, Robinson bought the *New Statesman*, the weekly left-wing magazine, and awarded a lucrative contract to Hobsbawm Macaulay, Sarah's public relations company, to promote himself and the magazine. His rented flat in the Grosvenor House Hotel in Park Lane, inherited from Joska Bourgeois, was used by Macaulay for champagne receptions, and rapidly became the communal drinking hole for Brown, Balls and Whelan, alias 'the Hotel Group'. Even in Robinson's absence Balls and Whelan would let themselves into the flat, help themselves to alcohol, order food and watch football matches on television. Regularly in the evenings Brown also arrived for pizza and wine and discussions about policies and strategy. In that all-male conclave there was no small talk, except about football. For the first time Brown relaxed in London. In the mornings he would go up to Robinson's flat for breakfast after pounding the running machine in the hotel's gym, an improvement

on the Livingwell Health & Leisure Centre in Millbank. The
shadow chancellor owed Robinson an enormous debt. He
seems not to have asked any awkward questions about the
financing of his safe haven.

The Hotel Group became Brown's sanctuary, in which he
could secure a stronghold in the party to offset Blair's natural
authority. In preparation for the 1995 shadow cabinet elections he began to marshal a considerable operation to secure
the election of his nominees. Andrew Smith, a relatively
unknown shadow Treasury spokesman, lobbied MPs in support of Tom Clarke, a Monklands MP and spokesman on
disabled rights. Others called on behalf of Clare Short's nomination in the same election. Clarke and Short would be elected
and Jack Cunningham, not a friend of Brown's, would be a
casualty. Brian Wilson, a Scottish MP, described the operation
of Brown's machine as 'a very bitter episode'. Other colleagues
in the shadow cabinet who increasingly questioned Brown's
policies for changing British society were similarly scalded by
his abrasiveness.

The cost of social security, which accounted for 40 per cent
of the government's expenditure, was £15 per day for every
working person. That expenditure, Brown believed, was
financially and morally corrosive. Life on the dole for the
young and healthy was, he felt, unacceptable. To define the
party's policies in his own terms he wilfully ignored Chris
Smith, who was the first to be asked by Blair to 'think the
unthinkable' for a 'New Beveridge plan'. Smith, Brown
believed, was incapable of devising reforms to limit payments
which abandoned old socialist dogma. Brown was leaning
towards 'incentives' and the cessation of universal benefits.
In short, he was becoming attracted to means tests, which
formerly he had vociferously opposed. The battle lines with
the traditionalists were drawn at the party conference in
Brighton in 1995. Brown worked hard on his speech. The

jokes at the outset were magnificent, but his sermon about inflation and limiting public spending lost his audience. His pledge that under Labour there would be 'no massaging of the figures' and 'no car-boot sales of national treasures' evoked only poor applause. A worse reaction greeted his proposals in November 1995 to punish the work-shy.

The disagreements started after the rejection of Gordon Borrie's report. Chris Smith was the target of Brown's spleen. The battleground was Smith's proposal to increase unemployment benefit and restore other allowances. Brown exploded. The party, he told Smith, must 'break for good' the idea that high spending was a measure of success. 'Tough choices have to be faced,' he raged as Smith's embarrassment grew. Brown refused to restore the link between pensions and average earnings (he advocated a 'guaranteed minimum pension'), and even speculated about introducing 'workfare', compelling the unemployed to work for their benefits. His support for means testing shocked his colleagues. 'Targeted is better,' said Brown. Money should be directed to people in need. True socialists, he continued, should support 'progressive universalism', the catchphrase that referred to extending tax credits to the middle classes. Brown was firing in every direction regardless of the antagonism he was attracting.

In November 1995, without consulting Robin Cook, Chris Smith or others responsible for the party's social policies, Brown pledged that a Labour government would deduct 40 per cent of claimants' unemployment benefits if they unreasonably refused offers of work or training. The old guard were outraged. Robin Cook protested at a shadow cabinet meeting, 'How can you square that draconian threat with your opposition to the Tories' Jobseekers Act? This is unacceptable. The contradictions are patent.' Around the table there was anger at Brown's conduct. 'This is objectionable,' protested Michael Meacher, the shadow employment secretary. 'Why haven't I been consulted?' Brown sat stony-faced, irked by the complaints. After they had ended, he mumbled his belief that there was support for his policy. Cook and Meacher glared. Brown clearly believed he could dictate changes in the party's domestic policy without the need for the approval of his colleagues. 'I don't want this argument being leaked,' ordered Blair. 'We'd better move on.'

Two days later, reports describing the dispute appeared in the newspapers. Brown ignored them. To display his power, he announced in a *Daily Telegraph* interview that he would introduce a 10 pence rate of income tax to 'reward hard work and effort'. Again he had not consulted the shadow cabinet, and faced ridicule that his 'hugely expensive' gesture might cost £10 billion, whereas entirely removing the poor from paying any taxes would be preferable.

At a meeting of the shadow cabinet on 22 November, Cook and Prescott again protested about Brown's cavalier behaviour. Brown was incensed. He was convinced that Cook and Prescott were uniting to destroy him. 'They're plotting,' he muttered, classing John Prescott as an enemy seeking revenge for Brown having opposed his appointment as deputy leader. Brown refused to apologise. Blair also rejected the criticism. 'Gordon has done a quite brilliant job,' he snapped. 'He has my 101 per cent support.' Blair found Brown's unpopularity useful to deflect the left's anger, but he failed to prevent Brown's retreat. Deducting benefits from the workshy was dropped as party policy, but means testing remained, and Brown's old grudges were re-energised.

To Brown, the facts were less important than his primacy over the footsoldiers. He would not tolerate any interference, as Chris Smith discovered one morning in mid-1996. Driving through London, Smith heard on BBC Radio 4's *Today* programme about a change of Labour's policy. Brown, it was announced, had decided to abolish the universal weekly

£10.80 child benefit for 1.1 million sixteen-to-eighteen-year-olds. In its place he proposed means tested allowances for the poorest children attending full-time education, and possibly penalties for children at private schools. 'I hit the roof,' Smith complained. 'What the hell is going on?' he asked Alastair Campbell. 'He's changed the policy without telling me. He didn't even consult me.' The fingerprints of Charlie Whelan were all over the leak. 'Oh, shit,' said Campbell with apparent surprise. In reality, not only had Whelan briefed the *Today* programme, describing Brown's proposals as 'egalitarian', but Campbell himself had briefed the *Mirror* that Brown's 'tough decision' was that the middle classes did not need benefits.

Later that morning, Brown telephoned Smith. 'You're bouncing us into decisions before the policies are agreed,' said Smith accusingly. Oozing humility, Brown apologised: 'I had absolutely no intention of pre-empting anything or jumping the gun.' That was of course untrue. 'I've got a flavour of Brown's style,' Smith told a confidant afterwards. 'He's authoritarian, impatient and arrogant. He believes in laying down the law rather than negotiating.' By the end of their conversation Brown had agreed to consult Smith about a speech he would make later that day. His one worthless concession was to replace the phrase 'we are considering' with 'we are consulting'. 'This has left me with a bad taste in my mouth,' rued Smith, who joined David Blunkett and John Prescott in mid-May 1996 to complain to Blair that Brown risked blowing up. 'There's no safety valve,' said Robin Cook and Blunkett after another argument over Brown's frenzied promotion of welfare-to-work. 'He's got no life beyond politics,' was a common conclusion. Prescott added his resentment of Brown's plan for Treasury control over the domestic agenda as a 'dangerous obstruction' to economic and social development. Blair dismissed the disputes as 'fevered nonsense' and 'tittle tattle', but Brown's critics agreed that his lust for power was damaging relationships among normally reasonable men. Few could grasp the incandescent anger gripping the slighted chancellor. Regardless of the damage to the party and to him personally which inevitably followed reports of arguments and splits, his rage against those he perceived as critics or enemies was uncontrollable.

Brown blamed the arguments on the absence of any binding ideology in the party. There was, he lamented in a private conversation with Paddy Ashdown, the Liberal Democrat leader, 'a lack of intellectual force behind the movement. There is no intellectual coherence about the position so nothing to fall back on.' The disagreements coincided with embarrassing publicity about shadow health secretary Harriet Harman sending her children to a grammar school. Without an overriding faith, Brown admitted, the party's leaders had resorted to 'being a bunch of control freaks'. Discipline was the palliative to the lack of a 'core idea' to hold the party together. Although publicly Brown smilingly insisted 'There are no disagreements,' privately he was resolute: in his personal disputes, engineered to increase his power, he would take no hostages, nor would he forge alliances with his rivals. Always conscious of a possible future bid for the leadership, he was attentive to those standing on the rungs below him – 'Bring on the young eagles,' he would say – but scornful to those known to have favoured his removal from the spotlight.

Fights and disgruntlement were the acceptable price of pursuing an abrasive agenda, especially against Peter Mandelson. The two politicians, Brown's adviser Michael Wills attested, were 'like scorpions in a bottle: only one of them will get out alive'. Brown's jealousy that Blair continued to consult Mandelson was a constant source of friction, causing Blair 'despair'. An attempt by Mandelson's staff to negotiate a peace treaty in 1995 with a written agreement demarcating the relationship between the three men was derided by Brown.

A climax of their feud occurred on 9 May 1996, after Blair had sided with Brown during a discussion with Mandelson. Abruptly, Mandelson left the room. 'Have you any conception,' Blair told Mandelson afterwards, 'how despairing it is for me when the two people that have been closest to me for more than a decade, and who in their different ways are the most brilliant minds of their generation, will not lay aside personal animosity and help me win?' If the 'Greek tragedy' continued, he warned, he would allow Mandelson to resign as Labour's election manager. 'Gordon,' Mandelson replied, 'is determined to kill me before I destroy him.' Patching up the row was Blair's priority. At his behest, on Monday, 13 May 1996, Mandelson arrived in Brown's office to negotiate a settlement. The following day Mandelson called journalists to praise Brown as the future chancellor. In return, on Wednesday Brown praised Mandelson as a 'brilliant strategist'. The truce was discussed during a small dinner party in Geoffrey Robinson's flat in the Grosvenor House Hotel. Anji Hunter spoke of a 'bitter, vicious, internecine war between Gordon and Peter'. Sue Nye nodded. The two men, she said, were indulging in 'immature, petulant and dishonest' methods against each other. The three resolved that the personality war could irredeemably divide the party between Blairites and Brownites. Robinson asked whether he should go and see Mandelson. Hunter and Nye approved. Robinson, although not a friend of Mandelson's, would be an ideal peacemaker.

On 23 May 1996, Robinson met Mandelson for dinner at the hotel. Candidly, he made his pitch: 'It's important to prevent an irreparable split between Tony and Gordon.' Mandelson agreed. There was no reason for him to contradict Robinson and continue the feud. The conversation drifted to Mandelson's own life, and his failure to accumulate sufficient money to buy a house in a fashionable area of London. Robinson spotted an opportunity to help him, and hopefully buy his allegiance, or at least his silence. By the end of the evening he had offered Mandelson a loan. Early the following morning Mandelson telephoned for reassurance that the offer was genuine. The eventual loan of £373,000 was more than Robinson had anticipated, but he savoured the notion of buying leverage.

The truce among the party leadership was endangered by John Prescott. The deputy leader disliked his exclusion from strategy meetings. He had protested about it in writing, and had been horrified when his memorandum was leaked – by someone in the Treasury, he suspected – to a journalist. In the aftermath, he feared that Brown's super-Treasury would threaten his own authority. Blair summoned Brown, Prescott and Cook for the tiresome chore of reconciliation. Public bickering, he warned, could cost the party election victory. While Brown and Prescott could be persuaded to pose together for a photograph at a football match between England and Scotland – both naturally supporting different teams – no one in the world could create harmony between Brown and Cook, a seemingly immovable obstacle in Labour's firmament.

That left Chris Smith. 'He'll have to go,' Brown told Blair. In July 1996 Smith switched portfolios with Harriet Harman, becoming shadow social security secretary. Not quite trusting Harman either, Brown appointed Henry McLeish, an old Scottish friend, as her deputy. Neither Harman nor McLeish was cautious when asked by the *Guardian* soon after their appointment whether a Labour government would implement Tory chancellor Ken Clarke's plans to cut £50 million of benefits for single parents. 'No,' replied Harman. Brown never reacted to that published commitment. Harman was directed to concentrate on his plans for the New Deal and welfare-to-work, targeting 1.3 million unemployed men aged between fifty and sixty-four.

Brown did not understand the full consequences of his manoeuvring. In the switch with Harman, Chris Smith became Labour's fourth shadow health minister in four years. The party was approaching a general election without experts in two key areas, the NHS and social security. Little had changed since 1990, when Robin Cook was shadow health minister. 'Have we got a policy on the NHS?' Cook was asked. Pulling a survey out of a drawer, he replied, 'Seventy per cent of the population think our policy on the NHS is better than the Tories'. I know we haven't got one, and I don't intend to change it.' Six years later, the party's only policy was to abolish the internal market, the Conservatives' attempt to make the NHS financially accountable and efficient. After seventeen years in opposition, Labour had not drafted an alternative plan to improve the NHS. Blair was uninterested, and Brown could identify no one he felt could be trusted with the task.

Brown rarely spoke well of any politician, and conversely he was ultra-nervous about anything said about himself. Beyond his rivals' gaze he was a vulnerable politician, needing approval as much as support. Other than his two brothers and his old friends in Scotland, the Hotel Group had become his supreme comfort. Bonded by Labour and football, he sat with Ed Balls and Charlie Whelan in Robinson's suite to eat, drink and raucously disparage their party colleagues. After the England versus Scotland match Brown attended with John Prescott, Balls and Whelan arrived at the flat first, and were singing football songs when Brown entered, furious about Scotland's defeat. Thanks to Robinson's hospitality, his mood had lightened by the time BBC screened the highlights.

Brown was at his most secure in the company of the two men. Balls was his thinker, and by 1996 Whelan had become more than a spokesman or someone who could be telephoned around the clock and asked, 'What do you think?' He was now Brown's weapon to denigrate rivals and destabilise his enemies. Befitting his membership of the Communist Party, Whelan was disciplined and obeyed his orders. He was thrilled by Geoffrey Robinson's purchase of a bottle of wine at lunch in the Savoy costing £300, a strange contrast to Whelan's delight in wearing a Che Guevara badge and his boast, 'I've never been interested in politics, per se.' Standing at the press gallery bar in the Commons, Whelan would chortle, 'I've got a great news story,' then proceed to promote Brown and disparage others in the coarsest terms. Described as 'a killing machine' and 'a serial killer', he would shamelessly admit to rubbishing ministers, but 'only if it was absolutely necessary', and approved by Brown.

The bitter arguments between May and July 1996 created targets for Whelan's black arts. Stories appeared in the newspapers undermining Chris Smith, John Prescott and Robin Cook. As Smith realised, Whelan had been deployed to brief against Brown's enemies: 'Anyone who disagreed with or challenged Gordon was fair game.' The jealous and the suspicious even suggested that Brown's strategy was to bring about Blair's failure by using Whelan to whisper complaints about his 'leadership by *diktat*'.

Considering Brown's Presbyterian background and his boast of moral probity, his use of Whelan was surprising. His old Scottish friends would insist that Brown was non-confrontational. 'He'd walk on eggshells to avoid an argument and find an accommodation,' one testified. Apologists would suggest that he tolerated Whelan as a 'necessary evil'. Having spent his childhood in a goldfish bowl where his behaviour was always scrutinised, Brown had learnt to avoid being caught *in flagrante*. Whelan was ideally placed to control or to warn about those who might act to his master's detriment. An example arose while Brown was drinking one evening in Geoffrey Robinson's flat. He was anxious about the revelation that Robinson had paid Julia Hobsbawm and Sarah Macaulay

a hefty £100,000 to launch their agency. Brown feared that
either Hobsbawm or Macaulay might say something embarrassing to a journalist, and, personally and through Whelan,
he warned them.

Thanks to the legwork undertaken by Robinson, Brown
was successfully wooing the City with speeches about public
spending and inflation. Purposefully, just as he was alienating
so many colleagues in the shadow cabinet, he was seducing
the party's erstwhile enemies during whirlwind visits to
boardrooms for lunches and dinners, seeking to prove that
business could trust Labour. Chanting the same mantra –
'capitalism has won' – he told the pinstripes and the younger,
casually dressed tycoons, 'We've learned our lessons, we're
not returning to Old Labour. We're like the Democrats in
America rather than European-style socialists.' Bill Clinton,
he repeated, was a hero. Reiterating phrases written by
Clinton's speechwriters Sidney Blumenthal, Bob Shrum and
Jeff Shesol, he promised that New Labour would champion
'popular capitalism'. In a tone not dissimilar to his father's
sermons, he attempted to convince the City sceptics that his
conversion was genuine. Endlessly pointing out that output
per worker in Britain was 40 per cent less than in America
and 20 per cent less than in Germany, he pledged to reshape
Britain to become like the tiger economies of the Far East.
'We're going to create a more entrepreneurial culture,' he
promised. 'We're going to improve Britain's productivity,
research and development.' None of his hosts were minded
to mention the developing catastrophes in Japan, South Korea
and across Asia.

Casting himself as the future iron chancellor, Brown
preached his tough approach to spending and tax. 'There'll be
a pay squeeze on the public sector,' he assured his audiences.
Across London, his hosts were intrigued by a Labour politician
incanting praise of the Victorian era's inventiveness and

commitment to hard work. 'What I call British genius,' he explained. 'I don't want government to intervene,' he stressed. 'I want to create an atmosphere where we create skills and pioneer research but leave much to society.' His endorsement of venture capitalists, especially Ronald Cohen, the founder of Apax, a leading venture capitalist company, and his support for tax breaks in poor areas – 'a more effective route to job creation' – was revolutionary from a Labour politician. For those who doubted their ears – Brown after all occasionally resembled Harold Wilson – he offered the assurance: 'Labour will be a pro-business party. We understand better than the Conservatives what makes for prosperity in the modern world.' Globetrotting executives marked Brown down as an original who could not be fitted into any existing box. He resembled no other politician they had ever met. Apparently unintoxicated by personal wealth, he personified old-fashioned decency. After his speeches there was rarely any small talk beyond politics and the odd joke about football, especially Brown's local team Raith Rovers.

The rush of converts swallowing their old scepticism included Martin Taylor, the chief executive of Barclays Bank, Keith McCullagh of British Biotech, Sir Peter Davis of the Prudential, Robert Ayling of British Airways, Dennis Stevenson of Pearson, and Lord Hollick. Alan Sugar and other mavericks who had formerly sponsored the Tory party publicly switched to Labour.

Others, especially the City's traditionalists, were more cautious about Brown's repetitive references to 'prudence' and the 'long term'. They wondered why Brown, like Harold Wilson, believed that governments could create new businessmen and enterprises, and questioned whether he grasped the financial struggles of the small employer – the tight margins, the constant haggling to solve problems and overcome human obstinacy. Brown boasted about his understanding of

business, but did he really believe that international conglom-
erates experienced identical problems to small businesses? He
referred the doubters to his association with a family timber
merchant, to prove that 'business is in the blood'. And his
mother, Brown explained, had been 'one of the small number
of women who were company directors' – of John Souter Ltd
in Insch, Aberdeenshire, founded by Brown's grandfather and
managed during his lifetime by Uncle Gordon Souter, a
staunch Tory. 'I was brought up in an atmosphere where I
knew exactly what was happening as far as business was
concerned,' said Brown. 'I was aware of all the difficult
decisions that businesses had to make, and you couldn't
escape the fact that there were challenges that they had to
face.' His mother, when asked to confirm his pedigree, was
self-effacing. 'I would have hardly called myself a business-
woman,' said Elizabeth Brown, aged eighty-two. 'Not really.
I only did light administrative duties.' Brown angrily attacked
those who maliciously misinterpreted his mother's modesty.
He suffered no retaliation. No one interrupted his voluble talk
in favour of 'incentives' and 'national action plans' and against
'wasteful subsidies' and 'old-style over-regulation' to ask
whether he really had ever picked up the Inland Revenue's
guide and spontaneously said, 'This is too complicated. Regulations should be kept simple.' The City wanted an alternative
to the exhausted, sleazy Tories, and although Brown would
later deny that sleaze had ever been an election issue, he
himself had led the chorus of the government's accusers.

The negotiations to convert the business community to
Labour had started in 1995. Howard Davies, the director general of the CBI, invited Tony Blair to his home in Islington. The
relationship was sealed by Adair Turner, Davies's successor,
an articulate former Tory eager to attach himself to the new
breed. In early 1996 Turner and Sir Colin Marshall, the president of the CBI, accepted that Labour would win the next

election, and that British business would be best served by
forging good relations with the party. To reinforce their new
commitment, Marshall advised his members for the first time
not to donate money to the Conservative Party, and invited
Brown to address the CBI conference in Harrogate, the first
time the organisation had invited a shadow chancellor to
speak. Excited by this breakthrough, Brown travelled north
by train, rehearsing an uninspiring joke he would tell the
delegates in his opening remarks to 'get the audience on my
side'. He asked Balls and Whelan whether the joke was 'too
risky', and took the chance. The audience's laughter was
polite.

Brown knew he was pushing at an open door. The opinion
polls showed a Labour lead over the Tories of 16 per cent,
despite the public's certainty that Labour would increase
taxes. 'Seduction is easy if the girl wants sex,' complained one
Conservative. 'They're opportunists.' Brown's success was to
persuade the public that his management of the economy
would be superior to Ken Clarke's. Nevertheless, he feared a
last-minute rebuff. His policies had been formulated in the
period after the ERM disaster. He had not expected the Tories
to escape from the recession. In 1996, unemployment and
benefit claims were falling fast, while house prices and sterling's value were rising. Britain was heading towards a boom
which threatened to undermine his criticisms. His tactics were
to ignore the truth and repeat his dire warnings. Fortunately,
the converts were prejudiced in his favour regardless of economic realities. The disgruntled were on his own side: the sight
of Brown supping with the enemy alarmed members of the
Labour left. Mark Seddon, the editor of *Tribune* and a future
member of the party's National Executive Committee (NEC),
complained about his inconsistency. One day, said Seddon,
Brown spoke emotionally about socialism to the Nye Bevan
group in south Wales, and on the next day in the City he

praised harsh capitalism. Some consoled themselves that he was masterminding a secret plan to achieve socialism by manipulating the market. Brown ignored the critics. He would do whatever was necessary to become chancellor. Once in office, he anticipated his biggest obstacle would be the Treasury's officials.

Secrecy and suspicion were instinctive to Brown. His spontaneous distrust of the Treasury's senior officials, shared by Ed Balls, was particularly directed at Terry Burns, the Treasury's permanent secretary. After serving the Tories for eighteen years, both believed Burns and his close aides were tainted not only by political prejudice but by Nigel Lawson's discredited policies and forecasts. Burns, they decided, could not be trusted to implement their policies, and might frustrate their ambitions. Their solution was to finesse the incumbents. On their arrival in the Treasury they would present impeccably researched policy documents on taxation and private investment in the public services for immediate implementation. The genesis of these documents owed everything to Geoffrey Robinson.

On 12 June 1996, Robinson proved his worth as an ally. He welcomed Stephen Hailey and others from the accountants Arthur Andersen to his flat. The team had been assembled to design new taxes to finance Brown's ambitions. Among them were members of the Labour Party who had worked for John Smith – Chris Wales, Chris Sanger and Chris Osborne. They rated themselves 'London's best brains'. Their fees would be personally paid by Robinson.

The previous year, Ed Balls had been persuaded that the New Deal could be financed by raising £10 billion from a windfall tax on the privatised utilities and reducing a tax credit granted to the pension funds worth £8 billion per year. At the meeting in Robinson's flat, the Arthur Andersen accountants agreed to design the windfall tax, codenamed 'Project

Autumn'. During that year, Brown went only once to their offices in Surrey Street, off the Strand, when he attended a presentation with Robinson and Balls. 'What have you got?' he demanded, dispensing with small talk. To the accountants' surprise, he asked few questions. Even Robinson remained subdued. As Treasury officials were to discover, Brown left the detail and the blunt questions to Balls. 'A low-profile meeting' was the accountants' summary.

Selling Brown's plans to the City was delegated to Robinson. With Chris Wales, a forty-two-year-old tax partner at Arthur Andersen and a member of the Labour Party for twenty years, Robinson toured the corporate headquarters. The millionaire politician and the accountant earning £250,000 per annum preached that Labour had willingly surrendered to market forces, in the hope that, like the CBI and the Institute of Directors, the bankers would at least remain neutral during the election.

Robinson's money was buying good research, but not peace. Two personal relationships were complicating Brown's life. Despite his insistence that politics and not personalities was his sole preoccupation, he refused to resolve the complications with Sarah Macaulay or to improve his relationship with Peter Mandelson. Brown found meetings with Mandelson to plan the election strategy intolerable, and Mandelson did little to hide his own contempt, provocatively writing notes to Blair while Brown was speaking. Mandelson's importance as a power broker still aroused Brown's envy. The Labour-supporting novelist Ken Follett's damnation of Mandelson as 'the rent boy of politics' would be one of the kinder outbursts against the oleaginous politician. As for Brown, his sentiments had become unprintable. He carefully prepared a vitriolic aside for a speech at a Tribune rally in the Royal Festival Hall. In large letters in blue felt-tip, smeared by the rain, his script written by Douglas Alexander included the joke: 'Peter asked me for 10p to phone a friend the other day. I said, "Here, take 20p and ring them all."' The raucous laughter was a delight for the speaker. After a pause, Brown added: 'When people ask me if I have a close relationship with Mandelson, I answer, "How would I know? I haven't spoken to him for eighteen months."'

Geoffrey Robinson was untroubled by his failure to broker an end to the warfare. At least, he believed, his generosity over the home loan had bought Mandelson's loyalty to himself. Similarly, his money had also bought Tony Blair's affection. Blair had agreed to spend his summer holiday with his family in Robinson's large villa in Tuscany, while Brown and his brothers had accepted his invitation to stay in a flat in Cannes inherited from Joska Bourgeois. The flat had frequently been used by Brown and Ed Balls, their work interrupted by ferocious games of tennis which continued into the midday heat, at Brown's insistence, until he had won a set. Robinson's largesse empowered him to remind Brown about his vulnerability on one issue: the ferocity of his feud with Mandelson suggested a politically unpalatable explanation for his continuing bachelorhood.

The unfounded gossip that Brown was a homosexual had not gone away. The 'evidence' was purely conjecture: three political friends – Tom Clarke, Nigel Griffiths and Nick Brown – were confirmed bachelors, and Brown himself was not only unmarried but was never photographed with a girlfriend. Moreover, no woman since Margarita had acknowledged having been to bed with him. Marion Caldwell had no wish to embarrass him despite his hurtful indecisiveness, while Sheena McDonald had asked for a reference to herself as a girlfriend of Brown's in a biography of Tony Blair to be replaced by 'one of his closest female friends'. For two years Brown's relationship with Sarah Macaulay had remained secret. Although they were seen together with friends, he deliberately kept his distance from her in public to prevent any suggestion of a relationship. Under his influence she had retreated from discretion into manic privacy. Frequently, at the end of a day, she waited to hear whether they would meet or even where she might be sleeping – in his flat or her home, or elsewhere. Late into the night she sat expectantly, and quite often fell asleep awaiting a telephone call that frequently did not come. Brown needed women to care for him like surrogate mothers, not as equal soulmates. Irritated by Macaulay's persistent demands for an old-fashioned relationship based on mutual friendship, he obstinately offered no commitment. When she was driving him in her car he regularly put on headphones to listen to music until she complained 'That's bloody rude,' and he stopped the habit.

It was at this time that Brown exposed himself to an unexpected threat. *Desert Island Discs* on BBC Radio 4 traditionally gives a famous person an innocuous, sentimental thirty minutes to reminisce about his or her life. The presenter Sue Lawley's normally unchallenging interview technique reassured Brown that his appearance on the programme, to be broadcast on 13 March 1996, would safely repair his tarnished image. With charm and laughter he regurgitated familiar biographical stories in between his eight chosen records, which included a song by the Scottish folk-rock band Runrig, Kirsty MacColl's 'Days', the Beatles' 'Hey Jude', 'Jerusalem' and 'Cry Freedom', the anti-apartheid hymn. Lawley's question arrived like an Exocet, unexpected and potentially fatal: 'People want to know whether you're gay, or whether there's some flaw in your personality that you haven't made a relationship.' Without a pause or show of embarrassment, Brown half-laughed and replied, 'People have a right to know about [politicians'] arrangements.' Lawley asked whether he was irritated by questions about why he had never married: 'Not at all. It just hasn't happened, and it's one of those things that

I'm surprised hasn't happened, but it hasn't . . . I've always assumed I would be married.' She conjured the image of a middle-aged loner living amidst a mess. The practised politician deflected the insinuations with some grace, coming across as tough, funny and capable of looking after himself. In the aftermath, Lawley was criticised by some as 'rude and intrusive'. Others noted that Brown never categorically denied that he was homosexual. He did not officially complain, but he did rage about the 'ridiculous and untrue rumour and smear campaigns cast around because I'm not married . . . It makes me angry that unfounded allegations have been thrown around by people who should and do know better . . . Substance is what people judge you by.' Although friends suggested that Labour women regarded Brown as romantic and a sex symbol, the damage could only be repaired by marriage.

The unseen confirmation of his sexuality in the summer of 1996 was the presence of Sarah Macaulay in the neighbouring aeroplane seat as he flew for his regular holiday in Cape Cod. That year she and Brown would stay at a country club rather than in Chatham's, the house without a sea view rented by his brothers and their families. As usual, he brought a bag of new books to devour. During those three weeks visitors observed evidence of Sarah's friendship towards Brown while she remained quietly in the background. Brown did not discuss politics with her. Instead she provided him with the right clothes, took the towels to the beach and helped adjust his clumsy NHS contact lenses. It appeared to some that she was confident about her place in his life, behaving not deferentially but as an equal who avoided challenging him. She offered sympathy and shared his ambitions for success. Others felt she was cowed, used and ignored by a man accustomed to unquestioned authority.

During the holiday, Brown's brother John did most of the

cooking. Although his parents had expressed surprise that
it was Gordon, their shyest son, rather than the extrovert
John who had become a political giant, friends regarded their
different fates as understandable. John, who was responsible for Glasgow City Council's public relations, was an
effective operator but not a heavyweight. In Cape Cod John
would quietly tend the big barbecues when Gordon's trusted
friends the television journalist Jon Snow and the lawyer
Helena Kennedy came with their families for the day.
Together they would eat, play tennis, swim and most importantly talk about football, films, books and politics. Other visitors included the journalists Harold Evans and Tina Brown,
Geoffrey Robinson and occasionally Elizabeth Drew and Ted
Kennedy, scions of America's Democratic Party. Brown and
Kennedy had seen together Andrew Lloyd Webber's musical
The Beautiful Game, about football and love across the Ulster
divide.

Brown felt particularly at ease with American academics
and politicians, especially Bill Clinton's advisers Bob Shrum,
Robert Reich and Stan Greenberg, all of whom had been convinced since 1994 that Labour would win the next election.
For some time Brown had emailed his speeches to Shrum for
vetting, and he was particularly grateful for the suggested
phrase 'hard-working families'. The unspoken irony was that
in 1991 Brown had attacked the Tories for 'relying on American-style election dirty tricks', referring in particular to
Shrum's negative campaign advertisements alleging that an
opposing candidate had used cocaine and marijuana. After
1997 Shrum would be welcomed to work in Downing Street
with Balls and Ed Milliband. That summer Brown would also
take the initiative in meeting Henry Kissinger, a hate figure
for many in the Labour Party. Having read many of Kissinger's
books, Brown wanted to discuss ideas with him. Unlike Blair,
who preferred meeting politicians it would be advantageous

to be photographed with, Brown enjoyed discreet scholarly debates.

Sitting in the sunshine, 'shooting the breeze', Brown praised Bill Clinton for making the nineties America's decade. As a laboratory for growth and progress, the country's dynamism sustained his idea of 'popular capitalism'. In the midst of the dotcom boom and an unprecedented bull market with soaring share prices, Brown pondered how his generation, now in their early forties, could escape the shadow of Thatcher. He persuaded himself that he could be the first chancellor to eradicate 'boom and bust' from the British economy. He would banish inflation, end unsustainable consumer spending and cure the structural deficit in public finances. In effect, he would abolish the historic economic cycle, a feat no chancellor had ever achieved. His conception of the New Era was reminiscent of J. K. Galbraith's description of the self-appointed demigods before the 1929 crash: 'The old laws of economics were for mortals, but not for us. With us, anything was possible. The sky was the limit.' Dismissive of the sclerotic European Union, he wanted to replicate America's model in Britain, but without the ugly elements of poverty, greed and fear. Greed was not, he believed, the best or the only motive to encourage innovation and growth. He opposed the notion that being generous to the poor or compulsorily redistributing wealth undermined the incentive to work. 'I believe in socialist values,' he reassured his listeners. 'Dynamism and fairness can go together.' His ideal was 'a truly classless society to promote opportunity'. America was a model for his dream of equality of opportunity. His friends politely refrained from mentioning the fact that America's growth was driven by privileged elites aggressively championing inequality as the justifiable price of wealth – hardly the gospel of socialism.

Brown's 1996 holiday in Cape Cod was a chance to reconcile those contradictions and clarify his philosophy. In the

contest between socialist ideology, the free market and the
benefits of privatisation, he was conscious that Labour had
been portrayed, with some justification, as intellectually bankrupt. Recently he had invited Lord Levene, a Tory banker
and businessman, to tea in Westminster. In 1984 Brown had
attacked Levene's proposal to privatise the Rosyth shipyard
and ridiculed his suggestion that the yard's financial accounts
were phoney. 'Look,' Brown said to Levene twelve years later,
'this has been on my conscience for some time. I now recognise what you said was right and I was wrong. And I wanted
to tell you that.' Levene was gratified by Brown's conversion,
but in fact it was limited. Brown remained a social engineer.
Britain, he enjoyed saying, was more unequal than it had
been at any time in the past hundred years. Equality was his
Big Idea. He was particularly influenced by Richard Layard's
figures which showed that the widening gap between rich
and poor had increased the number of British children in
poverty from one million in 1979 to almost four million in
1997. 'The social consequences are serious,' warned Layard.
Brown repeated that conclusion: 'We live in a Britain where
inequality is growing faster than ever before. Under the Tories
the number of people in poverty has grown to one in three.'

His proposed solution differed from that of others in the
party. While agreeing about 'the importance of equality and
a classless society', he diverged from Roy Hattersley over the
meaning of 'equality'. He dismissed Hattersley's dream of
'equality of outcome' as a nice idea but of no practical value
other than stimulating 'people's nightmare of socialism. It
denies humanity rather than liberates it. It is to make people
something they are not rather than helping them to make
the most of what they can be.' His credo was not to punish
those who had become rich through hard work, but to help
the powerless who had been denied the opportunity to realise
their potential. People had to be convinced that they would

be better off in work, and not on poverty wages. He castigated those who proposed higher taxation to compensate the poor for the consequences of inequality. They were ignoring the real challenge, namely the removal of the causes of poverty. Margaret Thatcher had argued that poverty could only be relieved by creating wealth. Brown believed that education would stimulate the poor to help themselves. While the Tories, he argued, sought to dismantle the welfare state, he would make it the role of the government to help individuals realise their full potential. New Labour's goal was 'equality of opportunity' – providing the unemployed and the low-paid with access to knowledge and skills. The mechanisms would be the new University for Industry and Individual Learning Accounts (ILAs). Government grants would provide free adult education. Brown began drafting a speech about building a new society based upon learning, skills and the work ethic. The unemployed would be exhorted to undertake training and to accept their responsibility to earn a wage. 'Work as the best form of welfare' would be the catchline. There was no fear of an embarrassing comparison with Norman Tebbit's 'on your bike' speech.

What distinguished Brown from the Old Labour herd was his belief in private enterprise funding the public services. But unlike raw capitalists, he did not believe that markets by themselves were enough. Markets needed the support of social and political institutions, and a culture of communal trust. His struggle was to define the relationship between the market and the state. Rather than regarding the market as a tool of personal freedom, he argued, the state should use it as a tool of public interest. The state, he believed, could improve markets by regulation and taxes. He would eliminate monopolies, impose competition and encourage more scrutiny of company directors, to make markets work more competitively 'where they create external costs and benefits that are not

fully priced in the market'. To balance raw capitalism and to
control markets in the interests of the state, he intended to
introduce contracts, rules and targets. The conundrum was
whether his new regulations would undermine his intentions.
Brown's American friends in Cape Cod were unsure whether
he understood that free markets are an expression of personal
freedom, allowing individuals to organise their lives without
government interference, a contradiction of his Scottish heritage of centralised control. Entrepreneurs, in their view, were
dynamic wealth-creators only when they were free of regulations and high taxes.

Taxation was a sensitive topic. In autumn 1996 Brown and
Ed Balls agreed to increase tax revenue by £8 billion per year.
Brown urged Blair to agree to a top income tax rate of 50
pence in the pound. Unconvinced, Blair consulted Peter
Mandelson, who warned, 'We've got to avoid the "tax bombshell" trap. We mustn't say that £100,000 a year makes a
person rich.' Focus group findings showed that the proposal
was unpopular. Mandelson's interference reinforced Brown's
refusal to retreat. Blair intervened. 'We have to make it clear,'
he insisted, 'that people pay too much tax already.' Brown
would not budge. With Blair's support, Mandelson organised
newspaper articles attacking Brown's proposals. Embarrassed,
Brown retreated, virtuously promising that Labour would not
increase the basic rate of income tax. In private he would
reassure Michael Meacher and other sympathisers of his
intention to redistribute wealth by raising other taxes. 'So it
isn't as bleak as it seems,' smiled Meacher. Brown nodded.
The trick, he repeatedly explained, was to convince the public
that taxes were not being imposed for their own sake, but to
pay for worthwhile services. The deceit would not be punished if it was delicately concealed by assurances rather than
expressions of vengeful spite.

Brown had disciplined himself to be 'very careful in what

we said'. The Conservatives, he told his colleagues, would be powerless if Labour stuck to 'generalised statements which cannot be quoted against us'. The corollary was to portray the Tories as dishonest, the perpetrators of twenty-two tax increases since 1992. Scrutinising every Tory statement, press release, article and quotation on taxes since 1992, Brown searched for evidence that the government were the authors of 'fudged figures', reckless spending and debts, leaving a 'vast black hole' of £26 billion in 1997 and £19 billion in 1998. In their defence the Tories claimed that Britain was on the verge of an economic boom, and that Labour's pledges to spend £30 billion on public services would cost the average family £1,200 a year in extra tax. 'Lies,' retorted Brown. 'It's the Conservative big lie technique. To state a lie, repeat it, spending millions on advertising and posters to promote it, hoping that the bigger the lie and the more often it is repeated, the people will start to believe it.' Brown's attacks against the Conservatives camouflaged the ambition of his intentions.

Helped by Geoff Mulgan and Ed Balls, Brown intended to redefine socialism and repair his relations with the left at the party conference in Blackpool in October. In his impassioned speech to the delegates he attacked the usual demons: the 'City cliques', the millionaires and the tax loopholes. Excited by the seemingly inevitable election victory, he pledged that the party's socialist bedrock – 'our idealism' – would never be abandoned. 'Our prudence and responsibility is not therefore an abandonment of socialism – it is the very essence of it . . . I don't want this party to stop dreaming dreams.' He won a standing ovation. The contradictions in his speech ought to have confused everyone, but Labour's huge lead in the opinion polls silenced the sceptics.

The polls also strengthened Brown's self-confidence. His insecurity was buried beneath bellicosity. Twenty-four years after stepping on the first rung towards becoming a politician, the prospect of imminent power was leading to the replacement of deference with impatient certainty. Scenting victory, Brown laid about him with a will. Labour would not agree to finance the replacement of the royal yacht *Britannia*; he would not be using Dorneywood, the chancellor's country house, because it was 'a complete waste of taxpayers' money', according to Charlie Whelan, who was apparently unaware that a trust and not taxpayers paid for the house; and he announced, without consulting his colleagues, that all Labour ministers would agree to a ministerial pay freeze. Any opposition would be crushed.

Sitting with his feet stretched on his desk, Brown called a political journalist at the *Guardian*, which had discovered Arthur Andersen's secret work for the party. Chris Wales, Brown heard, had told the reporter the story was 'balderdash' and threatened action if it was published. As Whelan, Sue Nye and Ed Balls stood watching, Brown told the journalist, 'If you print that I'll have you.'

At Brown's behest, Charlie Whelan adopted the same aggression. Leaks were, as always, his best weapon. Ken Clarke's private correspondence to Britain's two European Commissioners was given by an intermediary to the *Sunday Times*, and twenty-nine embargoed budget press releases were passed to the *Mirror*. 'No one can condone the leak of sensitive budget matters the day before the budget,' said Brown with feigned sincerity. He heard with some pleasure the complaint from Jill Rutter, the Treasury's official spokesman, that Whelan was 'doing a great if disreputable job. His guerrilla tactics are creating problems for us all the time. The leaks are spun in a damaging way to the government.'

Even on the eve of the election, Brown's colleagues were not spared from the familiar terrorism. Whelan suggested to selected journalists that Gavin Strang, the shadow minister for agriculture, should be 'dumped', and that Chris Smith, the health spokesman, should be 'demoted'. Smith had been struggling to survive what he called 'a nightmare'. On Brown's orders he was not allowed to match the Tories' pledge to increase spending on the NHS to match inflation. After several arguments Smith angrily called Blair while driving to the Midlands and protested, 'I'm only allowed to pledge an extra £100 million on basis of reducing bureaucracy. This is madness.' 'OK, leave this with me,' replied Blair. 'I'll get back to you.' The following day, Brown agreed to allow Smith to match the Tories' spending. His revenge was immediate. 'I don't care who becomes health secretary, but it won't be Chris Smith,' he authorised Whelan to say in the weeks before the election. As Smith discovered, 'anyone who disagreed with or challenged Gordon was fair game'. Shadow foreign secretary Robin Cook also tried to finesse Brown. Policy, said Cook, would be decided in the shadow cabinet, not by leaks. Eyeing each other suspiciously across committee rooms but rarely speaking to each other, Cook, a devotee of horseracing, snapped defiance after Whelan suggested that the Tote would be privatised, and questioned why Brown should consider privatising the national air traffic control system. Brown smiled wanly; Cook's attacks were a mere pinprick. With Whelan's help, he had made himself the hero of the hour.

On 20 February 1997, Brown entered the Queen Elizabeth II Conference Centre in Westminster to address a throng of Labour supporters. He was carefully targeting opinion-formers, especially the 350 leading industrialists, businessmen and City professionals who had been seduced by Geoffrey Robinson. The millionaire had attracted a glittering list to 'improve mutual understanding' and advise the government by joining panels, councils and 'task forces'. Among the packed audience were Greg Dyke, Gavyn Davies and Melvyn Bragg. The brotherhood were assembling ahead of the coronation. Deliberately, Blair had not been invited, allowing

Brown to announce major statements on taxation. The top rate of tax would not be raised, said Brown, assuming the credit for a policy which he had opposed. His rich supporters cheered. Gordon Brown inspired confidence. New Labour was truly their party. The only remaining obstacles were the incumbents in the Treasury and the Bank of England.

Discreet conversations with Terry Burns, arranged with the government's permission, had confirmed Brown and Balls's antagonism towards the fifty-three-year-old permanent secretary. The reason for their dislike of him was hard to fathom. Unlike Brown, Burns was the product of a working-class family, brought up in the Durham coalfields, who had graduated from Manchester University rather than Oxbridge and been recruited by the Treasury in 1980 from the London Business School as chief economic adviser. He was promoted to permanent secretary in 1991. That achievement was irrelevant to Brown. Even Burns's devotion to Queen's Park Rangers, an unglamorous London football team, did not impress the supporter of Raith Rovers. Burns's support for monetarism, his association with Nigel Lawson and his participation in the ERM disaster discredited him in Labour's eyes, although as yet Burns was unaware of Brown's dislike.

Eddie George, the governor of the Bank of England, was also disliked by Brown, who over the previous months had been noisily searching for a replacement. Two possible alternatives, Gavyn Davies and the former director general of the CBI Howard Davies, were deemed unacceptable. Eddie George, like Terry Burns, had become aware during their lunches and dinners that Brown was considering the Bank's future role. But he was not told that, under the influence of Ed Balls and Alan Greenspan, the chairman of the US Federal Reserve, Brown was thinking of assigning to an independent Bank of England the power to fix interest rates, which had previously been the prerogative of the government. He was also planning to transfer the supervision of the commercial banks from the Bank of England to a new agency. Those plans and Arthur Andersen's tax proposals were secret. All the policy papers were kept in Robinson's flat.

The only thing that remained was to win the election, which had finally been called for 1 May 1997. Although the party was 20 per cent ahead in the opinion polls, it was decided that the campaign should be fought as if the outcome was on a knife-edge. At seven o'clock every morning Gordon Brown chaired the strategy meetings. From a Spartan room in Millbank with a large window overlooking the press conference auditorium, he watched developments, dictating responses to every accusation and assertion, delicately avoiding mistakes. 'The campaign is about gaffes. The media are desperate for them,' he told his staff. Thanks to their pagers, everyone was kept rigorously 'on message'. Occasionally Brown's passion for politics still suggested an awkward, uneasy man with no feel for the populism so easily displayed by Blair. His stock phrases – 'I think most people think it's time for a change'; 'The long night of Tory rule is drawing to a close'; and 'a systematic pattern of arrogance and greed' – were those of someone nervous to seize the prize rather than of a statesman-in-waiting. 'It's not that the Conservatives don't deserve another five years,' he said, 'they don't deserve another five minutes.'

Brown's only irritation was Peter Mandelson, focused on the identical goal in Millbank's 'grid room', from where he detailed the campaign's strategy. Charlie Whelan was encouraged to spread gossip about the tension between the two, denying reports of any discontent directed towards Brown. On the contrary, sniffed Whelan, Brown had been summoned to Millbank to reassure the miserable staff about their inevitable victory and to free them from Mandelson's grip. 'Trousers,' he scoffed, 'thinks that Millbank is his exclusive area. That's wrong.' After a slurp of beer he added with a laugh, 'Even Cookie helped against Trousers.' Brown, chortled Whelan, was in full control. One only had to look at them together to realise that his boss was Blair's equal, if not Labour's real leader.

One story passed around by Whelan required no massaging to reflect on Brown's credit. Jimmy Airlie, Whelan's mentor, had died in March 1997. Despite the pressures of the forth-coming election campaign, Whelan told journalists, Brown made the pilgrimage to the communist trade unionist's funeral in Glasgow. The hall was packed. Brown refused offers to go inside. Among Airlie's comrades, some of them from Dunfermline East, dubbed 'Little Moscow', he stood outside in the rain, winning the hearts of those on the fringes of the Kingdom. By contrast with Blair's entourage, television cameras were not encouraged to follow Brown. His modesty precluded even friends from witnessing his intimate moments – although there were some self-interested exceptions.

During the months before the election Brown had allowed Ross Wilson, a well-respected television producer, to follow his campaign with a camera crew. On 27 April, four days before the vote, Brown was due to visit his parents' home in Insch, Aberdeenshire, to celebrate their golden wedding anniversary, and was undecided whether to allow the cameras to record the event, rejecting any intrusion into his family life. 'You can't come in,' he told Wilson, fearful that his parents would say something embarrassing. 'It'll be OK,' Sue Nye reassured him, understanding his desire for privacy yet realising the potential benefits of showing his human face. He relented. The pictures were endearing and unremarkable. Brown departed with a smile, but out of range of the cameras he looked troubled.

A disagreement had emerged with Blair about the advisers Brown would take to the Treasury. He insisted on Sue Nye,

Charlie Whelan, Ed Milliband and Ed Balls. Blair was uneasy, especially about Whelan. 'Charlie's a getting-there man,' Blair was told. 'The point of Charlie's existence is working for the victory. What purpose will he have in No. 11?' Blair agreed. Unlike Ed Balls, whose life was dedicated to achievement and who would manifestly insert himself into the Whitehall machine, Whelan was temperamentally unsuited to team-work and consolidation. He enjoyed breaking the crockery too much. In the months before the election, Brown had done little to restrain his praetorian guard. Unlike Blair's group, who shared a positive outlook, seeking to be reasonable and hopeful, Brown's spokesman mirrored Brown's own zero-sum game, constantly asking, 'Who shall we support and who should we knock down? What's in it for us?' Surely, Mandelson and Campbell reasoned, even Gordon would understand? They underestimated Brown's reliance on Whelan. Only recently, at Brown's request, Whelan had told journalists that Labour would appoint a minister for employment with cabinet rank, whose task would be to reduce unemployment. Brown was gleeful when this was reported on every front page. He knew it was untrue, but a purpose had been served. That was Whelan's importance, and his fate dominated a brief conversation between Brown and Blair on election night.

The mood inside Brown's house at North Queensferry in the last hour before the polls closed was muted. Brown, Whelan and Sue Nye ordered an Indian takeaway from a local restaurant and watched television, awaiting the result of the exit polls at 10 p.m. Sarah Macaulay had been left in London. While Whelan spent the time on the telephone, Brown ironed a white shirt in the kitchen. Few could understand the psychology of his childhood experiences in nearby Kirkcaldy, yet soon the values of life in the manse in that dismal town were to be imposed across Britain. Brown expected Labour to win with a majority of about sixty seats. Thirty-six hours earlier,

Balls and Robinson had sat in the Grosvenor House Hotel flat typing out the draft of a letter on a laptop to Eddie George declaring the Bank of England's independence. The envelope was placed with Arthur Andersen's tax proposals in Robinson's safe. The prospect of changing the City forever was materialising.

Just after ten o'clock, the BBC exit poll predicted a landslide for Labour. By the window, Sue Nye and Whelan silently embraced. Brown barely smiled. The euphoria was brief. For Brown, the satisfaction after reaching the goal was going on to achieve his next ambition. Restlessly, he was already contemplating the next problem. He telephoned Blair. There was no small talk. 'Charlie's coming with me,' said Brown. 'No,' tersely replied the man who later that night would be confirmed as prime minister. 'Sue can't come either,' continued Blair. Both Nye and Whelan, he said, had been vetoed by Terry Burns. That was untrue. A day earlier, Blair had asked an emissary to contact Burns and urge him to block the appointment of Whelan, who was 'a disaster'. Burns had refused, saying that Whelan's fate was for the new prime minister to decide. No one had suggested to Burns that Sue Nye should be banned from the Treasury. On the contrary, Burns was a golfing friend of Gavyn Davies, Nye's husband, and he had agreed during the long discussions with Ed Balls that both she and Whelan would be employed in the Treasury. 'She is coming,' Brown said emphatically to Blair. The notion that Nye, the purchaser of dozens of red ties and responsible for saving him from the consequences of his chronic untidiness, should be barred from the Treasury was risible. This was about territory, and the first clash about sovereignty. Outside Brown's house, no one could have imagined the turmoil that was already taking place between the two men who within hours would be the leading members of the new government.

As he emerged in the darkness to be driven to the airport

for the flight to London, Brown was rehearsing his soundbites: 'This result is not just a verdict against the Conservatives. It is a clear and positive endorsement of the desire of the people of this country for new politics.' He looked like a man on his way to a funeral, not a victory celebration.

SIX

'Do You Want Me to Write a Thank-You Letter?'

Inside the private jet flying through the darkness from Edinburgh to Stansted airport, across a nation which his party would now rule, Gordon Brown contemplated the struggle for power that he knew was about to begin. This was not Blair's victory, but his victory. Or at least, both their victories. His prize was the domestic agenda. He would enforce the Granita agreement. Whitehall's departments would be rigidly divided between Blair and himself, and that would include selecting the top civil servants. Keeping Charlie and Sue would be the first proof of his sovereignty. Someone would suffer for seeking to exclude them.

As he pondered his strategy, Brown was faintly aware of a minor power struggle on board the plane. Peter Jay, the BBC's economic editor, had secured a place, hoping for the first television interview with the new chancellor. He asked the camera crew hired by Scottish Television who were filming Brown to record his scoop. They refused. Defeated, Jay watched others record history.

Brown's team drove directly from the airport at 3.30 a.m. to the celebrations at the Royal Festival Hall. Sarah Macaulay was waiting for him, dressed in a striking red suit, her face gleaming with excitement. There was no hug or even any sign of emotion as they met. Enigmatic and unengaged,

Brown stared with a serious expression at the jubilant crowds, especially Peter Mandelson and John Prescott, who were jumping up and down like zombies. Either he was preoccupied by the prospect of embracing power later that day, or, as Blair stepped on cue into the spotlight at sunrise, he was hiding a simple torment: 'It should have been me.'

Shortly after Tony Blair's victory speech, Brown gathered with the Hotel Group in Geoffrey Robinson's flat to celebrate. Afterwards he slept in the spare bedroom. At three o'clock in the afternoon of Friday, 2 May, he was woken by Sue Nye. It was time to go to Downing Street. He had missed the emotional television coverage of the Blair family travelling by people carrier in bright sunshine to Whitehall, to be greeted by a carefully choreographed crowd of cheering supporters. The nation seemed united in greeting the dawn of a new era. Labour's landslide majority of 179 had encouraged widespread predictions that the Conservatives were destroyed forever. Downing Street, Brown told a friend, had been a Conservative street. To symbolise his idealism and democratic socialism it should be renamed 'The People's Street'.

New Labour looked destined to govern Britain for many years, and its two architects now assumed the authority permanently to change the country. Brown spent forty-five minutes with Blair. Their agreement to divide the governance of Britain was reconfirmed. Through the Treasury, Brown would control the domestic agenda, although there were some things he preferred not to reveal to Blair. He emerged at 5 p.m. During the hundred-yard drive to the Treasury's front entrance he could reassure himself that No. 11 Downing Street, his official home, would champion ordinary people, in contrast to No. 10's intention to promote New Labour. In a snatched telephone call with Tom Brown, a Scottish journalist friend, the new Chancellor of the Exchequer had said, 'We've had a long apprenticeship. The test now begins.' Blessed with a sound economy, he would be the first chancellor in many years with a chance to introduce the changes he had long plotted. 'To be radical,' he would say, 'to do what you want, you've first got to be clear in your analysis. You can't be credible without being radical. A left-wing party requires both.'

Terry Burns was standing on the Treasury steps waiting for the ministerial car. He appeared to share the widespread relief at the departure of an exhausted government and to welcome the new ideas promised by Labour. During his many discussions with Ed Balls and Gordon Brown, his respect for the two had grown. He hoped to prove that the Treasury would help to make the Labour government successful. Spotting Burns from the car, Brown disguised his own true sentiments. With a broad smile he shook the outstretched hand and entered the darkened chamber. The loud clapping was a surprise. Filling the entrance hall and crowding the elegant staircase to the landing were dozens of beaming civil servants spontaneously applauding their new boss. Unprepared to say anything more than 'Thank you,' Brown beamed and followed Burns up the staircase lined with portraits and photographs of his predecessors. The new chancellor was perfectly suited to an institution that employed austere workaholics who were usually politically to the left of centre. He was led into his office, a bare, oak-panelled room, twenty yards long, with a huge desk at one end. There was ample space for his computer on which he could surf the internet for hours in the future. The room was his prize after twenty-seven years of political agitation. His destiny was about to be realised.

To the surprise of his new colleagues, Brown's bonhomie rapidly evaporated. Older officials had learnt over the years that the character of every government was formed by its years in opposition. In those first minutes they became aware of an age gulf – Brown and Balls were respectively ten and twenty years younger than most of them, and their distrust was overt. Attempts to establish a cordial relationship were greeted with sternness. Brown spoke without warmth or humour; while Balls, sitting on his right, and Robinson, at the end of the table, remained expressionless.

The attitude of Brown and other Labour politicians towards Whitehall's senior civil servants had been conditioned by many influences, not least a special course of lectures at Templeton College, Oxford. Labour's success in government, Brown and others became convinced, would depend upon their avoiding capture by the mandarins, especially those who had worked closely with the Tories. They discounted the traditional notion of civil servants providing a neutral, Rolls-Royce policy-making machine. They could not understand that senior civil servants had been promoted on the basis of achievement, rather than by way of the greasy pole. In Brown's opinion, his officials were old, prejudiced and questionably competent. Strangely, Margaret Thatcher had voiced the same distrust, blaming Whitehall's defeatism as a cause of Britain's decline. Brown's doubts were more personal, and he meant to test the officials' loyalty to himself by challenging them. Terry Burns, the main focus of Brown's suspicion, was condemned outright, and others were equally suspect because of their service to the *ancien régime*, not least Alan Budd, the Treasury's chief economic adviser. Others, including Nigel Wicks, Steve Robson and Nicholas MacPherson, were more highly rated. Brown knew his intentions for the Treasury, and they were very different from those of his predecessor. He wanted to demolish imagined barriers, recruit more women and more task-oriented outsiders. The smug London Establishment would be expelled.

Brown's prejudices were shared by Tony Blair. Both were convinced that Sir Robin Butler, the cabinet secretary and head of the civil service, was 'non-strategic'. Blair complained that Butler was unable to analyse problems and 'produce a delivery plan for implementing solutions'. Both disparaged the civil servants' 'worthless' White Papers and their depressing talent for perpetuating the status quo. They represented paralysing inertia. Geoffrey Robinson voiced their common complaint that the Cabinet Office was 'the repository of every fizzled-out runt initiative that's been thought up. I've never seen such a mess in my life.' In their impatience to succeed, Blair and Brown were resolved to neutralise Butler's tribe. New Labour would rely on handpicked outsiders, labelled 'special advisers', for policy and relations with the media.

Late afternoon on Friday, 2 May had become dusk as Brown's officials completed their briefings and he issued his first orders. 'You'll have that on Monday,' he was told. 'I want it over the weekend,' he replied. Now was the moment for his bombshells. The first had been flagged, but was still unexpected: 'We'll be sticking to Tory spending plans.' Ken Clarke, the civil servants knew, would have abandoned his intention to increase spending in that year by just 0.5 per cent. To keep the annual increase below 2 per cent was ferocious, and would harm the welfare state and pensions. To prove Labour's economic competence, Brown proposed 'an eye-watering squeeze on public spending'. Then came the policy documents secretly prepared by Balls and Robinson with the accountants from Arthur Andersen: the windfall tax, the tax on pensions and the fate of the Bank of England.

Brown was proposing two earthquakes. First, the Bank was to become independently responsible for setting interest rates; and secondly, the Bank's supervisory powers over commercial banks were to be transferred to a new agency. Brown's reasons were unexceptionable. The recent financial scandals in the City, including BCCI, Barings, Johnson Mathey and Robert Maxwell had exposed the weakness of the self-regulation introduced by the Conservatives after 'Big Bang'.

Brown intended to invite Eddie George to the Treasury and issue a *diktat*: 'This is the way it's going to be.'

Brown believed that Burns understood his orders, although the official's face, normally the image of urbane unflappability, showed, in Brown's opinion, shock. Burns did indeed demur. Two simultaneous revolutions, he said, were too much for Eddie George, and would be difficult to achieve in just a few days. One problem would be George's reaction, and another would be the provocative tone of the letter about supervision that had been drafted by Ed Balls. 'I suggest we stagger the change,' said Burns. Most of his colleagues disagreed. The quicker the change, they felt, the better. The solution suggested by Brown was to publish one letter stating that the Bank's independence would be granted immediately, and to present a second, unpublished 'side letter' referring to the transfer of supervision, with the mention of 'consultations' to mollify Eddie George.

Terry Burns's challenge confirmed the new chancellor's suspicions of him. Brown also noted that Burns was nervous about his proposed £8 billion tax deduction from pensions. To Brown's irritation, Burns appeared to assume that he had licence to argue his own opinions. That was intolerable. Brown found it easier to work with people he could dominate. He resolved to avoid large meetings and to decide policy in small groups, or better still with his friends in Robinson's flat, and always to seek support for his own opinion in advance. The Treasury's officials would work energetically over the weekend to provide him with the documents he had requested.

The next issue was housekeeping. The civil servants who occupied the room adjoining his office, ordered Brown, were to be moved. Sue Nye would have that room, and Balls was to have a desk there as well as his own office. Burns was diplomatic. Nick MacPherson and the two secretaries who

currently occupied that room would dislike the reorganisation. He suggested that Balls sat in Brown's office for a few
weeks while 'things were sorted out'. His naturally affable
style, he hoped, had defused the tension. Shortly after, he
realised his mistake. Geoffrey Robinson was strutting through
the Gothic building inviting officials to 'Call me Geoffrey,'
boasting that orthodoxy was banished and that those who
hoped for a future should hitch their wagons to their new
masters'. 'He's a disaster waiting to happen,' Burns told a
colleague.

His fears about Charlie Whelan were worse. 'Charlie's going
to be the head of the Treasury press team,' Ed Balls had told
Burns before the election. 'Do you have a problem with that?'
'No,' replied Burns, 'but Whelan can't come as the Treasury's
official press secretary. It's better if he comes as a special
adviser.' Burns had good reasons to make the distinction. To
ensure accuracy, especially about statistics, the Treasury's
press spokesmen were always administrators or economists,
not media specialists. Whelan could not be given executive
responsibilities. 'We don't want a spokesman who openly sets
the agenda,' explained Burns. 'It's dangerous for a Treasury
spokesman to create stories, or' – here he chose his words
carefully – 'cause confusion.' On hearing about these objections, Brown puffed out his cheeks. Burns, he scoffed, did not
understand. Publicity was not a minor, grubby but necessary
element of the chancellor's life, but a political weapon for
attacking opponents, concealing mistakes and protecting his
reputation. Whelan was essential to his survival. Like Balls
and Robinson, he was too important to exclude. Moreover,
he felt that Jill Rutter, one of the Treasury's official press
secretaries, was unacceptable. Even if she accepted Whelan's
arrival, she was not culturally 'one of us'.

The following morning, Brown met Tony Blair. The prime
minister had decided that the flat in 10 Downing Street of

seven rooms, with only two bedrooms and a small kitchen, was inadequate for his family of five. Brown agreed to swap, allowing the Blairs to occupy the flat in No. 11. This was not a sacrifice. Brown would prefer to sleep in his own small flat in Great Smith Street. He disliked the idea of living under the glare of servants at No. 10, and accepted the decorations he inherited from Norma Major. His frugality extended to his office in the Treasury. After a moment's thought, the only changes he required were the replacement of a Gainsborough and other paintings by the works of Scottish artists, and the removal of a tattered carpet, leaving the wooden floorboards uncovered. The sumptuous adjoining staterooms left him uneasy. He would refuse to be photographed in Downing Street or its garden. Five years later he had spent just £410 on his home in Downing Street, compared to the £650,000 incurred by Derry Irvine, the lord chancellor, on refurbishing his apartments in the Palace of Westminster – a comparison which Charlie Whelan gleefully circulated, seemingly to embarrass Irvine and Blair.

Once the domestic chores were settled, Blair announced his first cabinet. The level of his consultation with Brown was unprecedented. Prime ministers always guard the power to make cabinet appointments jealously, but the new chancellor's cultivation of loyalty by patronage could not be ignored. The posts for the Brownite clan included Nick Brown as chief whip, Nigel Griffiths as minister for competition and consumer affairs at the DTI responsible for establishing the Competition Commission, Doug Henderson at the Foreign Office, Tom Clarke as minister of state in the department of culture, and Clare Short as the minister for overseas development – helping the Third World had been a special interest for Brown since childhood. His own ministerial team would be Alistair Darling as chief financial secretary, Dawn Primarolo as financial secretary, Geoffrey Robinson as paymaster general and Helen Liddell as economic secretary. Considering her fraught relations with Brown in Scotland, Liddell was surprised by her selection. She knew little about economics, and correctly assumed her appointment was due to the prime minister's influence. 'She's too Blairite,' Brown told a Scottish friend soon after.

On that first weekend, Charlie Whelan began spinning on behalf of his mentor. The new chancellor, he told journalists writing for the Sunday newspapers, was checking the finances and had already discovered errors and 'black holes' threatening 'a nightmare'. Inflation was heading for 4 per cent, and contrary to Ken Clarke's prediction that the economy would grow by 2.5 per cent that year, it would in fact be only 2.25 per cent. Brown, said Whelan, also described Clarke's forecast that unemployment would continue to fall as a 'massaged' statistic. In reality, Brown knew that Clarke's predictions were accurate, or might even be pessimistic. His intention was eventually to claim the whole credit for the economic recovery.

At a crowded meeting with all the Treasury's senior officials that weekend, Brown was given a presentation of the nation's finances. 'These are fantastically good figures,' the official concluded. 'The state of the economy is much better than predicted.' Eyes swivelled to Brown. 'What am I supposed to do with this?' he snarled. 'Write a thank-you letter?' The mandarins quietly smiled. Politicians were a unique breed.

Monday, 5 May 1997 was a bank holiday. At 9 a.m. Brown welcomed Eddie George to his office. Brown was noticeably ebullient. George feared dismissal. Ignoring the Treasury's ban on smoking, Brown ordered an ashtray to be brought for the chain-smoking governor. He intended to enjoy delivering his thunderbolt of granting the Bank its independence. After the earlier discussions he had reluctantly agreed with Burns to stagger his second decision and to hand George a side letter

about transferring the power of supervision. The letter contained a phrase about his intention to consider transferring
supervision with a promise of consulting the governor. There
was merit, Brown had accepted, in persuading rather than
compelling Eddie George to approve the change. Brown
signed both letters. Realistically he could not deny that he
knew their contents, although subsequently he would claim
to have been deceived.

Watching Eddie George open the first letter, about the
Bank's independence, Brown was gleeful about the governor's spontaneous joy. Both understood it was a historic
moment, the biggest change to economic decision-making in
Britain since the war. Implementing the policy outlined in
the second letter about supervision, said Brown, would be
delayed. A misunderstanding then arose. Brown referred to
the Treasury's briefing papers about the mis-sale of 600,000
pensions as 'horrifying'. Ordinary people had been badly
treated by twenty major companies but were powerless to
seek redress. Helen Liddell was to have an 'eyeball-to-eyeball'
session with the companies at which she would threaten to
name and shame the culprits. That was good enough reason to
transfer supervision from the Bank to an independent agency.
Eddie George believed the question of supervision was undecided and no decision would be taken until discussions had
been held. Brown knew that the transfer was certain.

The press conference the following day to announce the
Bank's independence and responsibility for setting interest
rates was carefully orchestrated by the Hotel Group. Gratifyingly, none of the journalists present had guessed the secret.
Most commentators hailed Brown's unexpected announcement as bold, brilliant and dynamic. Nigel Lawson joined the
praise. The criticism came from the left, notably from Ken
Livingstone and from Anatole Kaletsky of *The Times*. Even
William Keegan, an admirer of Brown, wrote, 'I believe, with

only modest reservations, that Labour has taken leave of its senses.' After eighteen years of struggling to seize power, the critics carped, Brown had thrown the prize away. Eventually, most of them would acknowledge that they were wrong.

The new chancellor was immune to criticism, and he was in a hurry. If he was to impose his rule over the government's domestic agenda, the Treasury had to be revolutionised. Instead of allocating money for other departments to spend at their own discretion, Brown's Treasury would micro-manage the entire agenda. This would extend beyond the economy. Brown had decided to renege on the agreed division of responsibilities with Blair, and to add the NHS to taxes, welfare, social benefits, pensions, transport, education and agriculture in his domain. Despite the Treasury's inadequate skill in managing projects, confirmed by its crass and costly supervision of the introduction of computers across Whitehall, it was to become the powerhouse for management. Brown's one thousand officials and four ministers were instructed to harden their traditional bloody-minded denials to demands for more cash from departments. 'Cash alone does not improve standards,' was his watchword. 'My predecessors were concerned about raising money. I want to know how it's spent.' One exception to his austerity emerged during his journey to Buckingham Palace to be sworn in as a privy councillor. He travelled with George Robertson, the new minister of defence. 'I've already been asked to approve spending £23 million on the refit of a submarine,' said Robertson. 'Hold it,' ordered Brown. 'Don't agree to anything.' 'Ask me where it would be refitted,' continued Robertson. 'OK, where?' asked Brown. 'Rosyth,' replied Robertson with a smile. 'Oh, that's all right then,' agreed Brown, laughing.

As Brown moved to his seat at the oval table opposite Blair for the new government's first cabinet meeting on Thursday, 8 May, he sensed his destiny. In the image of one seasoned eyewitness, he exuded the restless energy of an artist attacking a vast canvas with a reservoir of rage. Looking at the other twenty-one ministers, he felt his usual contempt. Not one of these mere political wannabes matched his roving intellect or experience – nor did the cabinet secretary Sir Robin Butler. Butler, Blair and Brown had decided, would not be told of their decision to divide up the government. Brown had not yet told Blair that he had also decided to assume control of the DTI. That could be raised when they next spoke, outside the hearing of other politicians and civil servants. He and the prime minister would talk alone, either in the Downing Street garden or in one of their offices with the doors firmly closed. Continuing the historic practice of allowing an official to listen to all ministerial telephone calls and take notes was too ludicrous to contemplate. If possible, nothing sensitive would be committed to paper. Secrecy was vital. There would be none of the leaks from Whitehall that he himself had exploited during the Tory years. Without a paper trail, the new chancellor reasoned, he could also avoid the possibly unpleasant consequences of an irrefutable record of their decisions. He would not be held to account by anyone. Blair, he was pleased to note, shared his desire for informality.

Brown's assault on traditional government would be matched by an offensive against society's attitudes. His first public opportunity would be at a CBI dinner two weeks after the election. The invitation stated 'black tie'. To Brown, that symbolised Britain's class system. Sue Nye was told to call the CBI. 'The chancellor doesn't like black-tie dinners,' she told a director. 'Well, he can dress however he likes,' he replied. 'No, you don't understand. The chancellor wants everyone to dress down.' 'What do you mean?' 'No one should wear black ties,' insisted Nye. There was a silence. Then, 'I see.' At the CBI's headquarters in central London there was uproar. For the son of the manse to ridicule convention was unexpected, perhaps even childish, but no one dared insult the new chancellor. Indeed, the CBI's leaders were eager to retreat. The bewilderment reflected the mood inside the Treasury. The chancellor was determined to break conventions. To re-engineer the welfare state, he dismissed any possibility of finding trusted experts among his staff. Only outsiders employed in the private sector, he believed, could improve public services. Before the election he had identified several capitalists with social consciences as perfect agents of change.

Martin Taylor, an intelligent forty-five-year-old Old Etonian and chief executive of Barclays Bank, was his choice to pioneer the reform of the welfare state. Taylor had read oriental languages at Balliol and been a journalist at the *Financial Times* before joining Barclays. Three months before the election, Brown and Blair had hosted a coffee morning to reassure thirty business leaders of Labour's trustworthiness. Taylor was on the verge of a risky strategy to expand Barclays. 'Do you know what you want to do about welfare reform, or will you react only after taking over?' he had asked Brown. 'Welfare expenditure has to be limited,' Brown replied. 'The sums don't add up. Housing benefits are a drain on public expenditure.' The crunch, Brown told his audience, was to get the unemployed back to work. The new environment, he continued, using the tax and benefit system as an incentive for work, would be built on Bill Clinton's system called 'Earned Income Tax Credit'.

Brown was motivated by more than a social purpose. The cost of welfare in Britain had more than doubled in real terms over the previous twenty years, consuming nearly half the national budget. His purpose was to realise Blair's pledge to the Labour Party conference in 1996: 'I vow that we will have reduced the proportion [of national income] we spend on welfare bills of social failure . . . This is my covenant with the British people. Judge me upon it. The buck stops with me.'

The possibility of cutting costs was obvious. Sacks of letters were regularly delivered to the Treasury from private citizens denouncing benefit cheats. Unemployment was falling in Britain partly because the cheats were applying, with the help of doctors, for incapacity benefits. The explosion of teenage single mothers committing themselves to a life on benefits was alarming. Over the next weeks, Brown pursued Taylor to become an architect of his revolution – a scheme to modernise the tax and benefits system. He discussed offering the banker a ministerial post with Ed Balls. Sensing that Taylor would reject such an offer, Brown suggested soon after the election that he lead a task force representing the Treasury, the Inland Revenue and the departments for social security and education, helped by Geoff Mulgan. Taylor accepted. The appointment was completed without Brown consulting the Treasury's senior officials.

The principal obstacles to the reintroduction of means tests were the high priests at the department of social security. Taylor's help was sought to outwit them. 'We can't use the term "means tests",' said Brown. 'The left hates them, but they're the best response to fraud.' The new euphemism would be 'working tax credits'. People would be compelled to work if they were to receive benefits. Brown preferred not to admit that this policy was a development of the family credits pioneered by the Conservative minister Peter Lilley, which he himself had robustly condemned as iniquitous. To adapt the criticism of 'deconstructionists', what began as 'a heresy soon turned into a dogma, and hardened into a theology, sustained by a network of evangelists and high priests and inquisitors'. Taylor set a frantic pace to realise Brown's plans.

Brown and Balls were working eighteen hours a day, refusing to delegate work, giving the impression that they could single-handedly run the country. Brown ignored those who questioned how the Treasury could both be the guardian of the public purse and also hand out benefits. For a man convinced of his judgement, the possibility of a conflict of interests did not arise. Brown's strength was understanding his goal. His weakness was an inability to focus on more than one topic at a time, refusing to consider any other question until his all-consuming appetite for the issue currently at hand had been sated. Critical officials would not be invited to his meetings. Brown's world, they would discover, had to be uninfected by awkward, challenging personalities eager for debate. 'Brown has difficulty distinguishing between disinterested advice and a knife in the back,' complained one senior official only weeks after the election. Neither Taylor nor, more importantly, the new chancellor troubled himself to consider the opinions of Frank Field, a veteran Labour MP and an expert on the welfare system. Ignoring Field was typical of Brown. His grudges fuelled a conviction that those whom he disliked had little useful to tell him.

On election night, Frank Field had had good reason to believe that he would be masterminding the revolution of welfare benefits. The previous year, Blair had promised that he would be the new secretary of state for social security. 'You reach those voters I don't,' said Blair. Then he asked as an afterthought, 'You do get on with Gordon, don't you?' 'Yes,' replied Field. Stepping out of Blair's office, Field bumped into Alastair Campbell and recounted his conversation. 'I don't know why he doesn't appoint me to the shadow cabinet now,' said Field. 'That's a good idea,' said Campbell. The appointment was not announced, although Field remained on Blair's list of prospective cabinet ministers.

The unravelling of the arrangement occurred during a brief conversation on election day. Peter Mandelson paid a fleeting visit to Blair at his home in Sedgefield. 'I'm going to make Frank secretary of state,' said Blair. Mandelson protested that

Field was unsuitable, and the conversation moved on. Two days after the election, Blair telephoned Field: 'I'd like you to be minister of welfare reform.' 'What?' replied Field. 'I thought I was to be the secretary of state.' 'Oh, God,' sighed Blair, 'there's so much blood on the carpet. Do you want more blood?' 'You'll never be more powerful than today,' countered Field, irritated that Blair was considering appointing Harriet Harman as his superior. Unknown to Field, Gordon Brown was insisting on Harman's appointment. Blair prevaricated: 'I'll call you back.' Over the following ninety minutes Blair sought to persuade Field to work under Harman. 'I wouldn't appoint Harriet,' said Field. 'She's not up to the job.' Blair was flabbergasted. The whole formation of his government was being held up.

Blair tried to find a compromise, but, bowing to Brown's insistence, continued to favour Harman. Jonathan Powell, Blair's chief of staff, called Field and told him, 'You do realise there'll be a reshuffle in six months' time? Do you understand?' Field was slow to grasp that Blair felt bound to approve Harman, Brown's nominee, at the outset, but that Field would inherit the post within a year. Nevertheless, he refused to retreat. Blair telephoned him again. 'I'll make you a privy councillor,' he offered. 'I also want to be a Church Commissioner,' said Field. 'If it's in my gift, it's yours,' replied Blair. 'OK, I accept,' agreed Field. The following day, Harriet Harman was appointed as Field's superior. The combination of the aesthete Field and the feminist Harman was hardly ideal. Field did not hide his disdain for her limitations, and she accused him of misogyny.

Gordon Brown enjoyed power-play, regardless of the consequences for others. Vetoing the appointment of Chris Smith as health minister was another coup. Frank Dobson, the compromise candidate, was bereft of any policies other than dismantling the internal market and halting the devolution of hospitals' management. Brown's single edict to Dobson was uncompromising: 'Health is a huge empty hole. There's no more money.' Dobson, a hardened party loyalist, replied, 'I've just addressed the Royal College of Nurses, and I said, "There's no more money." Everyone cheered.' Brown puffed. Quietly in 1997, without much warning to Dobson, he would release an extra £290 million of health spending. The effect on the NHS, which spent more than £100 million every day, was imperceptible.

The chancellor was hastily imposing his writ across the land. Among the early casualties was the Low Pay Unit, created by Tony Blair to establish a minimum wage. The unpaid chairman, announced Blair, would be Professor George Bain, a Canadian economist teaching at the London Business School. Bain was called by Geoffrey Norris, Blair's special adviser. 'Contact Gordon Brown,' advised Norris. 'He doesn't like to be surprised, so keep him on board.' Brown was already chafing. In the past he had supported the idea of a Low Pay Unit, but he switched once Blair encroached upon his territory without permission. To show his displeasure, Brown customarily used a variety of techniques. Bain received the cold blast treatment. Led into Brown's enormous office for an introductory meeting, he found the chancellor alone and aloof. Surprisingly, no officials were present. From behind his desk Brown offered no small talk and no laughter, and he showed impatience while Bain repeated the script prepared for him by his officials. Brown realised that Bain could not be ditched. An immediate confrontation was undesirable. The audience was terminated. Revenge, Brown decided, would be exacted on another occasion.

At midday on 19 May Brown took aim at Eddie George. The governor arrived at the Treasury unaware of the chancellor's agenda. Unusually, Brown was waiting for him alone. George was to be told about the transfer of the Bank's supervisory

powers to the new Financial Services Authority (FSA). There
was little doubt about the justifiability of this. The Bank of
England, the DTI and other regulators had failed to supervise
London's financial businesses adequately. The mis-sale and
mismanagement of insurance, pension and mortgage policies
demanded the creation of a strong regulator. Brown's announcement nevertheless shocked Eddie George, who had
assumed from the 'side letter' that there would be consultation before a decision was taken. He had not understood
that Brown's letter two weeks earlier was non-negotiable.
Brown intended to ask Howard Davies to lead the new agency.
George was not asked for his approval. Brown did not particularly like Davies, nor did he show any interest in mastering
the complicated details which were necessary to implement
his orders. Davies would be hastily recruited later that day
while he was at a formal dinner in Argentina.

Lost for words and 'volcanic' as he left the Treasury, 'Steady
Eddie' was said to have dictated a letter of resignation from
his car while returning to the City. The bush telegraph spoke
of an attempt to destabilise the governor and replace him with
Gavyn Davies, a Labour trusty. City big guns, especially the
non-executive members of the court of the Bank of England,
murmured their disapproval. Andrew Buxton and Robert
Scholey, the senior independent members of the court, protested to Terry Burns in telephone conversations. They questioned Brown's commitment to an independent Bank. Brown
was surprised by the hostility, and asked Burns to calm the
protesters and Eddie George. Burns helped to persuade George
not to resign, and the crisis was averted. Although saved from
embarrassment, Brown did not thank Burns. Rather, he
blamed him for the original confusion. Burns was expected to
negotiate the creation of the FSA with George, a complicated
chore. 'I think you should renew Eddie George's contract,'
Burns suggested to Brown during their discussions. Brown

ignored the suggestion. His permanent secretary's independence was irritating to him.

While Eddie George raged, Gordon Brown arrived at the Mansion House for the annual CBI dinner. The picture on the street outside the historic building was confused. The last message to Sue Nye about black ties had been that the logistics were too complicated. 'We can't send out new invitations,' she was told. 'The chancellor will just have to be dressed as he wants.' Dressed in his normal dark blue suit, Brown was welcomed by Adair Turner, Lord Marshall and other CBI executives also dressed in lounge suits. Most of the 1,500 guests were in black tie. Brown appeared unengaged. The election victory removed the need for any pretence of liking City folk. He was uninterested in how they earned their money. His true preoccupation was controlling 'fat cats' and 'vested interests'. His speech to his former enemies before the dinner was not fiery. Competition would be encouraged, he promised, the 'Whitehall knows best' attitude would be abandoned, and the University for Industry would be launched to spread equality of opportunity for all. After his speech he ate only the first course, then bade his hosts farewell. He had warned them beforehand that he might have to return to the Commons. Instead, he went to a party in the Barbican for trade union leaders celebrating Labour's election victory. The CBI's goodwill towards him was unaffected. The majority of Britain's business leaders supported Brown.

By contrast, the attitude towards the chancellor within the Treasury was divided. Some were puzzled by his intention to announce his discovery of a 'black hole' in the public finances. 'I'm pledging "honesty and openness" in public finances,' he repeated, while criticising Ken Clarke's 'optimistic' projections as unrealistic. He appeared unwilling to accept the Treasury's forecasts showing that, contrary to the £2 billion deficit in that year's accounts expected by the City, there would be a surplus of £36 million. His agenda, undisclosed to his officials, was to begin the campaign to win a second term for Labour, and to find an excuse to raise taxes. To that end he instructed the National Audit Office (NAO) to investigate Clarke's forecasts. The NAO was asked to prove that the prospects of the national accounts were worse than Clarke had admitted in his final budget in November 1996. 'There is widespread suspicion,' Charlie Whelan announced, 'that improper assumptions were made about privatisation receipts and revenues from "spend to save". We now want an open and accountable system with no cooking of the books.' To Brown's irritation, the NAO would fail to find an obvious 'black hole' in the Tory plans, although it did report that it was 'reasonable' to assume there might be a deficit in five years.

Brown was undaunted. The 'black hole' soundbite had registered, and the feelings of the vanquished were irrelevant. Six weeks after the election, the Hotel Group had established their position within the Treasury. Balls had proved his power. No visitor or document reached Brown without his knowledge. Alan Budd, the chief economic adviser, understood that the chancellor was taking his advice from Balls, whose ascendancy was displayed in the technical papers he published describing his intentions. His grasp of detail was impressive. Any resentment of Balls was tempered by general acknowledgement of his competence, although he was criticised for not understanding that during negotiations it was sometimes preferable to understate rather than overstate his intelligence.

Few, however, found any redeeming characteristics in Geoffrey Robinson. The paymaster general introduced himself as the architect of Labour's industrial policy, with the task to 'keep the Treasury in the real world'. Showing open contempt for the Treasury's culture and past performance, he took it upon himself to force-feed humble pie to an institution responsible, he believed, for 'a series of unforced errors'.

Insensitively, he reprimanded officials for 'what had gone wrong in the recent past'. Disregarding the comedy of his own record, he damned 'the Treasury's tendency towards optimism . . . and monetary laxity'. The cure, he said, was to provide his civil servants with a 'clear and firm direction'. Winning hearts and minds was usually Robinson's strength, but the cream of the Treasury's intellectuals were unlikely to be attracted by the same back-scratching as party workers and factory employees. 'I've never been so cuddled in my life,' complained one mandarin at the end of Robinson's third day in office. Robinson was 'touchy-feely', constantly putting his arms around shoulders and squeezing. 'It's a sad day,' muttered one observer of his behaviour. 'We've never previously allowed spivs to set a foot inside this building.' Terry Burns was puzzled as to why Brown trusted Robinson. 'I can't understand their relationship,' he said to colleagues. By mid-June, he had begun to understand.

Unprecedentedly, there was a state of permanent warfare between the chancellor and the prime minister. Although Blair was the most popular prime minister in the world, facing no effective opposition, Brown was already positioning himself to succeed him. There had not been a divorce between the two former allies, only an unspoken agreement to lead separate lives. Geoffrey Robinson, like Charlie Whelan, was committed to serve three purposes: to implement the agreed policies, to speed his mentor's coup, and to secure complete loyalty. 'We're here for a long time,' Robinson regularly told officials and outsiders, 'so why don't you get on with me and do it our way?' Caution was to be cast aside. For those in doubt, Robinson delighted in folding a napkin into a triangle; Brown and Blair, he said, were at the base, and he himself was at the apex, linking the two. Brown's regular arrival at his flat late in the evening with Balls and Whelan for drinks to discuss their plans, confirmed his opinion of his own importance.

Empowered by Brown's sponsorship, Robinson, Balls and Whelan adopted his grudges, dividing the world into friends and enemies, focusing especially on their personal and ideological dislike of Blair. One overriding imperative was secrecy. To protect himself from the kind of ruinous leaks he himself had previously deployed to undermine the Conservatives, Brown purposefully excluded from his inner sanctum anyone whose trustworthiness had not been proven, especially civil servants. Working in a cell structure, he dispatched his memoranda to Balls on floppy disks, avoiding a paper trail for officials to read or photocopy. He had been delighted to hear of a Treasury civil servant telling Helen Liddell, 'So this is what it feels like to be governed.' Ken Clarke's judgement was less flattering: 'In rushing into these things, this government is showing all the signs of inexperienced men and women being intoxicated with their new power. They are like eighteen-year-olds in a saloon bar, trying out every bottle on the shelf.' Clarke was derided as a forgotten dinosaur.

Jill Rutter noticed the self-importance during the first week. 'We are the Treasury,' Whelan told the Scottish Television crew who were completing their documentary of Brown's progress to Downing Street. He made a few denigratory comments about the 'opposition' in No. 10, and confessed his frequent ruses to plant false trails for journalists. 'You just have to be economical with the truth,' he boasted, adding that he would drop hints about tax rises while knowing that Brown would leave taxes unchanged: 'Gordon then looks good. You have to say things. You should never lie, but it's very difficult. They understand. They'll certainly understand tomorrow and forgive me.' Whelan was acting on Brown's orders. With his blessing, Balls and Whelan plotted to manufacture a 'victory' for Brown over the European Commission about an alleged proposal to fix the level of VAT on fuel. Whelan emerged from the meeting to declare that Brown had won, but since the whole dispute had been invented by Whelan, the victory was wholly fictitious.

'These are not the standards I would have expected,' Jill Rutter told Ed Balls. She was surprised that such an obviously intelligent man should stoop so low. She had no idea what else Whelan or Balls were telling the media on the Treasury's behalf. Balls, after all, had been recorded by Scottish Television saying, 'I tell everyone what to say,' and also insulting the Bank of England's governors. Rutter found Brown's endorsement of this behaviour puzzling. She failed to understand the new chancellor's distrust of an independent woman having any responsibility for his image. He wanted his trusted friend to be his sole spokesman as he prepared his first budget, due on 2 July 1997.

In the weeks before the election, Brown's soundbites had been honed to perfection. He pledged to stick to Tory spending plans. 'I repeat,' he would say, 'we have no public spending commitments on Labour's part that will lead to increases in taxes.' He would react to the Conservatives' plans for reforming state pensions by warning, 'Your pension is not safe with the Tories.' The protestations of honesty and innocence voiced by the son of the manse appeared sincere: 'I have nothing to hide. I never have had. In politics I believe you have to be cleaner than clean.' Now, writing his budget speech, Brown sought to present himself as the chancellor dedicated to cleaning up the Tories' mess. He would describe his inheritance as 'instability, underinvestment, unemployment and a waste of talent', and would pledge that under Labour Britain's rate of growth would increase, taxes would be as low as possible, savings and investment would be higher, red tape would be cut, and training and productivity would increase. Even house prices would be stabilised, he promised, by increasing stamp duty from 1 per cent to 4 per cent. Under Brown, Britain would be revolutionised. On taxes, he planned to be tough in the first two years and generous in the last two before the next election. He would take £5 billion in a single windfall tax from the privatised utilities, and, more important, he would tax savings and particularly pensions. By abolishing the tax credits on dividends received by pension funds he would receive £8 billion every year. The middle classes, he believed, would not feel any immediate pain.

To some, Brown appeared to be attacking pensions, but in his opinion he was completing Harold Wilson's policy of reducing the political power of the almighty financial institutions, which controlled funds worth £650 billion, by terminating their excessive tax advantages. Focused on welfare-to-work, he dismissed the many protests during June 1997 which predicted catastrophe for Britain's unique pension funds. Actuaries sent evidence to his office that his plans would push the country's pension schemes into a £50 billion deficit, that final guaranteed salary schemes for millions of employees would be closed, and that the Treasury would lose £2 billion every year in corporation tax, because companies would be obliged to top up their pension funds. BT, for example, would have to pay an extra £166 million per year to compensate for the loss, and British Gas £92 million. Experts warned that without the annual £8 billion, payments to pensioners and savings would fall. Employees, Brown was told, would move back into Serps – pensions paid by taxation – placing a greater burden on the economy. He was also warned that his campaign against the mis-selling of pensions and endowment policies and his encouragement to savers to invest in tracker funds rather than pay fees to fund managers were also undermining trust and savings.

To those who warned that his policies would cause permanent damage to savers and pensioners, Brown retorted that the stock market was booming and the funds were richer than ever. 'Many pension funds are in substantial surplus,' he repeated. It was 'the right time to undertake a long-needed reform'. He dismissed any contradictory opinion. Privately, he urged fund managers to invest in Britain's fledgling dotcom and technology companies. Brown and Ed Balls had never personally experienced the cautious investor's adage 'Whatever goes up comes down.' Neither realised that stock market booms occur only once every twenty years, distorting the economy.

Pensions were not on Brown's agenda. The battle was taken up by Derek Scott, an economist and special adviser in 10 Downing Street. The £8 billion suggested by Chris Wales, Scott advised Blair, was excessive. In the chancellor's mind, it was clear, pensions were the benefits handed out by the state to workers like those in Kirkcaldy, and nothing more. People who wanted to save for their old age were irrelevant. Blair was urged by Scott to restrain the chancellor, and with great difficulty a meeting was arranged. Across the table facing Blair in 10 Downing Street were Brown's senior civil servants Robert Culpin, a cerebral, uncombative official, and John Gieve, similarly quiet, and not noted as a mathematical genius. Neither had vigorously challenged the chancellor. Beside Brown was Ed Balls, the real influence. Blair opened the meeting by telling Brown that everyone agreed that taxing pensions was 'not a good idea'. 'It's a manifesto commitment,' replied Brown inaccurately. 'It's got to come down,' said Blair. They compromised at taking £5 billion every year from the pension funds. Scott discovered, as many others would over the following months and years, the price of the prime minister refusing to support his staff: they would be mercilessly bullied by the chancellor.

Shortly before his budget speech, Peter Mandelson and Alastair Campbell asked Brown when he intended to disclose his proposals to other ministers. He ignored them. They were to learn that the Treasury was Brown's sovereign territory.

Their irritation was compounded when they read a leaked report about the pensions tax in the newspapers. Robin Butler was asked by Blair who he suspected was responsible for the leak. Butler suggested Ed Balls. Brown denied this, and accused Terry Burns of disloyalty. For the first time since university, Brown was fearless. Sarah Macaulay sought to take advantage of his unprecedented self-confidence.

For three years she had pursued Brown, forcing him to split with Sheena McDonald and proving her suitability for the role of political wife. She wrote the constituency letters and organised his life and his home – there was new furniture in the North Queensferry house, videos and books were no longer scattered across the floors, the disorder was controlled. She had shown her skill at managing the 'Gordon Project' by placing him in the limelight in the right contexts, especially the world of charities. He had given her little in return. Her enforced anonymity and insecurity was becoming crushing. Brown was determined to outwit the paparazzi's desire to snatch a photograph of them together. Like Princess Diana, she felt embarrassed by his public discussion of marriage. In an interview with the *Daily Mirror*'s Mary Riddell before the election, Brown had scathingly dismissed any prospect of marriage. 'If it were true,' he said, 'I would tell you.' 'So it's nonsense?' Riddell asked. 'There's lots of speculation and no truth in it.' Brown, Riddell concluded, was married to the Labour Party. Equally humiliating was Whelan's boast to the *Daily Star* that Brown had enjoyed 'hundreds of girls'. Regularly, standing at the bars around Westminster, Whelan rolled into action, telling journalists, 'Gordon fucks loads of women and he's bloody good at it.'

Even this was not as embarrassing as a profile in the *Guardian*, clearly influenced by Whelan's hype. Brown was referred to as 'The handsome personification of brooding intelligence . . . He is a Gallagher-jawed enigma . . . It's that mystery that makes him a sex symbol ... Brown is Byronic right down to the slight deformity.' The blind left eye had never before been described in those terms, but in this profile even his jaw was identified as special: 'The way Brown constantly grinds the lower jaw as he talks, it always looks like he's just taken a load of rough cocaine off a Hell's Angel.' Perhaps the most irksome passage of the profile for the frustrated Macaulay was its summation of Brown as 'the ideal boyfriend who will take care of everything', allowing the woman to 'get on with the important things in life'.

This had to stop, Macaulay decided. She wanted their relationship cemented, and she turned to Whelan for help. Her proposal was the publication of a photograph of the two of them together. Brown, in the midst of his rampage through the Treasury, resisted the idea as a tiresome diversion, but Whelan persuaded him that his bid for the leadership depended upon proof of a relationship. Grudgingly, Brown agreed to pose with Sarah on the eve of the budget in Vasco and Piero's, a Soho restaurant, and a photographer from the *News of the World* was duly ushered up to their table. Brown was moody. The picture was snatched, and Brown walked to the exit. The result was miserable. 'Do it again,' ordered Whelan. Grumpily, Brown agreed to pose for another shot. The published photograph showed the two gazing lovingly into each other's eyes.

The photo's appearance prompted Macaulay and Whelan, both professional publicists, to promote the image of the 'hot couple'. She, willingly standing beside her man, ambitious to save the world; and he, the brooding, sexy bachelor who, besides running the country, had time for love. The only victims were the Blairs, who were annoyed to be portrayed, if only implicitly, as unintellectual adjuncts to the golden couple. Brown loathed Cherie. Ever since she had confronted him in the prime minister's office in Downing Street about his

offensive behaviour towards her husband, their relationship
had been fraught. 'For God's sake, Gordon,' she had shouted
with emotion, 'stop treating Tony with such rudeness. There's
more to life than all this.' Brown could not cope with an emotional reprimand and had steered clear of his neighbour ever
since. In obedience to Brown, Sarah made no effort to broker
a rapprochement with Cherie, telling her confidantes that she
had nothing in common with the oddball next door.

Over the previous twenty years, Gordon Brown had often
dreamt of presenting the budget. The realisation of his dream
on 2 July 1997 would be managed with care. His ministers
were invited to his flat in No. 10 for breakfast, cooked by
Balls and Whelan. Standing on the steps of No. 11 Downing
Street for the traditional photograph, he held aloft a new
budget case made by apprentices at the Rosyth dockyard who
were standing beside him. Whelan whispered that Gladstone's
case, made in 1860 and used by generations of chancellors on
budget day, had been 'dumped'. The stunt was only a small part
of a more sophisticated operation that was carried out throughout that morning. London's most important journalists had
been invited to the Treasury to be briefed about the budget's
details. After Brown's speech in the Commons that afternoon,
each received a call from Sue Nye. 'Gordon wants a word,'
she announced. 'What do you think?' asked Brown. In a
move intended to 'negative the negatives', he emphasised his
opinions, liberally sprinkling his replies with compliments. As
desired, the newspaper reports reflected his glory.

The enjoyment was not shared by everyone in the Treasury.
There had been a major leak of the budget before Brown's
speech, with substantial information being published by the
Financial Times and other papers. If anything similar had happened during the previous 150 years, the outcry would have
been deafening. On this occasion there was not a whisper of
protest, especially from the Treasury. Sir Robin Butler, the

cabinet secretary, was bewildered by the astonishing breach of precedent. Tony Blair agreed with Butler that the Treasury should be asked to discover who was responsible. Suspicion fell automatically on Charlie Whelan and Ed Balls. In self-defence, Whelan told his friends that Terry Burns had, on his own initiative, complained about Whelan to the prime minister.

That distortion successfully inflamed relationships in the Treasury. Burns had been embarrassed. Many suspected that the leaks had been authorised by Brown himself. His response was bravado. He confronted Burns and challenged him, 'There's a suggestion that you know who's leaking this stuff. If you have any evidence I want to know, and we'll take action.' Burns was surprised. He had never accused anyone of leaking, he told Brown, because unless the actual act of leaking had been witnessed, the person responsible could not be found. Brown affected dissatisfaction. 'I want a written minute about what you know,' he ordered. 'Find out who's responsible and tell me.' He knew that Burns had no evidence, but his imperious tone challenged him to risk naming Whelan or Balls. Burns agreed to send Brown a note of what he knew, but added that there was no evidence against any Treasury official. Becoming entrapped in a row between Blair and Brown, Burns discovered, was perilous.

The manipulation of the media disturbed Jill Rutter, and Terry Burns heard about her unhappiness. 'At first I thought Whelan was good for Brown,' she told him, 'but he's really an aggressive hooligan. His methods are the same as in opposition.' Confronting Whelan, she realised, was pointless. He would brazenly rebut any criticism. Even if other officials found him 'outrageous', 'patronising', 'a bullying maverick' and 'malicious', no one cared beyond the Whitehall village. The arrival of dozens of special advisers across Whitehall had caused Robin Butler and many of the permanent secretaries concern, but they accepted that the politicisation of the civil service was irresistible. Burns urged Rutter to be patient while he arranged for her transfer to another post or department, and told Brown that she would be transferred in two months, after her holidays, to avoid giving the impression of dismissal. Brown was impatient, and cared little for Rutter's feelings. 'I want her out by the end of July,' he ordered.

The success of Brown's budget demanded celebration. Scottish friends were welcomed for drinks in his flat on the first floor of 10 Downing Street. Their raucous laughter echoed similar joy of other politicos over generations who for years had peered through the gates and finally entered the hallowed Kingdom. The first official party at 11 Downing Street, on 29 July 1997, was for the British film industry. Brown's interest in films was indisputable. As a board member of the Edinburgh Film Festival in 1992, he had blamed Tory cuts in funding for the 'catastrophic collapse' of Britain's film-makers. Now, against the advice of the Inland Revenue, he had introduced new incentives to transform the industry. The director Alan Parker, a Labour supporter, was appointed chairman of the British Film Institute. Wilf Stevenson, Brown's student friend from Edinburgh, had been a director since 1988. Brown announced that there would be 100 per cent tax relief for films costing under £15 million, and 40 per cent write-offs for loans to make films. 'Our British genius for creativity,' he told his guests, 'has made Britain a world leader.' He intended to extend similar incentives to creativity in science, computer software, communications, design, fashion and music. As predicted by his officials and ignored by Brown, the concession would be used by the rich to avoid over £100 million of taxation.

Chris Smith, who as the new minister of culture was responsible for the film industry, was invited to the party. He had first heard of the plan at breakfast time that morning from Brown himself. Smith understood that since Brown and the Treasury had arrogated the power to decide the fate of all money, Brown would announce every department's good news. 'Gordon wants to grab the glory,' he told a fellow guest enjoying the Chablis and canapés. Complaining was pointless, he knew.

The chancellor was planning many more parties. To repair the damage wreaked over the previous five years between himself and the party's activists, he intended to invite a thousand people including Labour MPs, trade union leaders, Tribunites and each of the six hundred secretaries of constituency associations to drinks in Downing Street. Unlike Blair and Mandelson, who scoffed at union leaders – the little fat men bursting out of brown suits – Brown began actively to seek their friendship to rebuild his power base.

It was not long before the repercussions were felt. That summer Paisley South, a safe Labour seat, fell vacant when its MP Gordon McMaster died unexpectedly at the age of thirty-seven. Tony Blair nominated Pat McFadyen, a speechwriter and his liaison with the trade unions, as the candidate, but Brown deployed his new influence to defeat McFadyen and insert the young lawyer Douglas Alexander, his own speechwriter. The manoeuvre reinforced the Blairites' suspicions about the chancellor's ambitions for the premiership.

Unknown to them, at the end of July Brown was driving with Sarah Macaulay to Heathrow for his annual summer holiday in Cape Cod. In the car with them was Paul Routledge, a friendly journalist employed by the *Daily Mirror*, who was confirming some facts in the last interview for his biography of Brown, to be published in the autumn. In the moment of Labour's triumph, Brown wanted his version of history to be written. He particularly wanted it to be put on record that 1997 was not just Blair's victory but also his, after his masterminding of the reconstruction of the party. Blair's recent rapturous reception in New York, where he was hailed as the celebrity of a New Camelot, had riled Brown. Ever since the election the Blairites, especially Campbell and Mandelson, had been undermining himself and his supporters. 'Mandelson's poisoning the atmosphere,' Brown complained. With Whelan's encouragement he had sought to embarrass his former friend by mentioning an 'undisclosed' budget detail to Mandelson before his speech. This was a ruse intended to discomfort Mandelson after the phoney story was published in the *Sunday Times*, based upon his tip.

Gordon Brown was using Paul Routledge to give notice that his bid to become prime minister had not evaporated. In interviews, Tony Blair had always denied that there was ever a deal between him and Brown. 'There is no gentleman's agreement,' was his formulaic dismissal. Brown's plan was to accuse Blair of reneging on their deal at the Granita, a deliberate distortion. Speaking to Routledge earlier in the Treasury, Brown had portrayed himself as the victim of dishonourable actions by others: 'The newspapers, with a few notable exceptions, did not back me – not least because I was out of fashion. I was never part of the London scene anyway. But that did not in my view mean much once the campaign started among ordinary Labour Party members and indeed backbench MPs.' Routledge's interpretation was that Brown believed 'he could have beaten the political *beau monde*', and that 'Blair had repeatedly promised Brown he would not stand against him in a future leadership election'. To give the book substance, Brown had arranged for Routledge to interview all his family, his closest friends in Scotland and Westminster, and allowed him access to his personal archives. They had agreed that his elder brother John would check the manuscript.

Bidding farewell to Routledge at the airport, Brown and Macaulay flew to America. He was looking forward to the holiday with his two brothers and their families, shooting the breeze with the usual gang of friends, watching some films, playing tennis, reading a stack of books and trying to stop biting his nails.

SEVEN

Fevered Honeymoon

America inspired Brown. His impatience, even rudeness, familiar in London, disappeared. The jovial party host re-emerged, energetic and eager to discuss his ambition fundamentally to change British society. One hundred years earlier, William Gladstone had ended his monumental career and, unlike so many other politicians, remained a famous legend. Gordon Brown was, not dishonourably, seeking a similar legacy.

Talking with his American visitors Bob Shrum and the pollster Stanley Greenberg, and his usual English friends in the garden at Chatham's, the house in Cape Cod rented by his brothers, Brown announced, 'There's going to be the biggest change in the welfare state in fifty years.' The challenge was daunting. Too many healthy Britons, he complained, were receiving benefits. There were forty-three different social benefits, and too many people lacked hope. The annual cost of welfare in 1997 was £92.2 billion, nearly half the national budget. Tony Blair had pledged to freeze and even reduce that amount – a 'covenant' with the British people, he had said.

One model to transform the underprivileged and the work-shy into self-sufficient citizens was Bill Clinton's welfare programme. In his admiration for the American dream that everybody should have the opportunity to better themselves, Brown had dispatched special advisers to Wisconsin, a laboratory for Clinton's policies, to see welfare-to-work in operation. Their reports were encouraging, but he despaired about the quality of the civil servants tasked to implement his reforms, especially in the department of employment. 'They're useless,' he had exploded to Geoffrey Robinson and Frank Field. 'They'll never do the changes necessary.' His dissatisfaction focused on grey-suited, quietly-spoken civil servants. They were Londoners, they had served the Tories, and they were not clever. 'Why not get rid of all the Whitehall officials,' said an exasperated Brown, 'and hand the whole thing over to the private sector?' Field was puzzled. He knew the officials admired Brown's qualities and wanted to help him carry out his reforms. Encouraging senior civil servants to be proactive and to promote new policies required leadership. Inspiring strangers was not Brown's skill. Rather, he remained in his bunker, dispatching his pro-consuls to implement his rule.

To Brown's good fortune, over the previous weeks Geoffrey Robinson had smoothed the tensions. As a former manager of car workers he could energise subordinates, precisely the talent Brown lacked. With the gratitude of a younger brother, the chancellor had watched Robinson cheerfully encouraging the baffled officials to pursue his ideas. He was equally grateful that Robinson had recruited business leaders to endorse his welfare-to-work programme, including Ian McAllister, the chairman of Ford UK, Brian Moffat, the chairman of British Steel, Sir Richard Greenbury, the chairman of Marks & Spencers, George Bull, the chairman of Grand Metropolitan, George Simpson of Marconi, Allan Leighton of Asda and Terry Leahy of Tesco. Even Alan Sugar, the former sponsor of the Tories, had been recruited to travel around the country to encourage young people to become tomorrow's entrepreneurs.

Brown had not understood one reason for the officials' bewilderment. He had launched his reforms to introduce tax credits and change the welfare system without consulting Harriet Harman and others at the department of social security. By default, three different agendas – Brown's, Harman's and Field's – were competing for implementation.

Under Brown's plan, money would no longer be paid to claimants as 'benefits'. Instead, poorer families would be means tested and paid tax credits through their wage packets by the Inland Revenue. The attraction of this was that some tax credits would not be included in the national debt, unlike benefits, which were classed as expenditure. 'This is pure Orwellian Animal Farm,' his senior officials protested. 'This will lead to deadweight,' Nick MacPherson and Robert Culpin, the Treasury's tax experts, told the chancellor. 'John Major wanted to do the same, but realised that self-certification and relying on employers would encourage fraud.'

Brown's reaction was silence. Briefing papers from the DSS advised him that the same idea had been rejected in the 1970s because of cost and technical upheaval. Twenty years later, the problems would be compounded by the incompatibility of Whitehall's computers. The welfare system, Brown was told, would either collapse or become hugely expensive if it was extended to the highly paid. 'This requires massive reorganisation at breakneck speed,' he was told by a senior civil servant. 'The Benefit Agency needs to be restructured, taxation policies need to be re-engineered, and you are extending the power of Treasury.' Brown gazed at him. Clearly the Oxbridge-educated mandarin did not understand that that was precisely his objective. The Treasury was to rule Whitehall. 'You're going to suck the middle class into the benefits system,' explained Terry Burns at the end of a presentation of a mathematical model. 'The credit can't be effective and will be a disincentive for the poor to seek work.' Brown was dismissive. 'I don't think it will happen like that,' he told the group of officials. He had no intention of further discussion. They all failed to understand that his purpose was to use money as power.

The same misunderstanding affected Frank Field. Field had been charged by Tony Blair to 'think the unthinkable', but he had failed to grasp Brown's blueprint. At the first meeting of the cabinet's welfare-to-work sub-committee, Field condemned Brown's proposed plan as unworkable. Irritated, Brown abruptly terminated the discussion. Afterwards he confronted Field. 'How could you disagree with me?' he asked. 'I thought you were my friend.' 'It's just because I am your friend that I could disagree with you,' replied Field, puzzled by the furious chancellor. With a lifetime's experience of helping the poor, Field agreed with Brown's advocacy of self-reliance, but he believed that individuals should be compelled to contribute to their own pensions through insurance, without means testing. He was not aware of Brown's determination to reintroduce means testing, nor that the ultimate arbiter of change would be Brown, and not the prime minister. The support Field had anticipated from Blair was illusory, and Blair was unwilling to mediate between the two. Worse, Harriet Harman, sponsored by Brown and ostensibly Field's superior, supported the chancellor's preference for means tests and targeting. Four disagreements was not a good start to the reform of Britain's welfare system.

The differences between Frank Field and Harriet Harman were deep. After their appointment in May, they had not met for several weeks. Over the course of a year they would only speak twice privately without aides. Field was untroubled by this, as he had been given to understand that he would soon be replacing Harman. To accelerate that process, during the summer while Brown and Harman were on holiday, Field remained in London and told journalists, 'Civil servants are rolling their eyes about Harman. She's so thick.' Brown was uninterested in the personality clashes. Although Harman was part of his team, he felt little affinity with a London feminist who did not enjoy beer and football.

On his return from Cape Cod, Brown's concern was establishing his credentials as the iron chancellor. He sent a message to Harman that one benefit would have to be cut in the future – either for housing or single parents. Eager to obey, Harman chose to cut housing benefits. Her reward was Charlie Whelan's praise. 'Harriet's brilliant on TV,' he chortled at the Red Lion pub in Whitehall. 'You should see the focus stuff we've got on her.' Categorised as a Brownite, Harman was safe.

Blairites, by contrast, earned Brown's contempt. Brown and Blair were meeting and talking up to five times a day, either in person or on the telephone, agreeing their strategy without any witnesses or written records. Brown left the party's other heavyweights – Robin Cook, John Prescott and Jack Straw – in no doubt that they were excluded from the inner sanctum. He ostentatiously displayed his lack of interest in their contributions during cabinet meetings by reading papers or scribbling notes while they spoke. Blair confirmed the unusual nature of their relationship. 'Have you cleared this with Gordon?' he frequently asked his senior ministers.

John Prescott was easily squashed, albeit after a monumental argument, by Brown ordering a cut in the transport budget. Vital road schemes to relieve London's traffic congestion, especially the A40 to the west, were among the casualties, but the Scotsman was unconcerned. Peter Mandelson was another target. The minister without portfolio's attempts to concentrate power in Blair's office would be resisted by the Brownites, a stronger, more manipulative court. Brown's enmity towards Robin Cook had prompted the newly appointed foreign secretary to tell his permanent secretary soon after his arrival, 'I know that the foreign secretary must

Brown arrived at the Treasury in 1997 determined to remove Terry Burns, the permanent secretary (above), and Eddie George, the governor of the Bank of England (below).

Chris Smith (top), the minister of culture, had been undermined by Brown whil shadow health minister; Robin Cook (bottom), the foreign secretary, had fallen ou with Brown in the 1970s; Brown had tried desperately to prevent the appointmer of John Prescott (opposite, above) as the deputy leader; Nick Brown (opposite below), the chief whip, who as one of Brown's few friends could be relied upon t help destabilise Blair.

Increasingly, the chancellor relied on Sarah Macaulay to manage his domestic life, and on Ed Balls and his wife Yvette Cooper (left, after their marriage in Eastbourne) for economic advice.

work closely with the chancellor, but I want you to know that this foreign secretary has not spoken to the new chancellor for more than twenty years.' Cook tried to resist Brown, but was undermined by him. Whereas Brown had briefly visited Dorneywood and declared his lack of interest in the grand estate, Cook had enthusiastically embraced Chevening, the foreign minister's country house, and snatched all the other perks of his office. Vehemently, Cook protested at Brown's unilateral declaration that ministers should forgo a £16,000 pay increase. 'We're entitled to the money,' he told Blair. The prime minister aligned himself with the chancellor.

Brown felt no regret on hearing at the beginning of August of Cook's messy separation from his wife at Heathrow airport after the *News of the World* exposed the foreign secretary's affair with his secretary. Cook had been neutralised as a rival. With delight, Brown ordered him to produce a list of possible savings at the Foreign Office by selling embassies, reducing the number of diplomats and cutting down on entertaining. 'I want from all of you,' he told ministers, 'ideas of what to sell from the "national asset register".' He estimated that the state owned land and buildings worth £200 billion, and wanted sales, he said, in order to pay for hospitals. Posing as the champion against extravagance and status-seekers, he even wanted savings from Jack Straw, the home secretary and an emerging rival. On one occasion Brown became upset on hearing that Blair was taking Straw to the United States. Storming into Blair's office, he insisted, 'You've got to take me to America, not Jack.' 'I'm taking Jack,' replied the prime minister. 'No, me,' shouted Brown, slamming the door. An hour later he returned to Blair's office, again demanding that he rather than Straw accompany him to America. By nightfall a whole day's work had been lost. Unusually, on this occasion the chancellor was defeated, and a new grudge established.

Reports of Brown's churlishness had circulated among the

delegates as they gathered in September for the party conference in Brighton. Some were upset by the increased petrol
taxes and higher mortgage rates. Others had witnessed
Brown's strange insistence that he speak before the veteran
former minister Barbara Castle at a Tribune rally. Castle, they
gossiped in the bars afterwards, had won the duel, staging
her entrance to win huge applause.

Nevertheless, Brown expected that, as the first Labour
chancellor for nineteen years, his speech to the conference
would receive rapturous acclaim. Diligently he hammered out
on his laptop a Kennedyesque appeal for equality and the
redistribution of power to the people. His soundbites, honed
by Douglas Alexander, were heartfelt: 'We govern and we
seek to serve as a new political generation . . . No more barriers
of privilege dividing us, but a society where opportunity is
open to all . . . We are the people's party. Now delivering the
people's priorities. As once more the people's government.'
Disappointingly, there was no standing ovation. Brown
blamed his stern warning to the conference that he would
not tolerate irresponsible wage demands and would keep a
stranglehold on spending. But others knew that the conference's true hero was Blair, the miracle-worker. The simple
fact that Blair's popularity – even among a majority of Tories
– had soared in the opinion polls to unprecedented levels was
reason enough for Brown publicly to assert his superiority.

Real power in Whitehall was Brown's consolation. On his
premature return to London from Brighton, he did not review
the implementation of his socialist vision. Considering his
ambition, his indifference was curious. He dictated the objective, but delegated the detail to others. If Brown was lazy,
that nonchalance would have been understandable, but for
such a diligent politician the inattention to the execution of
fundamental changes in spending and savings was unusual.
Brown's comfort was his reliance on Geoffrey Robinson.

During the first four months in government Robinson had proved his value, especially by driving through the Public Finance Initiative (PFI), an unorthodox method of financing the construction of schools, hospitals, prisons and roads. Devised by Norman Lamont ten years earlier, PFI's attraction was the transfer of the risk of overspending and late completion of state building contracts from the Treasury to private contractors. Before 1997, Gordon Brown had loudly criticised Lamont's scheme as a cynical distortion of the public accounts. The Tories, he asserted, were seeking short-term gain at the cost of long-term pain, although few PFI schemes had actually been approved by the Conservatives. Civil servants objected to the accumulation of vast debt, and Ross Goobey, responsible for the scheme, was concerned by inadequate accounting controls. Once in office, Brown abandoned both criticism and caution. He wanted schools and hospitals built immediately, without increasing taxes. The beauty of PFI, just like the tax credits, was that they excluded new debt from the government's balance sheet. Billions of pounds of debt could be concealed. In November 1995 the Conservatives had promised to build a new PFI hospital every month. In June 1997 Frank Dobson promised the same, except that Brown promised the new buildings at no cost. The detailed mathematical calculations of profit and loss were to be ignored.

Five days after Labour's election victory Steve Robson, a senior Treasury official responsible for the privatisation of the railways, was persuaded by Robinson to mastermind the redesign of PFI. Robson's first task was to telephone Ross Goobey. 'Robinson wants you to resign,' said Robson. 'Why should I resign?' replied Goobey. 'If they want me to go, they'll have to fire me.' Next morning, Robinson called him: 'We thought you would like to resign.' 'Since until this moment,' answered Goobey, 'we have neither met nor spoken, how could you possibly know that? If you want me to go, you'll have to fire me.' 'I was pleased to oblige,' wrote Robinson in his memoirs. The next day's draft press release announced Goobey's resignation. His successor, Adrian Montagu of Dresdner Kleinwort Benson, was given a two-year contract at £160,000 p.a., more than Robin Butler, the cabinet secretary. Montagu would meet Brown only twice after his appointment. The chancellor, he discovered, deliberately disconnected high policy from its implementation. Selling PFI to the trade unions was more important than mastering the details of the contracts.

Presentation of government successes depended on favourable official statistics. Brown was mindful of Nigel Lawson's complaint that 'official economic statistics were seriously unreliable', causing major mistakes in his management of the economy. The changes to the government's statistical service since 1989 were unimpressive. Tim Holt, the director of the Office of National Statistics (ONS) since 1995, had made life difficult for Ken Clarke. At their monthly meetings, Clarke had been briefed about developments to improve the collection and analysis of statistics. There were arguments over Holt's refusal to agree to changes which would improve the government's image, but nevertheless in opposition Labour had protested about nineteen alterations to the measure of Britain's unemployment statistics. Holt justified them as 'modernisation', earning Brown's scorn.

Four weeks after the election, Holt was invited to Brown's office. While Holt spoke, Brown performed his disengaged act. He regarded the former academic as mousy, not suitable for the job and clearly mystified by government. The Treasury's forecasts, complained Brown, were also woeful. In his opinion the ONS was responsible for avoidable blunders. After twenty minutes Holt was shown the door. They never met again. Brown distrusted the ONS's reliability, and was determined to remove its director. Responsibility for statistics was delegated to a succession of junior ministers. Holt found each of them antagonistic. Their dissatisfaction, he believed, was not based on questioning the mathematical process, but on seeking political advantage by challenging the integrity of the statistical service. The government, he suspected, wanted either to privatise the service or to use figures provided by more compliant Treasury statisticians.

Despite his previous complaints about Tory manipulation of statistics, Brown wanted changes to improve the image of his performance. His expectations became apparent during the preparation of the economic statement due in November. On Brown's instructions, the public would be given less information about taxation since 1993, and some tables showing the Treasury's spending would be removed. In their place Brown would use the Treasury's analysis to damn both the Tory legacy and the Treasury officials themselves for their over-optimistic forecasts for the public finances in the mid-1980s, which had supposedly led to a huge deficit. Simultaneously, he ordered that the strong growth of the economy should be concealed to avoid giving the Tories any credit. The resulting picture would assist his arguments with Labour MPs about his freeze on spending.

Social security was his principal target for the freeze. The department was due to exceed its annual £90 billion budget by a small amount. For a chancellor to demand savings was normal, but neither Harriet Harman nor Frank Field realised that Brown was not simply scrutinising expenditure but, with the help of policy units for education, health, transport and social security similar to the prime minister's Cabinet Office, was intent on dictating a fundamental change of culture from the Treasury.

In social security, Brown relied on Richard Layard's research programme to reduce welfare dependency. His goal was 'to turn Britain into a nation of victors over adversity rather than victims trapped on benefit'. The Tories, he claimed, had rewarded people for maximising 'the extent of their illness, their disability, their poverty and their dependence on others'. Brown wanted to reward them for working, and to tackle the causes of poverty. He ignored Layard's warning that there were many unresolved problems, including an absence of any cost-benefit analysis. 'Just stick to a few major objectives,' Brown was advised by a senior official. Brown also ignored the warning that the Inland Revenue's new computer systems needed to pay the benefits would cost over £1 billion. The redistribution of the nation's wealth, his unannounced masterplan, would not be stalled by such considerations. He took comfort from the assurance of his senior tax official that tax credits would affect 'few' people compared to income tax – five million as opposed to twenty-two million. A greater problem, said the official, was the loss of revenue on tobacco.

Brown promoted Nicholas MacPherson, his principal private secretary, to the magic circle as 'head of work incentives policy' to implement his plans. MacPherson was ordered to oversee the conversion of family credits into the working families' tax credit (WFTC), to replace the disability working allowance with the disabled persons' tax credit (DPTC), and to introduce the childcare tax credit and the employment credit. Simplicity was abandoned.

Under Brown's plan, responsibility for paying all of these benefits would be transferred from the department of social security to the Inland Revenue. Just to administer the new childcare tax credits, the Inland Revenue would become responsible for paying benefits to 5.75 million families. Brown was warned that the Revenue, inevitably inundated by questions from those newly embraced by his system, would not be able to cope with merging tax and benefits. While most people fulfilled their responsibilities towards their families, some refused, and the Revenue, geared to collect individuals' taxation, would be incapable of supervising the payment of benefits to a whole family. He was also told that the Inland Revenue's involvement would deter claimants. The basic statistic illustrated the problem. Four million people were receiving one benefit, but only 24 per cent of them paid income tax. Brown replied that the government would save on the cost of administration by charging employers to undertake the calculations.

Any advice which contradicted his own opinion was rejected. Finally he was reminded of his own commitment to 'a more open and transparent approach to economic policy'. The Treasury's statistics showed that, contrary to his pledges that welfare costs would fall, they would in fact substantially increase. Again, that advice was ignored. The complications of reporting tax credits in the government's accounts, Brown believed, would prevent critics from discovering their real cost. His confidence was boosted by his conviction that he was reproducing Bill Clinton's successful scheme. One flaw was spotted by experts in the department of social security. In America, welfare benefits are mostly paid to disenfranchised blacks, while in Britain the majority of recipients are whites, especially the elderly. Interfering with welfare payments in America was politically safe. That was not the case in Britain.

Tax credits alarmed Tony Blair's advisers. Carey Oppenheim, a civil service expert, composed a well-written, damning indictment of Brown's plan. The cost, she warned, would be enormous, and the complications insoluble. Blair was urged by Derek Scott to confront Brown. He was given a detailed brief, and after bitter haggling a meeting was arranged. 'The prime minister was reluctant to engage the chancellor,' the official notes of the encounter reported. Blair was either uninterested or intimidated. Without his intervention, Harriet Harman was helpless. The chancellor's docile protégée could not protest about the revolution. By contrast, Frank Field sought to influence Brown, and an 8 a.m. meeting was arranged in the Treasury. The chancellor was late as usual, because he had arranged another meeting before the 'first' official engagement. Even as a minister, Brown's concept of time was hazy and his diary unreliable. His assistants regularly apologised on his behalf, and on his eventual arrival he would courteously repeat the apology, extending the conversation and thus compounding his unpunctuality for the remainder of the day.

The disagreement between Brown and Field concerned the new Winter Fuel Allowance for pensioners. 'No one told me!' screamed Brown about the expense of the system, which he had approved. 'You were told, Gordon,' protested Field, 'but it's difficult to argue with you if you're shouting. Even the civil servants just give up and walk out.' Brown was shocked. Treasury officials, he knew, had complained that while he possessed a 'good brain', he became overwhelmed if he had to deal with more than one subject at a time. In their opinion, his mixture of arrogance and inflexibility converted every disagreement into a personal insult. 'Tell me about these books,' soothed Field, pointing at a huge pile stacked at the end of the chancellor's desk. 'You've got some lovely paintings too,' he added. 'I've never looked at them,' replied Brown unconvincingly.

At their next meeting Field protested about Brown's reduction of family allowances and his plans to deny women their right to separate taxation. 'Your policy is anti-family,' he said. 'What's happening to our commitment to the family?' Brown did not reply. He hated confrontations. Disputes were best delegated to officials, so he could be sure of winning.

Field made a third attempt to influence Brown in the cabinet committee on welfare reform, chaired by Blair. To protect himself, Brown was flanked by Ed Balls and Ed Milliband. Their presence, Field knew, was intended to intimidate Brown's opponents. Rather than stay in the background, both advisers personally rebutted Field's criticisms. At Field's request, Blair asked Brown to stop them participating in a ministers' meeting. Brown agreed, but insisted that Balls continue to sit next to him. At the next meeting, Field again criticised Brown's plans. Brown refused to speak until Balls had given his advice in a loud whisper.

Brown planned to scrap the £11 per week benefit for single mothers. 'We've got a million lone parents on benefit,' he said, 'and everybody knows a change has to be made.' To avoid a confrontation, he delegated Alistair Darling to summon Harriet Harman and inform her of the cut. Harman was appalled. Before the election she had publicly pledged to restore the benefit cut announced by the Tories. To protect her reputation, she arranged to meet Brown. The chancellor who occasionally spent £75 for a haircut at Michaeljohn in Mayfair was merciless. Denying her a chance to make use of the brief prepared by her officials, she was given a curt order to obey. 'The chancellor has behaved unreasonably,' Harman was consoled by Chris Kelly, her senior civil servant. Her choice was either to resign or to carry out a complete somersault. Despite her label as a Brownite, her relationship with Brown was tenuous, and she lacked support from other party members. She chose to keep her job and obey Brown's order to find 'substantial savings from sick and disability benefits' to pay for health and education. In mid-November Ken Livingstone confirmed that a hundred Labour MPs threatened to vote against the government if the cut in lone parents' benefit was made. 'There's no loose change,' retorted Brown. 'Too many are fearful of change.'

Among the many urging Brown to reconsider was John Monks, the general secretary of the TUC. The delegation of trade union leaders who came to the Treasury were eager to be wooed, but their conversation in the chancellor's office was discomforting. Their tough talking made no impression.

'We thought it was a tactic, not an orthodoxy,' rued one
unionist, realising his misjudgement of Brown's zeal against
tax-and-spend. Brown responded with 'an air of menace
about him'. He enjoyed repeating, 'Compare the *Guardian* job
ads with the *Sunday Times*'s. There'll be 500,000 extra public
sector jobs over the next five years, but not right now.' Outside the Treasury in Whitehall, Monks consoled himself that
even if Brown was over-impressed by American capitalism,
at least the Tories were gone. 'He's not worried about making
enemies,' he reported to his staff. To deflect criticism, Brown
appeared to be spurring Charlie Whelan on to undermine the
fractious Field and Harman. In Westminster's bars Whelan
briefed journalists that Harman was losing both her grip and
the confidence of her colleagues. Field, sniped Whelan, was
also losing favour. 'Charlie Whelan's doing me a great deal
of damage,' Field confided to his friends.

Whelan was enjoying life. Empowered by the chancellor to
promote the alternative government in Downing Street, the
Treasury's official spokesman joyfully combined drinking
pints and flaying his master's enemies. Mandelson was a frequent target of his mischief, but more succulent still was the
prime minister. 'Blair's lightweight,' chuckled Whelan, tipping more ale down his throat. 'He's not real Labour. Gordon's
doing all the real work'; and, 'Blair doesn't understand anything about economics'; and, 'Gordon has all the power because
Tony's so useless,' followed by the stricture, 'And you didn't
get that from me.' Journalists who failed to oblige received a
late-night call jovially threatening, 'I'll break your legs.' Those
journalists labelled as 'the enemy' fared worse. Paul Eastham
of the *Daily Mail* believed he was being deliberately targeted
with planted stories in order to humiliate him. 'You're blacked,'
said Whelan to another who was perceived as unhelpful. He
showed no remorse about his methods. 'If you're not hard,'
he explained, 'you're going to get walked over.'

Whelan's carping about Blair's 'uselessness' outraged the prime minister and Alastair Campbell. Brown ignored their criticisms of his spokesman, even after Whelan wrongly predicted interest rate cuts, which were no longer under the control of the Treasury, at an IMF meeting in Washington. To sustain himself, Brown needed adoring sycophants who knew that a single criticism would spell ostracism, and none was more loyal than Charlie Whelan. Consequently, there was nothing unusual in the sight of Whelan clutching a glass of Guinness at the bar of the Red Lion in Whitehall on the evening of 17 October 1997. That week he was tipping journalists about Britain's position regarding the euro, a critical government policy.

Before the election, Brown had been inclined to support Britain adopting the euro. His enthusiasms always increased if Robin Cook supported the opposite argument. 'If the conditions are right,' Brown said, Britain would join the new currency's first stage in 1999. In Europe he had been fêted for his promise to deliver Britain into the club. Although the Labour manifesto mentioned 'formidable obstacles' to membership, many were convinced that Brown's endorsement was irrevocable. In early summer 1997 he mentioned his support for a debate about the euro, and dismissed pessimism about it as 'overdone'. Blair was confident that the Treasury would support him in his enthusiasm to abandon sterling at the first opportunity. He was mistaken. Many in the Treasury were sceptical about the merits of joining the euro-zone, and, more important, Ed Balls was a steadfast opponent.

Encouraged by Balls, Brown began privately to express his doubts about joining the euro before the next election, which would probably be held in 2001. The euro, he realised, would not guarantee growth, and the referendum Blair had promised would be a distraction. He had always been irritated by Blair's agreement to a referendum, and he would derive pleasure from preventing the prime minister from taking this historic decision. Nevertheless, some of his officials, including Nigel Wicks, and others in Blair's office, hoped Brown could be persuaded to return to the fold. Wicks telephoned an official at the CBI to deny the appearance of confusion. 'Don't rule out entry in 1999,' he said. 'We haven't closed our minds to this. We may still want to join.' He would later say that he had been pressing for a delay. Others briefed Robert Peston, a respected journalist at the *Financial Times*, that the government was considering joining the euro before 2000, in the national interest. Brown, it was suggested, ardently approved entry. Peston reported this on 27 September 1997, and the pound fell as dealers anticipated devaluation. 'Lies and bollocks!' shouted Whelan, confusing everyone, not least when he whispered in the Red Lion that Brown himself was trying to pull the sceptical Blair into early membership of the euro.

By early October 1997, the contradictory voices were causing mayhem. The value of the pound and of shares gyrated wildly. Peter Mandelson, a pro-European, said he was 'flabbergasted' by Brown's somersault, and insisted that there was a consensus in favour of joining the euro. Brown was irritated that he was not in complete control. Doug Henderson, a Brownite junior Foreign Office minister, murmured that Brown was pushing Blair into deciding to join. Eddie George's suspicions of Brown and Balls were reinforced.

Brown's tactics during the second week of October reflected his bid to recover control. Whelan was ordered to convey the chancellor's anger with newspapers that had suggested there was a disagreement between himself and Blair. Thereafter, Brown repeatedly walked into Blair's office and argued about the euro. Brown, his officials agreed, was enthusiastic to join, but was not in a rush after having received a Treasury review highlighting dangerous disparities between the British and

European economies. To neutralise Blair's enthusiasm, Brown told him that joining the euro was 'not an imminent issue'. The confusion was complete.

Tony Blair, Gordon Brown, Robin Cook, Peter Mandelson, Alastair Campbell, Ed Balls and Charlie Whelan successively met in groups with officials to discuss the euro policy and its presentation. The ministers were unanimous only in disagreeing. Since doing nothing barely suited the dynamic image of the new government, Brown and Whelan decided that a definitive policy statement in *The Times* would extinguish the uncertainty. On Thursday, 16 October 1997, Philip Webster, a trusted conduit of Brown's thoughts, was contacted. Brown had agreed a statement, Webster was told. In composing that statement, his difficulty had been his unwillingness to utter the simple truth which firmly ruled out joining the euro. He preferred to use convoluted phrases suggesting that he had almost decided against membership but that the options remained open, and to rely on Whelan to smooth out any uncertainties in his favour. After receiving the statement, Webster called Whelan for an explanation. Whelan was more truthful. As the *Times* headline would accurately state, 'Brown Rules Out Single Currency for Lifetime of this Parliament'. Whelan gave the same message to Stuart Higgins, the editor of the *Sun*. 'Brown Saves the Pound' would be the tabloid's headline. The spokesman then crossed Whitehall to the Red Lion.

In the early evening, other newspapers began telephoning Whelan to confirm Brown's veto. After the first few calls he might have wondered whether it was advisable to call Brown or even Alastair Campbell, but instead he answered the journalists' questions in a loud voice. As dusk was turning into night, he grimaced as his telephone rang again. This time the caller was Tony Blair. Prompted by Mandelson's fury at the newspaper reports, the prime minister was trying to get to

the bottom of the chaos. What exactly, he asked, had Brown
said was his government's policy?

Moving from the bar into a quiet side street, Whelan
explained that joining the euro had been ruled out for the
life of the parliament. Blair was puzzled. He and Brown had
agreed that for the time being the best policy was to put off any
final decision.Whelan's honesty would cost the government
credibility. Blair's courtiers were encouraging the notion that
the confusion had been deliberately manufactured by Brown
to delay entry until he was the prime minister. As usual, said
Brown's critics, he had struck by stealth rather than mount-
ing an open challenge. Unfortunately for the government,
Whelan's telephone conversations that evening were over-
heard by Robert Blevin, a Liberal Democrat press officer. Blevin was naturally excited to hear Whelan saying that Brown
had excluded membership during that parliament, at the same
time that the Treasury's civil servants were insisting that
Brown was keeping his options open. He delighted in
revealing to the world that the prime minister had had to
resort to Cheerful Charlie's barside briefing to find out his
own government's policy.

Flying down from Scotland, Brown well understood the
cause of the shambles, the ridicule in the media and the fury
of other ministers. He was shaken. He knew that he and
Whelan had botched a delicate manoeuvre. Saving face would
best be achieved by twisting the argument. He would, he
agreed with Whelan, claim the high ground by attacking the
Tories for *their* indecision. The audacity was breathtaking, but
the unusually prolonged post-election honeymoon gave him
some licence. 'We are not going to make the same mistakes
the Conservatives made over the ERM,' Brown told a television crew summoned to his flat, 'where indecisiveness
caused speculation and damaged the national interest.' He
would not be 'bounced' by the Tories, he declared, into

making an early statement about the euro. Whelan reassured Brown that his sophistry was successful. 'Tell the press that Blair overruled the pro-euro Brown for political reasons,' was the chancellor's final instruction to his spokesman.

The following morning, Monday, 20 October 1997, was the tenth anniversary of 'Black Monday', a mammoth stock market crash. Inconveniently, Brown was fulfilling a pre-arranged invitation to switch on the stock exchange's new computerised dealing system. He pushed the button with trepidation. All the illuminated share prices behind him showed red, representing £10 billion wiped off the value of London's market. 'Brown Monday' was the gleeful headline heralding a chaotic week.

The chancellor returned to the Treasury to begin an intensive operation to repair his credibility. Surviving a crisis was the mark of a skilled politician. He needed to demolish his enemies. His real foes were not the pro-Europeans like Roy Hattersley who complained that popular prejudice rather than economic logic was dictating government policy. Hattersley's hyperbolical claim that Britain was at 'an economic crossroad' which would 'determine our political influence and standard of living for the foreseeable future' could be ignored. The Tories, feeble and divided, were also irrelevant. The real foes were Blair's courtiers, the rivals to Brown's power base. He relied during continuous meetings on Alan Budd, Nigel Wicks and Ed Balls. Together they devised five economic tests to determine whether joining the euro would be beneficial to the British economy.

Brown's own test would be his statement to the Commons on 27 October. The country would see that the decision on the euro would be taken by Brown, rather than Blair. In a battle for power with Blair, Brown threatened to resign if he could not make the announcement to Parliament that Britain was delaying its membership of the euro. Blair surrendered, and even failed during the days before the speech to influence Brown's statement. The chancellor rejected any suggestion of a public apology. Pacing up and down his room, advised by Balls, Whelan and Colin Currie, specially summoned from Edinburgh, he crafted a wily speech. Whelan could be relied upon to target sympathetic journalists to spread his message.

Over the years, Brown had perfected the routine. Whenever there was a clash between himself and the Blairites he would seclude himself from journalists and others, protesting that a 'team player' would not demean himself by discussing 'tittle-tattle'. Policy, he preached, was his exclusive concern with the prime minister. While he maintained that piety, his cohorts, especially Nigel Griffiths, Andrew Smith and Nick Brown, spread gossip to the detriment of Mandelson and Campbell. One anecdote describing Blair snubbing Mandelson was particularly relished. By the time the speech was prepared, Brown was content from his cabal's reports that the waters had been suitably stirred.

He rose that afternoon in the House of Commons to deliver a pledge to join the euro, but not yet; and a promise to support a single European state, but not at Britain's expense. To give credibility to his equivocation, he revealed that the final decision on joining the euro would depend on the five economic tests. Initially drafted, according to lampooners, on the back of an envelope while Brown was travelling with Balls in the back of a taxi in New York, the tests would have to be met in a 'clear and unambiguous way'. Seemingly objective, each in fact depended upon personal prejudice rather than economic judgements. Pledged to transparency and honesty, Brown had proved his mastery of obfuscation. While the Conservatives continued their internecine feud over Europe, he had defused the issue for his own party until 'early in the next parliament'. His relief was tempered. He had contained the embarrassment, but had not understood the principal cause of the turmoil – namely, his unwavering loyalty to his acolytes. He resented any criticism of Whelan, and disliked new questions that were being asked about Geoffrey Robinson.

Chris Blackhurst, a respected journalist on the *Independent on Sunday*, had discovered that Robinson's shares in his engineering company TransTec were held by Orion, a secret trust registered in Guernsey. Despite his appointment as a Treasury minister, Robinson had continued to advise the offshore trustees about share transactions, financed partly by the money he had secretly transferred from Switzerland. Blackhurst telephoned Charlie Whelan for a comment on Friday, 28 November 1997. His discoveries were embarrassing for Brown. At the 1996 party conference he had pledged ruthless measures against the rich who used foreign tax havens. 'A Labour chancellor,' he had said, 'will not permit tax relief to millionaires in offshore tax havens.' He had been echoing Tony Blair's assertion that 'We should not make our tax rules a playground for revenue avoiders and tax abusers who pay little or nothing, while others pay more than their fair share.'

Brown was nonplussed by the revelations, and asked Robinson for an explanation. The trust, replied the paymaster general, had been established without his knowledge by Joska Bourgeois for the benefit of his family, and there was no reason for him to discontinue a perfectly legal arrangement. Brown was grateful for the assurance. Considering the generous hospitality and expensive research, worth hundreds of thousands of pounds in total, he had received from Robinson, he was unwilling to confront him. Robinson knew too many secrets. But if Brown had been objective, he should have reproached himself for accepting Robinson's money without totally satisfying himself about its provenance. For the chancellor who had mouthed 'Tory sleaze' countless times to have accepted champagne, lobsters and accommodation financed by a secret tax haven was more than ironic. Any self-criticism, however, would be damaging. Less than three weeks earlier he had been scarred by an allegation of dishonesty.

On 9 November 1997 the *Sunday Telegraph* had revealed that in January of that year Bernie Ecclestone, the owner of Formula One racing, had made an undisclosed donation of £1 million to the Labour Party. Unknown to the newspaper, Ecclestone had met Tony Blair in Downing Street on 16 October 1997, with no civil servants present, to seek an undertaking that Formula One would be exempt from a proposed new law banning tobacco sponsorship of sport. He had also offered another £1 million donation. Blair tentatively accepted the money, and discussed the required changes in the proposed legislation. That meeting remained a secret, but, aware of the appalling truth, Downing Street had been alarmed by the newspaper's unfocused enquiries during the first week of November. A prime minister agreeing to change a law in return for money was a more damaging example of sleaze than Mohamed Fayed's payments to backbench Tory MPs for asking questions in the House of Commons.

Gordon Brown had been consulted by Blair about the potential disaster soon after the *Sunday Telegraph* story broke. He had agreed with Blair to pose a seemingly innocent question to Sir Patrick Neill, the chairman of the commission on standards in public life. The ruse, partly designed by Brown, would cast the politicians as honest brokers. Neill was asked for guidance on whether the party could accept a second unquantified donation from an existing donor. He was told neither the phenomenal size of the donations, nor that the prime minister had already effectively accepted the second donation and had agreed to change the law. In reply to an unexpected question on BBC Radio 4's *Today* programme after the sham was exposed, Brown would bluster, 'You'll have to wait and see, like I'll have to wait and see when the list [of

donors] is published . . . Because I've not been told, and I
certainly don't know what the true position is.'

The Ecclestone saga reinforced Brown's determination
never to be embarrassed by another newspaper revelation.
Avoiding a scandal over Geoffrey Robinson was vital. On the
night of Friday, 28 November 1997, while Robinson sat drinking champagne, the chancellor typed a statement for the
media in an attempt to save his benefactor. Robinson was
insisting that, as required by the rules, he had declared the
details of Orion, the secret trust, to Terry Burns, the Treasury's
permanent secretary; and further, that both its creation and
the trustees' transactions were beyond his control. Tellingly,
Brown did not probe Robinson's explanations. The scourge
of 'fat cats' and the City's vested interests was willing to be
convinced by Robinson's performance. He preferred not to
know that Orion was merely the tip of an iceberg of concealment. Together, the two men planned their salvation. The
critical success, Brown told Robinson, would be to gain Terry
Burns's acceptance that the offshore trust had been properly
declared after Robinson's appointment as paymaster general
in May 1997, and that the money had been deposited in a
blind trust to avoid any conflicts of interest. Burns's instant
reaction, however, dented their optimism. The punctilious
permanent secretary had recorded in a small notebook a contemporaneous note of Robinson's declaration in May. 'I don't
remember you mentioning an offshore trust,' he said. Robinson, said Burns, checking his notes, had specifically mentioned a 'family trust'. This unwelcome news was ignored by
Brown. By Saturday morning the press statement typed by
the chancellor included the phrase, 'I also told the permanent
secretary about the family offshore trust and he told me it
would not be necessary to include that in the blind trust.'
This implied that Burns had 'approved' Robinson's blind trust,
which explicitly included Orion, the offshore trust.

Having completed the text, Robinson telephoned Burns: 'We just need your agreement for its release.' 'I've got two problems with that statement,' replied Burns. 'It was never my job – nor is it now – to approve your offshore trust; and I have no recollection of you mentioning it.' The regulations concerning a minister's disclosure on appointment required officials, if consulted, only to give advice. Brown and Robinson appeared unable to grasp the awkward truth that permanent secretaries were not policemen, there to give 'approval' to ministers' financial arrangements or to pass official judgement on them.

Burns's refusal to help angered Brown. To meet the newspapers' deadline, he returned to his computer. 'Mr Robinson is quite clear,' he typed in his new version, 'that he has acted correctly in the performance of his ministerial duties and in registering his interests, and the permanent secretary is as well.' Contacted while watching a football match to give his approval to the new version, Burns was emphatic: 'I'm not going to be associated with that release. That's impossible.' 'You must say that you approved my arrangements,' urged Robinson. 'I can't,' replied Burns, 'because to the best of my knowledge you didn't say anything about an offshore trust.' Robinson was persistent. 'What have you got against me? Why won't you do this?' Charitably, Burns would later say to friends, 'I wasn't being asked to outrightly lie, but I was being asked to say something which I didn't believe to be true.' Brown's statement was released to the papers by Whelan without the phrase referring to Burns's approval. 'Are you saying that I am not fit to be a minister?' Robinson later asked Burns in desperation. Their conversation ended in an atmosphere of mutual suspicion. Burns, in Brown and Robinson's opinion, had confirmed himself as an enemy. Brown and Balls believed Robinson's version of events. To protect their own reputations, the only other alternative was Robinson's resignation, and that was unacceptable.

The reaction in Westminster on Monday, 1 December 1997 was sympathetic to Robinson. Influenced by the endorsement of Gordon Brown, most Labour MPs voiced a shared opinion: 'Lucky bloke. If he inherited millions by shagging a rich old woman, he was cleverer than most.' Tory cries of hypocrisy aroused their contempt. 'I'm just an ordinary guy. Why should anyone take an interest in me?' Robinson asked Peter Mandelson, relieved that he had escaped censure. Brown was less pleased by the press's depiction of Robinson as 'possibly the richest Labour MP ever', with 'money coming out of his ears', and as the source of his own finance. Robinson's loyalty and money, though, smothered his doubts. The following day, his sponsor's true qualities began to emerge.

Gordon Brown delighted in repetitively announcing his masterplan for a 'prudent' economy and a fair society. He enjoyed hammering out the speeches, fine-tuning the soundbites and stepping into the spotlight among the power brokers to repeat his message. He disliked micro-managing the specifics. Implementing his plans on taxes, savings and benefits required tiresome committees with pernickety officials. Not only was mastering the data exhausting, but he risked humiliation if he revealed any ignorance. That nearly occurred soon after his arrival in the Treasury. He had been asked by a senior official, 'What is your strategy for tax?' He was baffled. He could offer neither principles nor ideas, other than slogans about incentives and helping the unemployed and the poor. He was among officials who had spent their professional careers determining the intricacies of economic policy. Rather than face embarrassment, he ordered that Ed Balls, Alistair Darling and the others took care of those chores. The reform of savings had been assigned to Geoffrey Robinson.

Robinson's policy was to limit the tax advantages for savings. He wanted to abolish PEPs, a popular savings plan which

had attracted £70 billion. Before the election, Tony Blair and
Alistair Darling had pledged that PEPs would not be abolished,
but that promise was now deemed irrelevant. In America,
said Balls, PEPs had been successfully terminated. Balls and
Brown were apparently unaware of the sharp differences
between the savings culture in America and Britain. Both
were propelled by a visceral dislike of the middle classes in
southern England benefiting from tax incentives on their savings. If the level of savings fell, both believed, only the rich
would suffer. Their proposed replacement was Individual
Savings Accounts (ISAs), with a top limit of £50,000 compared
to PEPs, which had no upper limit. ISAs, under the plan
approved by Brown, were designed especially to encourage
the poor to save. The inconsistency of appealing to the poor
– who by definition had no money – to save while limiting
the amount the middle classes could invest on the stock
market was outlined to Brown by his senior officials. The
relationship between investment, savings and the balance of
payments, he was told, would be disturbed, undermining
mortgages, pensions and other savings plans. Combined with
the annual loss of £5 billion for pensions, the stock market
would be hit. That was all ignored, and the officials, having
fulfilled their duty, did not repeat their advice.

Derek Scott in Tony Blair's office heard about the impasse.
Reducing savings, he believed, was unhealthy for the economy. He urged Blair to intervene. Before the prime minister
could be galvanised once again to confront the chancellor,
Robinson was scheduled to unveil the flagship policy. Unfortunately, the public launch coincided with the newspapers'
exposure of his secret tax haven.

Like a fugitive, Robinson was smuggled by Whelan into the
Queen Elizabeth II Conference Centre near parliament. Under
any circumstances, Robinson's task that morning was difficult.
ISAs were ill-conceived, and he had failed to master his brief.

He was also under pressure to explain the incongruity of limiting legitimate savings by the middle classes while he himself enjoyed the benefits of a secret tax haven. Robinson had never wanted to rebut the accusations of hypocrisy and dishonesty publicly, but Gordon Brown resisted his plea to withdraw from the presentation of ISAs to journalists. Robinson's fears proved justified. Unable to answer the technical questions about ISAs, he imploded and abruptly fled. The embarrassment was bewildering. 'Are you sure there's nothing more to reveal?' the paymaster general was asked by Brown's aides. Readily, he gave the reassurance. There was no reason for his resignation. On Friday, 5 December 1997, Brown agreed that Robinson should say nothing more, and that he would be safe. The worst, he assumed, was over.

That afternoon, Brown telephoned Terry Burns from New York. He could not contain his anger towards the Treasury's senior official. By then, Brown must have been aware that Robinson was lying about his declaration of financial interests. He had never told Brown about his secret trust, and the Treasury's written records revealed the same concealment towards Burns. Yet Brown directed his anger towards Burns, an honest man, rather than Robinson. 'What's he done wrong?' Brown asked. 'What more could he have done?' He was angry that Burns would not endorse Robinson's story. 'I refuse to be involved,' replied Burns. That honest independence was unacceptable to Brown. He was outraged when Burns stipulated that Robinson should be barred from working on a new Capital Gains Tax to avoid a conflict of interest. 'I won't have Geoffrey's involvement in Treasury work limited,' Brown retorted frostily. But Burns obtained the approval of Tony Blair. The civil service had struck its first blow against Robinson, a minister whom they no longer trusted.

In that weekend's newspapers there were more revelations about Robinson's murky business activities. Labour sleaze

became an issue. Mohamed Sarwar, the member for Glasgow
Govan, had been charged with electoral fraud; Robert Ware-
ing, MP for Liverpool West Derby, had been suspended from
the Commons for a week for failing to register a directorship,
a shareholding and a £6,000 retainer; and Lord Simon, a minister of state at the Treasury, was criticised for retaining BP
shares worth £2 million after his appointment to the government. Even Ken Livingstone had failed to register his considerable earnings from speeches, and his private company
had failed to submit its accounts to the Registrar of Companies
in time. Tony Blair's pledge that Labour would be 'purer than
pure' required restoration.

On Sunday, 7 December, Geoffrey Robinson rejected
Brown's advice to 'keep quiet'. He threatened writs for libel
against critical newspapers and insisted that his two beneficiaries, Blair and Brown, issue endorsements of his probity.
Neither could refuse. 'Geoffrey Robinson,' said the Downing
Street spokesman, 'has the full confidence of the prime minister . . . [and] the rules have been carried out.' Gordon Brown
described his friend as 'a highly successful businessman', as
was proved by his declaration that he had paid £1.5 million
in income tax over the previous five years, and asserted that
he 'has not broken any ministerial code'. Brown agreed that
Will Hutton, the sympathetic editor of the *Observer*, should
interview Robinson on 13 December. The encounter would be
supervised by Ed Balls.

In the interests of the Labour government, Balls believed,
Hutton should 'trim and back off'. The interview, he demanded, should not embarrass the paymaster general. Balls
threatened to terminate the Treasury's favoured treatment of
Hutton if he did not assist Robinson's defence. Neither Brown
nor Balls was willing publicly or privately to admit prior
knowledge of Orion, and Balls was asking others to support
their version. The loyalty developed over many evenings in

the Grosvenor House Hotel had compromised their judgement. Hutton agreed to review the evidence and Robinson's answers during the interview carefully. The results, he discovered, were contradictory. Refusing to be cowed by Brown, he published in the *Observer* the authentic voice of Robinson's evasions. 'He's lied, lied and lied again,' the Tories chanted. The damage limitation had failed. Brown and Balls were outraged. They were unaccustomed to left-wing journalists declining to comply with their wishes. Brown ordered the Treasury's relations with Will Hutton to be permanently frozen.

Under pressure, Brown was rarely cool. Angrily, he shouted and cursed. Allowing Robinson to resign, and thus losing the expertise of an energetic, reliable friend would be a self-inflicted wound, and would please his enemies. Seven months after the election, he loathed the Tories more than ever. Demonising his enemies fuelled his hunger to protect Robinson. He would orchestrate a counteroffensive. Blair was prompted to say that Robinson was a 'brilliant minister' who had 'done everything according to the rules' and abided by the ministerial code; Alastair Campbell declared, 'He is staying.' Charlie Whelan scoffed about a 'pathetic attempt to smear him. He has nothing to hide'; and the *Guardian*'s Polly Toynbee, a matriarch of Labour zealots, pronounced Robinson to be 'an honest man' and the victim of a vendetta. Robinson believed that his troubles would pass. Gordon Brown readily agreed. There was a more pressing problem.

On 10 December 1997, Harriet Harman was humiliated. Forty-seven Labour MPs voted against the government's plan to reduce child benefits, and twenty-five abstained. Brown had been warned about the rebellion in the lobby by Clive Soley, the chairman of the parliamentary Labour Party, who had told him, 'You're going to lose this vote.' Brown's eyes glazed over and he jabbed his finger at Soley. 'We'll get these bastards,' he seethed. 'It's those you ought to be worried about,' replied Soley, referring to the government's reluctant supporters. Brown had never anticipated, Soley realised, how many were prepared to rebel. Brown was defiant: 'I need more savings.'

The vote to reduce benefits for Britain's poorest children coincided with a party in Downing Street hosted by the Blairs for the rich and famous, part of the government's £7.4 million celebration of 'Cool Britannia'. In another era, the juxtaposition would have embarrassed Brown, but his brief record as chancellor stood him in good stead. Nevertheless, his continued disengagement from traditional Labour surprised his friends.

The memory of John Smith appeared to be being deliberately tarnished. At a party gathering just before Christmas at the Thistle Hotel in Glasgow, Tony Blair had told the guests, including Smith's widow and one of his daughters, that Labour would not have won the election if Smith had been leader. 'What's he saying?' Smith's daughter asked George Galloway. 'That Labour before him was shit? That my father was a shit?' Galloway wandered over to Brown. 'What Tony said is a disgrace,' he said. 'Smith would have won.' Embarrassed, Brown said nothing. He and Blair wanted John Smith airbrushed out of history. Labour's old headquarters had been renamed John Smith House. Now there was just a John Smith Suite at the new headquarters in Millbank. After the party headquarters moved back to Walworth Road there would be nothing.

The former leader was a reminder of disaster, while New Labour's future was certain to be remarkable. The economy was growing at 4 per cent, much faster than the previous forecast of 3.25 per cent in July. Hidden beneath the chancellor's pessimistic projections of tax revenues, his plan to build a huge surplus by the end of the second year to win a second term was materialising. That summer, a Treasury official had given him a copy of Nigel Lawson's memoirs. He had devoured the readable account of his predecessor's triumph and despair, and was determined not to repeat the mistake of relying on the 'wishful thinking' of so-called experts and forecasters. Brown would never admit to mistakes. Over his first Christmas as chancellor he had every reason to be content.

EIGHT

Demons and Grudges

In the early morning of 8 January 1998, George Galloway spotted Gordon Brown pounding on an exercise machine in a private gym at 4 Millbank. The Scottish Catholic had never warmed to Brown. Irritated by his rise since their youthful disagreements in Scotland, Galloway dubbed him a sociologist or anthropologist – a witness to their nation's plight rather than a true fighter for the poor and supporter of the trade unions. Seeing the chancellor sweating reminded him of Bob Monkhouse's quip, 'If you can fake the sincerity, the rest is easy.'

'I saw your biography yesterday,' Galloway said to Brown. 'What biography?' replied Brown. 'Routledge's. It was on sale at Glasgow airport. I bought a copy.'

Brown's face froze. The book was not meant to go on sale until after its serialisation in *The Times* the following week. His agony was compounded by Galloway's next statement. 'It's got a lot of whoppers in it.' 'Like what?' 'That I tried to block your rise in the party with Bill Speirs. That's untrue.' Brown said nothing. Galloway smiled. In 1994 he had won a bet that Brown would not stand for the leadership. 'He doesn't have the balls,' he said. 'No courage.'

Within five minutes Brown had showered, dressed, run to his official car and, while speeding towards Whitehall, was alerting Whelan about the potential disaster. Whelan and

Routledge were close friends. Shortly afterwards, Whelan was begging Galloway, 'Do us a favour and don't mention it to anyone.' 'But it's on sale,' replied Galloway, who had already given his copy of the book to the *Guardian*. Paul Routledge also called Galloway. The hapless author was incensed. The mistake had endangered his income from the serialisation of his sensational revelations in *The Times*. 'It's my pension,' he pleaded. Galloway bore as little affection for Brown's allies as for the man himself. Embarrassing Brown, whom he condemned as a compromiser and 'a man of straw', was a delight.

Until that moment Brown had been pleased with Routledge's work. His book described the secret pact with Blair not to stand against Brown for the leadership, and Mandelson's betrayal in 1994. On the cover was the bold statement, 'written with Gordon Brown's full co-operation'. Indeed, the book's editor retained a manuscript with Brown's handwritten corrections. The raw truth of the feud appeared in the *Guardian* on 9 January, under the headline: 'Gordon Brown is convinced he could have beaten Tony Blair in a contest for Labour's leadership and that the prime minister broke a secret pact between them.' Brown was aghast at the consequences of his own intrigues. Across Westminster, his allegation that Blair had betrayed him provoked uproar among Labour MPs. Brown, they knew, could never have won the leadership. The injustice the book conjured up was a fiction.

The anger coincided with an important Brownite celebration, the wedding of Ed Balls to Yvette Cooper, a newly elected Labour MP. Brown arrived at the reception in Eastbourne with Sarah Macaulay, dismayed about Tony Blair's reaction to the book. Tony Blair and Alastair Campbell were visiting Japan. They had read the newspaper reports, faxed from London, with disgust. The publisher's assertion about Brown's 'full co-operation' was undoubtedly true. Considering the round of parties held in No. 11 for a thousand Labour activists, those around Blair construed that a coalition was forming to topple the prime minister. In three incidents – the Commons rebellion in favour of single parents' benefits, Robinson's murky finances and the euro – Brown's reliability had been shaky. Under pressure now, the chancellor protested, 'This is not an authorised biography, not in any way at all. Any suggestion that it is, is completely wrong.'

Alastair Campbell was incensed. First he sought to vent his fury via John Williams of the *Mirror*. After that paper refused to publish his attack on Brown, Andrew Rawnsley of the *Observer* was summoned. On Sunday, 18 January 1998, under the headline 'Blair Reins in Flawed Brown', the report revealed: 'According to someone who has an extremely good claim to know the mind of the prime minister, he still regards Mr Brown as a great talent and great force. But he is wearying of the chancellor's misjudgements . . . It is time, in the words of the same person, for Mr Brown to get a grip on his psychological flaws.'

Early that morning, Brown telephoned Whelan. 'Psychological flaws' was the authentic, crude voice of Campbell. 'Gordon was more upset than anybody could say,' Whelan told a friend, 'particularly as it looked like it came from high up in No. 10.' The headlines describing Blair 'reining in' and 'slapping down' his chancellor, and anonymous warnings that Brown's career 'could be jeopardised' encouraged Gerald Kaufman, an ill-disposed Labour politician, to scorn Brown as a moody political obsessive without a normal life, living alone in his small, untidy flat. Compared to Blair's growing stature, his charm and his appeal to all classes, Brown was criticised for refusing to accept his fate, and unintentionally tempting Blair to stay in office forever, or at least until Brown's chance for the succession had passed.

Brown was embarrassed by the opprobrium. Accustomed to the media's sympathy, he was even stung. He blamed everyone except himself and Whelan. Both cast themselves as the victims of Campbell, Anji Hunter, Blair's political secretary Sally Morgan and, particularly, Peter Mandelson. In Whelan's characterisation, the 'Poison Squad' were 'complete control freaks' outraged by their inability to control him. Loyally, he professed himself happy to 'put the boot into the bastards'. His task, reflecting Brown's mindset, was to 'prevent them getting away with murder', rather than to mend fences in the interests of a unified government.

Tempers were calmed at a summit in Chequers. Showing his usual diplomacy, Blair apologised to Brown for Campbell's comments, warned against splits and agreed to blame their advisers for instigating the argument. The camp followers' chatter, they agreed, was inflammatory. Both knew that the government's success depended on their continued good relations. Brown, they decided, would meet Mandelson in 11 Downing Street to repair their relationship. Over the next days Brown re-evaluated his stance. He would always publicly deny a rift with Blair. Indeed, he would praise his rival's character and performance; but he would avoid denying the existence of a deal outright by adhering to a suggestive code: 'I have always refused to talk and won't talk about that.' The resulting uncertainty, he judged, would reinforce the Treasury's increasing authority over the rest of Whitehall.

The Treasury's special advisers and policy units were becoming an alternative government. All they needed was a new permanent secretary. Terry Burns, isolated by the Hotel Group, was ready to retire, but on his own terms. Casting around for a successor, Brown sought to avoid the civil service choice, Andrew Turnbull, a fifty-three-year-old career official, currently the permanent secretary at the department of the environment, who was endorsed by Blair and Richard Wilson, the new cabinet secretary. He considered vetoing Turnbull, but there was no suitable alternative. Turnbull would be joined as his deputy by Gus O'Donnell, an economist presently attached to the British embassy in Washington, whom Brown knew from his visits to America. Although O'Donnell had served as John Major's press officer in Downing Street, his laddishness had eased his transition from the Conservatives to Labour. While Turnbull would be excluded from influence by Brown, O'Donnell skilfully adapted himself to the Hotel Group's expectations. The chancellor preferred not to consider the consequences of destabilising the Treasury's hierarchy.

During those first weeks of 1998, as attention switched from party rows to the next budget, Brown realised his good fortune. Income from normal taxation was rising faster than he had anticipated, and unemployment was falling. The economy he had inherited from the Conservatives was more robust than even his predecessors had realised. Instead of borrowing £9 billion that year, as he had predicted in November 1997, he needed only £3 billion, the lowest in seven years, and by some methods of accounting it would be just £922 million. The 'stealth' taxes levied since the election, especially on petrol, property, travel and pensions, had produced an extra £7.5 billion with barely any public protest. The silence encouraged his conviction that he could safely raise billions more in taxes to re-engineer society.

Typing on his personal laptop to avoid snoopers, he drafted a scheme likely to confuse. While insisting that he was still sticking rigidly to Conservative spending plans, and once again highlighting the supposed Tory 'black hole', he proposed to increase spending from £334 billion in 1997 to £437 billion in 2002, an increase of almost a third. Officially he had forecast that spending would increase annually by 2.25 per cent, but in fact it would be considerably higher. He intended to obscure the increase by splitting the extra expenditure in the official 'Blue Book' between current and capital expenditure.

This obfuscation was astutely packaged: 'The British economy, for the first time in decades, will establish a virtuous circle of low inflation, high investment and a higher level of sustainable growth.' He would repeatedly use the phrases 'prudence', 'toughness', 'stability', 'the long term' and 'fiscal stability'. While placating his left-wing critics by granting an extra £750 million to education and the NHS, the victims would be the middle classes. The beneficiaries would be the poor and multi-millionaires.

Some senior Treasury officials and his own special advisers were urging Brown to curb the huge tax benefits enjoyed by millionaires living in Britain while claiming to be domiciled overseas. Under British law since 1914, they paid tax only on the income which they brought into Britain, and paid no tax on income and assets which remained abroad. The Inland Revenue argued that there were glaring loopholes. By using offshore accounts, at least 100,000 wealthy people avoided paying a total of between £1 billion and £1.5 billion in tax every year. Instinctively, Brown wanted to tax them. In the past he had roundly condemned the situation as a 'scandal . . . in need of being cleaned up'. Nothing had happened to change his opinion.

The opposition to taxing non-domiciles was led by Chris Wales, the Andersen accountant seconded to the Treasury. Wales warned of an exodus of international businessmen, employees of multinationals and ship-owners which would undermine the City's international status. Brown wavered. Unlike the English middle classes, the foreigners could simply leave Britain, and he would be mocked for failing to abandon costly ideologies. He preferred to avoid a confrontation with that powerful lobby, and the scathing headlines it would entail. Among the beneficiaries were Labour donors including Lakshmi Mittal, the Hinduja brothers and Lord Paul, and many British supporters whose companies were based in tax havens. Socialism, Brown consoled himself, could not be created in one year.

The chancellor's mixed messages riled trade union leaders. One week before the budget, a delegation led by John Monks, the TUC's general secretary, visited Brown at 11 Downing Street. There was more than just the strained finances of the public services on their minds. Monks put their feelings bluntly: 'What's the point of these meetings if Charlie Whelan is trashing us?' Brown looked sheepish. 'Every time we meet,' continued Monks, 'he briefs against us. What's it all about?' Brown replied, 'Yes, yes. He's just being Charlie.' 'No,' said Monks looking directly at Whelan's master, 'we know Charlie of old. It must stop.' 'Right,' agreed Brown, without any intention of keeping his promise. He wanted to distance himself from Old Labour, and Whelan's activities suited his plan. He bade the dinosaurs goodbye. In the new era, they were irrelevant. The atmosphere, like the economy, was buoyant. The earlier troubles had been forgotten. Sarah Macaulay and Whelan had agreed the moment was right to relaunch the loving couple to humanise the chancellor.

On 15 March 1998, on the eve of the budget, photographers were invited to witness Brown and Sarah Macaulay attend the third birthday party in north London of Ben Davies, the son of Sue Nye and Gavyn Davies. Brown was to be shown as the smiling, family man. Sadly, the child refused to smile, and Brown looked awkward handing out jelly and singing 'Happy Birthday'. But the colour photographs which appeared on the front page of every newspaper the following day, including the *Financial Times*, were hailed by Whelan as a 'masterstroke'. The fact that a forty-six-year-old man, an unmarried loner, needed to borrow a child to prove his humanity was unfortunate. While Brown would gush, 'I do hope I have children. I love seeing them grow up. Of course, having a family is part of my ambitions,' he had done nothing to realise this aspiration.

For a man who disparaged personality politics to involve Sarah Macaulay in such a charade provoked carping that the 'psychological flaws' were not wholly imagined. The critics highlighted his solitary 7.30 a.m appearances at the health club, and his refusal to acknowledge other people. But others knew a different man. Brown's flat in Downing Street had become the scene of regular parties as friends from Scotland were welcomed to drink, laugh and watch football matches on television. Occasionally Brown would be uneasy. The thirty guests invited to celebrate his brother John's fiftieth birthday noticed his disappearances to see Blair and his irritation about a noisy demonstration in Whitehall. Since it was a family party and the staff had been sent home, there were no eye-witnesses to the hilarious competition to sit on Margaret Thatcher's bed, Churchill's chair and John Major's lavatory seat. The public's impression of the iron chancellor, however, remained grim.

The nitpickers were temporarily silenced by the euphoria and relief which greeted the budget on 17 March 1998. While Brown stood at the dispatch box, specially raised to compensate for his poor eyesight, Blair sat behind him reading the chancellor's script, suggesting an apprentice silently admiring his master. As Brown spoke, the stock market was soaring to a record high, echoing the chairman of the US Federal Reserve Alan Greenspan's prediction that the dotcom companies would herald a prosperous new era. Although the doomsayers in London were predicting inflation, boom and bust, none could undermine this transatlantic endorsement of Brown, who won praise for the certainty of his economic management and his worship of orthodoxy. The problem was Brown's brutal enforcement of his strategy. Unwilling to trust government officials and their departments to deliver visible improvements to justify tax increases and spending, he introduced a weapon euphemistically called 'targets' to modernise the economy.

Both Brown and Blair believed that anything measurable could be improved. By setting targets for each department and each public service, and creating a delivery unit in Downing Street to enforce these targets, they hoped that human inadequacies would be overcome and Britain's public services would be improved. During the nineties many corporate executives had become addicted to McKinsey's and other management consultants. Brown shared their taste for systems and formulas, ignoring each individual's immeasurable motives, habits and weaknesses. He did not seem to wonder why, if targets worked, the Soviet Union had failed to become the world's richest power, and ignored those who mentioned the historic disappointment of 'market socialism'.

By March 1998 over six hundred Labour sympathisers had been recruited under the banner of Public Sector Productivity to implement targets aimed at achieving greater economic efficiency. Based in the Treasury and 10 Downing Street, their presence reflected Brown's conviction that the Treasury could manage every Whitehall department. The mechanics were agreed between Ed Balls and Jeremy Hayward, an apolitical Treasury statistician employed as Blair's private secretary. Hayward was the trusted bridge between No. 10 and Brown and Balls, who were grateful to discover that Blair was uninterested in the detail. With the help of expensive management consultants, huge effort was devoted to imposing the official responsibility on each Whitehall department to define, refine and deliver the agreed target for its performance. The presentation was impressive. Public Sector Agreements (PSAs) were contracts between the Treasury and Whitehall departments to renew public services. They required the department to guarantee that their service to the public would be improved. If their target was not met, theoretically the Treasury's funds would not be released. By mid-1998 the Treasury had supervised agreements with twenty departments of 347

targets and 428 sub-targets to be fulfilled by 2002. The government's spending in 1996–97 was £317 billion. By 2001–02,
Brown projected it to be at least £390 billion. The test would
be whether the public services had improved.

In parallel, Brown extended the spending budgets from one
to three years, an intelligent reform to avoid the violent
lurches of the Conservatives' 'Star Chambers', when ministers
met in hotel bedrooms during their annual conferences at the
climax of weeks of arguments. The corollary of reform was
the new powers assumed by Brown. Without negotiation or
allowance for protest, he, Balls and Blair would ordain how
much each department would receive from the £333 billion
budget, in consultation with Robert Hill of the Policy Unit and
the Treasury civil servant responsible for that department's
spending. Brown fondly anticipated that the meetings of the
Public Services and Public Expenditure Committee (PX) under
his chairmanship, which would enforce the comprehensive
spending review, would be bloody. Those ministers who
believed that spending was an opportunity for favourable
publicity and the exercise of power would be crushed.

Under Brown's supervision, in early summer 1998 the
Public Expenditure Review Committee was scrutinising each
department's budget. Lowly assistant secretaries in the Treasury were authorised by Brown to summon senior civil servants and even ministers to justify their expenditure plans.
Not all ministers understood Brown's delight in testing their
obedience. Those who protested met Brown and Blair in an
office behind the speaker's chair. David Blunkett, the education secretary, 'threw a wobbly' and received more money;
Chris Smith, the arts minister, appealed three times to Blair
that Brown's allocation was unacceptable, and received a
small amount extra; John Prescott, the transport minister,
sanely asked for and got nothing; Frank Dobson lobbied Blair
to get more for health, and received an extra pittance; Jack

Straw, the home secretary, asked for more and was invited to be cross-examined by Derry Irvine, the lord chancellor.

Brown watched quietly, enjoying Irvine's evisceration of Straw. 'What's your department going to look like in five years?' asked Irvine. Straw hesitated, uncertain. 'Well,' said Irvine, 'if you carry on spending in this way, every penny of your budget will be spent on prisons. Nothing else. You haven't got a plan.' Brown smiled. Vicariously, he was earning a reputation for 'holding feet to the fire to enforce his spending targets'. His clear political priority was to appear as a master of detail to demonstrate his invincibility. 'Are we going to treat all our colleagues as criminals?' asked Margaret Beckett, the DTI minister. Brown's smile widened. 'I want extra performance for the money,' he exhorted. Naturally, he rejected the complaint that the targets were delivered as tablets of stone, with no remedies to cure failure.

The humiliated Straw was unaware that the image of the Treasury's supreme competence was a charade. Brown's staff preferred to conceal the uncertainty and errors bedevilling the Treasury's own budget forecasts and undermining the credibility of their targets. Brown in turn denied that error was possible. 'But who is going to scrutinise the Treasury?' one slow-comprehending official had asked. 'We're setting targets for every department to be judged by, but who judges whether the Treasury has met its own targets? Especially for spending.' Brown was deaf to that singularly unenlightened official, who obviously had a brief future. At the end of a final session about welfare payments, Brown stood up. 'That's it,' he said. 'Thank you very much. I'll take this away and make my recommendations to the cabinet.' 'Hang on,' protested Frank Field. 'Aren't we all going to discuss our list of priorities?' 'No,' replied Brown. 'I will decide.' Unknown to the beleaguered politicians, about £10 billion would be wasted by the Treasury on the working families' tax credit while the 'local authority capital receipts initiative' to fund Labour's heartlands was a camouflage for extra expenditure. Brown resisted any scrutiny of his growing empire.

The Home Office escaped lightly compared to the ministry of agriculture (MAFF). Brown distrusted both farmers and the department's civil servants. The ministry, he believed, was inefficient, old-fashioned and protective. Farmers, he felt, should not be subsidised. The mismanagement of the BSE crisis, costing £4 billion, had incensed the Treasury, and Brown ordered his officials to set tough targets for MAFF without consultations. Savings would be imposed. Richard Packer, the permanent secretary, and Jack Cunningham, the minister, were summoned to Downing Street, where Alistair Darling informed them how much money the ministry of agriculture would receive. Unknown to Packer, the reduction of financial support for British agriculture had been privately agreed between Brown and Cunningham. Brown, senior civil servants understood, did not realise the consequences, and Cunningham was uninterested. Ignoring Packer's brief, Cunningham assured the expenditure committee of his ability to achieve 'massive savings'. Packer had been comprehensively humiliated.

Among the Treasury's curious targets for MAFF was the eradication of BSE within 'two years' – incubation of the disease in cattle could take five years. The ministry was also given a new target to 'stop increasing production', although that had been the policy for over fifteen years. Other targets ignored the European Union's directives. 'This is completely crippling,' protested Packer. 'Brown's reinforcing the Treasury's viciousness and arrogance with megalomania.' Packer would never discover which individual Treasury official under Robert Culpin, the permanent secretary responsible for expenditure, set the targets for MAFF's drastic cuts in expenditure, but he dubbed them 'below the salt', and a few of them as 'nutters'. 'We've been trashed,' Packer told Culpin. 'MAFF's policies have been deliberately distorted. The Treasury has gone too far.' 'I'm surprised that you're so mild,' Culpin replied. 'I'll never get the truth,' complained Packer. 'I blame Brown. He's a control freak.' He also blamed Jack Cunningham. 'He can't look at a wine list without picking the most expensive,' he said of their meals in Brussels. 'He has a compulsion to spend.' When accounts of Cunningham's expensive lifestyle at the public's expense appeared in newspapers he received little support from his colleagues, including Brown. He had served his purpose, and the chancellor was disenchanted by him. To undermine his credibility, Charlie Whelan whispered unflattering comments about him, and smiled on hearing the echo of Cunningham's anger. That was Brown's way, as Margaret Beckett also discovered.

In early May 1998, George Bain delivered his first report on setting a minimum wage. Brown was displeased. The Low Pay Unit (LPU) had recommended a figure of £3.20 per hour. That was excessive, Brown believed. Worse, Bain wanted the minimum wage to be paid to twenty-one-year-olds. To save money, Brown decided to make it payable only to employees of twenty-two years old and over. On a Sunday morning, Brown telephoned Bain and quizzed him for twenty minutes about the detail of the statistics which, Bain insisted, showed that paying employees from the age of twenty-one had no economic significance. Brown did not trust the statistics. 'I won't allow twenty-one-year-olds to be classed as adults,' he announced. He was annoyed that the minimum wage had been set by a committee rather than by himself. The LPU, he hinted to Bain, should be scrapped.

Bain sought the support of Margaret Beckett. Because of her full diary, the only opportunity for an hour's meeting was in a VIP lounge at Heathrow airport. Bain described Brown's threat to the minimum wage, a manifesto pledge, and urged

her to fight for his report and the unit in the cabinet, and she
agreed. Like Jack Straw and Richard Packer before her,
Beckett would be astounded by the chancellor's reaction.
Quiet warfare against Bain continued throughout May. In
order to assert himself, the prime minister realised, Brown
was content to antagonise many of his colleagues.

The only hope for a peaceful resolution of the minimum
wage was to neutralise Brown's veto of the report's recommendations. Blair arranged a meeting on 4 June 1998, after
the cabinet. 'I want the commission abolished,' Brown told
him. 'The Treasury should set the minimum wage.' Beckett
fought back, and won. The commission would survive, but
the minimum wage would be set at £3 per hour, as Brown had
demanded. In gratitude, George Bain sent Beckett a bunch of
flowers. Annoyed, Brown directed Whelan to disparage
Beckett to the *Observer*. The newspaper's report on 21 June,
under the headline 'The Neighbours from Hell', described
Brown's 'crushing defeat' of the 'pulverised' Margaret
Beckett. The DTI's budget of £6 billion, suggested Whelan,
would be cut by £1 billion.

Whelan was also told to humiliate Robin Cook by alleging
to journalists that the Foreign Office had not disclosed to the
Treasury the amount of wine in its cellars; and to knock
George Robertson for failing to reduce the budget of the ministry of defence. Whelan's next target was Frank Field. 'His
ideas,' declared Whelan, 'don't work.' Field discovered from
the newspapers that Downing Street had rejected his proposed
reforms, described in a draft Green Paper, as 'unworkable'. To
his chagrin, Blair's staff, with Brown's help, had transformed a
coherent plan into a confused potpourri. Whelan also advised
his audience that the fate of Harriet Harman, unkindly dubbed
'that flaky woman', was also precarious. 'I don't think she
can be saved,' he whispered.

Once again, Blair summoned the warring factions in an

attempt to broker peace. Sitting on a sofa in his small office, Blair gazed at Frank Field and Gordon Brown. The chancellor had arrived with a thunderous face. Blair had announced that No. 10 would take responsibility for welfare reform. That, Brown said, was intolerable. The constant rows between Field and Harman had persuaded him to assert himself and take responsibility for everything, neutralising the prime minister's initiative. He had thought a lot about solving poverty, even publishing at his own expense a pamphlet, 'A Modern Agenda to Tackle Poverty', describing his proposals to reduce dependency. Housing benefits claimed by 4.7 million people were costing £11 billion every year. Fraud on single benefits cost at least £1 billion. He wanted the benefit curtailed.

Although Brown had agreed to restore the single parent benefit, the planned reduction to which had provoked the rebellion by forty-seven Labour MPs, he exerted pressure on Harriet Harman to limit expenditure. 'I've always supported what Harriet has done,' he told the meeting, although many felt he had done the opposite. He was determined to defeat the spenders, but refused to engage in a debate with Field. Field wanted to remind Brown of his pledge to 'break the spiral of escalating welfare spending' and the fact that he was allowing social security spending to rise by 2 per cent above inflation at a time when unemployment was falling. So far the social security budget had increased to £100 billion, and it was projected to rise to £108 billion in 2001–02. Brown was creating a system in which forty-six million Britons were entitled to at least one welfare benefit, and overall fraud was, according to Sir Nicholas Montagu, the chairman of the Inland Revenue, 'endemic', accounting in some benefits for 'at least 23 per cent of all payments'. Unofficially, Revenue experts estimated that 40 per cent of all claims were fraudulent.

'Where's your paper on pensions, Gordon?' asked Blair. Brown scowled. Blair smiled. Like an understanding father, he tolerated the chancellor's naughtiness. Pensions were a dry subject, and the prime minister was unwilling to protect Field from the chancellor's intimidation. Yet their dispute was critical to the budget and to Brown's social engineering. Brown favoured state pensions subject to means testing, while Field believed that everyone should contribute compulsorily to private pensions. 'Planning for pensions requires a dynamic analysis,' Field told Brown. 'Your way is static. You don't realise how normal people react. Means testing encourages fraud.' Brown refused to engage in a confrontation. Nor would he discuss why the state pension was essential for society, nor why those who saved for their retirement should be means tested. In his 1999 budget he would deliberately exclude pensioners from the 10 pence tax rate on income from savings, which would save just £55 million out of a budget surplus of £4 billion. 'Your pension plans will create chaos,' Field predicted. 'As Gladstone said, "Any fool can give the poor money. The question is whether the money gives them freedom."' Brown was unmoved. He knew that Harman and Field disagreed about everything. Field was livid about Harman's inability to argue for welfare reform and about her sabotage of his draft Green Paper, which she firmly denied. Blair looked flummoxed. The meeting ended inconclusively. 'You're pathological,' Field raged at Harman after they left Downing Street. 'Your department is chaotic. I'm resigning.'

In the first of three meetings with Blair to explain his departure, Field asked, 'Is this a way to run a government? A minister needs protection from Gordon.' The prime minister adopted his expressionless gaze. 'I know nothing about all of this,' he replied. Richard Wilson, the new cabinet secretary, was asked to mediate. Brown was uninterested. Wilson invited Field to discuss an alternative government post. Field rejected the offer. To avoid further disagreements and to win the argument, Blair accepted Field's resignation, also deciding to fire Harman and start afresh. Brown had successfully hijacked Blair's agenda to reduce the cost of welfare. He received no thanks from Blair's critics.

The turmoil provoked by Brown's tactics and policies disturbed the party's left wing. Tony Benn, a leader of the unconverted, criticised Brown for having no industrial policy other than to 'protect the rich'. Ken Livingstone condemned him as 'a September socialist . . . the most backward-looking chancellor for sixty years' who, after rousing speeches to the annual conference, spent the rest of the year being 'awful'. In a newspaper column, Livingstone demanded Brown's dismissal: 'Gordon is not up to his job . . . The end result of this charade is that Britain is now heading towards a recession entirely of Gordon's making . . . Quite clearly, he is not on top of his macro-economic policy.' To add salt to the wound, Livingstone also condemned Brown for appointing Deanne Julius, an economist formerly employed by the CIA, as a member of the Bank of England's Monetary Policy Committee: 'How on earth a Labour chancellor could feel that a former CIA employee would be of value in pursuing Labour's wider agenda on the MPC is a matter that "passeth all understanding".' (Two and a half years later, Livingstone appointed Bob Kiley, a former employee of the CIA, as the commissioner of transport for the London Underground.) To Livingstone's delight, Brown was hurt by the criticism, and was impatient for revenge.

On the stock market, the FTSE index had risen to a near-record 6,100 points, interest rates were falling and the national debt had been reduced. Brown assumed the credit. At the annual Mansion House dinner on 10 June 1998, he serenely appealed to the middle classes, promising to privatise air traffic control, the Royal Mint, motorway services and the Tote. Simultaneously, he reassured Labour's traditionalists that the old faith has not been abandoned. But by now even

his allies criticised him as a bully, his relationship with Blair
had cooled, and Mandelson had persuaded Blair to tilt the
balance of power in his own favour against Brown and his
unruly camp followers.

Brown was still unreconciled to Blair's leadership and
appeared to resent his personal success. Despite Blair's obvious concern to placate Brown, praising him in public and
private as 'the very best', Brown was unconsoled. He provoked arguments in Blair's office, inciting the prime minister
to ponder aloud whether he might act to prevent Brown's
eventual succession, knowing that the gossip would annoy
Brown even more. Usually Brown's rage was revealed to sympathisers by Whelan, but on some occasions Brown resorted
to comedy, as he did in a speech on 2 April 1998 to the
Westminster press gallery. He complained about the noise of
guitar playing, Oasis and French lessons coming through the
party wall with Blair's flat in Downing Street, concluding,
'And that's before the kids come home from school.' By July
the jokes had evaporated. The cycle of happiness–argument–
crisis in their relationship, Blair decided, could only be
resolved by a reshuffle to remind his next-door neighbour of
the true pecking order.

Brown was privately told by Blair about a proposed cabinet
reshuffle on 28 July. Horrified, he discovered that his supporters were targeted. Two friends, Nigel Griffiths (consumer
affairs) and Tom Clarke (film and tourism minister) were to
be sacked; and Doug Henderson was to be given the less
glamorous job of minister for armed forces instead of minister
for Europe. Harriet Harman was to be dismissed. The unexpected and shocking decisions were the proposed demotion of
Nick Brown, the chief whip, to agriculture, the dismissals of
Geoffrey Robinson and Charlie Whelan, and the promotion
of Peter Mandelson to become secretary of state at the DTI.
This was a testing moment for the clan chief who promised

protection in return for total loyalty. 'I've never seen Gordon so low,' Whelan told a journalist. 'I told him that this shows that Blair cannot be trusted.'

Geoffrey Robinson had become an embarrassment. He had been formally reprimanded by the House of Commons for not registering his business interests, he was under investigation for failing to declare a payment of £200,000 from Robert Maxwell (an accurate accusation which he still denied), and, to avoid humiliation, he was refusing to answer questions at the dispatch box. Encouraged by Campbell, Blair asked for Robinson's resignation. Robinson appealed to Gordon Brown for support. Brown was torn. Robinson represented the very sleaze that Labour had exploited to win the election. If he had been more courageous, Brown would have told Robinson to resign. But he hesitated, compromised by Robinson's generosity and the fear of revelations if Robinson was cast out. After a brief pause, Brown telephoned Blair and urged that the request for Robinson's resignation be cancelled. Blair agreed, but then had second thoughts.

To avoid a direct confrontation with his summertime host, the prime minister persuaded Richard Wilson, the cabinet secretary, to deliver the new message demanding Robinson's resignation. As he shuttled between Blair, Brown and Robinson, Wilson must have realised how, by seeking to oblige a fearful prime minister, his position had been compromised. He, as a decent public servant, trusted politicians not to lie, and judged that politicians believed themselves to be honest. Placed in the midst of the developing feud, he was naïve about his masters' motives, especially Brown's. To pre-empt Blair, Brown arranged for Robinson to pose with the Treasury team for a new photograph, while Balls told journalists that Robinson was 'a fucking brilliant minister'. The chancellor's tactics forced Blair to retreat. Subsequently, Brown would say that in July 1998 he had urged Robinson's dismissal but Blair had refused it, and would also mention his 'failed attempts' to save Harman. Richard Wilson's reward from Brown was harsh. He summoned Wilson to his office, where he told him, 'I don't want our relationship to be damaged by all this.' Wilson agreed. But the appearance of reconciliation was clearly unsatisfactory to Brown, who judged Wilson to be loyal to Blair rather than himself. He refused to speak to the cabinet secretary for the next three years, unprecedented behaviour from a chancellor towards the country's most senior civil servant.

At considerable cost, Gordon Brown had preserved his sovereignty. Robinson and Whelan remained in place, but Blair refused to appoint Douglas Alexander, Brown's former speechwriter, as a junior minister. To demonstrate the value of his patronage, Brown published his correspondence with Don Touhig, his parliamentary private secretary (PPS), who had resigned after being revealed to have secretly passed Treasury officials an unpublished and critical report by a select committee about child benefits. Brown wrote to Touhig, described as 'one of Brown's closest allies' and 'a trusted lieutenant', in commiseration: 'You have done an outstanding job . . . I know you will be back soon and I look forward to working closely with you in the future.' The following year Touhig became a whip, and was subsequently promoted as a junior minister in the Welsh Office.

Acknowledging unpleasant truths was difficult for Brown. He would flee the Commons to avoid hearing Frank Field's resignation statement. Criticism was as unacceptable as the appointment of Peter Mandelson as the secretary of state at the DTI. 'He'll be trouble,' Brown told Blair. The prime minister rejected the warning, and encouraged Brown to initiate a reconciliation with Mandelson over a drink in his flat. Opening a bottle of champagne on a Sunday evening, Brown effusively welcomed Mandelson to the cabinet. The welcome was not genuine. Recently he had lampooned Mandelson for keeping Labour 'in touch with the countryside' by regularly visiting the royal homes at Highgrove, Sandringham and Windsor. But Mandelson, he knew, would be grateful to be welcomed back into the fold. Despite all the bad blood between them, Brown's menace – used both creatively and destructively – preserved their bond. Mandelson remained, he knew, in awe of his magic and his power.

Peter Mandelson's visibility among London's social glitterati had increased just as Brown's Treasury team became unsettled. Alistair Darling had become the new chief at the department of social security, and his replacement as chief secretary, Stephen Byers, was a Blairite. Helen Liddell had been removed to reluctantly restore the Labour machine in Scotland. She replaced Alec Rowley as the party's general secretary. Rowley, appointed on Brown's recommendation, had not been a success. The new economic secretary was Patricia Hewitt. Robinson remained, albeit wounded. A photo-opportunity was arranged for Brown, Darling, Mandelson and Byers to pose as a united economic team, but the image aggravated suspicions that the opposite of what it presented was the true case. Clive Soley, the chairman of the parliamentary Labour Party, noticed that Whelan had become more important than ever as a means to promote Brown's opinions against the Blairites. 'I've heard Whelan briefing John Humphrys against the prime minister, Alastair Campbell and Peter Mandelson,' Soley told Brown, adding that Labour MPs had complained at the regular Wednesday meeting of the PLP about Whelan. 'We're very loyal,' said Soley, 'but see what's happening.' Brown listened but, as usual, was dismissive of protests about Whelan. He would not admit that, with his agreement, Whelan regularly briefed journalists to embarrass Robin Cook, Chris Smith, George Robertson and Mo Mowlam. 'Mo's useless,' snipped Whelan, reheating an old grudge.

Brown's enemies in the government might carp, 'He goes around Whitehall in jackboots, then ducks when the flack begins to fly,' or mock, 'He's brilliant but of course he's a nutter,' but they could not deny his success in cultivating a social revolution while retaining the sympathy of some opponents.

Thanks in large part to Brown's efforts, Labour had passed a watershed in its relationship with business and industry. He regularly met Britain's richest business leaders to secure their support for 'enterprise forums' and the New Deal, and often agreed to attend expensive dinners to toast a famous plutocrat. 'Twenty-nine thousand companies,' he would boast, 'have signed up to the New Deal and 30,000 people have found jobs they would not have had.' Three hundred thousand, he claimed, would benefit by April 1999. Although Brown gave the impression that his 'New Deal', costing £3.5 billion, was unique, in fact every developed nation had tried a combination of incentives over the past ten years to reduce unemployment, despite the evidence that expensive job subsidies yielded limited benefits.

One year after the election, about ten advisers in Brown's private office were engaged in restless rethinking of policies, constantly submitting ideas to help the disadvantaged. Among his favoured projects was a programme to teach literacy and numeracy to 750,000 illiterate adults by 2004. His 'National Skills Strategy' involved five new agencies: the University for Industry, Learndirect, Union Learning Funds, UK Online and Independent Learning Accounts (ILAs). Under his inspiration Tessa Blackstone, an education minister, proclaimed that the University for Industry would 'lead the learning revolution', and David Blunkett, the secretary of state for education, added his 'vision' that the university would 'revolutionise the way people learn'. There were hours of discussions over whether the name, the University for Industry, might deter the poor.

Eventually, the word 'university' was dropped. After consultations, conferences and seminars between civil servants and
employers, Brown issued a Green Paper grandly titled, 'The
Learning Age – A Renaissance for a New Britain', promising
to exploit new technologies to boost productivity, employment and competitiveness. Soon afterwards, a 'Pathfinder
Prospectus' set out in stirring vocabulary the opportunities
for adults to improve their abilities. Computer literacy was a
priority. Over the years Brown had spent long sessions surfing
the net, especially American websites. 'I want to see more
people equipped with the best skills,' he said. About £250
million was earmarked to supply computers to schools.
Another £200 million was assigned to ILAs for adults to pay
private companies for vocational studies, including textbooks
and CDs.

ILAs were not a new idea. In 1994 the Tories had proposed
and then rejected them as complex and ineffective. Brown
took a different view, but relied on his officials to grapple
with the problems of implementing his initiatives. He was not
interested in how the pricing mechanisms for the self-
financing organisations would be calculated in the Private
Public Partnerships (PPPs), or mastering the details of providing training in the 'university'. He was never heard to say,
'Let's keep this simple,' and only rarely asked to be briefed
about the results. Brown was seldom persuadable that his
ideas were spawning increased bureaucracy. His aura of power
dissuaded Treasury officials from explaining that anything
complicated would be unsuccessful. Brown had vowed to cut
red tape, and that was sufficient. He believed in his creations
because he was their star.

He flew to Cape Cod in July convinced of his power to
change Britain. At a recent meeting with Rupert Murdoch in
Sun Valley, Idaho, he had extolled the virtues of competition
for private business. 'I want to reward risk,' he said, while

complaining about a lack of enterprise in Britain. His principle was to inject the private sector's money, ideas and expertise into protected state monopolies. Still inspired by Harold Wilson's philosophies as translated by Geoffrey Robinson, he was attracted by any proposal combining the universities with industry to reproduce Silicon Valley in Britain.

During that holiday, Charles 'Chuck' Vest, the president of the Massachusetts Institute of Technology, made Brown a proposition. Vest had been invited to Brown's rented house, and in the course of their conversation he described MIT's collaboration with business. MIT graduates, explained Vest, had founded over 4,000 corporations, including Hewlett-Packard, McDonnell Douglas and Intel. Impressed, Brown wondered whether MIT could forge a research and business alliance with a British university. 'Well,' replied Vest, 'we want a partnership with a European university. In Britain, it would have to be Cambridge.' On his return to London, Brown would order his officials to organise a partnership between MIT and Cambridge, to be called CMI Ltd (Cambridge Massachusetts Institute). He was proud to bridge the gap between business, science and the universities. Although he castigated corporate Britain for its excessive pay and perks, he was pleased that its executives, lobbyists and publicists, flocking to the party conference in September, trusted Labour's reputation as the friend of enterprise.

But the mood in London turned unexpectedly nasty in September 1998. Brown's optimistic predictions in July proved wrong. There were rumours of an imminent worldwide slump. The London stock market had fallen; the employers' organisations had warned that business confidence was ebbing and unemployment would increase. 'Hours away from recession' was the TUC's judgement of Britain's 'crisis'. Ken Livingstone and other old socialists were delighted to concur, and urged Brown to end the spending freeze. UNISON's

Rodney Bickerstaffe, a trade union leader of the old school, told Brown, 'Don't just give us a vision of the promised land, give us a place in it.' Bickerstaffe wanted 'a bit of jam today' – a pay increase. Brown was facing his first real test as chancellor. His standard response to censure was either to flee or brazenly to insist upon his righteousness. On this occasion, he chose boldness. He composed a statement asserting that Britain would escape a recession. To maintain his spending freeze he needed to juggle authoritative announcements. First came the reassurance: 'There will be no recession but a moderation of growth.' Second, the defiance: 'I did not come into the Treasury to court day-to-day popularity. I always thought we were beginning a journey that would take time, patience and effort.' Third, the pledge of spending an extra £40 billion on education and health. That pledge was grossly misleading. The Treasury had added together three years of spending increases, and other increases previously announced, including extra spending due to inflation. The real increase, after deducting the double counting, was £18 billion rather than £40 billion. This misuse of statistics was instantly ridiculed as 'fantasy forecasting and Peter Pan economics'. The Treasury's data was criticised as 'poor' and 'unreliable', and the Treasury itself castigated as 'no longer . . . the place to get information'. Brown was unperturbed. His enemies had not grasped the reason for his optimism. Tax revenues were higher than anticipated, and his forecasters' predictions were positive. Brown's self-confidence and patience would prove well-founded.

He was again tested during a private meeting with Rodney Bickerstaffe and John Edmonds at the party conference in Brighton. Both demanded that the government should restore the link between the state pension and earnings. Brown faced the trade unionists alongside Sue Nye, Ed Balls and Alistair Darling. His refusal to retreat froze the atmosphere. 'I think you'd better leave,' he told his three colleagues. The three men remaining in the hotel room were tense. 'We don't like means testing,' said Edmonds. 'All the research shows that the poorest and oldest suffer. They just don't claim.' Brown's reply was short: 'You must concentrate the money on those who need it.' 'Yes,' replied Edmonds, 'but the research shows that with means tests those who need the money don't get it.' Brown's reply was familiar: 'You must concentrate the money on those who need it.' Over the next hour, as voices rose, Bickerstaffe and Edmonds found that every example they quoted was rebutted with mechanical regularity by exactly the same slogan: 'You must concentrate the money on those who need it.' Like an automaton, Brown ignored opinions other than his own, even from members of his own tribe.

Three months later, on 8 December 1998, the inspiration for Brown's stubbornness, his father, collapsed in the snow while returning home from shopping. He died immediately. John Brown had retired eighteen years earlier as the minister at St John's Church in Hamilton, after forty years' service to the community. His son was naturally distraught. Friends recalled that he spoke frequently about his father but rarely about his mother. The reasons were difficult to discern. Absolutely no one was allowed to pry into the fabric of his personal relationships, although two weeks later one result of his contrariness towards others once again gripped the country.

Brown's biographer Paul Routledge had completed a biography of Peter Mandelson, whom he loathed. In return for the promise of an extraordinary bombshell, Routledge reputedly received a newspaper serialisation deal worth over £100,000. One impetus for the book had been Geoffrey Robinson's secret loan to Mandelson for his house in London's Notting Hill. The secret, described by Whelan and Balls as 'the nuclear device', had emerged after the two Treasury officials told Robinson about a housewarming party at Mandelson's new home. Having lent Mandelson the money for the house, Robinson was furious not to have received an invitation. Impulsively, he revealed the existence of the loan. In fact, Balls and Whelan appear to have known about it ever since it was offered. Mandelson had faxed Robinson an agreement drafted by his lawyer for the money, unaware that Balls and Whelan, letting themselves in to the Grosvenor House apartment, would see it before Robinson did so himself. Brown heard about the loan from Robinson, and by summer the knowledge had spread to the Blairites. Michael Wills, newly elected to parliament, told Charles Falconer, the solicitor general, about the loan during a summer holiday in Spain. Brown knew that the loan had become ultra-sensitive since Mandelson's appointment to the DTI. As secretary of state, Mandelson was responsible for the department's investigation of Robinson's undisclosed relationship with Robert Maxwell. Mandelson failed to disclose his financial relationship with Robinson to his permanent secretary as required.

Over the weeks following Mandelson's appointment, Brown's feelings towards him had deteriorated. Mandelson had proved eager to embarrass the chancellor. To promote the privatisation of the Post Office, the new DTI secretary had privately spoken about Brown's 'defeat' while trying to prevent the sell-off. 'Garbage' and 'rubbish' were how Whelan described Mandelson's plans to reduce the Treasury's share in the Post Office from 85 per cent to 40 per cent, a policy opposed by the trade unions. Mandelson appealed to Blair for support, but the prime minister, after Brown's intervention, switched sides and opposed Mandelson. The privatisation of the Post Office, a vital reform, was halted on the chancellor's orders. Obsessed with Mandelson, Brown was resolute. Routledge's publicising of Robinson's loan was certain to damage Mandelson and weaken Blair. Brown was unconcerned that Robinson would also be a casualty. New revelations about his unethical business activities had transformed the paymaster general into an unacceptable liability.

Brown was delighted to hear on 16 December 1998 that the manuscript of Routledge's biography of Mandelson had been leaked to the *Guardian*. The newspaper's headlines about Robinson's secret loan were sensational. For a week Blair and Mandelson attempted to ride out the storm, but to Brown's satisfaction, on 23 December Mandelson resigned. At the Red Lion, Whelan ordered champagne to toast his enemy's destruction. Brown telephoned Robinson to ask for his resignation, mouthing sufficient words of regret for Robinson to believe that he was 'genuinely upset'. Brown's priority was to ensure that Robinson did not disclose any more secrets.

Chris Smith was among many Labour MPs disturbed by Mandelson's downfall. On a visit to Brown's office, he challenged the chancellor about a suspected plot. 'Charlie Whelan leaked this loan to harm Peter, didn't he?' asked Smith. Brown looked Smith in the eyes. 'Oh no, Chris,' he replied with seeming sincerity, 'I'm sure Charlie would never do anything like that.' Smith departed, unsure what to believe.

During the turbulent Christmas holidays, Brown's relations with his colleagues were strained. 'I won't sack Charlie under any circumstances,' he told Blair, and in constant telephone calls to Whelan he restated his solidarity. Initially, Brown appeared to have won. 'Charlie is entirely a matter for Gordon,' admitted Downing Street. But by Monday, 4 January 1999, he was defeated. On Blair's insistence, the man branded an 'oik' by Campbell, and by others as far worse, resigned. Many observers believed that Whelan was responsible for leaking the details of Mandelson's mortgage to Routledge, and that he would not have done so without Brown's knowledge. Whelan has always denied that allegation.

In an attempt to counter that impression, Brown met Mandelson at Sue Nye's about two weeks later for a drink.

Nye worked in many capacities for Brown, and that evening
her role was to rebuild the bridges that others in Brown's
camp – especially Whelan and Balls – delighted in burning.
Mandelson was inconsolable, especially by Brown. The chancellor had clearly enjoyed his destruction, the more so in
the knowledge that Blair felt scarred by the events. Furious,
Mandelson gave vent to his opinions on Brown's sexuality.
'I don't know whether Gordon is gay,' he said later, 'but on
balance I don't think so.' Few slurs could hurt Brown more.
'It angers me,' he said, 'because I've got nothing to hide.'

Just eighteen months after the election, Brown's inner
sanctum had been disrupted. Only Ed Balls of the Hotel Group
remained. Brown avoided the official photocall with Dawn
Primarolo, Robinson's successor. He regarded her as a poor
substitute, especially with regard to PFI, but acknowledged
her appeal to sections of the parliamentary party. The rows
and resignations contaminated the semblance of harmony
among New Labour's aristocrats. As usual, the peacemaking
diplomacy was conducted between Sue Nye and Anji Hunter.

Gordon Brown expected Tony Blair to take the initiative to
repair their relationship. At Alastair Campbell's behest, the
prime minister obliged by lavishing praise on his chancellor,
testifying that New Labour could not have existed without
Brown. The two, Blair insisted, were 'closer than any prime
minister and chancellor in living memory . . . I know that
conflict will always make more headlines than partnership,
but this partnership is built to last. This is a government without any of the kinds of ideological divides which destroyed
the Tories.' Brown delayed for a week before reciprocating,
acknowledging Blair's 'historic achievement'.

The culmination of all the various reconciliations was
Brown's appearance on Saturday, 27 February 1999 at a party
to celebrate the twenty-fifth anniversary of Robin Cook's
entry into parliament. Brown, as guest speaker at Living-

stone's football stadium, reminisced about his work towards the foreign secretary's first election victory in 1974. The evening was marred by the news that Sheena McDonald had been hit by a speeding police car in London, and was seriously injured. Sarah Macaulay sat by Brown's side as he momentarily gazed into the distance. His sorrow was interrupted by Robin Cook's speech. His old rival sought to make amends. 'Without Gordon Brown,' said Cook, 'I might not have been there at all.' In his reply, Brown was unable to ignore the old enmity. 'The important thing,' he said, 'is that we have been working together for twenty-five years and continue to do so.'

Over the years, Gordon Brown had perfected the theatre of political deception. He used that talent to promote his own financial genius during his budget speech on 9 March 1999. Critics were once again warning of minimal growth, falling productivity and an economy on the brink of recession. Brown ignored such warnings. Boldly, he claimed the credit for falling interest rates, although they were a worldwide phenomenon, and disregarded the risk of a huge balance of payments deficit from increasing imports. He denied that taxation was increasing, although his extra taxes had raised £8.5 billion. To confirm that unemployment was falling, he ordered that the statistics should be based upon the number of those who were claiming benefits, the very measure he had condemned during the Tory era; and he quoted the Bank of England's finding that unemployment was falling fast, ignoring the fact that the £3.5 billion spent on the New Deal jobs and the extra £1.5 billion spent on working family tax credits meant that each job created cost £50,000. Brown's success could only be proven over the long term, and the omens were fortuitous. Unexpectedly, taxation in 1998 had produced a surplus of £12.4 billion, which, combined with the income from his own extra taxes, was used to fund a cascade of tax cuts 'to help innovators and entrepreneurs for an enterprise economy'. Few noticed that these cuts, the news of which Brown delivered in a rapid, dense monologue, assuming an air of unquestioned triumph, amounted to only £5 billion, just 0.4 per cent of the Treasury's total income. Tinkering satisfied him that he was in charge of the whole engine room.

'The budget,' he told listeners to BBC Radio 4's *Today* programme, 'did cut taxes by £13 billion . . . Taxes have fallen to their lowest level in twenty-eight years.' Brusquely, he denied another truth. By raising taxes on company cars and abolishing mortgage relief, allowances for married couples and allowances to divorced fathers for child maintenance payments, the overall tax burden had increased. He was accused of presenting 'fiddled figures'. With audacity, he turned the facts on their head. The working family tax credit, he insisted, was a 'tax reduction' rather than a benefit. Tim Holt at the Office of National Statistics disagreed. The tax credit, he said, was clearly government spending. Brown was outraged that his word should be doubted, and restricted the publication of Treasury statistics which would show that taxes had risen. Tim Holt became a marked man. Brown asserted: 'There's a great deal of misinformation around and a great deal of allegations being made here, there and everywhere.' Assiduously, after his budget speech he telephoned journalists and editors to hail his own success. His word was believed. The following day's newspaper headlines echoed his self-congratulation. 'Everyone's a winner – there's real cash inside this budget,' declared the *Mirror*. Obligingly, Brown received the IMF's confirmation that his 'skilful management' had protected Britain from the worldwide recession. The news that his unexplained sale of Britain's gold reserves for £4 billion had resulted in a direct loss of £1 billion when the gold price rose was barely reported.

Soon after the budget, at a meeting of the monitoring committee for targets, Richard Packer, the permanent secretary at the ministry of agriculture, protested to Brown about the consequences of the Treasury's spending cuts in 1998. 'You agreed to them,' said Brown. 'No we didn't,' replied Packer. 'You did,' insisted Brown. 'No, they were imposed on us.' 'Well, let's move on,' grunted Brown. Packer was incensed. 'This isn't Hitlerite Germany,' he complained. 'He's got to expect to hear the truth.' Packer was marked for early retirement.

George Bain, the chairman of the Low Pay Unit, became another casualty of Brown's displeasure. Bain's plan to implement the second stage of his report, recommending a minimum wage of £3.70 for 1.3 million workers, antagonised Brown, who wanted to set the minimum wage at £3.50. Bain visited Brown in his office to present his argument. The trade unions, he said, wanted £4, and the CBI were prepared to offer £3.70. Without commenting, Brown signalled that the meeting was completed. On this occasion he had not reckoned with the ire of John Monks. The TUC general secretary was puzzled that Brown, posing as the champion of the working class and diligently attending the birthday parties of the movement's leaders, could suggest that the economy was unable to afford the increase. Monks went to see Brown, and warned him, 'I'll blacken your name if you block anything.' Any interference, Monks continued, would put an end to Brown's bid to become the Labour Party's next leader.

Brown planned his retreat. His intention was to embarrass Stephen Byers, the hapless secretary of state for trade and industry. Byers had publicly argued for a 10 pence increase to £3.60. Whelan leaked to journalists that Brown favoured a 20 pence increase, but had agreed to compromise with Byers at 10 pence and accept a £3.60 minimum wage. In private, Brown again resisted Bain's recommendation that twenty-one-year-olds should be included in the minimum wage. 'It's only 8,000 people,' Bain told Geoff Norris in Blair's office. 'The chancellor does not budge on points of principle,' replied Norris. Bain was surprised that this was the same Gordon Brown who expounded his dream of 'a seamless system without disruptions in financial support to provide a secure income for families with children in transition from welfare to work'. Brown was dismissive towards those who carped about his behaviour; there were others who knew him as a man of genuine compassion.

In summer 1999 Brown paid an undisclosed visit to the New Horizon Youth Centre in Camden Town, a deprived area of north London. His unannounced arrival, scheduled for forty-five minutes, was intended to help him understand how the state might help the dispossessed. He stayed for two hours, witnessing the anguish of young people whose aspirations were limited by their circumstances. He would, he said, measure his success in public life by the improvement of those children's lives, finding a solution to social isolation and poverty.

Their plight inspired his speech to the party conference in Bournemouth on 27 September. His text was social justice and an attack on the Tories' 'short-termist, take what you can, selfish irresponsibility'. Classifying him as usual as 'a leader in waiting', the headlines were a vindication of his optimistic predictions about growth and the recovery. Taxes had raised £316 billion in 1997–98, £12 billion more than predicted, and two years later the Inland Revenue would collect £345 billion. 'The years of responsibility', he preached, had just begun. There was no reason to disbelieve him. He had transformed the Treasury into a powerhouse of initiatives rather than a brake on progress. By granting independence to the Bank of England he had established himself as both savvy and politically dominant. Aided by his attacks on familiar scapegoats – the 'old cartels', the complacent old-boy networks and particularly the banks – his popularity among the delegates had improved, despite their complaints about the stamp duty, levied on share and property sales, and his £1.75 billion climate tax, levied on industry's use of fuel. He offered to repay just £5 million to meet their grievances.

Brown's resentment towards banks was ingrained from his youth in Kirkcaldy. Ever since his father had denounced them for disenfranchising the poor, Brown was convinced of their malevolence. Regulation and competition, he believed, would reduce charges and tilt the balance in favour of the poor. He ignored the competition introduced by the internet and the conversion of building societies into banks. His favoured method for imposing change was to hold an official inquiry. His tool was Don Cruickshank, an unspectacular businessman whose reputation, some felt, occasionally exceeded his achievements. Cruickshank's record at Virgin, the London stock exchange and the Scottish Media Group, and in countering the fanciful Millennium Bug, had given him limited credibility beyond Brown's coterie. But the chancellor knew he could be relied upon to denounce banks for overcharging.

Cruickshank's appointment reflected Brown's confused ideology. Since 1992 he had posed as a convert to enterprise in a free market. He appeared to have abandoned his anger at 'free market dogma', expressed in 1988 in his pamphlet 'Where is the Greed?'. There he had criticised Margaret Thatcher for blaming society's faults on state interference in the market, and for creating a more unequal and deprived country. Since then he had regularly criticised state interference, but in reality he was trying to influence every aspect of society.

Echoing Harold Wilson forty years earlier, Brown spoke confidently about combining science, technology and business so that 'Britain will lead the way in the next stage of the high-tech revolution'. He spoke lyrically of Britain as 'the business capital of the world', with Labour 'on the side of

the inventor, the innovator and the risk-taker'. Over the following two years, he promised, one million uneducated and
poor people would receive free computer courses. With Alan
Sugar he would tour areas of high unemployment in the
regions to encourage the creation of 100,000 new businesses.
To boost the replication of Silicon Valley in Britain, he introduced incentives for new share ownership by employees and
pledged £100 million in tax relief for investment in small
companies. In his vision, shares in 180 new companies would
be traded on the Techmark, the new London stock exchange
modelled on Nasdaq in New York. 'Techmark,' Brown said,
'is a new market for our new generation of dynamic entrepreneurs.' His ideal model was his own creation. On 4 November
1999 he allocated £68 million to CMI, the partnership
between MIT and Cambridge University that had resulted
from his summer conversation in Cape Cod with Chuck Vest.
Brown had driven through the agreement in what an NAO
report would subsequently call 'an unorthodox way', without
offering the project to public tender and excluding the DTI
from conducting its customary examination of costs.

The company, chaired by Lord Trotman, a cross-bencher
and chairman of ICI, would ostensibly own the rights to the
research it carried out, although, with Brown's approval, it
lacked any formal objectives, targets or contract. 'We can
create entrepreneurs,' Professor Sir Alec Broers, the vice-
chancellor of Cambridge University, pronounced, 'who can
use their inspiration and perspiration to build a stronger
British economy. They can change the face of business and
wealth creation in the UK.' However, Professor Michael Kelly,
a future executive director, would confess that the £68 million
project was 'a punt'. Academic protesters complained that
that money would have been sufficient to pay the debts of
all Britain's universities. Brown was unimpressed. During the
signing ceremony on 8 November 1999, he applauded Vest's

description of CMI Ltd as 'the building of a bridge of the minds'. There was an unworldliness in Brown's endearing faith that politicians' pronouncements and legislation could invent wealth creators.

A similar attitude influenced the financing of the London Underground. The hesitant announcement in 1996 by Sir George Young, the Conservatives' transport minister, that the Tube would be privatised had been derided by Brown. The privatisation of the railways was flawed and many believed that privatising the Tube would produce similar results. After the election victory, Brown admitted that the alternative to privatisation was unattractive. Over the previous decade the Underground had wasted £10 billion buying faulty trains, escalators, tracks and lifts. The Treasury's history of erratic investment had been compounded by the absence of financial controls. Dishonesty was rife, and yet more billions were required to repair the decrepit system. The absence of good managers led Brown to consider granting long-term management contracts to private consortia. He was supported by John Prescott, who had long advocated private investment through a Public Private Partnership (PPP) scheme. Notionally, PPP was similar to Gordon Brown's PFIs, except that the word 'public' was included and 'finance' excluded. In practice, the differences were considerable. Both Brown and Prescott believed that a PPP scheme would mean that the Underground would be self-financing rather than dependent on a subsidy from the Treasury. Brown cited predictions prepared by PriceWaterhouseCoopers that a PPP scheme for the Underground would save £4.5 billion over fifteen years in comparison to raising money on the markets by issuing bonds. Initial work in the Treasury using PWC's figures, which were later shown to be based on incorrect assumptions, had produced achingly complicated outline PPP agreements which were not understood by Prescott or Brown. The politicians' motives were not purely professional. The Treasury had constructed the PPP package to thwart the proposals of Ken Livingstone, who had been expelled from the party for opposing Labour's mayoral candidate Frank Dobson, and was now standing as an independent candidate. Livingstone favoured financing the Underground by issuing bonds.

Brown's antagonism towards his old critic was guiding his policy. In the London *Evening Standard* of 19 January 2000, beneath the headline 'Livingstone Must Not be London Mayor', Brown attacked Livingstone's many 'mistakes', including his bias against wealth creation. The same day he and Blair addressed 1,400 members of the London Labour Party, predicting 'disaster' if Livingstone was elected. Originally Brown had supported Glenda Jackson as Labour's candidate for mayor, but he later endorsed the official candidate Frank Dobson. His warnings were rejected by the London voters, who on 4 May 2000 elected Livingstone with a large majority. Dobson was humiliated, finishing third behind the Tories' Steve Norris.

Thereafter, whatever Livingstone suggested, regardless of its virtues, Brown opposed. Livingstone's proposal to issue bonds, Brown argued, would produce less investment and would burden London with an additional £8 to £10 billion debt. Livingstone hit back, 'You can raise as much money as you want with bonds, as long as you can repay them. Gordon shows a lack of grasp of the issues.' The mayor was right. John Prescott had used bonds to finance the Channel Tunnel Rail Link, and New York's subway was successfully financed by bonds.

He might have lost the argument, but Brown was resolved not to lose control. Rather than concede to Livingstone's plan, Brown promoted his PPP contracts, guaranteeing annual profits of about 18 per cent to the private contractors, a generous return. With Blair unable to overrule him, Brown appointed the businessman Malcolm Bates as chairman of the Underground, in order to discredit the mayor's plans. The first unrecoverable cost of Brown's grudge against Livingstone was £455 million, the salaries of lawyers and accountants employed to produce the PPP contracts.

NINE

Enjoying Antagonism

Brown's demons and grudges were celebrated by Labour's critics after the humiliation of millennium night at the Dome in Greenwich. Deliberately, the chancellor spent the night in Scotland. He had refused the prime minister's request to use Treasury money to finance what he correctly anticipated would be a disaster born of extravagance. The flop on the Thames would squander over £1 billion, tarnishing Tony Blair and Peter Mandelson. Brown escaped any blame.

At that temporal moment, Brown was focused on the big picture rather than trivia – the general election Blair planned to hold the following year. His ambition was to rescue Labour's lost soul and transform the country into 'Greater Britain' by reforming its institutions and economy. The unspoken theme of his 'big picture' was the redistribution of wealth and power. Hitting the rich, he believed, would help the poor. 'Fairness' would be stimulated by higher taxation. After a lot of thought, he readopted the slogan 'progressive universalism'. The expression defined his ideal society. In his hatred of hierarchy and disdain for the monarchy, Brown envisioned replacing the class system with a community of equals motivated by a spirit of contribution to the common good. Like all socialists, he believed mankind could be influenced to change its habits. His repeated use of the words

302

'rights and duties', and 'opportunities and obligations', emphasised his conviction that Britain's army of the work-shy and benefit fraudsters could be persuaded to become model citizens. 'I want to encourage civic patriotism,' he explained, 'to empower the forces of compassion and care in our communities.' By 2002, he hoped, the nation would give an extra £1 billion a year to charities, not least to compensate for the extra £400 million those charities were paying every year in his new taxes. He blamed the Conservatives for spreading the cynical view that 'nothing is possible, that big ideas cannot be achieved' and feeding the conviction that in politics 'everyone is just in it for themselves – that politics has no real purpose but the advancement of an elite and that Labour is just the same as the Tories used to be . . . The right equates Britishness with institutions,' he went on. 'It thinks modernising them would destroy Britain. I believe Britishness is far more subtle.' Brown's thoughts reflected Kirkcaldy in the 1950s rather than the realities of Britain's multi-cultural inner cities forty years later. Destroying the nation's historic institutions threatened to replace the community's few binding ideologies with a rootless pseudo-meritocracy. Devolution of power risked exacerbating that self-destruction. But at least, unlike Blair, Brown was genuinely searching for a supreme faith or 'core idea' to bind not only Labour but Britain together.

The realisation of Gordon Brown's vision depended upon camouflaging the redistribution of wealth while reassuring the beguiled middle class. Despite his denials, the Treasury had received £100 billion more than forecast in 1997 from taxation, not least by refusing to raise the level at which the top rate of 40 per cent income tax started. Every year, 9 per cent more people were included in the higher tax band. In addition, the Treasury had astutely raised £22.5 billion by the auction of mobile telephone licences, used to reduce the national debt and consequently lessen interest payments. By

denying the truth about higher taxation Brown risked unpopularity, but he hoped that loyal party members would be
attracted to his 'fairness' philosophy, and would patiently wait
for the rewards. To his frustration, he was misunderstood and
mistrusted by his own supporters.

The government was spending proportionately less on education and health than the Tories had in 1997 – 4.67 per cent
compared to 4.98 per cent. NHS waiting lists had risen to
about 1.2 million people. The squeeze, which was intended
to prove Labour's economic competence, was compounded
by Brown's decision to limit the annual pension increase to
75 pence per week, prompting eighty Labour MPs to sign a
Commons motion on 14 January 2000 condemning him. He
was perplexed. Surely his supporters understood his strategy?
Left-wing MPs and trade union leaders were summoned to
pledge their support. They refused.

Sitting with hunched shoulders in the Commons, aggrieved
by the snub, Brown refused to retreat, so as to avoid appearing
to be a loser. 'We must change Gordon on this,' Sally Morgan,
Blair's political secretary, said to Mark Seddon during a coffee
break at a meeting of the party's National Executive Committee in Milbank. 'Why doesn't the prime minister himself
change Gordon on this?' Seddon smiled. Eventually Brown
would award an extra £5 a week to single pensioners and £8
to couples, but by then his approval ratings in one poll had
fallen from 22 per cent to 6 per cent.

Despite an independent economist testifying that the condition of the poor had improved thanks to increased taxes
funding tax credits, Brown was condemned by some Labour
MPs as insensitive. Partly, his conduct was to blame. Spotting
Peter Kilfoyle, a Blairite, drinking with Fraser Kemp, a friend,
in the Strangers Bar, he could not restrain himself. 'Don't
worry,' he told Kemp. 'I don't hold you responsible for the
things that Kilfoyle says and does.' Both men were startled

by Brown's aggression. There was an absence of humour in his public appearances. Whenever he faced Michael Portillo, the fourth shadow chancellor since 1997, in the Commons, he monotonously regurgitated in response to every question the words 'prudence', 'caution', 'sound finance' and 'Britain in 1997 was heading for a boom and bust recession'. He was untroubled by the weariness of his audience. Accurate criticism was much more hurtful.

Tax credits had proven to be as sterile as Frank Field had predicted. The new system had failed to create an incentive to work; fathers were benefiting at the expense of mothers after the family credit was replaced by the working families' tax credit; and a poverty trap had materialised because the unemployed feared losing their tax credits if they accepted work. Told that his innovations were not working and that the number of applications for the credits was low, Brown ordered the whole system to be changed. Between 1999 and 2003, four different tax credits would be scrapped and five new ones introduced. The work was done in the Treasury. The department of social security was only told of some changes twenty-four hours before the public announcement. The dysfunctionality, Brown hoped, would be as much concealed as the real cost, but his ambition was thwarted by Tim Holt, the director of the government's statistical service. In 1997 Brown had promised to limit increases in social benefits. To achieve that, he wanted the tax credits to be classified as a tax refund. Holt refused, classifying them instead as customary welfare costs. On that criterion, welfare expenditure was projected to rise to at least £117.7 billion, £25 billion more than in 1997, contradicting Brown's pledge to reduce the cost of benefits. Brown was furious. To Holt's misfortune, the ONS had admitted to providing faulty statistics about unemployment. Brown encouraged his resignation and ordered the creation of an Independent Statistical Service.

Holt's departure coincided with Brown reconsidering his attitude towards party loyalists and especially the trade unions. Union leaders were bewildered by the government's approval of unlimited immigration to keep wages down, and its refusal to solve the skills shortage by introducing laws compelling companies to train British workers. While they expected Blair to intone, 'We can't get re-elected if the voters perceive that we are anti-business,' they were irked by the Blairite view that the CBI was more important to the party than the TUC. The fissure between the unions and Blair was an opportunity, Brown perceived, to recover some personal support. He considered various possibilities. He had been invited to lunch at the TUC on 25 May 2000 to celebrate thirty years of the Equal Pay Act. The atmosphere threatened to be uncomfortable. To prove his socialist credentials among the union barons he needed a topic that would highlight 'progressive universalism'. He decided to invent a diversion. The chosen theme was Oxford University and in particular Magdalen College, the most beautiful of the city's buildings and among the best colleges academically. Attacking Oxford, Brown reasoned, was certain to be popular among the party faithful.

For some years, Brown had warned the universities of Oxford and Cambridge that their special funding from the government would be terminated. In his opinion Oxbridge perpetuated elites, disproportionately benefiting privately educated children. He chose to ignore the failure of many state secondary schools to educate children to a sufficiently high standard. Rather, he believed that the most intelligent state-educated children suffered discrimination because of their social background.

On 23 May 2000 Brown was told about a newspaper report that Laura Spence, a 'brilliant' eighteen-year-old pupil from a Tyneside comprehensive with ten 'A starred' GCSEs, had been unfairly rejected when she applied to study medicine at

Magdalen. Without contacting Magdalen to clarify the facts, Brown denounced as 'absolutely scandalous' the college's failure to grant Spence a place after she had achieved 'the best A-level qualifications you can have'. In fact she had not yet taken her A-levels. With perfect class-war rhetoric, Brown blamed the 'disgraceful' decision on Oxford's prejudiced admissions system. While Margaret Thatcher had attacked Oxford's anti-capitalist culture, Brown complained about its pro-capitalist bias, obstructing the enfranchisement of the dispossessed. His onslaught, carefully publicised, was intended to re-establish Brown as a class warrior among the party faithful. Lurking within his conscience was undoubtedly his regret, admitted years earlier, of missing the personal relationships which Britain's rulers forged at Oxford.

Unlike other universities, Oxford set its own short entry examination and rigorously interviewed each applicant for a place. The interview, Brown asserted, was discriminatory, favouring the children of the middle classes over the lower classes. 'This is an interview system,' he stormed, 'that is more reminiscent of the old boy network and the old school tie than genuine justice in our society. It is about time we had an end to that Old Britain when what matters to some people is the privileges you were born with rather than the potential you actually have.' The public's reaction pleased Brown. To the uninformed, his stereotype was credible. He was readily supported by Alastair Campbell, the Oxford-educated Downing Street spokesman, on behalf of the Oxford-educated prime minister. The fact that all eight senior officials advising Brown in the Treasury also went to Oxbridge was not interpreted as an own-goal. Rather, Brown took comfort in their agreement that their *alma mater* should do more to attract pupils 'with real potential' from state schools. Brown's facts were assumed to be accurate. After all, the chancellor boasted about his rigorous research.

Gradually, Magdalen's staff responded to the attack. Having been demoralised by Thatcher, they were determined not to be cowed by Gordon Brown. Their revelations undermined his case. Twenty-two applicants had applied for five places to read medicine at Magdalen. All twenty-two had ten 'A stars' in their GCSEs, and all of them, including Spencer, had been interviewed by six world-class professors. Contrary to Brown's assertion, Spence's marks in the interview ranked among the best; she had failed in the written exams and the structured discussion. The identities of the five successful candidates also damaged Brown's argument. Three were women, three were from ethnic minorities, and two came from comprehensive schools. Spence was rejected simply because there were five better candidates. She subsequently turned down offers to study medicine at other British universities, and opted to study biochemistry with a £65,000 scholarship at Harvard. Brown remained convinced of his righteousness.

Labour's traditionalists applauded Brown's attack on privilege, and urged him to do more. By contrast, Labour's middle-class voters believed he had scored an own-goal. Loudly, he welcomed an investigation by Barry Sheerman, the Labour chairman of the House of Commons Education Select Committee, but discreetly hinted that Sheerman should bury the topic. Sheerman's private doubts were soon justified. Despite their best efforts, his committee could find no evidence of bias against pupils from state schools in Oxford's admissions procedure. On the contrary, the MPs established that interviews were helping state school children, and that Brown's outburst had reduced the number of applicants from state schools. The leaking of their conclusions irritated Brown, who ensured that Sheerman removed any criticism of himself from the published report by omitting to mention the Spence case. His facts, he sniffed, were indisputably correct.

The committee's obligingly bland conclusions coincided

with the launch of Individual Learning Accounts (ILAs), hailed by Brown as the cutting edge of Britain's future. Under his original plan, the ILA scheme gave £200 to every applicant over nineteen to spend on any course classified as educational. Brown anticipated that many of the one million applicants would learn computer skills, an essential qualification for many jobs. The first trials revealed, however, that few of the unemployed were attracted to the scheme. To extend the ILAs' popularity, Brown improved the offer. Instead of receiving £200, applicants would be given an 80 per cent discount on any chosen course. The money would be paid direct to the company providing the lessons. To reclaim the fees, the provider would invoice both the student and the government.

In 1999 Sir Michael Bichard, the permanent secretary at the department of education, told the Treasury that the pilots had failed. His experts advised that the plan should be reconsidered. The Treasury's education advisers were not pleased. The chancellor disliked bad news. As Brown did not pressure them to request more information about the reason for the failure or a description of the expenditure, his officials did not consider questioning the department of education's inexperience in pioneering and managing a business. Instead, Bichard was reminded that ILAs were 'a manifesto commitment to deliver a million accounts by 2002', and that the chancellor was taking a 'close interest'. Everything was focused on fulfilling Brown's ambition to realise what one teaching association later called 'a licence to print money'.

In September 2000, Capita, the only bidder, was awarded the management contract for the ILAs. By then Capita had won ten other management contracts from the government, worth approximately £1 billion. Although Brown described the ILAs as a PPP scheme, suggesting that Capita was risking its own money to earn profits, the final contract approved by the Treasury relieved the company of any financial risk. In autumn 2000, to make people aware of ILAs, the government launched an advertising campaign to support the door-to-door salesmen aggressively offering courses to thousands of potential clients. Besides computer studies, the public was offered many other courses, including 'Glastonbury 2001' and 'Chronic Cats'.

No cabinet minister dared to question the chancellor's initiative. The Treasury's colonisation of welfare, work, the NHS and education was unshakable. Even the prime minister's special advisers were frustrated by Brown's frenetic pace. Supported by the extra £100 billion collected in taxation, his status had recently been entrenched by his reappointment as chairman of the party's election strategy committee. Although Peter Mandelson had simultaneously been chosen to arrange the details of the campaign's plans, Douglas Alexander, Brown's protégé, was the real deputy. The chancellor's pre-eminence was guaranteed by Blair, who relied upon his intellect and smokescreens to conceal bad news.

Three years after the election, Brown recognised that targets were proving to be a hostage to fortune. Without admitting defeat, he ordered his officials to reduce the Treasury's targets from forty to eight, justifying the reduction, by a lexicon of new jargon, as 'slippage', 'measure changed', 'target changed', 'no baseline', 'watered down' and 'no target'. Simultaneously, the chancellor made a stream of announcements: he appointed a two-hundred-strong 'mortgage police force' to help homebuyers find better deals; an investigation into 'rip-off Britain'; an investigation by Martin Taylor to curb tobacco smuggling; an investigation by Lord Grabiner into the £80 billion black economy; a new 'war' against benefit fraudsters; and a plan to withdraw allowances from the unemployed who refused offers of work. All those announcements distracted the public gaze from any new faults in the PFI projects and transport.

The Treasury's management of the PFI contracts had

become complicated and expensive. The civil servants were not trained to negotiate commercial contracts, and their lawyers were charging huge fees. Brown's solution was to transfer responsibility for PFI to Partnerships UK, a company established by the Treasury. He wanted to sell a 51 per cent share in the new company to private investors in autumn 2000. He issued the order without being bothered by the detail. Initially, no suitable executive could be found to manage the company, and private fund managers resisted his enticements to invest. Newspaper reports about his insensitivity to the commercial world were buried in the business pages. The problems in transport were on the front pages.

In 1997, John Prescott had stopped most major roadbuilding projects in order to promote the railways instead. The deputy prime minister described a ten-year transport plan costing £180 billion as 'the biggest public investment programme in transport history'. Two years later, road congestion had worsened and the government's promise to improve the railways had not materialised. Costs were increasing and revenue was falling. Prescott responded with a mixture of unenforceable threats and undeliverable promises. Brown became alarmed. The solution to privatisation, Brown agreed with Prescott, was to impose on the railway companies a Strategic Rail Authority (SRA), with a ten-year plan to invest £60 billion in repairing the dilapidated network. The SRA's first executive chairman would be Sir Alastair Morton, a tough financier renowned for overcoming obstacles to complete the construction of the Channel Tunnel. Morton did not underestimate the railway's problems, or Prescott's intellectual incapacity to master his responsibilities. Frustrated by incompetence, he sought to engage Brown in the complications of rail finance and project management. The chancellor rebuffed the approach. Persistently, Morton demanded a meeting, and eventually Brown relented.

Adopting the impatient, unfriendly attitude familiar to Tim
Holt, George Bain and others, Brown glared silently as Morton
expounded the problems and his proposals to repair the
consequences of privatisation. Brown's reaction depressed
Morton. The chancellor, Morton concluded, regarded railways
as 'a nuisance interfering with his political vision'. Throughout
the presentation, Brown did not ask a perceptive question,
nor did he request any information afterwards. 'He's a radical
reactionary, not interested in detail,' Morton told his staff.
Brown was not prepared to enmesh himself in any detail,
except that the subsidy was to be classified as 'investment',
to avoid increasing the public expenditure deficit. Morton
complained about Brown's engineering of the figures to be
presented to the Treasury. On Brown's orders, Ed Balls and
others in the clan discouraged Morton from seeking further
meetings. Balls understood Brown's dislike of Morton. He was
educated at Oxford, he had earned money in Africa and the
City and, worst of all, he was independent.

The responsibility for supervising the expenditure of £60
billion on transport was assigned to Andrew Turnbull, the
Treasury's permanent secretary, and John Gieve, the Treasury's deputy chief. But neither was wholly trusted by the
chancellor. Brown preferred to rely on Shriti Vadera, an
Oxford-educated half-Sri Lankan banker formerly employed
by UBS Warburgs. Vadera had been recruited by Brown for
her expertise in Third World debt, one of his particular interests. Her lack of experience of transport combined with her
stubbornness would, Brown calculated, antagonise Morton,
who he sensed would resent the diminutive Vadera challenging his expertise.

Brown's assumption was correct. 'She's the assassin of the
SRA,' observed an insider after her second meeting with
Morton. Morton invited John Gieve to meet him to explain
his dilemmas. The emollient official listened as Morton

described the government's failure to invest sufficient money to realise its plans, and offered his solution. Unexpectedly, Vadera burst into the room. 'No one told me about this meeting,' she exclaimed excitedly. As the astonishment subsided, she launched into a forty-minute monologue, hurtling from idea to idea. At the end, she rose and insisted that Gieve accompanied her.

Brown had destabilised Morton's reforms. The deadlock was compounded by the appointment of Gus McDonald, a television tycoon, by Tony Blair as a transport troubleshooter. 'The ten-year transport plan is perfect,' McDonald told Morton. Caught between Vadera, with her limited knowledge of transport, and McDonald, supported by the former director general of the BBC John Birt, an unpaid adviser in 10 Downing Street, who were equally inexperienced, Morton could not even appeal to Prescott. Any initiative undermining Brown's pre-eminence was certain to invite the chancellor's retaliation. Brown's grip on transport was unbreakable, as it was on so many other policies.

On 15 March 2000 Brown successively shook hands with a hundred Labour MPs for photographs to be published in their local newspapers. On the same day he was reawakening animosities in a renewed mild struggle over Britain's membership of the euro. Until 1997 Brown had barely spoken about the euro, except to endorse his own pamphlet, 'Prosperity Through Co-operation', written in 1993. After the election he refused to consult Robin Cook, the foreign secretary, about the euro, and before 1999 he excluded the cabinet from any full discussion. He told Blair that any notion of a referendum on the euro before Labour had won the next election would be 'madness'. Not only would an attempt to converge Britain's economy with Europe's lead to inflation, but the policy would be electoral suicide. 'We need to wait another five years for a referendum,' said Brown.

Brown's scepticism about the euro had been nurtured by Ed Balls. The adviser listed the success of the independent Bank of England, the strength of the British economy contrary to the sceptics' warnings, the developing recession in Europe and the advantages of American entrepreneurship to reinforce Brown's doubts. The European Central Bank's rigid conviction that preventing inflation was more important than stimulating growth was, Brown and Balls agreed, folly. Brown was particularly alarmed by the pressure being put upon Britain, co-ordinated by the German government, to accept a withholding tax on interest payments. One casualty would be the City's lucrative Eurobond business, which employed 10,000 people and generated annual profits of £3 billion. Germany's purpose was to prevent tax avoidance, but representatives from the City convinced Brown that the tax would damage London, and would not solve Germany's problem.

Brown's willingness to accept the City's view was encouraged by his experiences at the monthly meetings of the European finance ministers. In 1997 he had been welcomed by his European counterparts, but by 2000 he was loathed. The ill-concealed sentiments were mutual. He often arrived late in Brussels or Luxembourg, and made excuses to avoid staying for lunch. The tortuous sessions bolstered his conviction that European politicians were building a protectionist, anti-American fortress. Regardless of the formal agenda, he would use the meetings to deliver finger-pointing lectures about Europe's insularity and failure to adopt Anglo-American policies. Without shame, he quoted President Bush: 'When Europe and America are divided, history tends to tragedy. When Europe and America are partners, no trouble or tyranny can stand against us.' Brown promoted Britain as the link between the two blocs, but with limited success.

In that uncomfortable atmosphere, Brown was accused by one senior Commission official of 'treating us all like dirt'.

European ministers complained that he was unwilling to listen. Echoing so many bruised civil servants in Whitehall, Commission officials experienced their own humiliations. Mario Monti, the Italian competition commissioner, complained that a meeting at the Treasury was cancelled at the last moment by Brown on the grounds that he was with Blair. He blamed Brown's impatience on a clash of temperaments. Conciliation and diplomacy, the essential ingredients of European negotiations towards collective decisions, did not appeal to the chancellor.

All those factors confirmed the chancellor's opposition to Germany's proposed withholding tax. 'The bottom line,' he told European finance ministers, 'is that we will stand up for the interests of Britain in this matter.' Berlin's pursuit of a policy contrary to Britain's interests encouraged scepticism among previous British enthusiasts. At the end of the millennium, a Mori poll reported that popular support for the euro had declined among the British business community from 48 per cent to 38 per cent. As the chancellor's doubts grew and the prime minister's enthusiasm reluctantly cooled, Robin Cook's antagonism increased. Cook blamed Brown for the loss of support for the euro. The former Eurosceptic, actively supported by Peter Mandelson, adopted the opposite stance to his old rival. He lobbied the prime minister to commit Britain to early membership. Portraying himself as the only minister making pro-euro arguments in public, and urging surrender on the withholding tax to prove Britain's commitment, Cook spoke enthusiastically while visiting Japan on 6 September 1999 about Euroland's economies enjoying 'real benefits' from the new currency, and promised that Labour 'would not let Britain lose by staying out'. Cook's speech had been cleared by Tony Blair. Brown was infuriated. 'He's plotting,' a Treasury official heard the chancellor grumble. In January 2000, Cook spoke openly in favour of the euro. In

response, Brown's officials called friendly journalists to disparage the foreign secretary. Cook retaliated. Through leaks, conversations and speeches, he complained that the government
was losing control of the euro debate. In particular, he was
irritated that Blair did not reprimand Brown for encouraging
the sceptics. He gave a speech in the House of Commons
warning of problems if Britain was excluded from the euro.

Brown understood the context. With Blair's support,
Stephen Byers and Peter Mandelson were also making pro-
euro speeches. To suppress those cabinet colleagues, Brown
decided to undermine Cook. He demanded to read another
of Cook's speeches in advance, and ordered the removal of
four sentences supporting the euro. Cook retaliated by releas-
ing the unexpurgated speech. Brown's antagonism was aggravated. With some pleasure, he refused in March to fly in the
same plane as Cook to a European summit in Lisbon. Blair
also flew separately. Their separate travel in three chartered
aircraft cost £30,000 instead of the £9,000 it would have cost
with BA.

At the annual Mansion House speech on 15 June 2000,
Brown presented himself as the 'guardian of the tests'. He
declared himself solely responsible for the government's
decision that entry would only follow proof of 'sustainable
convergence' between the euro and sterling. Shortly after, at
Brown's insistence, Blair told the cabinet to stick to that
'agreed' policy. Cook was furious, and on 18 June again
refused to fly in the same plane as Brown on another trip to
Lisbon. Cook's petulance was leaked to a journalist by the
Treasury. The previous embarrassment, Blair decided, could
not be repeated. Two private planes were cancelled, and Blair,
Brown and Cook flew together. Two days later, Brown
claimed victory. Standing alone against fourteen governments, he succeeded in having the withholding tax replaced
by a commitment to an exchange of information. Brown's

triumphalism provoked his enemies. Mandelson accused him of being 'neuralgic and totally unrelaxed' – a pain in the neck – about the euro. The chancellor, he said, had developed a 'territorial fetish' about the policy. Mandelson was supported by Cook. The Foreign Office had leaked a confidential memorandum from Sir Stephen Gomersall, the British ambassador in Japan, warning of a loss of Japanese investment if Britain did not join the euro. British industry, added Cook, was close to 'meltdown'. This hyperbole, Brown suspected, was encouraged by Blair and Mandelson. On 29 June 2000 Mandelson greeted the chancellor as they passed in a Commons corridor, but Brown ignored him. A few minutes later Mandelson walked by again and repeated his greeting. Brown ignored him for a second time. He enjoyed displaying his enmities in public.

Brown's coercive diplomacy alarmed Alastair Campbell. The chancellor was undermining Blair's primacy. The Treasury's veto over every policy except foreign relations was intolerable. The prime minister resented the suggestion that his only historic legacy would be constitutional reform and neutralising the British establishment. 'I don't want to be remembered just for that,' he told a senior adviser angrily. He remained bruised by the slow handclap admonished by the Women's Institute on 7 June 2000. On Campbell's recommendation he summoned a meeting with Cook, Brown and Byers, at which he reiterated the government's policy to join the euro. 'All I'm doing is arguing for that,' said Cook. Everyone stared at Brown, seeking his agreement. In Cook's version, the chancellor sat sulking, 'his face like a wet winter's morning in Fife'. He mumbled a refusal, demonstrating his veto over Blair. He found their antipathy refreshing. Either as the hero or the villain, he was winning his battle against Blair.

Only one person avoided Brown's resentment during those

months. After five years, Sarah Macaulay had replaced their clandestine liaison with a more public relationship. At forty-nine, Brown had been persuaded that a bachelor would have difficulty in being elected as the Labour Party's leader. Sarah's disgruntlement had been supported by his closest friends. All urged him finally to agree to marriage.

On Wednesday, 2 August 2000, a group of about twenty-five close friends and family members of Gordon Brown and Sarah Macaulay gathered for dinner in an Edinburgh hotel. The guests, including Ed Balls and Charlie Whelan, had been told two weeks earlier that Brown intended to marry on 3 August. John, his elder brother, had heard on his mobile telephone. 'I've got good news,' Gordon announced. Secrecy, everyone was told, was vital. Not even Tony Blair knew. Until then, Sarah's continuing embarrassment had not troubled Brown. He had brushed aside John Prescott's public appeal from the platform during the party conference in 1998: 'Gordon, forget about Prudence and name the day for Sarah. She's a lovely lass.' In the same year, he had also admitted wanting children. 'Oh, I do hope so,' he told Mary Riddell. 'It was amazing watching my brothers' children and seeing how much they altered over a few months.' But he had let Sarah Macaulay wait another two years, often not calling her for days. The unbearableness of her life had been evident at Nick Brown's recent birthday party, when her red eyes suggested a terrible recent argument. 'Gordon Dumps Sarah' were the headlines.

The guests at the prenuptial dinner in Edinburgh knew better than to ask their host to explain his change of mind. Over the previous years they had witnessed few obvious demonstrations of true love between the couple. Brown's overtly unloving attitude towards women had not been changed by his commitment to Sarah.

The ringing of a mobile phone interrupted the celebration.

The message was half expected: their secret had been exposed. Within moments, the party disintegrated. Brown, Balls and Whelan left the table, taking positions on different sides of the room to work their own phones. At 11 p.m. newspaper editors were called to be briefed. The guests who remained at the table were baffled. The wedding seemed to be no longer a personal attestation of love, but a media event about Gordon Brown. Even the bride had disappeared to her room to issue some last-minute invitations to what had become a publicity operation with the certainty of 'a great picture'.

How the secret emerged was predictable. The banns were posted, and Tom Donald, a local journalist and old friend, was asked not to report the announcement until the last moment. As the wedding plans developed it became apparent that the ceremony and the reception, partly arranged by Mary Goudie, a good friend of Brown's who was given a peerage in 1998, were always intended to be media events. Some cynics suggested that the marriage was no more than a gesture to advance the groom's ambitions for the premiership. Those inside his house in North Queensferry the following morning, however, would disagree. The ceremony at 10.15 a.m., conducted in the living room by the Reverend Sheila Munro in front of thirty guests – few had been able to accept the last-minute invitations – was genuinely emotional. The thirty-six-year-old bride, dressed in cream, smiled at her mother Pauline and stepfather Professor Patrick Vaughan shortly after Brown, standing beside his brother John as best man, completed his vows. At the conclusion, the simplicity was replaced by the surreal.

Unlike the calm, dignified mood inside the house, on the pavement outside, the army of journalists laying siege had become restive. 'Turn on the TV,' suggested a guest. Sky News was broadcasting a live report about the guests being besieged by journalists. Turning away from the television to look out of the window, the viewers confirmed the reality and turned back again to watch Sky confirm their plight. The biggest smile was Charlie Whelan's. The wedding had become a big story. 'I'll take them some champagne,' said a guest. A bottle of Sainsbury's 'Blanc de Noir' – a special offer at £11.99 chosen by the groom – was delivered to those outside on the pavement. The food for the reception, it transpired, had been prepared by students at the local technical college. 'Fine Day for a Tight Wedding' would be one newspaper's headline the following day.

Gordon and Sarah Brown unexpectedly appeared, walking through the garden towards the journalists. They posed for photographs while Whelan provided information. One photograph showed Brown awkwardly kissing the bride. 'How often have they done that?' asked a witness. By the time the nation was reading the newspaper reports of the event, Mr and Mrs Brown had arrived in America courtesy of Virgin Atlantic, which had upgraded their economy tickets. The Wequassett Inn, a resort club on Cape Cod, did not emulate the airline's self-promotion: the chancellor and his new wife spent their honeymoon in a standard room without a sea view, overlooking a patch of grass and a wall. The only cloud was the confessions in the *Mail on Sunday* of Ken Lukowiac, a Falklands veteran and a former boyfriend of Sarah's.

Sarah immediately ordered new stationery headed 'Sarah Brown'. That signalled a mission as much as a marriage. Her purpose was to promote her husband and the image of 'The Browns'. Carefully, she had verified which individuals were unquestioning allies, and which would not be outrightly helpful to the cause. She publicised the NSPCC's 'Full Stop Campaign' against child violence, and conveniently combined in her meetings with newspaper editors and other media executives promotion of both the charity's interests and her husband's. Any doubts about her intentions were extinguished by the party held on Monday, 18 September 2000 at the Jerwood Space art centre in Southwark. Unlike their festive party in Fife earlier that month for three hundred Scots, their personal friends in London were swamped by celebrities. Five hundred guests were invited without their spouses for a major networking operation, offered real champagne and sushi canapés. In the ensuing post mortem, the topic was not who was there – among the guests were the Archbishop of Canterbury, the Chief Rabbi, Richard Littlejohn, Ben Elton, newspaper editors, union leaders and Sir Richard Wilson, the cabinet secretary, as a sign of reconciliation – but who had been deliberately omitted. There were, it was noted, few English Labour MPs. Gordon Brown gave a hilarious speech based upon the euro debate – how he and Sarah had agreed 'in principle' to get married but had to pass five tests, especially 'convergence' and 'long-term sustainability'. His delivery was perfect. Unlike his parliamentary speeches, expressed in a dull monotone, he spoke with an engaging naturalness he deliberately excluded from his political life. Tony and Cherie Blair arrived through the back door, and stayed only twenty minutes. The party coincided with the government's worst crisis since 1997. The responsibility, Blair complained, was Gordon's. Antagonism ruled again.

Over the previous decade, Brown's assertion of control over Labour's economic policy and his disengagement from backbench MPs had isolated him from the resentment of Britain's working people to the highest fuel prices in Europe. Fuel taxes had risen automatically but unexpectedly fast, on the basis of a formula introduced by the Conservatives. Despite the protests of road hauliers that the additional costs were intolerable, Brown had described allegations that the government had received a huge windfall as 'absolutely ridiculous'. In the past year, he retorted, they had only received an extra £400 million. As so often, the facts contradicted Brown's assertions.

Oil prices had risen over the previous six months from $22 to $34 a barrel, earning the Treasury an additional 8 pence per litre, or £4 billion in VAT.

Road hauliers, who found themselves working at a loss, had begun to blockade oil refineries. Television news programmes dug out grainy images of the 'winter of discontent' in 1979 to remind Britons of Labour's last confrontation with the trade unions. Brown adamantly denied any wrongdoing. A cut in fuel taxes, he said, would mean less money for health and education. Despite the spread of blockades and fears of petrol rationing, he refused to retreat. The mention of emergency laws to force the striking tanker drivers to deliver oil and of the mobilisation of the army created a sense of panic. The public was bewildered. Brown, the non-driver who had 'never bought a litre of petrol in his life', was assailed for his dubious judgement. Despite his self-declared passion for enterprise, he did not understand the arithmetic that high fuel taxes had deprived road hauliers of any profits.

A personal appeal by Tony Blair to consider a tax reduction was ignored. Brown mentioned the sanctity of the '£40 billion extra' he had pledged to spend on health and education, forgetting that his sums had been exposed as inaccurate. He seemed isolated from the national mood. The blockade and the petrol shortage dominated the nation's life. 'I'll listen,' he said, but he did not convince many, especially beleaguered Labour MPs who recalled his destabilisation of Harriet Harman and the 75 pence pension increase. The trade unions were angered by his support for means tests and maintaining the link between pensions and inflation rather than average earnings.

By 14 September 2000, Brown's stubborn refusal to bow to deadlines and threats had shaken Blair. His chancellor seemed unable to distinguish between greedy public sector workers and the genuine plight of small businessmen. There was a damaging blur between his political instincts and tactics. Two months after winning enormous popularity for increasing expenditure on health and education, Brown was now widely disliked. For the first time since 1992, the Tories were ahead of Labour in the opinion polls. Gaunt and exhausted, Blair held a televised press conference inside 10 Downing Street to assert that the government was in full control of events, and would bring the fuel dispute to a speedy end. He hinted at cuts in fuel taxation in the spring budget. That was sufficient to end the blockades and the panic.

The respite was short-lived. Five days later, on the eve of the party conference, both Blair and Brown were excruciatingly embarrassed. Andrew Rawnsley, a political columnist and author, alleged that both men had given inaccurate accounts of the Ecclestone donation in 1997. Brown was challenged to explain whether his profession of ignorance about the size and source of the donation on the *Today* programme was true or not. Rawnsley suggested that Brown had been told the details of the donation by Blair during a car journey four days before his denial of any knowledge on the BBC radio programme. Brown was shaken by the allegation; not only by its substantial accuracy, but by the fingerprints of Downing Street's assistance to Rawnsley. Quite clearly Anji Hunter, Peter Mandelson, Alastair Campbell and other intimate associates of Blair had helped to discomfit the chancellor, possibly in retaliation for the Routledge biography. Brown denied lying on the *Today* programme, although his denial was equivocal. He admitted having been aware of a 'sizeable' donation, but denied knowledge of the precise amount. Blair, he explained, had asked for his advice, but he had replied, 'Look, I'm not getting involved in the details of this. I can't.' Few were convinced. The notion that Brown's natural curiosity would not have prompted questions to find out the full story was unrealistic.

The disbelief destabilised both Blair and Brown. The word 'crisis' was mentioned, despite the government's successes and enormous parliamentary majority. There was a mood suggesting an irrecoverable slide towards defeat in the next election. All this anxiety undermined Brown's self-control inside the Treasury. Biting his nails again, he behaved uncertainly as chairman of successive committee meetings. Frequently, his temper flared. The pressure was hateful. He resented the suggestion that the pension and fuel debacles were caused by himself, but sensed that he was trapped in a hopeless cul-de-sac. While he recognised that he would have to retreat on fuel tax, he would not surrender on pensions.

With relief, Brown flew to a Commonwealth finance ministers' meeting in Malta, and then to talks with G7 finance ministers in Prague. During those days he complained about 'taking the flak for Tony'. His predicament, he convinced himself, was caused by Blair's staff; the same people who accused him of suffering psychological flaws. Focusing on the enemies within galvanised his efforts to prepare a rousing speech for the party faithful at their conference in Brighton on Monday, 25 September 2000. Attack would be his best defence. His theme would be the poor and their real enemies, the loathsome Tories. Helped by Bob Shrum, an adviser to Al Gore, the Democrat candidate in the continuing American presidential election campaign, Brown inserted pledges of help to 'hardworking families', and comments about the good fortune of citizens who had 'a government on their side'. The content of the speech was influenced by the analyses of his own focus groups, recently organised by Deborah Mattinson.

Sarah was in place in the hall on Brown's arrival direct from the airport. His forty-five-minute oration successfully stirred his audience. The four-minute standing ovation was followed by Sarah's appearance on the platform, and the couple kissing – unawkwardly on this occasion – in striking similarity to Al Gore's appearance with his wife Tipper at a recent rally. Shortly afterwards, to avoid personal contact with his critics and to miss Blair's speech, he returned to Prague. He had not surrendered his position on pensions, and was not concerned that the trade unions would force a vote to defeat the party's leadership. He had correctly judged that pro-Tory opinion polls would soon swing back towards the government. The electors did not trust the Conservatives.

Retaliation was never far from Brown's mind. The unflattering suggestions in Andrew Rawnsley's book *Servants of the People* of his volatility and lack of candour rankled. He blamed the usual suspects in Downing Street, and particularly Peter Mandelson. With Brown's agreement, Geoffrey Robinson, tarnished but still credible, had written his political memoirs. In the continuing battle of the books, Brown had little choice but to support Robinson's attempt to restore his reputation as an effective Treasury minister traduced by vindictive enemies. Robinson had sufficient embarrassing information about his financial and personal relations with Blair and Brown to remain potentially dangerous. On the other hand, he could be relied upon to give a colourful account of his loan to Peter Mandelson, irking the resurrected politician, appointed minister for Northern Ireland in 1999. Newspaper serialisation of Robinson's book was timed for just after the party conference.

Brown's continuing trust of Robinson cast doubts upon the chancellor's judgement. By then he must have known that Robinson had not been straightforward about his secret trust in the Channel Islands, and should have suspected that Robinson had not told the truth to the Commons about his financial relationship with Robert Maxwell. When the truth did emerge in March 2001 – that he had concealed receiving £200,000 from Maxwell – Robinson was reprimanded and suspended from the Commons for three weeks. Even then, Brown denounced the truth to the Treasury select committee as 'fictional nonsense' and 'gossip'. He refused to acknowledge that for four years his entertainment and research had been financed by a tarnished man who had profited from suspicious deals. In Brown's opinion, Robinson remained a trusted ally able to help his cause, especially against Mandelson.

The chancellor was obsessed by Mandelson's close relationship with Blair, which rivalled his own influence. He was irritated by Blair's shared enthusiasm with Mandelson for the euro. Mandelson had been allowed to demand the cabinet's reconsideration of its 'tactical error' in not working towards membership. That decision, Brown believed, broke his agreement with Blair to maintain silence about the euro until after the next election. Thereafter, they agreed to campaign for a 'yes' vote in a referendum to be held two years after the election. Neither Blair nor Mandelson quite trusted Brown's commitment. On occasion he would speak about the combined strength of Europe and its ability to survive America's growing economic crisis and unexpected stock market collapse, while on other occasions he lamented that the single market had not lowered prices or created new jobs; that the Commission's advice to cut public spending in Britain was folly; and that the promised removal by Brussels of restrictive regulations across Europe had not materialised.

As a committed European, Mandelson minimised those discrepancies, compounding Brown's resentment of his rival's resurgence. Geoffrey Robinson's book, describing his loan for Mandelson's house and portraying him as an extreme pro-European, was deliberately hurtful. Mandelson was stung by the revival of warfare. Irritated by Blair's neutrality and Brown's smug silence about Robinson's allegations, Mandelson vigorously rebutted them. 'It is a piece of terrorism,' he exclaimed about Robinson's book. 'They are trying to smear me personally and destroy me politically. They want to take out a pro-European minister.' He felt that Brown was manoeuvring to forestall his appointment as foreign secretary; and that Robinson's book was a prelude to more discomfiture.

Three months later, on 21 January 2001, the *Observer* reported that Mandelson had helped Srichand Hinduja, a controversial Indian businessman, to receive British nationality after contributing £1 million to the Faith Zone in the Millennium Dome. Mandelson denied that he ever sought to influence the decision on Hinduja's application, but three days later he was forced to resign for the second time. His departure delighted Brown, whose position was immeasurably strengthened, especially on Europe. Appearing on the *Today* programme, he refused eleven times to answer the same question about how long the assessment process to join the euro would take. 'I won't be bounced into this,' he replied, with no fear of any challenge from other ministers. Within just four months, his status had been transformed.

To have travelled from widespread unpopularity before the party conference in the autumn to 65 per cent approval in the opinion polls by the spring of 2001 was remarkable. The 'most popular chancellor since the war' was the *Daily Telegraph*'s headline. Some carped that Brown was 'the master of illusion', but others acknowledged him as a man of substance rather than spin. He had emerged as a modern politician of principle, enjoying good relations with Labour's heartland, and relatively untouched by New Labour's scandals. In contrast to the Blairs, who apparently sought celebrity, his modesty was endearing. At the recent funeral of Jill Craigie, the wife of Michael Foot, Brown was seated at the rear of the hall while Cherie Blair and Fiona Millar marched straight to the front. That modesty in public was not replicated in Whitehall. His certainty about the finance and management of the public services, especially transport and the NHS, had frustrated improvements. His stubbornness, misjudged by Blair

and his advisers in Downing Street, was leading towards a
dead end.

John Prescott's management of transport had failed to bring
about any improvements in Britain's roads and railways. The
fault was not entirely his. Repeatedly, his department's proposals were questioned by the Treasury. Brown was seeking
to encourage private investors to finance the necessary work
on the Channel Tunnel rail link, the London Underground
and the rail network, but was loath to allow those risking
their money to control the projects or to earn an unestimated
profit. He did not understand that financiers charge high rates
of interest for those risks they cannot control. The result, after
four years in government, was depressing. A report by the
NAO about the Tunnel and its link to London concluded that
the public was not receiving value for money; during the
previous four years the management of the rail network,
battered by the government's criticism, had deteriorated; and
the proposed investment in the Underground by the Treasury's PPP scheme was still obstructed by London's mayor Ken
Livingstone, who favoured bonds and state management.
Prescott's advisers mentioned their exasperation with the
chancellor, and Treasury officials reciprocated with similar
complaints.

While reorganising the rail network baffled the Treasury
and the government's advisers, the disagreement about the
Underground's finances was a personal battle between Brown
and Livingstone. The Treasury bore much of the historic blame
for the Tube's decline. Constant interference by the Treasury
over previous decades, failing to adhere to long-term plans,
restricting investment and appointing poor managers, had
caused waste and poor performance. Brown's solution was the
semi-privatisation of the network, financed by a PPP scheme,
which avoided borrowing for investment and, in theory,
imposed the financial risk on the private contractors. Under

the scheme, the existing unified management of the network was to be replaced by two managements – one for maintenance and one for running the trains – which in turn would supervise three separate businesses. A similar division of responsibilities on the national rail network had caused chaos, but Brown refused to acknowledge the parallels. Ignoring the party's manifesto commitment, he expressed his hostility to public ownership of the Tube, and instructed Shriti Vadera, the expert on Third World debt, to impose his solution on Bob Kiley, the American manager appointed by Livingstone.

Vadera's abruptness, simply saying 'no' at meetings, successfully alienated Kiley and others, and by the end of January 2001 negotiations between the Treasury and Livingstone were deadlocked. Tony Blair was persuaded to intervene. The solution agreed between him and Kiley was a revised version of PPP and a unified management under Kiley. Blair asked Brown to reach an agreement on that basis, but Brown brusquely disagreed and refused to meet Kiley. Instead, on 12 February he delegated Vadera to see the American. Quoting the flawed study by PriceWaterhouseCoopers, Vadera told Kiley that she 'could not sanction public control of the Tube under any circumstances'. A few days later, a compromise agreement between Prescott and Kiley was aborted on Brown's orders. The chancellor had no patience for a man appointed by Ken Livingstone. Under no circumstances would he sanction the continued public control of the Tube. No resolution would be possible before the election. Brown would reject accusations that his grudge against Livingstone was the reason for four years of paralysis. Solving the problems of the Tube and the railways, he replied, required time and finance. Money could not be spent without careful scrutiny.

That excuse was arguably acceptable for transport, but lame for the government's failure since 1997 to improve the NHS.

In the 1997 election campaign, Labour had warned the country that there were only 'fourteen days to save the NHS', and then 'twenty-four hours to save the NHS'. Brown had blamed the Tories for wasting £1.5 billion in 'costly red tape' and a vast bureaucracy. Within two years, he said, Labour would cut that waste. Two years later, the opposite had occurred. Frank Dobson, the secretary of state for health, had abolished the new Health Authorities which had just mastered effective purchasing, and appointed regional Primary Care Trusts. All those employed by the Health Authorities had been compelled to reapply for their jobs. Many skilled administrators abandoned the NHS, to be replaced by inexperienced recruits. The new system had proved to be less amenable to improving the efficiency of management.

In June 1999 Dobson had handwritten a memorandum to the prime minister warning about the crisis in the NHS. To prevent leaks, the text was given to his parliamentary secretary for typing rather than to a civil servant, marked 'secret', and placed inside a plain brown envelope. Dobson himself personally delivered his doom-laden message to Downing Street. The NHS, he wrote, was 'bleeding and it could lead to a haemorrhage . . . The situation is now chronic rather than acute . . . We need money to save the patient.' In graphic language, he described the alarming gap between Labour's aspirations and reality: 'We have raised expectations without the funds to deliver.' During the two-year squeeze Brown had provided an extra £290 million for the NHS, but that was a pittance compared to the scale of the problems. Dobson concluded that only billions of pounds of extra spending could save Labour's historic flagship.

Dobson's secret plea had been made in the midst of a self-created crisis. In the name of 'modernisation', his principal reform had been the dismantlement of the 'internal market', the Conservatives' scheme to devolve power to individual hospitals, empower patients to decide where to seek treatment, and to impose stricter financial accountability upon the hospital trusts. In Dobson's opinion, if the trusts continued, the NHS was destined to be replaced by privatised health care. His solution was to invest extra billions into the NHS and to trust its staff – about one million employees – to produce the world's best health service. He ignored research that had revealed the NHS's financial sloppiness and the inefficiencies created by centralised control from London. His reorganisation had coincided with an outbreak of 'flu and shortages of medical staff in hospitals. Personal horror stories and pictures of the victims of what the *Daily Mail* vigorously condemned as Britain's 'Third World health service' were unhelpful. The fault was partly Dobson's. Unaware of the complexities of the NHS, he had failed to ask the right questions to discover the consequences of Tory spending cuts, not least the unexpected increase in waiting lists.

Brown dismissed Dobson's letter to Blair as intemperate. Although he was himself among the NHS's most uncritical advocates, he had never studied its problems. Like Dobson, he believed that more money was the solution to its ills. Unlike Dobson, he hoped that his restrictions on NHS spending would provoke managers to reduce waste. A credible contemporary study by Tim Ambler of the London Business School had found that 8 per cent of the national budget – £30 billion – was wasted on bureaucracy and inefficiency. One fifth of the NHS's budget was estimated to be lost to waste and fraud. At the Treasury's suggestion, the department of health imposed targets to cut waiting lists and to reduce spending on bureaucracy. 'We have set tough efficiency targets and reordered departmental budgets,' Brown had announced on 14 July 1998. Four months after his dubious claim to have increased the health and education budgets by £40 billion, he also pledged that NHS spending would rise by a further £21 billion over three years. Seventeen months later, the NHS's crisis had escalated. The government, as Dobson had predicted, was blamed. Brown's plan was to present himself as the saviour in his budget in March 2000. The prime minister's edginess interrupted his timetable.

In January 2000, television news bulletins showed patients lying on stretchers in hospital corridors for days. The reports publicised the plight of Mavis Skeet, a cancer patient, whose long wait for treatment had possibly condemned her to a premature death. Blair's advisers understood the electoral risks of not offering an instant solution. On 12 January the prime minister had repeated in the Commons Brown's pledge that an additional £21 billion had been spent on more doctors and nurses since 1997. In fact the extra expenditure had been calculated as £10.3 billion, and the number of medical staff employed by the NHS had declined. Brown was criticised by Blair for failing to provide sufficient funds and frustrating reform. Four days later, appearing on BBC TV's *Breakfast with Frost*, Blair unexpectedly promised that NHS spending would rise by 5 per cent every year until 2006. 'At the end of five years,' he promised, 'we will be in a position where our health service spending comes up to the average of the European Union.' Brown was appalled, especially after he discovered that Alan Milburn, the new health minister, had secretly encouraged Blair's announcement. 'You've stolen my budget,' he screamed at Blair, and demanded to know where he was going to find an extra £12 billion every year. (In reality, to match European spending the true figure would have been £29 billion extra every year.) Within twenty-four hours, Blair's spokesman had modified the pledge to an 'aspiration'. 'It's a long-term challenge,' confirmed Brown, after lecturing the cabinet on the need to avoid promising unaffordable spending commitments reminiscent of Old Labour's tax and spend.

That, however, was precisely Brown's solution: extra money plus targets. In his budget speech on 21 March 2000 he announced extra spending on the NHS of £20 billion over the next four years. That would be real money, he promised, without double counting. Naturally, he would disguise the necessary tax increases and write a budget speech emphasising how taxes had been cut. By 2003–04, he promised, health spending would increase by 80 per cent above Tory expenditure, and education spending by 60 per cent. Seven days later, Tony Blair uttered similar undertakings. Since 1997, he said, NHS spending had increased to 7.6 per cent of gross domestic product, a good comparison with Europe. In fact, spending on the NHS was 6.3 per cent. The difference of £13 billion had been spent on private health. The flummery was illustrated by Brown's claim about nurses. 'In the last year alone,' he said, 'there has been an increase of 4,500 nurses working in the health service. This is just a start.' He pledged to recruit 'at least 10,000 more nurses', and even more 'in the years to come'. In truth, there would be no more nurses than Dobson had promised two years earlier. Nevertheless, Brown's budget speech won an ecstatic reception. The Tories' predictions of gloom and recession were dismissed, despite the beginning of the crash of high-tech shares on Wall Street.

Statistics could not conceal the absence of a solution. The 1997 Labour manifesto had included, at Brown's behest, a heartfelt sentiment: 'The myth that the solution to every problem is increased spending has been comprehensively dispelled . . . The level of public spending is no longer the best measure of effectiveness of government action in the public interest.' Three years later, his prediction had been vindicated. The lengthening hospital waiting lists showed the inadequacy of relying on money and targets. Targets had been imposed without understanding how hospitals could falsify statistics, thereby giving an impression of increased inefficiency. Tim

Ambler's study on waste had been endorsed by other studies. Between 1993 and 2000, one researcher reported, NHS funding had increased by 45 per cent, but there was no evidence that patient care had improved. Another researcher would later suggest that between 1997–98 and 2000–01, health spending increased by 41 per cent, yet the NHS treated only 2 per cent more patients (although many other patients were treated by GPs and in new clinics). By the government's own calculations, the dismantling of the internal market had saved £264 million rather than the £1.5 billion Frank Dobson had promised.

In reality, even those alleged savings had not occurred. Extra money had been spent on bureaucracy and monitoring targets. Over the previous four years an additional 13,000 administrators had been recruited at an annual cost of £400 million, or cumulatively £1.6 billion. In 2001 there would be more administrators in the NHS than qualified nurses – 269,080 administrators and 266,170 nurses. Private hospitals employed only 25 per cent of their staff as administrators. Since 1995 the number of managers in the NHS had increased by about 30 per cent, but there were only 8 per cent more nurses. Money had proven not to be the sole answer to improving health care. The alarming spread in hospitals of the resistant 'superbug' MRSA could have been prevented by better hygiene, not least by the simple expedient of staff washing their hands. Remedying that malaise would not cost money, but did require effective management. Extra money was not the only answer to the NHS's problems. The NHS in Scotland received about 18 per cent more money per person than the NHS in England – the same percentage as in Europe – but life expectancy in Scotland was, on most indexes, significantly lower.

Those statistics staggered Brown and Alan Milburn, the health minister. No one in the Treasury could accurately explain the NHS's problems and offer ideas for improvement. Public pressure demanded a response, but the Tories' solution – patients' choice and devolved independent hospitals – was unacceptable. Despite his assertion in *The Times* that he had terminated the 'Whitehall knows best' syndrome, Brown could only imagine the NHS managed by central government. Concerned by Blair's order to search for a solution, Brown's remedy was to commission his own independent report to offer a plan for the NHS's development until 2022.

In April 2001 Brown approached Derek Wanless, a mathematical statistician who had spent most of his career at the NatWest bank, rising in 1992 from chief executive to chairman. In 1999, after the bank's demise and takeover by the Royal Bank of Scotland, Wanless retired with £3 million in compensation. The two had met before the 1997 election at a bankers' meeting. Brown had been tense, appearing as if he wished he were anywhere else other than accepting hospitality from bankers. Wanless was not Brown's first choice, but at that moment of political desperation he was the best man available. 'I want to know whether Britain can continue to afford the NHS,' Brown told him. 'But before you start, I want to know that you believe in the NHS.' 'I do,' replied Wanless, although he admitted to using private health care. 'I'll do the job on condition that I can also consider "patient's choice", allowing people to select their hospitals and choose their treatment, and that my report will be published.' Brown agreed. 'Can I have the costings the Treasury has used for the past ten years for the NHS?' asked Wanless. Brown's eyes glazed. 'I need to know if the funding of the NHS is the driver of the total cost,' said Wanless. Brown clearly did not understand the question.

Inadvertently, Wanless had touched on Brown's weakness. There were vision and ideas, but there was an impediment to their implementation. He lacked the detachment of an accomplished technician. Inexperience of management and accountancy was a common limitation among Labour politicians. At the ministry of agriculture, Nick Brown's delayed reaction to the outbreak of a foot and mouth epidemic in Britain's herds and the mismanagement of its control and eradication would cost £8 billion. A colossal 1.2 million animals were being slaughtered, 70 per cent of which were healthy, and contractors and farmers were being paid recklessly inflated fees and compensation. Gordon Brown was blameless for that fiasco, but he did not support an independent inquiry into it. Labour had learnt from the Tories' candour in commissioning a judicial inquiry into the BSE outbreak that independent scrutiny was a self-inflicted wound and best avoided.

Gordon Brown however did bear some responsibility for the developing mismanagement of the scheme to encourage the purchase of ILAs. By May 2001 a million adults had subscribed for ILAs, and each had received about £200. The government's target had been achieved a year earlier than forecast. Five months later, the number of subscribers was heading towards 2.5 million, and the providers were chortling that the ILA programme was 'a victim of its own success'. Brown was ecstatic. His inexperience led him to pay little attention to reports that the department of education had received letters from the public reporting fraud.

The total budget for the ILA scheme had originally been set at £199 million. By May 2001, the department of education had spent £273.4 million. Officials in the department were surprised. None of those responsible understood how to monitor the distribution of money to the public. At the most senior level, the civil servants consoled themselves that, on the Treasury's orders, they could rely on Capita. Nevertheless, they were concerned. If ILAs continued to prove so popular, the cost over two years was projected to be £600 million.

Instead of stopping the scheme, David Normington, the new permanent secretary, under pressure from the Treasury to keep it operating, was assured that nothing was amiss. ILAs, he knew, were among Gordon Brown's favoured projects. Yet the scheme's flaws were blatant. Any provider could make a false claim for providing the service, or invent fictitious 'students' who would automatically receive £200 each. The government's lawyers had also failed to include in the contract a requirement for Capita to report frauds, allowing its operations director to plead that the possibility of fraud had never 'crossed our minds'. Brown had never asked, 'How will we check that the scheme is genuinely successful?' He planned, after the next election, to promote John Healey as the new Adult Skills minister to supervise ILAs, but meanwhile he persuaded Estelle Morris, the new minister of education, to continue the scheme. The letters alleging fraud to the department of education continued to be ignored by the Treasury. The confused management of ILAs was a microcosm of the complexity introduced into the tax system since 1997.

In the weeks before the 2001 election, Brown and Ed Balls pondered how to present Labour's taxation policy to the party's best advantage. Four years earlier, Brown had given the impression that taxes would not increase. Since then they had risen to 37.8 per cent of gross domestic product, compared to 35.2 per cent in 1996–97. In 2000–01 they would reach 38 per cent of gross domestic product, representing an extra £17.7 billion in taxes. The Institute of Fiscal Studies projected that taxation in 2002 would rise to 40 per cent of gross domestic product. Despite Gordon Brown's assertion in his 2000 budget speech that the typical family was 'paying less tax than at any time since 1972', taxation was, with the inclusion of VAT, excise duties and the end of mortgage relief and personal allowances, at a near record high. Brown prided himself on the mirage. Among his coterie, it was boasted that even the best economic commentators, Neil Collins of the *Daily Telegraph* and Will Hutton of the *Observer*, could not embarrass the chancellor. The majority of voters supported higher taxes to improve public services. The 'stealth taxes' had not proved electorally unpopular. In the 2001 election campaign, Brown intended to conceal his intention to raise National Insurance contributions by 1 per cent and not increase the 40 per cent tax threshold in line with inflation, catching more people in the higher tax band.

Increasing taxes was a means to his goal of changing the nation's culture. After four years, he had begun the redistribution of wealth by abandoning the simplicity of the tax system he had inherited. While paying lip service to the essence of good taxation, namely neutrality to encourage work rather than penalising income, Brown had increased the number of tax rates from eight to fifty-four. In three years, *Tolley's Standard Tax Manual*, the accountant's Bible, had grown in length by 21 per cent, or nearly eight hundred pages. The tax system, complained the Institute of Chartered Accountants, had 'spun out of democratic control', and was 'detached from the principles of good revenue raising'. With the exception of skilful refinements to capital gains taxes, there was no evidence that the complications had produced any economic benefits. According to Tim Ambler's research, British income taxes were four times more expensive to collect than their American equivalent.

Brown's critics on the Treasury select committee accused the chancellor of levying taxes without considering their impact, a charge he naturally denied. With pride, he asserted that his tax changes had lifted a million children out of poverty since 1997. Others said the figure was 500,000. He claimed that the £5.2 billion spent on the New Deal had created 200,000 new jobs. In contradiction, the Institute for the Study of Civil Society said that barely 18,000 new jobs were created at a cost of £1.7 billion, and even that was disputed. Only 10 per cent of entrants had actually completed training courses, and at least 50,000 were back on benefits within three months. Some experts would assert that by the time the New Deal started, youth unemployment was no longer a problem, and the £5.2 billion was wasted. Many employers had abandoned their participation because of the scheme's complexities. Brown would prefer to ignore the unpublished study by the National Audit Office which demonstrated that the DTI's grants for new jobs between 1991 and 1995 had been near-worthless. Only 5,000 of the 27,600 jobs costing £750 million created in the previous decade by the Conservative government still existed. One statistic did, however, prove Brown's success. Britain's poorest had received an additional 15 per cent in income, while the rich had lost 3 per cent of their net income. The quiet redistribution of wealth was successful, but the cost was considerable.

In 1997, Blair and Brown had pledged to reduce social security costs. Paying benefits, Brown had said then, confirmed the existence of a problem but did not provide the solution. Tax credits were his answer. By 2001 the cost of social security had risen from £92 billion to £117 billion, one third of public expenditure. The increase was less than Brown had anticipated. As predicted by the trade union leaders, means tests had deterred applicants. Twenty per cent of the five million parents eligible for the children's tax credit had failed to apply, just as 80 per cent of eligible mothers would fail to claim the baby tax credit launched in April 2002. Brown had not appreciated the irony of his own statement that taxation should 'help families, particularly children and pensioners'.

The waste was noticed by Blair's staff. Billions of pounds which should have been spent on health and education, Blair had been told by Jeremy Heywood, his private secretary, had

been squandered. At a heated meeting, Blair confronted
Brown about that startling mismanagement. The chancellor
scoffed, and refused to consider the failure of any policy.
Rather than demand changes, the prime minister retreated.

Brown adopted the same nonchalance when summoned to
Blair's office to discuss the fragmentation of Britain's pensions
policies. He had been reluctant to agree to a meeting in early
2001, and only attended under protest. The pressure from
Blair, galvanised by his civil servants and special advisers, had
compelled Brown to face his critics. As predicted in 1997, his
withdrawal of the annual £5 billion tax credit from pension
funds and the inevitable decline of the stock market had
wrecked the retirement plans of tens of thousands of Britons.
Over the previous four years he had invented a pension tax
credit. Robert Culpin and other senior civil servants had
warned him that the state would be unable to fund the credit,
but Brown ignored them, and they chose not to raise the
subject again.

In 10 Downing Street, Derek Scott, the prime minister's
special adviser, decided to investigate. Brown was displeased.
Scott was disparaged as too right wing, but the chancellor
could not ignore the submissions by Carey Oppenheim, a
talented official seeking to analyse the consequences of his
indifference to the pensions crisis, which had not existed
before 1997. Over the next weeks Brown forbade officials at
the Treasury and the Inland Revenue to provide information
to the prime minister's office. Scott called on Brown, and
warned him, 'Your plans are financially unsustainable.'
Brown exploded, accusing Scott of interference. Blair called
a summit meeting. The Treasury delegation led by Brown and
Balls arrived in a truculent mood. In an emollient tone, Blair
suggested that the combination of the pension tax credit and
the plight of the private pension funds was a timebomb.
Brown's response was breathtaking. In a combination of

aggression and insolence, he defied Blair's entreaty to consider the problem. Supported by Balls, the chancellor refused to consider the plight of those who had saved throughout their working life for private pensions or had contributed to failing company schemes. The argument became fierce. Blair ended the meeting, but insisted that another would be held.

During the next months the same scenario was re-enacted: Blair urging a considered pensions policy, Brown refusing Scott access to information from the Treasury and Inland Revenue, and finally Brown's intimidatory response. The introduction of a new pensions minister, Ian McCartney, an uneducated former manual worker lauded by Brown as the architect of a new and complex stakeholder pension scheme, was a calculated snub. 'You're just steamrollering,' complained one of Blair's advisers. Brown shrugged. 'The stakeholder scheme will fail and the pension credits are too expensive,' continued the adviser. Brown said his proposed pension credit, which guaranteed a minimum income, was the solution. The Treasury forecast that the credit would cost £2 billion in 2004–05. Independent experts predicted that since 50 per cent of the population would immediately be eligible for the credit, and it could rise to 70 per cent by 2025, the real cost could rise to £10 billion a year. This unsustainable cost was aggravated by the corollary disincentive to save, and the £5 billion deducted from pensions every year. The facts undermined Brown's argument. He twitched uncomfortably, and looked across at Blair. 'We're only committed to pay the credit for the next five years,' he said. 'We can change it after that.' The prime minister and his staff were flabbergasted. 'But what about after?' asked a member of Blair's staff. 'People save for twenty years for their pensions. They won't believe in you, and they won't save. And what happens to their pensions after five years?' Brown shrugged. There was nothing more to say. Pensions were his territory.

These perplexities were not costing Labour any popularity. Even statistics suggesting that Brown's chancellorship was a mirage rather than a miracle were making no impression. The growth of Britain's gross domestic product under Labour had fallen from 3.1 per cent to 2.6 per cent; Britain's share of world exports had fallen from 5.1 per cent in 1997 to 4.5 per cent in 2000; while tax and social security payments took 46.1 per cent of income, up from 42.1 per cent in 1997. Warnings of a recession were effortlessly brushed aside by the evidence of a record £35.4 billion surplus in the accounts, a reduction of the national debt from 44 per cent to 30 per cent, and tax revenues rising by 4.6 per cent per annum, compared to an average of 1.8 per cent during the Conservative government. Above all, Brown predicted that the British economy, despite the recession across the world, would grow in 2001 by 2.75 per cent. In the past his optimism had usually proved to be well-founded, and there seemed to be no reason for that to change. Even if productivity failed to rise and manufacturing jobs continued to be lost – in April 2001 Motorola closed its factory in Scotland, costing 3,100 high-tech jobs – there would be more '*Guardian*' jobs in the public sector, just as Brown had promised the trade union leaders. His formula for success was untested and audacious. Instead of the government accumulating debt to stimulate the economy, he would encourage an explosion of personal debt through cheap loans secured against rising house prices, and accumulate over £120 billion of PFI and rail debt off the government's balance sheet; and to keep unemployment down, he would use taxes to increase the numbers employed by the state.

The impression of success over the previous four years and the Tories' failure to reconstruct their party guaranteed re-election. Brown predicted that Labour would increase its 179 majority and win more seats than in 1997. The essence for

Brown, as the director of the party's re-election campaign, was not so much to secure the victory as to produce a defining theme to reassure the party and its faithful. While Blair declared the second term's purpose as 'delivery', Brown sought ideological criteria. Henry Kissinger had once remarked that governments were elected to office with a store of intellectual ideas and ousted when the store was exhausted. Brown was searching for new policies and new ideals.

He approached that challenge with confidence. Unlike the unintellectual opportunists around the cabinet table, he had spent endless hours throughout his life absorbing history, biographies and political theory. A serious politician, he understood, required a hinterland. Throughout his chancellorship he sought explanations to establish a new philosophy justifying Labour's history. The discussion at private seminars in 11 Downing Street had extended beyond socialism to attempt new definitions of old values that would attract the support of interest groups preoccupied by the dynamic of a changing society. The public's acceptance of higher taxation was, Brown prided himself, proof that the majority of the population had been persuaded that politicians could be trusted to spend wisely. What his critics condemned as meddling were attempts to re-engage the poor and disenfranchised in communal and family life. Just as he was proud of committing more money to aid in the Third World, which, bizarrely, he never visited, he sought to alleviate poverty among Britain's dispossessed without personally confronting the unpleasant realities on the grimy streets. His pride was that Britain's labour force had increased by about 30 per cent since 1997 to 7.7 million, including 1.2 million young people, and unemployment had fallen to a historically low level.

That success was overshadowed by the permanently unemployed, lacking any intention of ever working, who had reclassified themselves as 'disabled' and would receive everlasting incapacity benefits. Defiantly, that huge underclass – at least one million relatively healthy people out of the 2.7 million receiving the benefit – were uninfluenced by Brown's tax credits, just as they had been immune to similar blandishments introduced ten years earlier. Claimants for incapacity benefits received a basic £84 per week compared to £55 per week for jobseekers, plus other entitlements. His optimism that he could reverse that trend remained. The solution was 'Brownism', a capitalist society with a moral sense, fair rather than selfish. He wrestled to find a slogan encapsulating a fusion of several political ideals to present as his doctrine.

In 2001 he spoke about 'civic renewal' and the 'renaissance of local government' to combat the disproportionate affluence of London compared to other regions. Such words were hardly inspirational. Devolving power was an old chestnut, and lacked credibility when espoused by a politician who had himself centralised government power within the Treasury. His second attempt focused on the economy. He acknowledged that while employment had increased, productivity was static. 'I think,' he said with evident need for reassurance, 'that we are moving into the second phase in Britain where we are able to combine employment growth with productivity growth.' Again, that was an old theme, barely made credible by Britain's annual growth since 1997 of 1.3 per cent, compared to 3 per cent in the early 1990s. Brown's antidote was to commit 'hundreds of millions of pounds' to promote small business start-ups in poor areas, copying Bill Clinton's 'Business Improvement Districts'. In politically correct language he promised quangos and initiatives which DTI officials would be incapable of translating into reality and which the public, deterred by stifling regulations, rejected. His Wilsonian approach ignored an essential cause of Britain's low productivity. The employment of immigrants as cheap labour was a disincentive to industry to invest in expensive but cost-

saving high technology. Using cheap labour rather than computers had blighted the construction industry, which
languished twenty years behind its international competitors.
The source of that information was an expert employed by
the DTI, but his warning was ignored by the Treasury.

Brown's third idea was 'a quiet revolution' to reconstruct
society, which had allegedly been destroyed by Margaret
Thatcher. Her comment, 'There's no such thing as society,'
regardless of her complaint that her opponents had maliciously distorted her meaning, provided fertile territory for an
evangelising socialist. Beyond the slogan, there was little originality. Brown claimed that the work ethic had failed under
Thatcher but had revived under his welfare-to-work programme. The proof of his commitment to the new era was
that over the previous three years he had handed out £370
million to children and charities to buy computers. No independent audit verified that expenditure.

His fourth attempt to define the new era was the most
convincing. In a speech at the annual CBI dinner on 23 May
2001 he condemned his party's former ideology, and promoted Labour as the true party of business, pledged to cut
taxes. 'For too long after 1945,' he said, 'British society was
ideologically divided, locked in a sterile and stifling debate
between those who wanted the government to do everything
and those who wanted governments to do nothing ... I
believe that those old cold wars between capital and labour,
business and government, public and private, are not just over
but must never return.' He praised those ambitious to earn
higher profits, promised to create an enterprise culture open
to all, and urged everyone to adopt the work ethic. 'I tell you
honestly,' he concluded, 'that the Labour Party of the 1980s
was wrong and irresponsible to become, contrary to its history, an anti-European party.' He had learnt, he confessed,
the 'historic lesson'. Three weeks later, he expanded on his

admiration for Thatcher in the *Wall Street Journal.* 'In the 1980s,' he wrote, 'Margaret Thatcher rightly emphasised the importance of the enterprise culture. But this did not go far enough.' If at that moment Margaret Thatcher could have suspended her cynicism about a Labour leader ditching his prejudices, she would have hailed 'Brownism' as a profound conversion.

The foot and mouth outbreak delayed the election for a month. Tony Blair's ministers had suggested that the disease was contained, but their own mistakes had allowed the outbreak to rage for four more weeks. Brown bluntly rejected Michael Meacher's request for £300 million to help the rural recovery. Meacher, the environment minister, appealed to Blair: 'I need money quickly.' 'I'm seeing Gordon tomorrow,' replied Blair. 'I'll raise it then.' The chancellor told the prime minister, 'No.' There was no appeal.

On 8 May the prime minister announced that the election would be held on 7 June. Brown began his eighteen-hour days running on the treadmill in Millbank's gym for thirty minutes before embarking at 6.30 a.m. on endless meetings and appearances. The party's private polls were all positive – and there was an added bonus. The electoral system was now more loaded against the Tories than previously. The Conservatives had failed to argue their case with the Boundary Commission which had redrawn the constituency boundaries in Scotland and some inner cities. They would consequently need an 11.5 per cent swing if they were to win an overall majority. In the circumstances, that was impossible.

Labour's challenge was to retain the votes of those electors in 1997 – one third of all the party's supporters – who had not voted for the party in 1992. Brown believed that regardless of their gripes about increased taxes, the electorate would decide to vote on future expectations. Labour's performance would depend upon his own management of the economy as the foundation for the reconstruction of the public services. In 1997, private polls had shown that the Conservatives were more trusted than Labour on managing the economy. By November 2000, Labour was substantially more trusted. That was Brown's success. He anticipated that the Tories would propose tax cuts, and planned to exploit that traditional ploy. His fifth budget on 7 March had made a virtue of not offering tax cuts, and his election campaign would challenge the Tories with the question, 'Which public services are you proposing to cut?' That was certain to expose the Tories as out of touch with the public's desire to rebuild the NHS and schools. His theme would be to emphasise the danger of change and past mistakes. The manifesto's title, 'Ambitions for Britain', encompassed Labour's achievement and optimism.

The party's only vulnerability was Scotland, where devolution had undermined Labour's and Brown's strength. In the elections for the Scottish parliament in April 1999, Helen Liddell had been blamed for failing to counter the Scottish Nationalists. Brown and Douglas Alexander had saved the party from embarrassment by attacking sectarianism and emphasising the vigour of the Union. Quixotically, Brown had criticised the SNP's commitment to higher taxes, especially their proposal to abolish the ceiling on contributions to National Insurance. The sleight of hand was impressive. His own agenda was to do precisely the same to avoid raising income tax.

As Brown predicted, Labour's vulnerability to criticism about the deteriorating performance of the NHS and schools was ignored by the Conservative leader William Hague. The Tories campaigned on Europe, immigration and tax cuts. Hague's unexpectedly rapid launch of the Tory manifesto on 10 May promised £8 billion in tax cuts. Brown was blamed, especially by Mandelson, for allowing the Tories to seize the advantage. Four days later, that advantage had evaporated. In a thoughtless interview, the shadow chief Treasury secretary Oliver Letwin predicted to the *Financial Times* that the Tories would reduce public spending by £20 billion by the end of the new parliament. That was a golden gift to Brown. Mercilessly, he repeated the mantra that the Tory cuts would destroy the public services, and effortlessly deflected accurate accusations that he intended to increase National Insurance contributions as 'a typical Tory slur'. His own slurs were impregnable to Tory criticism.

With Labour's success assured, the electorate became bored. The campaign's desultory pace over the following three weeks would culminate in the lowest turnout – 59.3 per cent – since 1918. Certain that his mastery of the election machine would deliver victory, Brown was talking to his confidants about his secondary concern: his eventual inheritance of the leadership. He looked forward to a definitive confrontation with Blair in the near future. History suggested that prime ministers became tarnished during their second term, and an ideological battle with Blair would hasten that process. His tactics would be to preach purity and pledge loyalty, hoping to become the beneficiary of inevitable disillusion with the prime minister. The eve of the election was an ideal moment to assess his prospects.

Brown had become aware of Blair's desire for greater control over the government's domestic agenda. The prime minister was weary of his chancellor ignoring every criticism and challenge in the cabinet. His regular tantrums and offensive behaviour had become debilitating. Too frequently, Brown had won their exhausting arguments. Although both occasionally gave the impression of enjoying the heat of debate, Brown too gleefully demonstrated that he regarded the prime minister as little more than an unintellectual master of slogans. That behaviour, Blair believed, reflected Brown's unforgivable obsession with sabotaging his legacy.

Dismissing Brown may have been a dream, but it was not

an option. As both men clearly understood, any prime minister who broke with his chancellor risked destroying his government. On those occasions when Blair wished the chancellor would permanently disappear, he would mention his determination to serve a full second term and even hint at a third term before bequeathing his office to Charles Clarke. Brown fumed, and exacted his revenge by combining with John Prescott to resist Peter Mandelson's bid to return to the government. Continuing his vendetta against Mandelson was more than mere animosity. The level of Mandelson's status proportionately undermined his own influence.

Having decided he had no option but to tolerate the chancellor's intemperate behaviour, Blair sought ways around his vetoes. Joining the euro and fundamental changes to the financing and management of the public services were two Brownite hurdles for Blair to overcome. More private involvement and an end to the monolithic public services governed from Whitehall would improve the NHS, but he was baffled at how to overcome Brown's obduracy. The chancellor resisted real devolution and objected to the introduction of market principles.

During meetings without officials – but never, on Cherie's orders, in Blair's private quarters – the prime minister and the chancellor had endlessly debated their disagreements, and occasionally Brown was finessed. Blair's announcement in the Commons in February 2001 that the final assessment of whether the five tests to join the euro had been passed, which in turn would trigger a referendum on whether or not to join, would be announced within the first two years of a new parliament, was one of those surprises. Infuriated, the chancellor had stormed into Blair's office, pushing aside an official, to protest. A referendum, he shouted, would risk irreversibly splitting the country, weakening the government. 'Impossible' was the word the expelled official heard as the door closed.

During those confrontations, Blair invariably felt squashed. While Brown was supported by the incomparable Ed Balls, the prime minister's advisers were less impressive. Only recently Robin Cook had asked Blair about the economic conditions for entry. Blair had replied, 'I've no idea what Gordon is proposing,' and added, 'Even the Treasury officials can't find out what's going on over the economic assessment, let alone us at 10 Downing Street.' To secure Brown's support for the euro, Blair had hinted that he would be inclined to stand down once Britain had joined the monetary scheme. Together we can win the referendum, Blair told Brown, but the chancellor was sceptical, since about 60 per cent of the electorate opposed membership. On that question, Blair knew, Brown was unfortunately right. Changing British public opinion on this issue would take at least another five years. The prime minister could hearten the enthusiasts with the promise of the government's 'courage' to stand up for its European convictions, but the chancellor would remain cautious. Carefully, Brown had chosen his vocabulary for a thousand near-identical soundbites: 'The Treasury's assessment will not be fudged,' and 'Britain's stability will not be put at risk.' Their quandary was not helped, Brown suggested to Blair, by Robin Cook's enthusiasm for the euro. The foreign secretary's opposition to the Treasury was destabilising, said Brown. For his own reasons, Blair had decided that after the election Cook would be replaced. He would pay the price of interfering in the relationship between Blair and Brown. Sensitive about his weak power base in England, Brown would not tolerate any challenge, not least because his influence in Scotland since the sudden death of Donald Dewar on 11 October 2000 was also eroding.

Long before his tumultuous entry into the Treasury on 2 May 1997, Brown had understood the predicament of Scots as a minority in British politics. Under New Labour, Scottish

control of Whitehall and Westminster in 1997 was unprece-
dented. Besides Brown, Scottish senior ministers included
Derry Irvine the lord chancellor, George Robertson at the
MOD, Robin Cook, Alistair Darling, Scottish secretary Donald
Dewar, and transport minister Gavin Strang, while the prime
minister himself had been educated at a Scottish public school.
That over-representation of Scotland, combined with a raft of
junior ministers provoked some resentment among the party's
English MPs. Just before the current election campaign, at
the end of a late-night drinking session with a group of Scottish friends in Brown's Downing Street flat, one particularly
close ally had burst out during an unexpected lull in the
constant laughter, 'How will it go wrong? How could we lose
it?' The guffaws of 'We're here forever' that night were
reassuring, but the host was less sanguine. Devolution had
produced disappointing 'numpties' – nothing turnip heads –
in the Edinburgh parliament, just spending money given to
them by the chancellor. Their ferocious, factional arguments
were impossible to resolve. The Scottishness – the glue of
grittiness and clannishness – which had bound him to so many
people since the 1970s was disappearing. He could still rely
on Henry McLeish, the new party leader in the Edinburgh
parliament, and Wendy Alexander, the clever sister of Douglas
Alexander, to represent his authority in a country increasingly
uninterested in national politics, but he feared that if the
Scottish tribe's strength waned, he would be weakened in
Westminster. Accordingly, taking stock during the weeks
before the election was a volatile cocktail of optimism and
antagonism, an unsatisfactory combination offering no comfort for his speculation about his ultimate fate.

Brown's prediction of a second landslide was fulfilled. With
an overall majority of 167 seats, Labour had, for the first
time in its history, secured a second full term free of any reliance on other parties. Unlike 1997, there were no major

celebrations or euphoria. Rather, there was a slight feeling of anti-climax. The obligation now was to transform the aspirations and the propaganda into reality. Blair spoke about 'delivery', conjuring images of a mechanical process. By contrast, his chancellor envisaged laying the foundations of a new society, realising the dream of 'Brownism'. His success would depend upon maintaining his control of the government, and hopefully wresting its leadership for himself. His disagreements with Blair began soon after the election victory.

TEN

Turmoil and Tragedy

Gordon Brown did not hear from the prime minister for four days after the election. On Monday, 11 June 2001, Tony Blair finally telephoned. 'I assume you want to carry on as chancellor,' said Blair. 'Yes,' replied Brown stiffly. Nothing more was said. Brown understood the background to that frozen exchange. As he told a friend soon after, the same conversation after the next election would be more significant. Blair would again call, and would probably say, 'Look, Gordon, nobody does three terms as chancellor.' Brown was looking forward to replying, 'I have no intention of serving three terms as chancellor.' 'But what happens,' asked his friend, 'if Blair insists that you stop being chancellor?' 'That's when the conversation gets interesting,' replied Brown with a twinkle. Unmentioned was his hope that Blair would not be prime minister by the time of the next election. For himself, he would continue to preach teamwork and practise the opposite. His rigid control of the domestic agenda would infuriate the prime minister and destabilise Blairite ministers. The cost to the country of his pet schemes was at least £20 billion. The first to experience the consequences of 'Brownism' would be the new transport minister.

Blinking behind his glasses, Stephen Byers was pleased by his performance. For over an hour inside 10 Downing Street, the prime minister and the chancellor had listened to his presentation on the plight of Railtrack. Since the election, Byers had been plotting to renationalise the railways. This, he was certain, would enhance his reputation in the party, angered that Railtrack would pay £88 million that year as dividends to shareholders out of the subsidies provided by taxpayers.

Gordon Brown was unimpressed by Stephen Byers. The former polytechnic law lecturer was clumsy, and prone to mishaps. He had won some slight credit from Brown as secretary of state at the DTI for the department's investigation of Geoffrey Robinson, when Robinson had been adequately protected by Byers's refusal to publish an official investigation into his business conduct. But that single decision, the chancellor intimated, was insufficient to redeem him. Even Byers's decision to allow the corrupt American energy supplier Enron to build a gas-fired power station in Kent drew no comment from the Treasury. Brown usually failed to understand the detrimental effect his lack of sympathy could have for the objects of his contempt. Byers, in particular, was terrified of the chancellor, fearing his outbursts and his hatred of uncertainty. His nightmare, he confessed, was the image of Brown driving a four-wheel vehicle towards him in an underground carpark.

Byers also disliked Alastair Morton, the chairman of the Strategic Rail Authority (SRA). After the election, Morton had written a memorandum analysing Railtrack's financial problems and offering remedies for attracting more private investment. Byers rejected his proposals, and disclosed that he was searching for a replacement for Morton. Morton offered his resignation. Byers had not acted on his own responsibility. Shriti Vadera had been examining the possibility of renationalising the railways. Morton would be an obstacle to any such proposal, and was best removed.

The privatisation of the railways had, in the Treasury's opinion, proved disastrous. Incompetent managers and profiteering were blamed for fatal accidents and declining reliability. Only one year earlier, Prescott had unveiled his £60 billion ten-year plan to build 'a system for the new millennium and of which we can be justly proud'. The plan disintegrated after Prescott's hysterical overreaction to the Hatfield crash in October 2000, when a poorly maintained section of track had led to a derailment, causing the death of four passengers. The deputy leader had caused panic at Railtrack, leading to a collapse in productivity and an explosion of costs.

In April 2001 Vadera told Brown that the SRA and Railtrack had been awarded an increased subsidy by Tom Winsor, the rail regulator. Railtrack had received £10 billion during the five years ending in 2001. The network was told that for the next five years it would receive £16 billion. Vadera also told Brown that on 2 April 2001, to pay for the extra work after Hatfield, Railtrack's managers had asked for an advance of £1.5 billion from the agreed subsidy. Brown was exasperated. The privatised railways, he raged, had become an expensive mess. To allow incompetent managers to receive that subsidy was reckless waste. He wanted an end to the fiasco. Vadera cautioned against nationalisation. The shareholders, she estimated, would be entitled to £6 billion in compensation, but that payment could be avoided if Railtrack was placed in administration. The same result would be achieved without the need for special legislation or compensation. The plan, designed by herself and Byers, entailed the minister applying to the court for an administration order against Railtrack on the grounds that the company could not pay its debts. The court would grant the order, and the railways would effectively be renationalised at no cost. The shareholders would lose all their money. There was, however, one problem. On 23 May 2001 the company's accounts had been approved by its auditors and the company was declared to be solvent, with sufficient funds to pay its debts. The government, explained Vadera, would withhold the £1.5 billion advance. Without that money, Railtrack would certainly be insolvent.

Byers was pleased with the plan, which he presented to Blair and Brown as his own work. He would win enormous political plaudits, he assured himself, for taking back the tracks from the profiteers. The railways had become a rallying cry for Old Labour, and the minister excitedly anticipated the cheers in the Commons when he announced the takeover. The chancellor was especially receptive to the plan. Harming the shareholders would be popular. Neither Brown nor Blair understood that while taking over Railtrack would save the government paying £80 million in dividends, the interest charges for future bank loans would cost more. Nor did Brown consider the reaction to an administration order among businessmen and bankers. At dozens of meetings in the City over the previous years, the chancellor had endlessly repeated his desire to attract private investment in public projects through PFI and PPP. He had stressed the importance of competition and the protection for private investors provided by independent regulators. During his briefings from Vadera, it had not occurred to him that his denial of any compensation to Railtrack's shareholders would jeopardise his credibility. That problem was understood by Blair, but it remained unresolved by the end of Byers's presentation. After two hours, the prime minister was clearly bored. Pushing his chair back, he told Byers, 'There's some confusion which suggests an absence of an agreed strategy.' Turning to Brown, he said, 'You sort out with Stephen what to do, but whatever you do, don't renationalise Railtrack.'

Alone with Byers and the advisers, Brown was impatient. He disliked detail, especially when it concerned finance and the law. Although expensive lawyers and bankruptcy experts were available to be consulted, he failed to ask the questions which would have revealed the consequences of committing Railtrack to administration. Quite simply, the chancellor did not understand that his approval of Byers's plan would lead to huge additional costs. Nevertheless, he gave it his full support.

On 25 July 2001 Byers and his officials met John Robinson, the chairman of Railtrack. For a year the minister had listened to their descriptions of the extra costs incurred since Hatfield. Robinson would ask for an advance of money, and Byers would refuse it. On that day their lament was no different. Yet subsequently Byers described an alarming scenario. Robinson, he said, had revealed that Railtrack would become bankrupt if the government failed to provide further financial help. Byers never provided evidence to substantiate this allegation, and Robinson would emphatically deny saying anything to suggest the company's possible bankruptcy. But Byers's version of the conversation would be quoted to justify his subsequent application for an order of administration. One month later, on 23 August, Byers's officials secretly instructed lawyers and accountants to prepare the ground for an application to the court for Railtrack's administration. Brown and Byers prepared for a surprise move, withholding the extra grant to Railtrack to imperil its finances. At the beginning of October 2001, the company was solvent. The directors expected to receive a regular payment of £445 million from the government, they were legally entitled to raise a £1 billion loan, and they were awaiting an answer for an advance of £1.5 billion. John Robinson was unaware of the government's intentions.

On Thursday, 4 October, Stephen Byers's office telephoned the rail regulator Tom Winsor to invite him to a meeting the following day at 4 p.m. Winsor was not told the reason for the unexpected summons. His position, enshrined by statute, was unusual in Britain. He was empowered to decide how much the train operators should pay for access to the rail network, and his decision could not be challenged by the companies or the government. After he increased the charges for 2001–06, the Treasury was obliged to increase the subsidy paid to the operators to pay for his decision. During his regular checks on Railtrack's accounts, Winsor had not noticed any reason for particular alarm. The company, he was satisfied, was solvent, although he was unimpressed by its managers, especially after Hatfield.

Stephen Byers concealed his excitement as Winsor sat down to hear what was later described as a 'bombshell'. Railtrack, said Byers, was according to its financial advisers insolvent and unable to pay its debts. The government, he went on, intended to withhold the expected payment of £445 million, refuse the £1.5 billion advance and place Railtrack into administration. Winsor was incredulous. That, he told Byers, amounted to confiscation without compensation. The repercussions would 'severely' impair the government's ability in the future to raise private investment in the City, not least for the London Underground. Gordon Brown's entire policy of seeking private finance for public projects would be undermined. The chancellor's agreement effectively to renationalise Railtrack and override the rail regulator's statutory powers contradicted his repeated public pledges to create and protect independent economic regulators.

Byers was unconcerned by Winsor's protests. He was proud of his initiative. He hardly listened as Winsor mentioned the most pertinent objection to the plan: Railtrack had sufficient funds to continue trading. An application to the court on the grounds that Railtrack had 'no alternative source of funding' would be bogus, not least because Winsor was empowered to order extra money to be paid, and he alleged that the government intended to mislead the court. Reassured by Gordon Brown's complete support, Byers nevertheless executed his plan regardless of its legal or financial flaws. His only fear was that Winsor would use his statutory powers to order the train operators to pay Railtrack an extra £1 billion in access charges – money that the Treasury would be legally obliged to provide. 'If you try to intervene,' warned Byers, 'I'll get emergency legislation to stop you.' Winsor was amazed. 'This is all a bad idea,' he told the minister. 'Is the government really prepared to take all these risks in order to prevent an interim review?' Byers was uninterested. The meeting was over. Byers would subsequently deny in the Commons uttering any threats to Winsor.

Forty-five minutes after his meeting with Winsor began, Byers received John Robinson, and announced that the government was withdrawing all financial support and seeking an order for the administration of Railtrack. Robinson departed. That night, Brown and Byers waited for Robinson's reaction. Their plan could be scuppered if he asked Winsor to authorise an increase in charges of £1 billion from the train operators. That would require Winsor to undertake a review.

'They can't be so stupid,' Alastair Morton told Winsor on hearing the news. Morton blamed Shriti Vadera. The manoeuvre, he believed, would boomerang. The reform of the railways would be delayed, increasing the cost of London Underground's part-privatisation and threatening the credibility of the government's guarantees in the PFI projects. Worse, he was sure that the government had not considered how it would manage Railtrack after securing the administration. How could ignorant accountants run Railtrack better than its present directors? Winsor agreed.

On the evening of Saturday, 6 October, the day after the meeting in Byers's office, Steve Marshall, the chief executive of Railtrack, telephoned Tom Winsor and asked him to conduct an interim review and give the company 'hundreds of millions of pounds' by Monday morning. Winsor admitted

that he was inclined to help, but Marshall's details were
sketchy and his timetable was unrealistic. How could a review
of Railtrack's finances be completed within a few hours? And
why had Marshall left a potentially lifesaving call until beyond
the last minute? He concluded that Marshall had not really
expected him to help, and would comply with the government's edict although the company was not insolvent. 'Railtrack reached the high-water mark of their own incompetence
the night when they could have saved their own lives,'
recalled Winsor. 'Robinson was a disastrous chairman of
Railtrack.'

During Saturday afternoon, as Byers's press officers briefed
the Sunday papers that Railtrack was to be placed in administration the following day, Treasury officials were calling the
same newspapers to suggest that the Treasury rather than the
department of transport was masterminding the operation.
Brown wanted to reaffirm his authority on major decisions.
The result was not what Brown had imagined. The Sunday
papers' criticism of the government was universal. 'He's
making a mess,' Brown roared about Byers, stung by the
reaction. Just as Marshall agreed to surrender and not oppose
the government's application to a judge that Sunday afternoon, the Treasury's press officers were ordered by Brown to
distance his department from the decision. Even though he
had been present at the meeting when the fateful decision
was taken, and he had refused a £1.5 billion advance to Railtrack, the Treasury's officials told journalists that Brown was
involved only in 'contingency planning'.

On the Monday morning, Gordon Brown dived for cover.
The version of events offered to journalists by Byers was challenged by Railtrack's directors. City players were unanimous
that the government had damaged its credibility. Transport
experts complained that after four years, the government
lacked any policy for the railways. In the Commons, Byers

was basking in the adulation from the Labour backbenches. His promise not to pay the shareholders one penny in compensation evoked roars of approval. 'The government,' he swaggered, 'are not here to fund the shareholders of private companies.' All the work undertaken by Brown since 1992 to educate the party and the City about Labour as the party of business was strangled and buried.

By the end of the day, Brown understood his error. The Treasury's involvement, and his presence at the critical meeting, were denied. His officials were to report that he would clean up Byers's mess by touring the City to offer reassurance. As a preliminary, he dispatched Andrew Turnbull to reassure bankers, 'This isn't bad.' Their reply was categorical: 'You just don't understand. It's short-sighted, counterproductive, and will be more expensive than before.' There was, Turnbull was told, a loss of trust and a disincentive for further investment in government projects.

Brown did understand political survival. He slunk into the background, refusing to answer questions at a hearing of the Treasury select committee. Cross-examination on facts was a danger he avoided. The Treasury, the MPs were told, had no responsibility for Railtrack. Tony Blair did not sing from the same sheet. 'The chancellor,' he told a Labour Party meeting shortly after, 'deserves credit for decreeing that no more taxpayers' subsidy should be poured down the throat of Railtrack.' Despite their many entreaties to the City, neither understood the real repercussions. Some compared the panic to the ERM crisis in 1992.

Brown was influenced by aspirations rather than reality. The sparkling, refurbished Treasury building reflected his revolution. Nine years after the ERM debacle, the chancellor boasted that his Treasury, led by handpicked advisers, was determining the nation's future by controlling spending in every department. His team – Ed Balls, Shriti Vadera, Chris

Wales from Arthur Andersen, Maeve Sherlock from the
Council for One-Parent Families, Stewart Wood from Magdalen, Oxford, working on education, Paul Gregg, a welfare-
to-work expert, Tony Burdon from Oxfam, Nick Crafts, an
economic historian on the productivity team – were paraded
as experts for 'blue sky' thinking to infuse new ideas into the
civil service. Experts rather than established party activists,
they resented the accusation by the Blairites in 10 Downing
Street of being 'entryists'. They responded by encouraging
Brown's redistributionist agenda, expressing particular disdain about the idea of introducing 'choice' into the public
services. Above them, Ed Balls had been reclassified in 1999
as chief economic adviser, a civil servant rather than a special
adviser. Balls had not become impartial. On the contrary, he
remained fiercely partisan, and with Brown's agreement was
searching for a parliamentary constituency for the next general election. Like Vadera, he evinced the chancellor's piety
and certainty.

A different opinion was growing among some City players.
The gossip was of a looming global recession sweeping aside
Brown's reputation. In Britain, thousands of employees of
private companies were being dismissed, profits were slashed
and famous corporations – including Cable & Wireless,
Invensys, Reuters, British Airways and Corus steel – were
struggling to survive. The dotcom revolution, so lavishly
praised by Brown, had imploded. Marconi, led by Lord Simpson, a Labour star, crashed in a chase for worthless technology. Airline bookings were the worst for ten years, consumer
spending and personal debt were soaring and, as Brown's
critics carped, the economy's expansion was sustained by an
explosion of new jobs in the public sector – 93,000 in the
previous year – and only 71,000 new jobs in the private sector.
Despite Brown's exhortations for efficiency and enterprise,
the management of money in his world was one-dimensional:

it was taken from the taxpayer and redistributed according to government priorities. Only recently he had allocated £900 million to Glasgow council to repay its debt for building council houses. English cities did not receive such favours, but it no doubt delighted his brother John, who was employed by the council. Instead, the British Chamber of Commerce complained, an additional £39 billion would be taken in taxes between 1997 and 2005, including an extra £6.2 billion in 2001–02 alone. Members of the CBI noted the chancellor's endless speeches about productivity, but he resented their criticism of the DTI's 'initiatives' and new regulations costing, the employers estimated, £30 billion over eight years. Successful businesses, his critics said, depended on skilful management, not on civil servants without commercial experience administering subsidies.

Unlike his critics, the chancellor had never practised the subtle art of buying and selling for profit, yet he presented himself as the creator of an American-style 'enterprise culture' in Britain. But he remained suspicious of the public's vulnerability to profiteering and the glaring carelessness of the directors of City institutions. The investors' losses at the insurance company Equitable Life, the mis-selling of endowment mortgages and his conviction about excessive bank charges fuelled his belief that the market could be improved by government control, not least by increasing the power of the Competition Commission to destroy cartels. He trusted four businessmen to deliver the answers. Paul Myners, a former fund manager, was asked to investigate investment managers; Ron Sandler, a banker, to investigate the insurance companies; Derek Higgs, a corporate banker, to investigate the failings of directors in corporations; and Don Cruickshank, a trusted businessman, to again lambast the banks.

Brown's obsession with banks raised questions about his understanding of developments since Big Bang. The four clearing banks had become vulnerable to competition from building societies, foreign banks and internet banking. To take risks on investments and expand globally, the banks inevitably profited from 'safe' customers, but a substantial portion of their profits was earned from expansion overseas. In May 2000 Don Cruickshank had reported that the banks were overcharging and earning excess profits. Brown commissioned an investigation by the Competition Commission. That report in October 2001 ordered the banks to offer better and cheaper services which, it was claimed, would reduce the annual profits of the clearing banks – the 'greedy four' according to Brown – by £500 million. Brown then ordered another review of the banks, the seventeenth since 1997, to further reduce their profits from small businesses. Rather than trust competition, he preferred to impose price controls and regulations. Government departments had issued a record 4,642 regulations in 2001, and would issue even more in 2002. Brown's critics felt that Cruickshank and the others were powerless instruments of Brown's prejudices rather than independent investigators.

Brown was unembarrassed by the critics. His bravado reflected his sense of infallibility about the involvement of private enterprise in state business. On 18 October 2001, ten days after the rail imbroglio, a crisis erupted in the administration of ILAs, one of his favoured schemes. At an early-morning meeting in the Treasury, Estelle Morris, the minister for education, told Brown that evidence supplied by the police proved that ILAs had been the target of fraud. Two and a half million people had signed up for ILAs – three times more than expected – and at least £73 million had been stolen by phoney providers of courses and phoney students. The £200 paid by the government for each applicant had been stolen by fraudsters who hadn't even pretended to provide any training. Morris's officials appeared to be responsible for rejecting pro-

Using Whelan, Brown had undermined David Blunkett (third from left), the education minister, Robin Cook, Margaret Beckett and Frank Dobson.

At the Labour Party conference in 2003 Brown was accused of plotting a coup, symbolised by his appeal for a return to Labour's true values. Blair's rousing speech the following day squashed Brown and received rapturous applause – except from Brown.

'Gordon has to be incredibly optimistic about pensions,ect. He wants tony to retire early'

Gordon Brown's presentation of his seventh budget on 17 March 2004 (he is pictured with Paul Boateng and Ruth Kelly) confirmed his dominance of Britain's government and would, he hoped, be the springboard for his unchallenged coronation as Britain's next prime minister.

fessional advice that the scheme was vulnerable to dishonesty. Paralysed with fear, the minister suggested to Brown that the ILA scheme should be terminated. Brown refused.

Later that day her officials contacted Downing Street to explain their problems. Tony Blair agreed that the ILAs should end, but again Brown refused. In his mind there was a political risk. ILAs had been labelled by the Treasury as a PPP (Public–Private Partnership) scheme, similar to the London Underground. PPPs could not be allowed to fail. David Normington, the new permanent secretary at the department of education, confronted Brown. The PPP label, he said, was a fallacy: 'It's not a partnership. We were not sharing with anyone.' Brown was not listening.

Six days later, on 24 October 2001, Estelle Morris returned to Brown's office to obtain his approval to terminate the scheme. Again he refused. Instead, she was ordered to obfuscate in the House of Commons. Flustered, she rose in the chamber at 4 p.m. on the same day to announce a 'temporary' stop of the 'successful programme'. ILAs, she claimed, 'have opened up access for a great many people to a wide range of learning opportunities'. Shortly after, however, the police were authorised to announce a formal investigation. Compared to the original budget of £199 million, ILAs had cost so far £273 million. The fraudsters had stolen in excess of £100 million, yet the police would fail to convict anyone. Without scrutiny, Capita had earned commission on each applicant, including those later discovered to be bogus. Quite legitimately, the company pleaded that it was not required by the Treasury to vet each applicant.

Brown refused to accept any responsibility for the costly debacle. He heaped the blame on Michael Bichard, the department of education's former permanent secretary. David Normington, Bichard's successor, would subsequently concede, 'This is a very bad story. I am quite ashamed of it . . . I can only say I am sorry.' Ivan Lewis, the parliamentary under-secretary of state, would admit that ILAs were 'one of those glossy strategies which do not lead anywhere'. Like the four other ministers involved, Lewis would not accept any blame. Brown avoided any opportunity publicly to explain his responsibility. Just as for railways, he refused to allow Treasury officials to answer questions during the subsequent investigation by the Public Accounts Committee.

Similar stubbornness influenced the expensive fate of the 'University for Industry'. By 2001, Brown's dream of an education service delivered to millions by computer and satellite had become another layer of the 'skills industry'. Two thousand centres named 'Learndirect' had been established to steer a projected 100,000 people every week towards what Brown predicted would be self-financing training courses. Instead, 80,000 had enrolled for free courses after the Treasury spent £67 million a year to promote the scheme and £145 million to provide the courses. His grand vision of millions of deprived Britons benefiting from the 'superhighway' had evaporated. No inquiry into the waste was authorised.

The Treasury also did not scrutinise the management of CMI Ltd, the Cambridge Massachusetts Institute, established to exploit scientific research. On Brown's initiative, £68 million had been committed without any independent assessment of the costs or benefits. The first £13 million had been assigned to MIT rather than Cambridge. On Brown's insistence, British taxpayers were financing research at the richest university in the world. Dr Gillian Evans, a member of Cambridge University, was bewildered by the absence of any defined projects and her failure to obtain detailed accounts for the expenditure. Despite her requests, neither the Treasury nor the DTI could explain how the money had been allocated or who would own the benefits of the research. Brown was apparently unconcerned that the Treasury had failed to stipulate how CMI's performance would be evaluated. A review of the company by the NAO was not published on the orders of Patricia Hewitt, the secretary of state at the DTI, on the grounds that it was 'confidential'. (Subsequently, the report was published.) Once again, it appeared, Brown had waved aside any scrutiny of financial costs.

On three mishaps – rail, ILAs and CMI Ltd – the chancellor had hidden behind other ministers to avoid public responsibility. A lack of public interest had also protected him from repercussions following the costly shambles of privatising the national air traffic control system (NATS). Floundering with insufficient money and poor management, NATS required more money than had been anticipated, but was paralysed by a loss of nerve among its supporters and Brown himself.

Brown's footwork in avoiding criticism for the introduction of tax credits was less successful. In 1996 he and Tony Blair had pledged to reduce the cost of welfare benefits. Instead, spending on social security was forecasted to grow during an era of more or less full employment from £92.2 billion in 1996–97 to £126.7 billion in 2003–04. The 37 per cent increase funded the new tax credits. The advantages were mixed. In an unprecedented invasion of privacy, 5.7 million out of seven million parents were obliged to complete forms in order to qualify for benefits. The dependency trap, 'a form of permanent serfdom' according to Frank Field, meant that benefits were being paid to higher earners rather than to the poor. Families paying moderate and higher rates of income tax received childcare benefits, but 1.4 million couples had lost benefits for their children. Anyone earning less than £31,500 per year was better off claiming a tax credit rather than attempting to increase their income.

Any detrimental influence on society was denied by Brown, yet means testing the middle classes encouraged couples to calculate their joint earnings and often decide against

marriage for purely financial reasons, an unfortunate development for a chancellor intent on building community spirit.
There was also the predicted explosion of fraud which he had
ignored. The complexities of the housing benefit system were
one fruitful source of illicit income, and the chancellor's new
childcare tax credit was another. The childcare credit entitled
mothers to register their child at a nursery and receive £150
per week for six months to pay for the service. Contrary to
professional advice warning of possible psychological damage,
Brown was intent on encouraging the mothers of very young
children to return to work rather than care for their offspring
at home. Many accepted the enticement, but thousands of
dishonest mothers registered their children with carers, collected the complete six-month grant, then immediately withdrew their child from the carer and kept the money. Brown
had forecast that the childcare credit would cost £250 million,
but fraud had magnified the real cost to at least £1 billion. In
the 1997 manifesto Labour had estimated that £21 billion was
lost annually to benefit fraud. Since the election the figure
had increased to over £30 billion, only a fraction of which
was being recovered.

The warnings Brown had received from Treasury officials
in 1997 had been proved correct. The credits were too complicated for claimants to understand, they discriminated against
some working families with children, and since the cost of
administration fell on employers, many small companies
shunned the paperwork and rejected their obligations. The
most serious complaint was the declining number of genuine
claimants. Among the non-claimants were those parents
unable to read the forty-seven pages of instructions before
completing a twelve-page application form to qualify for the
children's tax credit. Other parents would be deterred from
applying for the baby tax credit: only 85,000 out of an eligible
500,000 applied after its introduction in April 2002. The credit

was abolished a year later. The same pattern affected the
working family tax credit. Brown announced that 90 per cent
of Britain's families would benefit from that, but in the first
year only 51 per cent applied for a scheme which would cost
£13 billion. Overall, the Office of National Statistics estimated
that only 500,000 people had benefited from the new tax
credits since 1997, despite an extra £24 billion of government
spending. During 2002 nearly £5 billion of benefits would
be unclaimed, despite a 900 per cent increase in advertising
costs since 1997, up from £4 million a year to £35.8 million
in 2001.

To balance those statistics, Brown announced in 2001 that
1.2 million out of 4.4 million impoverished children had been
lifted above the poverty line during Labour's first parliament.
His claim was revised by the Treasury to say instead that there
were '1.2 million fewer children in relative poverty than there
would otherwise have been'. Money, Brown remained convinced, could influence people's behaviour. A Treasury
adviser estimated that every child dropping out of school at
sixteen cost the country £97,000 in benefits, crime, lost productivity, ill-health and drug misuse. To prevent that social
calamity, Brown proposed that children aged over sixteen
with parents earning less than £30,000 per annum would be
offered £40 per week to stay at school, and that 76,000 children should be enrolled in a Young Enterprise scheme. Those
who refused offers of work would lose their benefits. The
announcement of the means tested money reflected Brown's
good intentions but also his lack of realism about the reasons
sixteen-year-olds were unwilling to study. One casualty of all
his ideas and soaring costs was Sir Nicholas Montagu, the
fifty-eight-year-old chairman of Inland Revenue.

Montagu, a former academic and the pioneer of rail privatisation for the Conservative government, had had an unimpressive record since 1997. The Revenue's computer systems

were inadequate, his officials had failed to anticipate the
problems arising from self-assessment for paying income tax,
they had failed to warn ten million taxpayers about their
inadequate National Insurance contributions towards their
pensions (a mistake not revealed by Lord Rooker, the pensions minister), and the general collection of income tax was
faltering. Tax collection depends upon effectively preventing
fraud. In 1994 the Revenue had recovered £6.9 billion from
tax evaders, but in 2002, although the national tax bill had
risen, the amount of unpaid taxes recovered had fallen to
£3.8 billion, at a time when the Revenue itself estimated that
evasion was costing at least £25 billion annually. Montagu, a
mild man, partially bore the blame for the deterioration. He
was unaware that in 2000–01 the Inland Revenue had mistakenly overpaid between £510 million and £710 million to
claimants, and that the error had continued for three years
without anyone noticing.

The Revenue's staff were overwhelmed by the remorseless
changes ordered by Gordon Brown. With limited discussion
and little foresight, Montagu realised, the Revenue had been
transformed into a 'social department'. Montagu was not prepared for the new culture. Ignoring warnings from Robert
Culpin and others, Brown imposed upon the Inland Revenue
responsibility for the administration of all National Insurance
payments, which had formerly been carried out by the Contributions Agency. To undertake that task, Sir Nicholas Montagu
had transferred some staff from the Revenue's non-compliance
units to work with EDS, the computer specialists, to organise
the payment of £16 billion every year for the child tax credit
and the working tax credit. The two tax credits, introduced in
1999, were to be radically changed in April 2003. To satisfy the
chancellor's instructions, Montagu approved a tight timetable
to introduce a unique computer system, and subsequently
compressed the preparatory period before the computers went

'live' from twelve to four weeks. In December 2002 his work was praised by the Office of Government Commerce, an agency blessed by Brown, as 'an exemplar of good programme management'. Consistently with the chancellor's distant relationship with the Treasury's technocrats, Dawn Primarolo, who as the paymaster general was responsible for taxes, did not meet Montagu for five months during 2002 to discuss the introduction of the revised tax credits.

In March 2003 Montagu was warned by the computer specialists at the Office of Government Commerce that the administration of the credits was at 'great risk'. In reality, the programme was doomed. The computer system was woefully inadequate, and there were insufficient staff. Montagu was now faced with the responsibility of preventing the upheaval from spilling into chaos. Strangely, he did not warn Primarolo about his struggle to meet Brown's ambitious demands, nor did he personally confront the chancellor about the problems. Possibly he lacked the courage to present Brown with unwelcome news. The Treasury's officials, he knew, were usually bereft of self-criticism. Montagu's diffidence and Primarolo's management style combined to make an already bad situation worse. Primarolo would be unaware at the launch of the revised family credits that two million people were forlornly calling the Revenue's helpline, and three months after the launch 375,000 applications had not been processed. The helpline for those without money would cost £53 million that year.

The blame for the 'totally unacceptable' chaos and 'chronic mismanagement' as the Inland Revenue 'struggled to cope' would be levelled by the House of Commons Treasury Committee at Brown personally. In their subsequent investigation, the committee would suggest that there were 'serious questions about how the department had been led' by Brown. Edward Leigh, the Tory chairman of the Public Accounts

Committee, described the introduction of the tax credits as 'nothing short of disastrous'.

The Revenue's mismanagement reflected disarray in the Treasury. The running costs of Brown's department had increased by 40 per cent since 1997, but its officials were unable to explain the reason. Sir Nicholas Montagu was more forthright. He would admit that his management had 'gone spectacularly wrong', and that at the very least the introduction of the tax credit should have been delayed. Brown, however, denied any personal responsibility, and refused to give detailed answers in the Commons about the precise amount lost by the Treasury.

Brown's expectation of escaping any criticism of his management was endangered by the contemporaneous exposure of an unusual property deal. Sir Nicholas Montagu had been ordered by the Treasury to sell and lease back six hundred properties owned and occupied by the Inland Revenue to a private property company. The contract, completed in March 2001, had transferred the properties to Mapeley Steps Ltd, a subsidiary of the similarly named Mapeley YK Company Ltd, registered in Bermuda, a tax haven. The intention of Robin Priest, the company's chief executive, and the financier George Soros, who owned 42 per cent of the company, was to minimise taxes on any profits, especially avoiding capital gains taxes when the properties were sold in the future. The chancellor had every reason to enquire about the progress of the negotiations of such a significant property deal, but refrained from doing so. Montagu, aware that Mapeley intended to minimise its taxes, failed to alert Brown or Dawn Primarolo about the potential embarrassment of selling all the Inland Revenue's properties to a company established specifically to avoid paying British taxes. Instead, he offered the company 'letters of comfort' to allay some concerns.

For years Brown had condemned multi-millionaires based

in offshore tax havens for exploiting tax loopholes or transferring huge sums of untaxed cash out of Britain. Annually, he
estimated, 100,000 people living in Britain avoided payment.
Many British passport holders were claiming 'non domicile
status' by showing their ownership of a burial plot or property
abroad. Repeatedly, Brown threatened to close the tax loophole, which coincidentally benefited Labour donors including
Lakshmi Mittal (a £125,000 donation), Christopher Ondaatje
(a £2 million donation), Gulam Noon (a £200,000 donation)
and David Potter. To the anger of his political advisers he
retreated from this pledge, admitting that he feared an exodus
of foreign businessmen from Britain, including prominent
shipowners. In order to deflect attention from his reluctance,
he threatened sanctions against Jersey if it resisted implementing EU rules against tax havens. Brown's gesture politics persuaded Sir Nicholas Montagu not to question the offshore
status of Mapeley Steps Ltd. The Treasury, Montagu believed,
could not discriminate against bidders for government contracts based in tax havens. He would claim that he had 'no
alternative' but to sell the buildings to the offshore company.

Montagu's silence compounded the effects of the Revenue's
maladroit negotiations with the property company's directors.
Although he praised his own agreement, Montagu failed to
reveal some inherent problems. Mapeley Steps paid £220 million for the properties, although some assessments valued
them at £370 million. Soon after the sale was completed, the
company complained that the Inland Revenue had provided
inaccurate information about the cost of running the buildings, and claimed £210 million in compensation. The dispute
remained unresolved until Montagu was persuaded that
Mapeley Steps risked bankruptcy and takeover by its banks,
which would entail the Inland Revenue losing control of its six
hundred properties. To avoid that embarrassment, Montagu
agreed to give undisclosed millions to Mapeley in compen-

sation. As part of the settlement, the Inland Revenue agreed
to pay Mapeley an annual rent for its former buildings of
about £307 million, contradicting a previous official disclosure
that the annual rent would be about £170 million. Montagu
again failed to disclose the commitment of extra money to
the Treasury ministers, which would be criticised as malad-
ministration and a lapse in standards. Montagu described the
criticism, especially from Brown, as 'very hurtful' to his family.
Brown's fury was curtailed when Partnerships UK, his own creation involving Steve Robson, Derek Higgs and Malcolm Bates,
began brokering a settlement between the Inland Revenue and
Mapeley to resolve what Montagu called 'an unfortunate
coincidence of mistakes'. His solution would be to order the
merger of the Inland Revenue with Customs and Excise, a
massive undertaking embracing 100,000 staff and hundreds
of systems which would, he pledged, reduce staff by 12,500
and save £200 million every year. The experience of past
reorganisation in Whitehall suggested that was optimistic.

As the senior minister, Brown was responsible for his
department's errors; not only because of the doctrine of ministerial responsibility, but also because of the complexities he
had introduced. Most officials had learnt to avoid challenging
his decisions, or to remain silent after he dismissed their
advice. Among the few exceptions had been General Sir
Charles Guthrie, the chief of the defence staff. The general
had been unimpressed by Brown's silence during the Kosovo
conflict, and his constant sniping at the defence budget despite
supporting the invasion of Afghanistan. 'You don't think I
understand defence, do you?' Brown snapped at Guthrie during a heated conversation about a proposed budget cut. 'No,
I bloody well don't,' was the reply. Guthrie found it difficult
to respect a man who wanted to risk soldiers' lives on the
cheap, and even proposed to auction some seventeenth-
century silver candlesticks owned by the state made in the

reign of William of Orange to raise £100,000 for 'public services'. Professionals like Guthrie could not understand the chancellor's principles. Labour was committed to education, yet he refused to give more money to universities or to increase student fees, leaving the institutions mired in debt. Similarly, he professed his faith in the public services, yet PFI deals had accumulated nearly £35.5 billion of debt, without definite proof of their financial benefits. The obfuscation about PFI's advantages was orchestrated by Brown's department. Andrew Smith, the chief secretary to the Treasury, told the House of Commons in July 2001 that 'two substantive reports on PFI ... have indicated that PFI is delivering value for money'. One of these reports, 'PFI and Value for Money', by the National Audit Office, had he said 'found an average saving of 20 per cent'. Strangely, the NAO had not yet examined the operation of PFI contracts, and the report did not exist. Smith blamed a 'typographical error' for the mistake. No one blamed the chancellor – except the prime minister.

Gordon Brown's control of the economic and social agenda had sapped Tony Blair's patience, and his disdain for the prime minister irritated Blair's advisers in the Downing Street policy units. The territorial clash in what the advisers called 'the border zone' had become particularly pertinent over the billions spent on benefits and tax credits – 'bills of social failure', in Blair's opinion. Some of that money, Blair believed, should have been used to finance his ambitions for 'delivery' in schools and the NHS. His frustrations were mentioned to trade union leaders during a party in 10 Downing Street on 25 June 2001. 'Four years of failure' was one of the phrases passed on to Brown with which Blair had expressed his anger about the non-improvement of the public services.

Blair was convinced that only the private sector's commercial values could revolutionise the NHS. He wanted to demolish old structures, introduce market reforms and recruit new managers. The dispute between the two men was ideological. Blair wanted to reintroduce Thatcherite devolution of the NHS, while Brown championed the NHS employees whose restrictive practices were hindering Blair's reforms. Brown was uncertain whether the prime minister, who favoured sudden action rather than prolonged argument, would dare to challenge the trade unions and his own promotion of himself as the true champion of the NHS. In the battle between old and new, Brown prepared himself to present an account of his journey to resolve socialism and the market. This was fertile territory, he reasoned, on which to erode the prime minister's authority and summon support for his bid for the leadership.

Gordon Brown's plans to undermine his rival were disturbed by the terrorist attack on the World Trade Center in New York on 11 September 2001. The reversal of fortunes was dramatic. The prime minister's elevation as the international champion of the war against terror overpowered the image of a chancellor grappling to repair domestic muddles. A swirl of gossip inflamed Brown. His old critics, he knew, were comparing the bright glow emanating from Blair with Brown's supposedly waning star, especially after the chancellor was heard to grumble that Britain's gung-ho support for George W. Bush's all-out war against Iraq was 'excessive'. Paul Routledge, the chancellor's first biographer, accused Blair's supporters of opportunistically exploiting the image of their leader striding the world like a colossus to humble the chancellor. 'Tony,' urged Routledge, 'should call his people to order.'

An 'evil mood', Brown's cabinet colleagues agreed, awaited most guests to the Treasury. His selective social skills were barely visible. He barely deigned to look his visitors in the face, and dismissed their contributions without pretending to listen to them. His temper, the private secretaries at the Treasury reported, was rising. 'Don't fucking tell me that!' he screamed at a junior minister. 'I already know that!' The door slammed. 'He's chewing the carpet,' was the gossip reaching senior officials. Any challenge provoked his ferocious rage. Alone, his temper subsided and he slumped into a solitary sulk. In the outer office were witnesses to the dark side of his charisma. He dismissed Alan Milburn as 'useless', Geoff Hoon, the defence secretary, as 'lightweight', and David Blunkett as 'far too right-wing'. In response, Blunkett derided the chancellor as 'The Money God', and encouraged whispers that the prime minister favoured either Charles Clarke or Blunkett himself as his successor. 'A disruptive, tragic figure,' sneered Charles Clarke, a veteran enemy.

Brown did nothing to restrain his own friends from complaining that Blair should honour 'the Deal', and consider retiring before the next election. In retaliation, his enemies' venom was unleashed in public. Frank Field called for the dismissal of an 'unpleasant' chancellor. Mo Mowlam asserted in an interview that the tension he caused was 'crippling the government'. Others whispered their anger anonymously. Brown was asked about the feud at a finance ministers' conference in Ottawa. Naturally, he sought to distance himself from it, pressing his spokesman to say, 'All the talk about rows with cabinet colleagues, and rows with the prime minister is from his point of view trivial garbage. It's not true and he's having nothing to do with it.' But denial was not enough. Nor was the customary Blair praise in the House of Commons. Even Brown's reciprocal praise in an interview with *The Times* in which he spoke of his 'hard-working and brilliant' cabinet colleagues, his 'utmost respect for the brilliant work our spending ministers have done', and declared 'Tony Blair is the best friend I've had in politics' failed to defuse the hostilities.

A conversation during the last week of November 2001 restored the balance. Although as usual no record was kept, Blair recounted to his advisers afterwards a version suggesting that a line had been drawn. He had told Brown, he said,

that his spending priorities had been mistaken, and that his
unpleasantness towards other ministers was causing harm.
The public services, it was agreed, would be reformed, and
the contradiction of Brown publicly urging devolution but
imposing centralisation would have to end. The atmosphere
was, as usual, tense. The chancellor hated being backed into
a corner, and he now began looking for a way out of his
troubles. Previously he had adapted an old adage, 'There are
only two types of chancellor: those who fail and those who
get out in time. That's why I'm still looking for a third way.'

On 27 November 2001, Derek Wanless was listening to his
car radio. One week earlier the former banker had submitted
his report on the NHS to Brown, and he was eagerly awaiting
the chancellor's speech in the Commons. After all his hard
work, the last few days had not been as rewarding as he
had anticipated. His first two-hour visual presentation at the
Treasury to Brown and Alan Milburn, the health secretary,
had revealed some of Brown's idiosyncrasies.

The headlines of his interim report, Wanless had told Brown
in his introduction, were bleak. His research established that
over the past decades the NHS had been bedevilled by poor
productivity and a lethargic attitude towards improvement.
The NHS lacked manpower, was undermined by targets, and
in the long term should be funded by another method. Brown
was surprised by those conclusions, and shocked by Wanless's
next statement. On most criteria, said Wanless, health care
in Britain was worse than elsewhere in Europe. Compared
with those of other countries, the NHS's services were poor,
and the Office of National Statistics had damagingly underestimated the growing numbers of the elderly.

Brown's reaction at the end of the presentation astonished
Wanless. Without apology, he voiced his suspicion that Wanless had deliberately highlighted bad comparisons. He refused
to believe that the health systems in other countries were

better. The NHS, he repeated, defined Britain. 'It's the envy of the world,' he said, echoing a traditional Labour cliché. The best comparison with the NHS, said Brown, was the American medical system. 'The private sector is less efficient at spending money than the public sector,' he insisted. The reason for his refusal to compare the NHS with European services, it became apparent from his questions, was that he was unaware of the state insurance schemes on the continent.

Wanless's factual replies failed to spark a reaction. Brown preferred to conceal his lack of knowledge. 'Financing evidence is not crucial,' said Wanless, meaning that money alone would not solve the NHS's problems. Over eighteen years, the Tories had increased health expenditure by 70 per cent after inflation, but few believed the service had improved. That was an area Brown also refused to debate. In 2000 the NHS had cost £44 billion. Brown had pledged to spend £57 billion in 2004. To match European expenditure in 2004 would cost £72 billion, an unattainable target. Privately Brown admitted that Labour had been too slow to act, and had made mistakes. 'We've had a long apprenticeship,' he told his Scottish friend Tom Brown, a columnist on the *Daily Record*, in May 1997. 'The test now begins . . .' In truth, nothing constructive had been achieved over the previous five years, and Brown was partially responsible.

Four days later Wanless, uncowed by Brown's frosty reaction, was completing an identical presentation to Tony Blair in Downing Street. Gordon Brown, Alan Milburn and others sat behind the prime minister. Like Brown, the prime minister had not realised that patients, informed by the internet and newspapers, would increasingly expect to be offered a choice of treatment, and would make both clinical and non-clinical demands which could only be supplied by personal payment to the NHS. 'I think you were mistaken to make the commitment to match European spending,' said Wanless, 'because you don't know how much Europe will be spending.' Blair stared fixedly. Brown did not conceal his smile. Like Brown, Blair did not seek to debate Wanless's conclusions. The legacy of Frank Dobson and Old Labour, both realised, was stagnation.

After thanking Wanless and bidding him farewell, Brown began to plan his speech to the Commons. He would have preferred to work in secrecy, ignoring other ministers including Alan Milburn, and present Blair with a completed package. But the prime minister insisted on a discussion. The two men occasionally enjoyed their arguments. Their fierce discussions about principles and policies could exhaust observers, but appeared to energise the two combatants. On the fate of the NHS, they were irreconcilable. Blair wanted a 'mixed economy under the NHS umbrella' and 'more market-oriented incentives', while Brown, fearing the end of universalism, favoured retaining the centralised economic foundations. Inside Blair's office their debate became so ferocious, with neither willing to surrender, that agreement appeared to be impossible.

The mediator, as so often, was Alastair Campbell. Perhaps surprisingly, the spokesman renowned as a vulgar bully possessed the insight to bring peace. 'This is bollocks,' he said, looking at both men sternly. He urged them to remember why they were there, to remain serious politicians, and to take the best of both of their arguments to fashion an acceptable narrative. He reminded them of the cement binding them together, not least their shared Christian faith. Blair was the more generous, embracing his colleague with all his faults. Brown was incapable of similar demonstrativeness towards Blair, although he had benefited from their unique relationship. Both agreed to compromise.

Brown returned to the Treasury to write his speech. He proposed to turn adversity into victory, relying on Wanless to support his prejudices. He decided to ignore the chapters in the report about the advantages of private care, diversity,

consumer choice and the requirements of regulation, and to
omit mentioning the deliberate absence of statistics in the
interim report. He would take the least important chapter
about funding out of context, suggesting that Wanless had
provided supporting statistics, to give the impression that the
report sealed the argument in favour of the NHS as an exclusively state-funded centralised institution, rather than to reflect
the report's suggestion that there were variations worth considering. Above all, he would use the report to justify future tax
increases to pay for the NHS, 'prove' that private health was
less efficient than the NHS, and quote Wanless as the justification that equality was best for society. To make that socialist
argument palatable to non-believers, he added a pledge: 'There
will not be one penny more until we get the changes to enable
us to make the reforms and carry out the modernisation the
health service needs.' No money without efficiency sounded
marvellous – but it was an empty threat. Brown never
intended to withhold a penny. Nor did he intend to support
Blair's commitment to match European spending on the NHS.

On his car radio, Wanless was stunned to hear Brown use
his name over fifteen times in his Commons speech, and then
partially misrepresent his report to justify his own conclusions. Unseen by radio listeners, Brown's right leg was
vigorously banging up and down in rhythm to his fast delivery,
as he theatrically barked out commands for other ministers to
implement. By the end of his speech the repeated mention of
'Wanless' provoked jeers from the Conservatives, but he sat
down to wild cheers from his benches and three slaps of con-
gratulation on his left leg from Blair. He did not acknowledge
the prime minister's thanks. Blair would, he realised, take some
time to understand how he had adapted Wanless to justify
making no major changes to the management and financing of
the NHS. Only gradually would the prime minister realise that
Brown, disappointed by Wanless's objectivity, would use the

report to protect his vision of Labour's traditions and would
ignore everyone's protests. Some might damn the government's policy as confused, but his supporters understood that
he was protecting Nye Bevan's legacy.

In his car, Wanless was oblivious of Brown's joy. And there
was an added discomfort: Michael Howard was condemning
his 'biased report'. Howard, he knew, had not been given a
copy in advance. By the end of the broadcast Wanless felt
traduced. That afternoon he telephoned the Treasury to complain about the misuse of his name. 'He doesn't realise he's
repeating one word so often,' explained a harassed official.
Two days later, Brown telephoned to apologise. 'I may have
overdone it,' he admitted. Wanless might have doubted the
sincerity of the apology. Brown had been delighted to quote
Wanless as justification for raising taxes. More money, he
was convinced, would transform the NHS. In a debate the
following day, Brown proudly announced another victory
over Blair. 'I don't rule out tax rises,' he declared, legitimising
his record of forty-five tax increases to raise an extra £22
billion, and turning the table on the Tories, challenging them
to drop their promise to cut taxes. 'On a day like today,'
concluded Blair's spokesman, 'we can see how fortunate we
are to have such a superb chancellor and how the very close
relationship which he has with the prime minister is one of
the great strengths of this government.'

This emollience from Downing Street achieved the opposite
of its intention. The party's cheers about the NHS and taxes
during the last week of November roused Brown from his
depression. The renewed esteem from his kin rekindled his
ambitions for the leadership. In the past he had equivocated
about the folklore surrounding the meeting at Granita, condemning it as 'all gossip'. Blair's last response to the rumours,
in May 2001, had been as usual dismissive: 'As Gordon and
I both say whenever we are asked about this, there's no

gentleman's agreement, no.' Blair was always amused by the image of Brown fuming about his frustrated dream.

But that weekend Brown accepted an invitation from David Frost for a live television interview with an explicit purpose. He prepared a surprise answer for Frost's question about the leadership and 'the Deal'. 'What Tony Blair and I have said to each other really is a matter for us,' replied Brown, implying that the two had indeed discussed and agreed the leadership succession. Frost looked speechless. 'This is the first time I've heard you silent,' smiled Brown. That exchange encouraged him. At the end of a turbulent year of highs and lows, he sensed the beginning of a new era, not least the forthcoming birth of his first child in the new year.

Just before Christmas Brown invited more than a dozen Scottish friends to a dinner party at 11 Downing Street. On such occasions, witnessed by so few, he shone. Expansive and funny, he spoke excitedly about politics and his personal life. Compared to the public image of a melancholic alternately biting his nails or pushing his tongue into his jutted jaw, Brown was, as usual among his clan, compassionate and witty. His only reflective moment was to lament that the resignation of Henry McLeish as first minister of Scotland in October amid allegations about wrongful claims for expenses had further weakened his position in the devolved government; and the demotion of Nick Brown for disloyalty and incompetence during the foot and mouth outbreak had not helped his cause at Westminster. The occasion also represented his unmentioned Achilles heel in English politics. Brown was rarely seen in London's theatres, concert halls or restaurants. His diffidence towards the metropolitan middle classes and the capital's heroes reflected the inner turmoil of the Scottish socialist partially converted to capitalism. That sentiment was shared by his boisterous guests. They were 'foreign occupiers', resented even by some English Labour MPs.

Those same people rejoiced on 28 December 2001. Seven weeks prematurely, Sarah gave birth at Forth Park Hospital in Kirkcaldy to a girl weighing 2lbs 4oz, to be called Jennifer. Tahir Mahmood, the consultant obstetrician, announced, 'The baby was crying healthily.' Brown appeared exhausted but elated as he left the hospital laughing. 'Baby looks like father,' said Mahmood. 'No, like the mother,' countered Brown, and the doctor agreed. Even Brown's critics joined the moist-eyed chorus of genuine congratulations to a man who was at last apparently able, at the age of fifty, to share the normal joys of those he sought to rule. 'It's the most beautiful baby in the world,' he said outside the hospital. 'I probably waited a longer time than most people to be a father, and it's just a superb feeling. Politics seems a lot less important to me today.' Speaking to his friends, he sounded like a new man. Tom Brown reported that he had never seen the politician, clearly infatuated by his new daughter, smile so much.

On the third day, the happiness turned to misery. An ultrasound scan showed that the baby had developed a haemorrhage in the brain. Premature babies with fragile blood vessels in their head are prone to that danger. The only disclosure was that 'a very rare series of events' had occurred. Inevitably, the parents were devastated. Although the baby was transferred to the Edinburgh Royal Infirmary, the situation could only end in tragedy. Within seventy-two hours the new father had experienced the extremes of emotions. With death imminent, Jennifer was baptised on Sunday night. She died in her parents' arms at 5.20 p.m. on Monday, 7 January 2002. Later that night, the anguished couple were photographed leaving the hospital. Some criticised the newspapers for intrusiveness, but Brown himself never complained. Death revealed the real human being.

The condolences were stark and honest. 'There is little that anyone can say of comfort at such a time,' said Blair wisely. 'We are just trying to stick together as a family,' wept Brown's brother John. 'Baby Jennifer may have known her parents for only a short time, but she will have changed their lives forever,' lamented Helen Liddell.

Friends who called at North Queensferry discovered that Brown was shattered, and relied on Sarah for support. At some stage he must have recalled his own account of James Maxton's grief following his wife's death in childbirth in 1922. 'Maxton was devastated,' Brown had written. 'It was a tragedy from which he never recovered ... The sense of loss and loneliness never left Maxton.' Ramsay MacDonald advised Maxton, 'You must do your best in your own way to trudge through the valley without losing heart.' And to recover, he urged, 'Get back to work, work, work. It keeps you sane.'

Even at Brown's moment of dire misery, there was no public glimpse of self-pity. At first he was distracted by organising the funeral, which was held on 11 January. Planned initially as a small ceremony for his family conducted by Rev Sheila Munro, who had married the Browns, it became a gathering of many politicians including Tony Blair, John Prescott and a large number of journalists. John Brown's sermon described the baby bringing her parents 'a joy so deep, a love so immediate and intense, that the anxiety, the loss that followed, are almost unbearable'. In the days that followed friends found that Sarah had collapsed, and in turn became dependent on her husband. Thousands of letters had arrived from strangers telling how they had suffered and coped with the pain of losing a child. 'I don't think we'll be the same again,' Brown would reply to all those unexpected condolences, 'but it has made us think about what's important. It has made us think that you've got to use your time properly. It's made us more determined. Things that we feel are right we have got to achieve. Jennifer is an inspiration to us.' Sarah would tell friends, 'I prefer to have been a mother for ten days than not be a mother at all.'

There was uncertainty about how Brown would emerge
from the trauma. The unexpected answer was that three
weeks after the death, he returned to the Treasury. The budget
had been delayed until 17 April, and he undertook no public
engagements. At lunchtime he would drive to his small flat
to keep Sarah company and write individual replies to many
of the thousands of letters. To his officials he gave a searing
account of his experience: 'I have definitely seen the best of
British. I saw the NHS fight to save Jennifer. Now I'll battle
to rebuild it. It'll be the greatest achievement of this Labour
government.' The media were savaging the government over
a catalogue of disasters in the NHS and the railways, where
workers were on strike for the first time in many years. Investment in the public services since 1997 had been the smallest
proportion of national income since records began. The reconstruction of the NHS could be financed in several different
ways, but Brown insisted that it would be on his terms.

One week later, Derek Wanless presented his final report
in the Treasury. Brown sat in the same room as previously
with Ed Balls and other advisers to hear the cost of change.
Wanless's headline figures were massive. To match the government's ambitions, annual spending would have to increase
from £68 billion to £154 billion in 2020 – without efficiency
savings, the figure would be £184 billion. 'Productivity,'
announced Wanless cueing a slide. The chancellor stared fixedly.
In public, Brown spoke repeatedly about the need to improve
productivity, but Wanless's remorseless description of the NHS's
gross inefficiencies, especially among administrators, dissolved
his interest. The rumour that a forthcoming report by the Office
of National Statistics would confirm that efficiency in the NHS
had fallen by 15 per cent between 1995 and 2000, despite a
25 per cent increase in spending, had irritated the chancellor.

'Localism,' declared Wanless, signalling another slide. Local
democracy, he predicted, would inevitably mean different

standards of care in different regions. Brown may himself
have preached the advantages of devolved government, and
even advocated the advantages of local solutions in the NHS,
but Wanless's assessment was irritating. 'There won't be any
unacceptable variations,' said Brown. 'That's what happened
when we devolved at the NatWest,' replied Wanless. 'In the
short term there were problems, but it's better in the long
term.' Brown waved his hand in dismissal. He emphatically
rejected 'the politics of secession' – the disenchanted buying
their own health, education and even security, to the detriment of the community. Somehow he would put an end to
that fragmentation.

'Targets,' announced Wanless, acknowledging the order to
move on. 'Targets are causing real problems, encouraging doctors to make the wrong decisions.' Brown grunted, clearly
unconvinced. For four years he had praised targets and Public
Sector Agreements (PSAs). The recent discovery that only 40
per cent of the three hundred PSAs started in 1998 had been
met raised no alarm. Despite his pledge of 'transparency and
accountability', there was no inquiry into the conduct of those
hundreds employed to monitor targets, and no one was reprimanded for the failure to meet 60 per cent of the PSAs.

'You're ignoring the human factor,' said Wanless. 'Get off
the target philosophy.' St Thomas's hospital in London, he
continued, had lost its higher star status because patients
receiving intensive treatment had been kept on trolleys for
over four hours. The doctors had insisted that they could not,
for medical reasons, be moved. 'This isn't a trolley. It's a bed,'
they proclaimed. The assessors disagreed. 'Health is too complicated to use targets,' said Wanless. 'I don't think there's
anything really wrong here,' countered Brown. 'I'm sure
that's not a widespread problem. Just a one-off.' Targets
appealed to Brown. They enforced centralised control,
removed any danger of regional variations and would deliver

uniformity. 'The problem,' he told Wanless, 'is not setting targets but the failure of the NHS to implement them.'

Wanless tried again. 'Targets are naïve and blunt. They're corrosive. They don't drive standards higher. Your targets are leading to misallocation of resources and poor productivity. A good auditing system rather than targets would be better.' 'I disagree,' replied Brown. 'We can get both. I have to get value for public money. I don't know any other way than targets to achieve that. In the long term it will get better.' 'But you haven't considered the advantages of regional variations.' 'I have,' insisted Brown, ignoring his own inexperience of management.

'Statistics,' said Wanless. Brown was intrigued by Wanless's discovery that the statistics used by the NHS were inaccurate, but he was antagonistic to his conclusions. Frank Dobson, said Wanless, had wasted five years by scrapping the internal market. 'I don't think you understood the damaging consequences,' he told Brown. 'The Tories weren't destroying the NHS, they were trying to make it more efficient. You should have tried to improve it.' Brown gestured his disagreement in familiar style. He seemed unwilling to understand that the NHS's problem was not only about money, but about delivery.

Wanless tried again: 'My report is four years too late. You should have commissioned this in 1997.' 'We didn't realise how bad it was, and we didn't have the money,' replied Brown. 'Commissioning a report would not have cost any money,' countered Wanless. Brown still did not understand. 'Your policies since then,' said Wanless, 'have made it worse.' There was an uncomfortable silence. Seventeen separate agencies audited Britain's acute hospitals and over thirty monitored the NHS's performance, said Wanless. Whatever the truth, the public perceived deteriorating services.

Brown was no longer interested in the conversation. He disliked challenges to his philosophy. He was convinced that the fundamentals should not be changed. Even though Wanless felt that financing the NHS by general taxation rather than by the social insurance system used all over western Europe was probably less expensive, Brown refused to entertain the idea that more money was not the only answer. His body had positively jerked when Wanless asked him to explain why the Scottish NHS was so dismal, given that its spending levels were as high as the Europeans'. Wanless's report could be used to justify creeping privatisation to dismantle what the prime minister damagingly called 'the old monopolies'. His criticism of targets categorised him as untrustworthy.

In Britain during the 1990s, McKinsey's and other management consultants had become an addiction to some executives and politicians. Brown's obsession with targets was a product of adopting the consultants' jargon of systems and formulas. He trusted the new breed of tieless bureaucrat, articulate about missions and milestones, without understanding their weaknesses. New NHS managers were urged to meet targets without understanding the real objectives. They were 'delivery merchants', bearing little loyalty to the institution. Long before the results of their tampering became evident, most of them would have moved on to assume a new title in another job. Above them, the target-setters and scrutinisers regarded themselves as more talented and important than was really justified. Proper scrutiny of a hospital's performance required prolonged and detailed study, but few scrutineers remained in the same job long enough to become sufficiently experienced to make proper evaluations. Meeting Brown's targets required only ticking boxes and providing statistics, without checking whether the evaluations were accurate. Insensitive to management and human motivation, Brown did not realise that introducing the target culture into the NHS had created measurements that encouraged dishonesty. The auditors –

who ostensibly had methodical, suspicious minds – were excessively eager to help their clients. Just like those accused of colourful accounting at Enron, Global Crossing and Swissair, all of which employed McKinsey's as advisers and all of which would become bankrupt, the health service had become tainted by conflicts of interests and aggressive accounting. To bury the failure of targets, Brown would order the Treasury at the end of the year not to publish reports on some of them. His remedy was more inquiries. He appointed Peter Gershon, a former executive at Marconi and, since 2000, the chief executive of the Office of Government Commerce, to investigate the government's efficiency; and he asked Malcolm Bates to report on obtaining better value in government procurement. He preferred not to comment on the European Central Bank's estimate that productivity in the British public sector had fallen 8 per cent since 1998, costing £70 billion. He was chasing a dream as much as confronting reality.

That confusion greeted Wanless twenty-four hours later when he entered 10 Downing Street to repeat his presentation for Tony Blair. In the centre of the room, Blair sat alert. To his right were Brown and Ed Balls. Brown was clearly nervous. Despite his mourning, he had reached the last stages of writing his budget. Reforming the NHS would be a major feature. Just ten minutes after Wanless began, the chancellor and Balls began speaking loudly to each other. Wanless halted, stunned by the interruption. Blair was embarrassed, but said nothing. He recognised Brown's familiar tactic to destabilise someone who was delivering an unwelcome opinion. Wanless resumed, addressing the prime minister, who was eager to find a solution to the increasing public criticism of Labour's policies. Brown continued his animated discussion with Balls. His officials from the Treasury, accustomed to such behaviour, understood that Wanless's report would be buried on the morning of the budget. Eventually the disruption petered out,

but Brown did not conceal his impatience. Blair and Alan
Milburn knew that a war with the chancellor was imminent.

Alone in his office, isolated from his officials, Brown hammered out the budget on his personal computer. Driven by
his misery, he sought phrases and sentiments to turn the
annual ritual into an inspiration for Labour's heartlands,
and an introspective justification of his life's purpose. His
chosen platform was to launch a counter-revolution against
Thatcherism. He would return to his spiritual roots and once
again become a hero of the left. In a recent speech to honour
Nye Bevan and damn the Thatcher legacy, he had expressed
those rousing sentiments. Repeatedly he had mentioned the
word 'socialist' as he eulogised tradition and condemned the
'walls of privilege' represented by elitist schools and private
hospitals. 'Today in Britain,' he had complained, 'most of the
children of rich families go to university but most of the children of poor families do not . . . It is the unfairness of asking
the sick to pay for being sick that is totally unacceptable.'

Naturally, he would not use that vocabulary in his budget
speech. To retain the support of the middle classes, he would
criticise 'taxation for its own sake' and praise 'wealth creation
to fund the social benefits we demand'. His record would
speak for itself: the lowest inflation for forty years, and the
smallest national debt and lowest unemployment for decades.
For the seventy-first time since 1997 he would include the
phrase 'boom and bust' in a Commons speech. He might have
paused before writing that overused phrase. House prices
were surging, share prices were slumping, savings were down
from 9.7 per cent between 1993 and 1997 to 5.1 per cent in
2002, pension funds were withering (contrary to the ONS
estimate, only £27 billion was saved for pensions in 2002,
rather than £86 billion), and manufacturing was depressed.
For twenty years he had preached the need for more investment, but his micro-management had failed to change the

culture. During the last five years of the Tory government the economy had grown by 3.2 per cent, but since 1997 growth had been 2.4 per cent per annum. Despite all his incentives, the growth of productivity had fallen from 2.4 per cent to 1.4 per cent – in manufacturing it had fallen back to the level of 1974 – and labour costs had increased, while investment in research and development had fallen from 2.2 per cent to 1.8 per cent of the gross national income, less than in all of Britain's major competitors. While growth had fallen, taxation had risen from 34.9 per cent to 39.3 per cent of the national income. Brown's forecasts of growth were also not quite accurate. In 2001 the economy had grown by 1.8 per cent, 0.2 per cent more than previously believed; and he would forecast in his April budget that the economy would grow in 2002–03 by between 2 and 2.5 per cent. In November he would reduce that forecast to 1.5 per cent. He would predict that the government's borrowing would increase by £10 billion over the year. Six months later the deficit would grow to £13 billion, and would continue rising. However, compared to other economies edging towards recession, Britain's growing economy was producing an additional £20 billion of taxes. That was sufficient for the chancellor to trumpet his claim to have defeated 'boom and bust' and to finance the expansion of the public services.

Brown's proposal to raise taxes was approved by Blair, who hoped it would help to secure 'delivery' in the second term. There was no alternative but to abandon the claim that Labour was the party of low taxation and hit the middle classes with a 1 pence increase in National Insurance contributions. The Treasury's receipt of taxes since 1997 had risen from £270 billion to over £400 billion as a result of removing tax relief on mortgages and pensions, and failing to raise the 40 per cent income tax threshold. An additional million people, including teachers and policemen, were now paying income tax at the higher rate. The chancellor anticipated that public spending would increase from £317 billion in 1997 to £511 billion in 2005–06. His plan was to announce in July the biggest increase in public spending in thirty years – £93 billion over three years. Asked to explain how the extra money would be generated, he replied that the economy would grow in 2003 by between 3 and 3.5 per cent. That prediction, he knew, was optimistic, but some felt a fatalistic trait had emerged in the grief-stricken man. Possibly the tumult of the previous weeks encouraged his gamble, but equally there was little pressure from the prime minister's staff to explain how the extra money would produce the benefits if Wanless's recommendations for greater efficiency were ignored.

Using Wanless's estimate of £184 billion to rebuild the NHS, Brown wrote out a commitment to increase spending on the NHS by 43 per cent to £105.6 billion by 2008. That promise, he believed, would reverse five years of disappointment among his supporters over his past sins – the 75 pence pension increase, the cut in benefits for lone parents, the privatisation of the Tube and air traffic control, and PFI – and clear the ground for a confrontation with New Labour about the NHS. This new stance required the abandonment of 'prudence' and the acquisition of faith in central planning for the state to spend over £500 billion in one year. Copying Bill Clinton, Brown had always planned delivery for the second term, and had even come up with a soundbite – 'prudence with a purpose'. Since Blair was going helter-skelter for war in Iraq, Brown relied on Ed Balls to negotiate with Jeremy Hayward, Blair's private secretary. In Brown's mind, he would assert his personal supremacy just as the prime minister was embarking on an enormous gamble.

Brown's entry into the House of Commons on 17 April 2002 to deliver his sixth budget was more than a personal milestone. The feverish expectation and cheers from Labour MPs disguised new turmoil in the party about the possibility of war with Iraq. Fresh speculation about the divisions between Blair and Brown had been sparked by another attack by Mo Mowlam about Brown's role in their 'destructive' relationship. The two men, she alleged, frequently failed to 'acknowledge each other's presence. That does not indicate a positive relationship. You could tell by the body language, the amount of eye contact, how poor the relationship was.' Insiders confirmed the accuracy of Mowlam's description. Gordon Brown's supporters exploited the opportunity to intensify their campaign of disillusionment with Blair. 'He never says anything memorable or profound,' was one complaint. Blair was disparaged as a smug, wealthy, privately educated yuppie, unaware of the party's principles or purpose. In contrast to Brown, the prime minister was described as an unfocused non-intellectual with no ideas other than the vague 'Third Way', who lied, spun and employed Thatcherite language to espouse business rather than Labour's core values.

Those fissures intensified the atmosphere as the chancellor rattled through his budget, particularly addressing the party's traditionalists with his promise to redistribute Britain's wealth. After Brown sat down to loud cheers, the prime minister praised his sixth budget as the 'defining moment' of Labour's second term. Brown managed a weak smile. 'He has made the rank and file feel proud again to be members of the party,' wrote Roy Hattersley, anointing Brown as Blair's unassailable successor. Brown felt he had every reason to behave as the dominant personality in British politics. At a press conference about the budget amid the striking architecture of the new Chelsea and Westminster hospital, which had cost £200 million more than estimated, he spoke about 'my decision to increase tax'. He clearly imagined himself replacing the prime minister. Brown's ratings in a Mori poll rose to +29, way above Blair's, and various other polls recorded that between 57 and 65 per cent of the population were satisfied with the budget. Supporters chimed that Blairism was buried, and hoped that Brown would lead a revolt if Blair agreed to join America's invasion of Iraq. 'Many are looking to Brown for a lead,' said Mark Seddon, a member of the National Executive Committee and the editor of *Tribune*. 'He thinks it's too gung-ho and is worried where it's all going to lead.' His aides spoke of splits, coups and the imminent demise of Blair.

The chancellor's undisguised ambition wearied Blair, but up to spring 2002 their extraordinary partnership had survived because the prime minister corralled Brown's persistent jealousy with a combination of concessions and seduction. Ceding responsibility on domestic issues to Brown had succeeded for ten years, but Blair was no longer willing to bear the brunt of the public's discontent about failing public services. He wanted substantial changes in policy on health and education. Command, he decided, would have to be retrieved from the Treasury. Among those told about the looming power struggle was Sidney Blumenthal, the former adviser to Bill Clinton.

On 9 June 2002 Blumenthal was visiting Brown in the Treasury for a 'brainstorming' session familiar to high-ranking Democrats who supported Labour. Unexpectedly, a Blair adviser had informed Blumenthal beforehand that the chancellor had become 'a consolidator'. The Treasury no longer generated new ideas. The reformers, he was told, now resided at 10 Downing Street. That was not Brown's opinion. Alan Greenspan's agreement formally to open the refurbished Treasury building was proof of the chancellor's radicalism and his regard for Americans. He understood their warning that relations between London and Washington would be damaged if Britain refused to support the war in Iraq. He would support the war, he replied.

'We've got to watch the match,' said Brown suddenly, interrupting his conversation with Blumenthal. England was playing Argentina in the World Cup. With the score at 0–0, David

Beckham took a penalty. Beckham scored, and like half the nation the chancellor shrieked and leapt out of his chair. The Americans were bemused not only by the chancellor's enthusiasm for football, but by his conservatism. He had become unreceptive to new ideas. His focus was on the succession, and the circumstances were improving.

In July 2002, at the Glamorgan Business Centre in Pontypridd, Brown gave a rousing inaugural lecture to celebrate Nye Bevan's life. At the end, amid cheers, Michael Foot presented him with an original drawing by Vicky, the famous cartoonist, portraying Bevan waving his finger in support of 'world socialism'. The cartoon, said Foot, should be hung in the Treasury 'and any nearby joints you may end up in'. For a brief moment, Brown's move next door seemed to be inching closer. Tony Blair's crass attempt to steal the limelight during the Queen Mother's funeral in April by seeking to place himself at the centre of events in Westminster Abbey, only to be rebuffed by Black Rod, an incorruptible Westminster bureaucrat, and the revelation that Labour, with Blair's knowledge, had accepted a donation of £100,000 from the pornographer and owner of the *Daily* and *Sunday Express* Richard Desmond, sullied the prime minister's reputation. Aloof from that sordidness, Brown appeared as the champion of honest socialism.

But, as so often, the glow evaporated. On 15 July 2002 the stock market recorded its biggest ever fall in a single day. The shine of Brown's economic competence was tarnished by events beyond his control. Within the party, the latest surge of enthusiasm for him dissipated. Although a handful of new dissidents joined his core of supporters, the overwhelming majority of MPs remained loyal Blairites, relying on the prime minister to retain their seats at the next election. As the inevitable summer reshuffle drew near, Brown became engaged in the customary haggling to protect his loyal outriders. The prospects of Nick Brown and Michael Wills, and of Nigel Grif-

fiths, damaged after revelations that he had claimed a total
of £40,000 for rental expenses for a constituency office that he
actually owned, appeared forlorn. In compensation, Alistair
Darling and Andrew Smith were promoted.

That summer Brown began writing *Courage of Heroes*. The
book, the royalties from which would be donated to the University of Edinburgh Development Trust for Perinatal Research,
would describe the bravery of, among others, the anti-Nazis
Dietrich Bonhoeffer and Raoul Wallenberg, the First World
War resistance heroine Edith Cavell, the Burmese opposition
leader Aung San Suu Kyi, the airline passenger Todd Beamer
who fought the hijackers on 11 September, and Eric Liddell,
the Scottish athlete and missionary. Brown's chosen heroes
reflected his sense of his own integrity. All were, he wrote,
'known for not taking the easy option. They are ten people who
have inspired us all with extraordinary feats of bravery and self-
sacrifice. They also shaped the world we know.' The project
revealed his emotional turmoil, as was appreciated by Dr Jonathan Sacks, the Chief Rabbi. 'I owe a special debt to the Chancellor of the Exchequer,' Sacks wrote in his own book, *The
Politics of Hope*, 'for his consistent interest in the dialogue
between faith, politics and economics, and for the strong commitment he has shown to the moral dimension of global economic policy.' Brown's book would eventually be abandoned,
but courage had become the essential virtue of his life.

His political courage was questionable, but his personal courage was irrefutable. His endurance of the solitude he had experienced during six months in hospital when he had lost the sight
in his left eye thirty-two years earlier had proved the strength
of his character, and the latest medical evidence suggested that
his surviving right eye had deteriorated. Watching David Blunkett cope during a weekend visit to his home in North
Queensferry provoked mixed feelings. The risk of total blindness inserted urgency into his bid for the party's leadership.

ELEVEN

Revolt

On 18 November 2002 Gordon Brown arrived at the *Guardian* newspaper offices in London with Ed Balls for breakfast with the editor and twelve journalists. His relationship with the newspaper's political writers was mixed. Some he liked, others he distrusted. Alastair Campbell's derision of 'the Gordian' suggested a certain partiality. Brown had accepted the invitation for a discreet conversation some weeks earlier. By chance the breakfast coincided with a new crisis between himself and the prime minister. Their disagreement this time was about principles, not personalities. Retreat for Brown was inconceivable, and here was an opportunity to influence an important publication. He planned subtly to describe the dispute and emphasise the virtues of his argument. He could rely on his intelligent audience to decipher his insinuations.

The hostility had been ignited seven weeks earlier at the party's annual conference. The normally sympathetic trade union leaders had buffeted the chancellor. Too many party members were uneasy about his refusal to concede a generous pay increase to the striking firemen, and did not grasp the social engineering achieved by tax credits. Led by John Edmonds, they had attacked the PFI contracts, booing Paul Boateng, the junior Treasury minister, with a slow handclap, jeering at him to 'Sit down.' From the platform, Bill Morris had lectured the chancellor that Labour 'was not elected to extend the private sector' or to approve worse working conditions for union members. Brown glared furiously when John Prescott publicly apologised and promised 'urgent discussions'. To placate his critics, the chancellor would promise an 'independent commission', but afterwards he ignored the protests. In an article for *The Times* he justified PFI for accelerating the modernisation of Britain's public services.

The gap between the modernisers and Old Labour, he feared, was reappearing. The party's new divisions reflected his own disagreements with Blair. 'How is it,' he asked Blair when they met in Downing Street with Alastair Campbell, 'that we have ended up with such an antagonistic relationship with people who should be so well disposed towards us?' Blair stared silently back. 'Why are we arguing with Bill Morris, a friend?' continued Brown, warming to his theme that Blair's insensitivity and style were alienating the party's bedrock – upon which he relied – by appearing to endorse the re-emergence of a two-tier society.

His argument with Blair, Brown hinted to the *Guardian*'s journalists, was about the devolution of power. Blair's conviction that reform of the NHS and universities should embrace market forces was anathema to the chancellor. Frank Dobson had recently attacked Blair's support of the market as 'elitist', a resounding characterisation of everything Old Labour detested about the 'Third Way'. Brown favoured local flexibility, rewarding success with a 'limit' to market principles. He wanted the private sector to produce the taxation to finance the state's health and education monopolies. Unlike Blair, he rejected the notion that state bureaucrats could not be efficient. Beyond a certain boundary, Brown believed, the market would endanger the ethic of public service for the community's benefit, and that included the financing of universities.

To satisfy the universities' need for more money, Brown had long favoured levying a graduate tax of 3 pence in the pound on students from the wealthy and the middle classes for the rest of their lives, with poorer students paying for possibly twenty-five years. The tax would raise £1 billion a year. He was unconcerned that non-taxpayers and graduates who moved abroad could escape payment, and he opposed the variable fees advocated by Blair's education advisers. Imposing huge debts on young working-class children, to be repaid during their twenties, would, he believed, create more disincentives for them to apply for university. 'Ridiculous and elitist,' he told the *Guardian* journalists. 'Elitist' had become his favoured term to denigrate the Blairites. Brown was particularly angry that No. 10 was encouraging Sir Richard Sykes, the rector of Imperial College in London, to lobby for £15,000 annual fees for students. 'There is a difference between elitism and excellence,' said Brown. His anger, directed against those who believed that elitism and excellence were interdependent, had fuelled his support for Laura Spence against Oxford University. Excellence, he believed, could be shared by every class. There was a self-imposed blindness in his pursuit of that class battle. His own education in Edinburgh substantiated the truth that excellent students did forge an elite, and that excellence could only be taught by elites. Over the years he had never voiced any criticism of his own education at grammar school and university, but he had ignored Labour's destruction of Scotland's heritage of outstanding education. He had remained silent as the working-class schoolchildren in Kirkcaldy were denied the excellence which he had enjoyed. Similarly, he had said nothing in public or private about Labour MPs, including ministerial colleagues, who chose to send their children to selective or fee-paying schools. The paradox, in the *Guardian* office, was the context of his sermon. He was addressing journalists who had also benefited from 'elitist' education, several of whom sent their own children to private schools.

His second battle with Blair was against foundation hospitals, which were supported by Downing Street's special advisers and by Alan Milburn, the health secretary. The evidence was accumulating against Brown's conservatism. Independent reports suggested that Derek Wanless had probably underestimated the chronic levels of bureaucracy in hospitals. A report by the Audit Commission showed that despite an increase in funding of 6 per cent in 2001, only 3 per cent more patients were being treated. Life-saving technical equipment was not being used to save cancer patients at Bart's hospital in London because no radiographer could be recruited for £26,000 per year. The hospital had however advertised for a project manager at a salary of £40,000 to supervise the operation of the unused machine. Forty-eight per cent more senior managers – twice as many as in the private sector – had been recruited since 1995, compared to only 8 per cent more nurses. The solution for Tony Blair and Alan Milburn was foundation hospitals – an imitation of the Thatcherite trust hospitals – offering choice, diversity and competition. During the summer, Milburn had carried out an aggressive campaign through television appearances to promote himself and the end of centralism.

Brown feared creeping privatisation. If the state financed foundation hospitals, he argued, the division between rich and poor would be entrenched at the state's expense. The managers would have, in his opinion, 'extreme power' over patients, and would rely on the government to bail out hospitals bankrupted by reckless spending. His edict to Milburn was explicit: foundation hospitals would not be allowed to borrow money and increase the national debt. Change without the chancellor's agreement was impossible. An attempt in early October by Blair to calm the antagonism

had not brought even a temporary truce between Brown and
Milburn. The subplot was Brown's dislike of opponents,
especially those promoted by the newspapers as possible
future party leaders. Milburn's private briefings against
himself had been wounding. Ever since Milburn's brief
appointment as chief secretary to the Treasury in 1998–99,
challenging Brown's decisions, their relations had been
fraught. He would rely on Ed Balls to tell journalists about
the Treasury's contempt for Milburn, and restrict himself to
extolling the virtues of socialism.

Barely mentioned as Brown drank coffee with the journalists in the *Guardian*'s newly-built Scott Room was the euro,
although that was another sharp difference between himself,
Blair and the Europhile ministers. That was one battle which
he was winning. Since the beginning of the year, Blair had
been unable either to silence or defeat the Treasury's heavy
guns. Gus O'Donnell, the director of the Treasury's macro-
economic policy, had emphatically announced in February
that the five tests would never be met. 'Economics,' O'Donnell
said, 'can never be clear and unambiguous. Ultimately, it will
be a political decision.' Shortly after, O'Donnell was contradicted by Ed Balls, who said political prejudice was irrelevant
to such a critical decision, which would depend solely upon
an assessment of the long-term economic advantages: 'If you
enter the euro at the wrong time you could end up damaging
the economy, jobs and growth.'

The disagreement would have been more embarrassing if
Europe had not been staggering in recession and the euro's
foundations – the so-called 'stability pact' – had not been
undermined by massive debt. Compared to Britain's national
debt, at 39.3 per cent of the gross domestic product, the European average was 68.8 per cent. Yet on 11 February 2002
the European Commission had ordered Brown to cut public
spending by £10 billion, because Britain was borrowing too

much. Winning a referendum in those conditions, Brown
laughed, was not feasible.

Three months later, unwilling to be marginalised by Brown
or to allow Britons to 'hide their head in the sand', Blair
had again sought to set the agenda. With his support, Peter
Mandelson predicted that Blair would ignore hostile polls and
'seize the chance' for a euro referendum before the next election. Blair also encouraged Peter Hain, the minister for
Europe, to announce that Britain's failure to join would be
'a tragedy' and 'an enormous blunder' perpetrated by the
'enemies of Europe'. Blair's surrogates had been curtly dismissed by Brown. Hain was ridiculed for 'idle speculation',
and others were castigated for uttering unauthorised statements. Blair's frustration was palpable. In an interview on
BBC TV's *Newsnight* on 17 May 2002, he volunteered his
ambition to be remembered as 'the man who took Britain
into the euro because it was in the national interest'. Not to
join, he added melodramatically, would be a 'betrayal'. There
would be a referendum, he said, before the next election.
But once again, events moved in the chancellor's direction.
Shortly before Brown arrived at the *Guardian*, Romano Prodi,
the federalist president of the European Commission, blurted
out in the midst of a euro crisis that the rules of the stability
pact – the euro's cornerstone – were 'stupid'. That own-goal,
just one day after Blair had extolled the euro in a speech as
'economic sense', reinforced Brown's credibility.

Brown's language and demeanour as he rattled through
the checklist of disagreements during that breakfast would
have been unfamiliar to the public. Deploying the charm
familiar to his friends, he eschewed the stiff posture and tedious talk of 'prudence', and spoke from the heart. After his
departure, the journalists discussed their impressions. The fact
that Brown had revealed his disagreements with Blair to such
a large group was clearly a deliberate escalation of the warfare.

None knew why he had chosen that precise moment to ratchet up the contest and clearly define his non-negotiable position. An article published in the *Guardian* the following day accurately described an 'ideological substance to the feud; some clear red water is opening up between our prime minister and his chancellor'. Brown's confirmation of the split was highlighted on the front page.

By then a minor dispute had arisen between Ed Balls and the *Guardian* about quoting Brown in another report. Balls said that Brown was unavailable to confirm a quotation – an unconvincing excuse – and the report was not published. By the end of the week a written summary of Brown's criticisms of Blair had reached the *Mail on Sunday*. Under the headline 'Markets can't work in healthcare', the newspaper reignited the image of Brown beseeching Blair to honour his Granita pledge and resign. As Brown had anticipated before the *Guardian* breakfast, the sensationalists would ignore his subtleties and rawly predict the 'endgame', the transformation of a creative partnership into 'a duel to the death'. The sad truth, Brown knew, was that the Brownites were in the minority. Only a seismic shift in the party could change the leadership.

The Blairites' retaliation confirmed the seriousness with which they regarded his challenge. Journalists close to Blair described Brown as an arrogant non-team player whose inflexibility and refusal to trust others made him unfit to lead the party. The first to mention 'government after Gordon' openly was again Mo Mowlam. She complained that the chancellor was making it 'so difficult for Tony to govern. I think the animosity between the two of them is counterproductive to good government. It has meant that things have not been delivered. It has meant crisis after crisis which didn't need to be a crisis.'

An old enemy newly recruited to the overt critics' camp was Charles Clarke. Clarke had supported a graduate tax in

the late 1980s, but recanted after his appointment as education secretary in October 2002. During their recent arguments about financing the universities, Clarke and Brown had
exchanged some scathing comments. Brown would have liked
to neutralise Clarke, but the privately-educated, middle-class
minister was immune to his intimidation. For his part, Clarke
regarded Brown's briefing to the *Guardian* as another forlorn
bid for the leadership. He referred enquirers to a comment
he made in 1995 about Brown's candidature in 1994: 'I started
out believing that Gordon should not run for the leadership,
but I have subsequently come round to the view that it would
have been better if he had, and had actually been beaten.
That would have humiliated him and meant that Tony did
not owe him a debt. There was never the remotest chance
that Gordon would be elected leader of the party.' To complete
the counterattack, Blair spoke about Brown in the past tense
during an interview with David Frost on 26 January 2003.
'Gordon has done a fantastic job in managing the economy,'
said Blair. 'So you are certain,' asked Frost, 'he will be chancellor next Christmas? Gordon shouldn't be looking for a new
home?' 'Well,' replied Blair, 'as I said, he has done a fantastic
job.'

The prime minister, Brown knew, had chosen his words
with care, but the effect was minimal. He welcomed the frenzy
of speculation his *Guardian* briefing had unleashed. Three days
later his spokesman issued an unprecedented statement denying that Brown was pestering Blair to resign. 'Ever since this
government was formed,' said the spokesman, 'people have
wanted to say that the Blair–Brown relationship is doomed
to fail; partly, they argue, because of historical precedent.
The press haven't had that, and it's obviously become very
frustrating. It is a vital and strong relationship and it remains
so. The idea that the chancellor has been demanding that the
prime minister move over is simply untrue.' The denials

simply confirmed Brown's ambitions. Over the previous days he had hosted two parties at 11 Downing Street to raise funds for charities. With Sarah's help, he was presenting the big tent of the leader-in-waiting, fostering newspaper reports describing his wide range of new friendships among actors, sportsmen, celebrity chefs and businessmen. There was also another agenda. The conflict over principle was intended to camouflage his vulnerability. On 27 November 2002, nine days after his *Guardian* breakfast, he was due to deliver a pre-budget statement to the Commons, and he foresaw problems.

Despite the commitment of an extra £61 billion over three years, there had been no perceptible improvement in the public services. Daily there were complaints that roads, railways, schools and hospitals were getting worse. In 2001, fewer patients were treated by the NHS than in 2000. Amid a world recession, the economy also appeared to be deteriorating. The London stock market had fallen more than markets in other countries, underperforming Wall Street by 40 per cent since 1997, reaching the lowest point for a generation (the S&P 500 was up 5 per cent, compared to the FTSE 100 which was down by 19 per cent); Britain's pension funds, the world's best in 1997, were paying pensioners on average 28 per cent less than in 1997, and two-thirds of final salary pension schemes had been closed to new members; taxes had risen faster than in any other European country, but the Inland Revenue's income from taxation had fallen; the budget deficit had increased and personal savings were still falling; and public borrowing would rise by £102 billion more than Brown had forecast over the next five years. He no longer concealed his preference for raising taxes from business rather than individuals. Annually, between 1997 and 2000, Whitehall produced about 3,000 new regulations, costing business, according to the British Chambers of Commerce, £20.6 billion in 2003, and according to the CBI, costing industry £12 billion.

The disenchantment with the chancellor in the business community was growing. Just before his Commons statement Brown met Digby Jones, the director general of the CBI, for their regular monthly meeting. Until then, Jones had been pleasantly surprised by Brown's willingness to listen, even on occasion to engage in a genuine discussion. But now Brown increasingly received Jones purely out of politeness. Within four months, he would give up the pretence and simply flick through papers while Jones spoke. 'Thanks,' he would say at the end of one presentation. 'I've got your slides and we'll take your arguments into account.' The CBI's assessment confirmed the warnings of many pressure groups and independent analysts. Brown's constant self-congratulatory statements disguised uncomfortable realities. The statistics which he never cited suggested that his vaunted success was partially an illusion. Government expenditure in Britain was rising towards 42 per cent of gross domestic product, compared to 30 per cent in the USA, and 35 per cent under the Conservatives. Manufacturing output was falling – in March 2002 by 6 per cent – while employers were enduring new 'nightmares', having to act as unpaid tax collectors for working family tax credits, and coping with complicated new laws for maternity leave, discrimination, and procedures for dismissals. Despite Brown's priority to raise productivity, the individual worker's output in Britain had risen by only 1.6 per cent under Labour, compared to 2.5 per cent in the last five years of the Conservative government, and remained about 25 per cent lower than in the United States, Germany and France. Economic growth had also been higher under the Conservatives, 2.75 per cent over five years compared to 2.5 per cent under Brown. Government spending had risen at the fastest rate since 1975. Rather than increasing at 2.9 per cent as predicted by the ONS, the rate was 5.7 per cent. In 2002 Britain's trade gap was £34.3 billion, the biggest in history. A CBI survey in November had reported that 66 per cent of the organisation's members believed that Britain had become a worse place to do business since 1997, 75 per cent complained about the government's poor understanding of business, and 80 per cent blamed increased regulations for inflicting 'significant damage' on their performance. The chancellor hated that criticism. 'I do not accept that Britain is a worse place than it was five years ago,' he snapped back. 'That would be defeatist and wrong.' He really believed that his talk, the taxpayers' money and low inflation and low interest rates would ensure that Britain would 'weather the storm'. Above all, he believed that the success of tax credits and the constant rise of property prices had augured a historic change confirming the New Era of Britain's economy.

The chancellor found it difficult to address failure, and his pre-budget report on 27 November 2002 was muddled. Two years earlier he had praised his own prudence in accumulating a £40 billion surplus in the year's accounts. Now he increased his forecast of the deficit from £11 billion to £20 billion, knowing that some experts predicted that net borrowing would rise in 2005–06 to £28 billion, and to £31 billion in 2006–07. He scoffed at those forecasts, predicting that the deficit would be £19 billion in both years, and would turn to a surplus in the current budget of 2004–05. He denied that he would have to raise taxes by £11 billion. His forecasts would prove to be wrong, but he gave no sign of weakness. In the manse fifty years earlier he had learnt the certainty of faith and the importance of infallibility. Maintaining the vision was critical to the government's continuing success.

Brown's speech was heard in silence by Labour MPs. He sat down to no applause. Hunched on the front bench, crossing and recrossing his legs, jerking his hand through his hair, he had to listen as Michael Howard, the shadow chancellor,

listed unflattering statistics, ridiculing Brown's previous forecasts of growth at 2.25 per cent, which had been reduced to
1.6 per cent, and challenging the self-proclaimed iron chancellor to learn from his mistakes. Brown hated this rare
humiliation, made worse by the lack of support from those
on the benches behind him. They should look at the facts, he
would tell them later. He had honoured his pledge to the
trade unions, increasing the numbers employed by the state
by 140,000 in 2002 alone. If they disliked his tactics of giving
to public sector workers with one hand and then uttering dire
warnings of a continuing 'squeeze' on their pay, they should
understand the politics. The pay of the public workers had
increased by 4.7 per cent compared with 3.9 per cent in the
private sector. The sense of economic well-being among a
nation of home-owners calculating the appreciation of their
capital had prevented any outcry from the middle classes and
frozen the Conservative vote. There was, however, little personal thanks. His approval rating in one poll fell from forty-
five points to six.

The impression that the country's finances were healthy
was reinforced by the fact that £35.5 billion of debt incurred
in the PFI contracts did not appear on the national balance
sheet. Eventually the taxpayers would be liable to repay the
money, but that would be long after the chancellor's retirement. The concealment of this debt depended upon the
approval of Len Cook, the new director of the Office of
National Statistics. The Treasury's accounts, presented to
Cook, showed that the government's guarantees on the PFI
contracts were not classified as state subsidies but as a 'contin-
gent liability' which was 'unlikely' to be spent. That classifi-
cation was challenged by Alan Beard, the head of accounting
at the department of transport, Sir John Kingman, the chairman of the statistics commission, and Sir John Bourn, the
auditor general at the National Audit Office, all of whom

agreed that the £35.5 billion was indeed part of the national
debt. Gordon Brown asked Len Cook to apply the accountancy rules of the European Union rather than Britain. Unlike
Tim Holt, his disobliging predecessor, Cook endorsed Brown's
accountancy. The issue, Brown declared, was closed. Yet the
reality of the PFI contracts could not be ignored.

Jeremy Colman of the National Audit Office had examined
a sample of five hundred PFI contracts and discovered that
the vaunted 'savings' were occasionally tiny compared to the
cost of the projects. On a £746 million contract for the ministry
of defence, the alleged saving was just £100,000, raising suspicions about the accounting. Colman's report criticised the
'spurious' calculations about the 'risk factor' and 'pseudo-
scientific mumbo-jumbo' of the 'Green Book'. The quality of
the buildings was also mixed. Many PFI schools and hospitals
had been poorly built and, threatened by the contractor's
bankruptcy, the repairs had been paid for by the taxpayer. A
study by the Audit Commission would also conclude that PFI
schools had not been built quicker, cheaper or better than
previously. Finally, the major advantage heralded by Gordon
Brown – that the building contractor would be obliged to
maintain the buildings – was disappearing. To obtain tax
advantages, the contractors were selling their projects to private fund managers who could claim 100 per cent tax relief
on their profits. The value of 25 per cent of the contracts had,
according to one survey, deteriorated.

In reply to those criticisms, Brown cited the NAO's statement that there was 'strong evidence that the PFI approach
is bringing significant benefits to central government in terms
of delivering built assets on time and for the price expected by
the public sector'. But, as the NAO countered, the speed of construction did not compensate for the cost of the long-term debt
or the extra costs incurred before the contracts were signed.
Brown's talent was to suppress any association of criticism

with himself, just as he had disassociated himself from the consequences of thrusting Railtrack into administration.

The renationalisation of Railtrack and its replacement by Network Rail had been hailed by Brown as a step towards financial sanity. At the end of 2002 Richard Bowker, the chief executive of the Strategic Rail Authority, supervising the passenger train operators, wrote: 'The rail industry now works together as a team better than at any time since privatisation.' The facts, Shriti Vadera reported to Brown, revealed something different. The accountants Ernst & Young, employed to manage the network on the government's behalf, had no incentive to save money. Every request for expenditure by engineers, especially on the grounds of safety, was approved by accountants unable to assess its importance. Contracts for work were awarded at 'cost-plus', a well-known recipe for profligacy. Network Rail's costs for renewing the tracks rose from £2.2 billion to £5 billion per annum, and were heading towards £7 billion a year. The government's boast in 2000 that passenger numbers would increase by 50 per cent was airbrushed from the record. The reliability of the service deteriorated by 30 per cent. Maintenance conducted by the old British Railways, experts calculated, was 67 per cent more efficient than under Network Rail. The imposition by the government of the Health and Safety Executive's rule over the railways, Alan Osborne, the director of HSE's rail safety, discovered, was 'grossly inefficient and dysfunctional'.

Dispensing billions of pounds had proved to be an ineffective instrument for improving the railways' management. The advantages predicted by Gordon Brown of the administration order in October 2001 had not materialised. State control of the railways was more expensive and less efficient than control by Railtrack's hapless managers. The extra billions in subsidies had been increased when Brown, alarmed by the new distrust in the City, made the abrupt decision to pay the share-

holders about £500 million in compensation. His peace offering was rejected, and a writ was issued in 2003 for about £2
billion compensation and costs. Brown was paying the price
for not anticipating the consequences of his decision. Without
considering a detailed plan of the railway's management after
obtaining the administration order, his officials grumbled,
'We'll have to find a way to put the toothpaste back into
the tube.' Tom Winsor's warning in October 2001 that the
government should be 'extremely reluctant' to threaten the
regulator had been justified. Ignoring it was costing billions
of pounds.

The SRA would find difficulty raising private investment
without government guarantees. Brown was faced with the
predicament he had sought to avoid: the responsibility for
underwriting Network Rail's loans of £21 billion had fallen
on the Treasury as part of the national debt, jeopardising his
boasts about reducing it. The problem was compounded by
Network Rail's need to raise a further £14 billion. Brown and
Vadera had ignored advice to raise the money from banks,
using the future charges to the rail operators for access to
the tracks as collateral. Instead, to preserve the fiction that
Network Rail was a private company, they had insisted on
pure loans, not guaranteed by the Treasury, which attracted
higher interest charges. With Len Cook's agreement, those
billions of pounds would not be classified as government debt.
The chancellor avoided the blame for the railway's ballooning
costs – the subsidy would double that year to £2 billion, or
£22 per passenger on Virgin West Coast – and poor performance. The responsibility, said Shriti Vadera in 2003, was
Richard Bowker's. The SRA was destined to be abolished.

Gordon Brown's grudge against Ken Livingstone prevented
the application of the same accountancy techniques to the
London Underground. Angry that Livingstone had been
elected London's mayor against the official Labour candidate

Frank Dobson, Brown spent about £100 million in 2001 to
persuade the City institutions to support a Public Private Partnership (PPP) for the Tube's reconstruction. He was unsuccessful, and would spend an estimated £300 million in 2002
on professional advice on how to block Livingstone's scheme
to finance the improvements by issuing bonds. His efforts
were forlorn. He had promised that his PPP scheme would
only be invoked if he could prove that it gave value for money.
He gave the order for the PPP scheme and delegated the implementation to Shriti Vadera. The contracts offered by Vadera
to the chosen operators were 2,800 pages long and contained
over 8,000 performance targets. Martin Callaghan, the architect and administrator of the contracts, admitted that he was
probably the only person who understood the complexities.
The contracts deterred the chosen corporations from accepting
any financial risks involved in maintaining the Tube, denying
the Treasury any opportunity to launch the PPP scheme.
Gradually, Brown retreated. The operators were guaranteed
sufficient profits, and the Treasury agreed to bear substantial
risk at public expense. On 18 July 2002 the House of Commons transport select committee asked Brown to give evidence about his involvement in the part privatisation of the
Tube. His refusal was criticised by the committee as 'disdain'.
By refusing to meet the executives of the Underground or
publicly to discuss his own policy, he avoided immediate censure for the expensive disarray. But two years later, the
National Audit Office confirmed that the PPP agreements
would not deliver the promised improvements and were probably a bad deal. Firstly, the interest payments on the £3.8
billion borrowed by the contractors were costing £450 million
more than they would have done had the government raised
the money; secondly, the administrative costs for creating the
scheme had wasted £455 million; and thirdly, the promised
improvements to the service still remained unproven.

Christmas 2002 was the end of a terrible year. Instead of a baby approaching her first birthday, there were only photographs and letters of condolence. Instead of praise for his economic management, there was criticism about a catalogue of ruses to conceal debt, tax increases and declining growth. Instead of certainty about his political ascendancy, the prime minister was refusing to reveal a date for his retirement. The atmosphere in North Queensferry during that holiday, visitors remarked, was gloomy. The isolation from Westminster did not calm Brown's nerves. 'I'm going to "kill" Mandelson,' he said, meaning that he wanted to neutralise Mandelson politically. 'Why?' he was asked. 'Because if I get him out of the way, and then Alastair goes, Tony will fall.' In the chancellor's mind, Tony Blair was a weak man whose demise was inevitable if his two props were removed. To his glee, the news from London soothed his restlessness.

Unexpectedly, Tony Blair had been embarrassed. Peter Foster, a convicted Australian conman, had been exposed as having negotiated the purchase of two flats in Bristol for Cherie Blair. Through the Downing Street spokesman, Cherie adamantly denied Foster's involvement, but remained under some pressure. Foster was the boyfriend of Carole Caplin, Cherie Blair's 'lifestyle adviser' who enjoyed access to the Blairs' home in Downing Street. Four days after Cherie's denials, the publication of emails between herself and Foster proved them to have been inaccurate. To compound her predicament, the exposure of the relationship between the Blairs and Caplin suggested that the prime minister's judgement was also questionable. The ideals of New Labour, especially Blair's exhortation in 1997 that the party should be 'purer than pure', were tainted. The ridicule of the Blairs coincided with protests against the imminent war in Iraq, the consistent defeat of Blairite trade union leaders in elections by candidates representing Old Labour, and substantial resignations of ordi-

nary members from the party. Those circumstances encouraged Brown to ponder whether there was a new opportunity
to present himself as the true leader of the traditional party.
At home in Fife, he resolved to strike for the leadership
although the timetable was ill-defined.

The dilemma for Labour MPs, even those dissatisfied with
Tony Blair, was whether Brown would be a superior prime
minister. Although he could not match Blair's facility with
slogans and emotional warmth, Brown displayed an
unrivalled mastery of policies and politics. But his character
was seen as a potential weakness. His unpredictability sparked
unease. Civil servants described his tempers, albeit mitigated
by his genuine sympathy for those who suffered. Potential
supporters were also deterred by the suspicion that behind
the image of indefatigable certainty lurked unknown anxieties. Ten years earlier, he had lost the race for the leadership
partly out of failure to project himself as someone able to
speak to the voters about lifestyle, relationships and weaknesses. Little had changed to attract greater popularity. He
asked no one to sympathise with the pleasures and strains of
his life, or even disclosed the food he cooked. There were
few satisfying signposts to his character and even his historic
heroes lacked resonance. James Maxton was not Charles
Dickens, Gustav Mahler or Oliver Cromwell. Maxton was a
forgotten idealist and political failure. Brown never glorified
men of genius or audacious pragmatists. He drew his support
from old friends and those disillusioned with Blair. Among the
newcomers would be Barbara Roche, a Home Office minister
who was unexpectedly dismissed in summer 2003. Tony Blair
did not telephone to commiserate with her. Gordon Brown did,
and won an ally. He would also telephone Chris Bryant, the
homosexual MP exposed for posing in his underpants on a
website, offering words of encouragement. Bryant received
no similar words of comfort from Blair. 'Customer care' from

10 Downing Street declined after Anji Hunter's departure. Since the summer of 2002 Brown had sent handwritten letters to all who had lost ministerial jobs, thanking them for service to the government. Most recipients felt gratitude, and gave him their allegiance. But they were still too few to tilt the party towards him. In January 2003 Brown set out to attract more support just as Blair's popularity soared as an internationally acclaimed hero of the 'war against terrorism'.

The first defiance misfired. The battleground was student fees. In the name of anti-elitism, Brown insisted on a graduate tax. In the name of reality – that it was wrong to charge students the same amount for attending Oxford as the lowest-ranking former polytechnic – Charles Clarke argued for variable fees. No one proposed to abolish the fraud-infested childcare tax credit and use the £1 billion that would save every year to fully finance the universities. During stormy meetings in January, Clarke was supported by Blair. On 16 January Brown had planned to ambush Clarke, but was foiled. He could offer no viable alternative. Variable fees were agreed as government policy. In the aftermath, Brown was accused of negativism and disloyalty. He appeared isolated and retreated. Some whispered that he had been wounded, and that Blair had 'cut him down to size'. This only strengthened his determination not to retreat on the NHS. Since Christmas he had been planning a counterblast against Blair, asserting the supremacy of Scottish collectivism over middle England's desire for a reduction in government.

Tony Blair's agent, the health secretary Alan Milburn, was emboldened by the chancellor's defeat on universities. While Brown paid lip service to devolution, Milburn had actually been converted to the policy. Instead of proposing that there should be fifty foundation hospitals, four times more than originally suggested, he conjectured that nearly all hospitals would eventually be released from central control. Brown was incandescent. His aides were encouraged to spread the suggestion among journalists that Milburn was 'running down the NHS'. The first skirmishes were coded. Milburn spoke about 'real localism'. To regain the high ground, Brown's aides adopted the same vocabulary. Ed Balls advocated 'new localism', and Paul Boateng urged 'an end to destructive centralism'. In retaliation, the health secretary responded with, 'The chancellor isn't scary any more.' 'He's irrelevant,' he said, suggesting that Brown was destined for the backbenches rather than No. 10. This was no longer a turf war but an ideological battle for power.

Conveniently, the organisers of the Social Market Foundation, a privately funded research group, had invited Brown to speak on 3 February 2003. He planned to appeal to the party for support. In an ill-lit basement he spoke for an hour at breakneck speed to over a hundred people, explaining how Labour could embrace markets without losing faith in traditional values. 'Brownism' was presented as an amalgamation of socialism and capitalism. 'Instead of being suspicious of enterprise and entrepreneurs,' he explained, 'we should celebrate an entrepreneurial culture . . . [and] enable markets to work better.' Dismissing the 'sterile and self-defeating' opposition to PFI, he criticised Old Labour's 'kneejerk anti-market sentiment'. He supported the enhancement of markets and competition, but emphasised the limitations. Building a PFI hospital was admirable, but managing it by the same market principles was abhorrent. In a convoluted phrase he recommended 'market-based government intervention to make the price mechanism work'. In other words, Brown supported rigged markets and was anti-market for health care. Patients, he said, lacked sufficient information and resources to choose the appropriate treatment, especially in maternity and emergency cases. Rather than giving individuals freedom, he exclaimed, the state knew best how to spend the billions.

No one should be able to buy better health care than that provided by the state. Britons should rejoice and rely on Whitehall. Derek Wanless's report was cast aside.

Mingling with his audience after his speech, Brown assumed that he had defeated Blair's counterattack. Although Blair's advisers were dismissive – irrelevant was the message from Simon Stevens, Downing Street's NHS guru – Brown was praised by the *Guardian* for 'a willingness . . . to grapple with the big ideas and truths of the world we live in. This was a speech which needed to be made and which needs to be studied and debated too.' His breakfast briefing two and a half months earlier had proven beneficial. The ideological split was firmly established. But one week later, on 11 February, Brown received an unexpected public snub. On Blair's initiative, Alan Milburn and Charles Clarke held a joint press conference to promote consumer choice and autonomy, advocating variable university fees and foundation hospitals. Brown appeared to be outflanked, yet he was quietly delighted by ensuing reports of a split.

On 30 March the American army was speeding towards Baghdad. Tony Blair expected to be empowered by a military victory to defeat Brown on foundation hospitals, and to hold a euro referendum before the next general election. That morning, Brown was the guest at a conference organised by the British Chambers of Commerce in Westminster. He led nine ministers to preach a favourite sermon, the successful marriage of Labour to enterprise. In the near future he would write a newspaper article, 'How I'll Start up the British Enterprise Revolution', describing all his corporate tax incentives; and in another article, 'Business Should Thrive in the Groves of Academe', he would exhort closer relationships between industry and the science departments of universities. He believed that his audience of businessmen in Westminster would appreciate those sentiments. He did not anticipate that they would complain that across the Atlantic excellence and elitism were rewarded, or that entrepreneurs were reluctant to take risks if their profits were confiscated by excessive taxation. Members of his audience would protest that Brown's increase in National Insurance would take an additional £4 billion a year from British businesses, part of the extra £54 billion taxed from them over Labour's two terms (a statistic disputed by the government). Lower profits, the businessmen argued, meant that there was less money to reinvest in industry. Their second complaint, organised by the Engineering and Machinery Alliance representing 4,000 companies, was that government assistance schemes were ineffective and complicated. 'When you ask what government can do for business,' one delegate told Brown's ministers, 'perhaps "less" is the answer.' The chancellor was heard in silence. His junior ministers were booed, hissed and jeered. Brown scowled as he left the hall. His enemies were everywhere.

On the eve of becoming the longest-serving chancellor since 1918, he returned to the Treasury to write his seventh optimistic budget speech. To defy his critics and prove that he was always right, he would predict a recovery and a new boom the following year. The economy, he would attest, was in good shape, and much better than those of the country's European competitors. Interest rates were the lowest since 1955, unemployment was the lowest for thirty years, and the housing market was still booming. Critically, inflation was uniquely low in all the major economies. As usual, Brown searched for appropriate phrases. Previously he had sought to attach his name to the success of films, computers and dotcoms. On this occasion he retreated from anything too brave. Reassurance was his theme: 'flexibility with fairness', 'steadfast for stability' and 'fairness to families'.

As usual, he did not reveal that taxes would continue to increase, from 35.6 per cent in 1997 to 41 per cent in 2005, reducing the average annual income by 1.9 per cent, or £500;

or that inflation, at 3 per cent, was the highest for five years, even excluding the increase in house prices. He would conceal the facts that employees in the private sector would earn on average 2 per cent less, while public sector employees would earn 5.2 per cent more. Although the economies of some EU countries, including Spain, Sweden and Ireland, were growing faster than Britain's, he would boast that Britain was outperforming the rest of Europe. He planned to speak at breakneck speed when he admitted his previous forecast of growth was 0.5 per cent too high, and that his prediction of an £11 billion deficit had been revised to £27.3 billion. He would certainly deny knowing that the real deficit could be £37 billion (in the event it was just under £35 billion), or that the economy was due to grow 1 per cent less than he forecast and tax revenues would be lower.

Instead, he would vociferously deride those who were broadcasting such awful certainties. 'Prudence with a purpose' had disappeared from his lexicon, because he intended to borrow £176 billion over the following six years. Instead of 'prudence', he would boast that by 2005 government spending would have increased by 66 per cent, or £200 billion, since 1997. As usual, he would bury the history of forty-eight tax increases in the barely read 'Red Book', the details of the nation's accounts, rather than give ammunition to his critics. He would surprise both those critics and the independent forecasters by predicting 3 per cent to 3.5 per cent growth, 1 per cent more than others. Nearly everyone else was predicting gloom and doom, but he was certain he would be proved right. The combination of a post-war boom, an astonishing 14 per cent increase in personal debt over the previous year, secured against rising house prices, and the expansion of the public services was pumping money into the economy, guaranteeing growth and optimism. Five years earlier he would have decried that explosion of personal debt, heading towards an unprecedented £1 trillion, as 'boom and bust'. He would have condemned the Tories for a spending spree and for widening the gap between the rich and poor. He would have protested on behalf of the most deprived: the single parents and their three million children, increasingly ghettoised amid high unemployment on sink estates, impervious to all his exhortations to work, learn and become self-reliant. But his audience and his purpose had changed. He was looking for a new theme while encouraging the impression, with the endorsement of respected economists, that the miracle continued.

Two days before his speech, Tony Blair invited the chancellor to outline his proposed budget. The routine had become familiar. Every year, Blair's staff would furtively seek information from Treasury officials about the budget. Sometimes they were fortunate and an informant, disobeying the chancellor, would reveal a nugget. On other occasions Brown had worked on his personal laptop to prevent any leak to the prime minister. There was no precedent for such conduct in Britain's entire history. On this occasion, the chancellor arrived with a senior official. The atmosphere was frosty. Brown might well have been contemplating the disappointments of the previous three months and the calculated belittlement he had suffered from Downing Street's advisers. A glowing interview with Britain's great war leader had just been published to coincide with Blair's fiftieth birthday. The prime minister appeared impregnable. Brown's reaction was churlish. To each question Blair asked about the budget he remained impassive until he either nodded to the official to disclose the details, or shook his head. Little was said. Thankfully the prime minister, preoccupied by the war, did not seek a confrontation.

On budget day, 9 April 2003, the pictures of Saddam Hussein's statue in Baghdad toppling to the ground overshadowed Gordon Brown rattling through his speech. There was little celebration that evening in the Treasury, nor the usual excited

expectancy about the following morning's newspapers. That
day's television news programmes barely acknowledged the
budget. Brown no longer anticipated the rapid disintegration
of Blair's eminence. But, as on so many other occasions, the
mood unpredictably changed.

The mayhem and deaths in Iraq during the days after the
fall of Baghdad invigorated those Labour MPs who had
opposed the war. On 7 May, four weeks after the victory,
amid persistent questions about the failure to discover the
weapons of mass destruction (WMDs) in Iraq that had been
the pretext for the war, the Commons was due to vote to
establish foundation hospitals. Quietly, Brown's aides spread
his message of opposition among Labour MPs. Little pressure
was needed to attract politicians disenchanted by the prime
minister's pursuit of 'an illegal war'. The revolt against the
government was more substantial than expected: Labour's
majority of 165 fell to seventy-four.

The atmosphere was unexpectedly febrile. Four days later,
on 12 May, Clare Short resigned as international development
secretary. Unlike before the war, Brown had not sought during their frequent conversations to persuade her to remain in
office. The agitation after her departure would, in his opinion,
tilt the party towards himself. He was not disappointed. In an
interview published in the *Guardian* the following morning
under the headline 'It's Time for Tony to Go', Short suggested
that Blair should 'organise an elegant succession' for Gordon
Brown. The momentum about the leadership was once again
gathering pace. Four days later, on 17 May, the government
faced another revolt, against the proposed abolition of juries
in complicated criminal trials. The prime minister was
described by Chris Smith as 'not part of the heart and soul of
the Labour movement'. The revolt was muted, but in July
the bill would be defeated in the Lords.

The decline in Tony Blair's reputation was dramatic. Unseen

and unheard by everyone except his closest associates, Gordon Brown was pleased by the unexpected reversal of his fortunes. The climax would be the anticipated announcement as to whether the five tests for entering the euro had been satisfied, leading to a referendum before the next general election. Two years earlier, Blair had been sure that after winning the election he could 'fix Gordon' and win the referendum. But as Iraq lurched into apparent chaos, his popularity fell. Ranged against him on the euro were those still scarred by the ERM debacle eleven years earlier. Gus O'Donnell, the Treasury's permanent secretary, had been John Major's press secretary, and Mervyn King, recently appointed as the new governor of the Bank of England, had been the Bank's chief economist. In the midst of the ERM crisis King had been humiliated in Frankfurt by the chairman of the German central bank's refusal to meet him, leaving him standing outside his office.

The opposition of O'Donnell and King was supported by Ed Balls. In 1992 Balls had written, 'the mistake is to let economic schemes run ahead of political realities'. He remained convinced that the euro could not work until Europe was more socially and politically integrated. His opinion was shared by Brown. The chancellor opposed a federal Europe, trade blocs and tax harmonisation, favouring liberalised markets in a global economy. British history, he had repeated to Blair in Downing Street on 1 April 2003, was littered with bad economic decisions taken for political reasons. Britain's economy would be ruined if the country joined the euro in the foreseeable future.

To Brown's satisfaction, nothing was moving in Blair's favour. His last minister for Europe, Keith Vaz, had been regarded as a joke, and then discredited by the commissioner for parliamentary standards, having to serve a one-month suspension from the House as a result of some unsavoury business links and 'serious breaches of the code of conduct'.

Vaz's replacement, Peter Hain, was regarded as unsentimen-
tally eager to relinquish British sovereignty. Hain's recent quip
that the European Convention to create a new constitution was
just a harmless 'tidying-up exercise' was so astonishing that
public anti-Europe feeling was easily incited by Eurosceptic
newspapers. Hain intensified this by opposing a referendum
about the constitution, foolishly accusing his opponents of telling 'a lot of lies frankly about what is going on'. Brown had
no affection for Hain, and saw the advantage of retaining the
affection of the anti-European tabloid newspapers, especially
the *Sun* and the *Daily Mail*. Everything was set for his challenge to Blair, who had been weakened by fraught relations
with the French and German leaders over the Iraq war.

On 15 May, after a heated discussion, Blair scored one
minor concession. The decision on whether there should be
a referendum to join the euro was to be taken by the whole
cabinet, each member of which would be given the Treasury's
eighteen technical reports. The majority, Blair knew, favoured
entry but would be bound by the reports' disapproval. Blair
accepted that the cabinet's decision would be against an
immediate referendum. In return, Brown would announce
the delay in a positive speech advocating entry. That was the
limit of Brown's indulgence. At the end of that day he leaked
to journalists that the conclusion of the five tests was against
membership. On BBC TV news in the evening, Andrew Marr
stood in Downing Street and announced that Blair had bowed
to Brown's decision.

Brown was chortling, and Blair was furious. To give the
impression that they were united, the following day, 16 May,
they issued an unusual joint statement. They had not disagreed about the euro, they announced. Both agreed that
Britain should join the euro when the five tests were met,
because entry was in the 'long-term national interest'. Few
were fooled. Over lunch in a West End restaurant four days

later, Peter Mandelson admitted to a group of political journalists that Brown had 'outmanoeuvred' and defeated Blair.

The Blairites' resentment towards Brown's victory was reflected by the *Guardian* journalist Jackie Ashley in three articles over the following five weeks. In the first article on 17 May she wrote, echoing Blairite ministers including Charles Clarke, that Brown 'might have won the euro battle but it will turn out to be a pyrrhic victory', and that Brown's chances of becoming prime minister 'look more remote than they ever have been'. The Treasury's power, she argued, was in terminal decline, causing Brown to be 'more isolated now in cabinet than he has ever been', and the rise in the power of Alan Milburn and Charles Clarke suggested that Brown would be better to resign.

Three weeks later, Ashley took a different view. Under the headline 'So Canny Gordon was in the Driving Seat All the Time', she reported that Brown was after all 'succeeding'. Her change of heart was prompted by the publication on 6 June of the original draft of the press briefing note agreed by Blair and Brown nine years earlier after their meal at Granita, which included Brown's crucial handwritten amendment, including the word 'guarantee'. It had been leaked to underline Brown's decisive influence over Blair. The change of mood was startling for Blair. In the wake of the scandal of Carole Caplin and Peter Foster, the resignation had been announced of Fiona Millar, Cherie Blair's personal assistant; and Alastair Campbell, whose resignation was also imminent, was accused by Andrew Gilligan on the *Today* programme of 'sexing up' the government's intelligence dossier, published in September 2002, claiming that Iraq possessed weapons of mass destruction. The continuing failure to find the WMDs prompted Clare Short to say, 'Blair duped us all along. We were misled. We were deceived.' The opinion polls reported that a majority of the population believed that Blair – 'Tony

B-liar' – had not told the truth. Doubts about Blair's veracity had shifted opinion among ministers and Blairite journalists towards Brown.

On 9 June 2003, the Commons was packed. Brown fidgeted on the front bench. He loved the limelight. Impatiently he waited for an inarticulate pensions minister to complete her statement before practically pushing her aside, piling three huge books onto the dispatch box and commencing a highly technical speech in praise of the euro, from which Britain, he claimed, could benefit by up to £3 billion a year, a mere £50 a year for every Briton. Brown's triumph could be seen in the misery on Mandelson's face. Four out of the five tests, Brown announced, had not been passed. That was the cue for the shadow chancellor Michael Howard. As Brown turned his back, Howard crowed: 'There they sit, united in rivalry, each determined to frustrate the other, to scheme against the other, to do the other down . . . Blair goes one way, Brown goes the other way, and bang goes the Third Way – lost in compromise and confusion.'

By the following morning, Howard's ridicule had been forgotten. Brown was sharing a press conference with Blair. That day's newspapers placed him at the centre of attention, accompanied by photographs of himself with Sarah, five months pregnant and under constant medical supervision. What was more, Brown was unaware that Alan Milburn had decided to resign from the government. The health secretary would plead the need to see more of his children, but to others it would seem that he had surrendered to the almighty chancellor. The prime minister appeared exhausted and even reticent. A growing majority believed that he had lied about WMDs in Iraq, and were unimpressed by his defeat on the euro at the hands of Brown. Earlier that morning Brown's spokesmen had playfully hinted that the chancellor's new enthusiasm for the euro had been induced by Blair's offer of a deal for the

succession. Asked to confirm that agreement at the press conference, both looked uneasy. There was neither denial nor
confirmation, which was sufficient to fuel more speculation.

Jackie Ashley was among those convinced that there had
been a profound change in their relationship. Less than four
weeks earlier she had written that Brown's hopes to be prime
minister were remote, but now she believed his accession
looked inevitable. The reason for this was her certainty of a
new, real deal. There might not have been a deal at Granita,
she wrote, but Brown's success over the euro had apparently
completely transformed Blair's plight. One year after the next
election, Brown's supporters were saying, the euro referendum would be fought and won, and Blair would hand over
power to Brown. By the end of the week Blair's popularity
had fallen further. Brown could look with satisfaction upon
the chaos of the normal summer ministerial reshuffle. The
abrupt dismissal of his friend Nick Brown, which four weeks
earlier would have been seen as evidence of his own weakness, was barely mentioned by a media bewildered by the
dismissal of the lord chancellor Derry Irvine, and the ill-
considered new constitutional proposals to abolish the post
and change the House of Lords. Tony Blair's slide implied the
unrelenting rise of Gordon Brown.

Ten days later, on 28 June 2003, Brown hosted a big party
at North Queensferry. Two hundred people were invited to
celebrate his twenty years as a member of parliament. The
event took place in a big marquee with real champagne and
'no great cuisine', and included many MPs representing the
awkward squad and Blair's critics. Ian Davidson, Bill Tynan,
Brian Donohoe and Mohamed Sarwar joined Alistair Darling
and Nigel Griffiths in wondering whether their host was on
the verge of becoming the new prime minister. Until that party,
Brown had discouraged his friends from discussing Blair's
departure. That evening, he encouraged the speculation,

especially during his hilarious fifteen-minute speech. 'He's manoeuvring into position,' those present agreed. The celebration was marred only by Charlie Whelan. Dressed in a kilt, unusual clothes for a south Londoner, Whelan argued with a member of the Scottish parliament. 'You fuckers are doing nothing in the parliament,' he shouted before being hustled out of the tent by local constituency workers.

The ecstasy of that weekend dissolved three days later. On 1 July Brown addressed the annual conference of the Transport and General Workers' Union (TGWU) in Brighton. The government's relations with the trade unions had deteriorated. Bill Morris, the retiring general secretary of the TGWU, was angry about the government's policies on PFI, immigration and pensions. Remarkably, he did not blame Brown for the pensions disaster, but Blair. John Edmonds, the leader of the GMB union, was also angry with Blair, not least for failing to appoint him as a minister in the House of Lords. 'I refuse to ever speak to Blair again,' he once said in half-jest. 'I'll only talk to Gordon.'

Brown could have used his influence to broker peace between Blair and the union leaders, but he preferred to avoid harming his own relations with men who would determine his own fate as party leader. His speech received an unexpectedly lukewarm reception in Brighton. As the politician responsible for Labour's election strategy, his theme was the Conservatives' threat to the NHS, his chosen battleground for the next general election. Effectively he was using the issue of the NHS's future to gather support. Yet his efforts to galvanise his audience in the dark hall by reminiscing about the union's proud history and by aggressive warnings about the dangers to the NHS failed. He pulled every emotional string, but the applause was muted and there was no standing ovation. Saving the NHS was clearly not a rallying cry for Labour's loyalists. On the platform, Tony Woodley, the

general secretary elect, explained the lack of reaction. His
members, he told Brown, were disillusioned by Labour's failure to reduce the widening gap between rich and poor, its
failure to repeal anti-union laws, and the war in Iraq. Woodley
received a standing ovation.

Brown returned by train to London in a sombre mood.
Woodley represented the new breed of trade union leaders.
None of them had had any exposure to mainstream political
life, but had emerged from minuscule enclaves. Woodley himself
had only recently joined the Labour Party, and wore his dislike
of his predecessor with open pride. 'You could see Bill Morris's
clawmarks on the walls as we kicked him out on his last day,'
one of Woodley's aides would boast, emphasising his disdain
for those who collaborated with New Labour. Even Brown
would find it difficult to forge friendly relations with such an
ideologue. Other union leaders were even more antagonistic.
These relationships required considerable work. In the meantime, Brown reasoned, his self-imposed silence would highlight
Blair's difficulties. He abandoned London to spend the summer
in Scotland to await the birth of Sarah's second child.

At the end of July 2003, Tony Blair overtook Clement Attlee
as the longest-serving Labour prime minister – six years and
three months. He spoke about his need to rebuild public trust.
Events had complicated that ambition. Dr David Kelly, the
government's expert on WMDs, committed suicide after
appearing before a House of Commons select committee;
Cherie Blair appeared in a fashion magazine posing in her
bedroom while Carole Caplin, with whom she allegedly
shared showers, painted her pouting lips; on 29 August Alastair Campbell resigned; and Blair approved the abandonment
of 'targets' and 'delivery'. Once again, Blair's vulnerability
was being debated.

Over the following weeks, Brown contemplated two conference speeches in the autumn – to the TUC and to the party.

Attacking Blair directly was inconceivable. To gather support, he needed to pledge his loyalty. His speech to the TUC on 9 September was written with his usual care. Once again he arrived expecting a warm reception. He listed Labour's achievements, gloried in the enterprise economy, praised Blair's 'strong leadership' five times, and made a few jokes. Long before the end of the speech, however, he sensed difficulties. His jokes fell flat, his praise of Blair backfired, and when he finished, the ovation was thin. Taking note of the unions' evident ill-will, Blair abandoned his own intention to ridicule the likelihood of the return of a left-wing Labour government to the same audience the following day. Both politicians left Brighton with contrary conclusions. While Blair wanted to defy the left, Brown returned to London to write a sermon for the party conference in Bournemouth at the end of the month about Labour's true values. He would emphasise the clear red water between himself and Blair.

During those weeks, his consultations were intense. Everyone assured the chancellor that the public was weary of spin, reheated Thatcherism and the seemingly unbalanced Downing Street wife with her bizarre entourage, and that he should capitalise on the prime minister's unpopularity and satisfy the yearning for tradition. He fashioned a tub-thumping speech, pandering to the party activists' prejudices.

On Sunday, 28 September, the eve of his speech, Channel Four broadcast *The Deal*, a television play dramatising the events surrounding the Granita dinner. The compelling production was biased in Brown's favour, and accordingly the newspaper previews portrayed him as the victim of a betrayal. Naturally, he refused to comment, but he was delighted by the speculation.

On the night of the programme Brown and Ed Balls were greeted by Geoffrey Robinson at the *New Statesman*'s annual party in the Royal Bath Hotel. The sight of the three laughing together was a reminder that Robinson's lack of candour had always been ignored by the chancellor.

The following day would be the climax of nine months of intrigue. In an anonymous hotel room half a mile away, Yvette Cooper, Ed Balls's wife, was working the telephones to gather support for the chancellor. Over the next forty-eight hours she would seek to influence delegates to vote in favour of foundation hospitals and against variable fees, swaying the mood of the conference in Brown's favour. Naturally, Brown would scathingly dismiss any suggestion of secret discussions and plots. No trace of evidence conclusively proving his disloyalty would ever emerge.

Brown's speech the following morning was crafted to delight and insult. Sixty-three times he mentioned the word 'Labour' as he sought to capitalise on the traditionalists' antagonism towards New Labour. 'I believe that at every point in our history Labour needs not just a programme but a soul,' he declaimed in a mesmerising homily reminiscent of a sermon from the pulpit calling upon the faithful to return to core values. He wanted a 'chain of hope' to encourage those striving for 'something more important than ourselves'. Long before its end, the speech was perceived as a bid for power, delighting the Brownites and annoying the Blairites. 'Have confidence in our principles . . . have confidence that Labour values are the values of the British people. The Labour Party [is] best when we are boldest, best when we are united, best when we are Labour.' There was a two-minute standing ovation.

The retaliation was planned before the gauntlet had hit the ground. Brown had allowed Blair to spot all his weakness. His oration was little more than a variation of a thousand speeches he had given over the past decade. Neither before nor after the speech had he adequately prepared his supporters to rally to his cause. The drama dissolved within an hour of the applause dying out. The anticlimax was confirmed the following day, 30 September.

Twenty minutes before Blair entered the hall, the atmosphere was fevered. Dozens of Blairites, scattered among the audience, were purposefully generating excitement. Blair's entry was dramatic. In an imaginative speech, he perfectly gauged his timing and audience with an alluring mixture of emotions. Unlike Brown's monosyllabic rant the previous day, he offered a modulated explanation and appeal for reform, and no retreat to the 'comfort zone'. Without Blair, the activists were left in no doubt, Labour would lose the next election. 'The true choice is forward or back,' he concluded. 'I can only go one way. I have not got a reverse gear . . . It's the only leadership worth taking.' There was a wild seven-minute ovation. Every member of the cabinet clapped enthusiastically, with one exception: Gordon Brown was photographed with a sour expression, his arms folded. Blair had won by conjuring the danger of the external enemy. Any notion of Brown's challenge had evaporated. He had rushed to Scotland, where his mother was ill. His opponents chortled that Blair would remain for at least another three years, possibly more. The insurrection had faltered, and worse. Later that week Blair told a confidant in anger that for the first time he no longer believed Brown would succeed him.

On Friday, 17 October, Sarah Brown gave birth to a healthy boy in the Edinburgh Royal Infirmary. He was named John, after his grandfather. Those visiting his house saw a smiling Brown, seemingly believing that his achievement was unique, a common blessing for all first-time fathers – even those aged fifty-three. The joy during his two weeks of paternity leave was occasionally suffocated by the old anxiety. The isolation of his home in North Queensferry rekindled the festering anger. Rather than relax his campaign for the leadership, Brown decided to intensify his agitation.

To disarm him, Blair had removed the chancellor from the Labour Party's National Executive Committee. Although the NEC was not as important as formerly, it would approve the next election manifesto and the campaign. At least twice Brown telephoned Blair and asked if he could remain a member. He was turned down. In between, Tony Blair spent nearly a day in hospital with heart palpitations. Brown's rejection by Blair, combined with reports that Mandelson was again frequently advising the prime minister, caused the new father concern. Mandelson, he knew, wanted the next election fought on the centre ground, supporting Blair's commitment to radical reform of the public services. Both he and Blair opposed wealth distribution. Blair had also asked Stephen Byers and Alan Milburn to help draft the manifesto.

Brown's insurrection was re-energised. Ignoring the inevitable damage that would result from the perception of a split, the *Daily Telegraph* was offered an article, which it published on 5 November, denouncing the EU in the language of the most uncompromising Tory Eurosceptic. To annoy Blair, Brown complained about 'Europe's rigidities, inflexibilities and lack of competitiveness'. In another newspaper he attacked the proposed introduction of identity cards, which was supported by Blair. And that night his spokesman telephoned four breakfast TV programmes offering interviews for the following morning about the pleasures of fatherhood. The next day's newspapers, Brown planned, would feature his anger about his exclusion from the NEC. He only found out about it, the newspapers were told, when he saw it announced on the Labour Party's website.

In each of his television appearances Brown would first describe the pleasure of changing nappies, then complain about his omission from the NEC, and finally deny that it was an issue. 'The decision was for the prime minister,' he said four times that morning. 'I've got plenty of things to do with

my time, with a very young son.' At 10.30 a.m. he was at a
cabinet meeting, mingling with bewildered colleagues before
launching an intemperate attack against identity cards. 'The
cost will destroy all your budgets,' he warned in a tone which
some complained was 'bullying'. His plan was to humiliate
Blair, who had advocated the introduction of the cards at
Bournemouth the previous month. But as he looked at the
ministers' faces, Brown realised that he was in a minority. He
could destabilise but not overthrow the prime minister. The
unopposed election of the shadow chancellor Michael Howard
that day as the new Tory leader, replacing the hapless and
ineffective Iain Duncan Smith, provided the balm. No other
politician in the Commons could destabilise Brown as effectively as Howard, and now the two would no longer face each
other directly over the dispatch box. The sudden transformation of the opposition, making a mockery of Philip Gould's
prediction three years earlier of the permanent extinction of
the Conservative Party, calmed Brown's emotions.

That night, Brown arrived at John Prescott's official flat in
Admiralty House for dinner. Tony Blair was also a guest. There
was an irony that the pugnacious Prescott, who had punched
a protester during the 2001 election campaign and had been
hostile to both Brown and Blair since 1994, should replace
Alastair Campbell as the peacemaker between the two.
Neither Prescott nor Blair was in any doubt that Brown was
deliberately agitating for a putsch. But both did doubt that he
possessed the courage or the parliamentary support to execute
his dream.

Prescott essentially told Brown, 'Gordon, you should one
day be the leader of the party. I want you to be the leader of
the party. Many others do as well. But the one thing that will
stop you becoming leader is if you continue trying to destabilise Tony. The party won't have it.' Brown's wrath was concealed by a well-rehearsed smile. By the end of the meal, the

three had agreed a public statement admitting and terminating their arguments. 'A line should be drawn on the events of this week,' said their spokesman, adding that Brown would be allowed to attend NEC meetings whenever he wanted, that he would be in charge of the next election campaign, and that in return he would cease attacking Blair in public.

Over the following days, Blair and Brown privately discussed their futures. Their intense relationship over twenty years had generated both suspicion and understanding. Blair's skill was to perfect the manipulation of Brown's insecurities. On this occasion, he raised the threat of a tarnished inheritance. Splitting the party, he reminded Brown, would not help his cause for the succession. The party would not forgive Brown for harming the chances of a third term. Blair explained how he wanted to secure his own place in history before retirement, and that required a third election victory to establish Labour as the natural party of government in the twenty-first century. He urged Brown to be patient, and to do his utmost in the next general election campaign. Labour would need a big majority in 2005, he said, to be sure of Brown winning his own majority in 2009. Brown owed loyalty, concluded Blair, to the Labour cause. He should not allow himself to be seen as a greedy wrecker. Both knew the dangers that loomed in the new year. Lord Hutton would report on the circumstances of David Kelly's death, and the Commons would vote on variable fees for universities. Criticism by Hutton or defeat in the Commons vote would endanger Blair's survival. On fees, he was particularly vulnerable. Both knew that Brown could influence the prime minister's fate.

Christmas 2003 was a particularly joyous occasion for Gordon Brown. Friends saw a new lightness in the chancellor's behaviour. Repeatedly he stood over his son's cot and smiled. His previous lack of public affection towards Sarah was replaced by a more solicitous attitude. Visitors were nevertheless struck by her coolness. While he played with the baby, Sarah sat at the table managing the domestic finances.

Over that holiday period he invited his closest friends to discuss his political future and to speculate about Tony Blair's fate. The state of Blair's health was unknown; the possibility of the government's defeat on university fees was real; and Lord Hutton's report raised the possibility of Blair's resignation. There could be a Brown government by summer 2004. Brown was not deluded. He had concluded that Hutton would not censure the prime minister. A reliable informant had revealed that the judge was writing a narrowly focused report on Dr Kelly's death, rather than highlighting the sensational disclosures about the controversial conduct of individuals who composed the intelligence dossier. 'Tony's clear on that,' Brown told his guests. 'Hutton will not criticise Tony.'

On variable fees, however, Blair was vulnerable. Over 140 Labour MPs were threatening to vote against the government. Brown was not yet discouraging the rebellion. Surprisingly, there was barely any resentment about Scottish politicians voting against the government on a bill that would not apply in Scotland. But since Brown's succession could be endangered by English MPs who opposed a Scottish leader, his best policy was ultra-loyalty. 'Heseltine,' he repeated. The anguish of the Tory politician blamed for toppling Margaret Thatcher and denied the leadership himself was a salutary lesson. If Brown was seen as responsible for bringing down the prime minister, he would not be thanked. Loyalty, even if fake, would eventually be rewarded. He was, Brown reminded his confidants, younger than most senior American politicians. Photographs with his baby John would reaffirm his youth. Although he was concerned by Michael Howard, an effective critic, no opposition in Britain's history had overturned such a huge parliamentary majority. Patience, Brown repeated, would be rewarded: 'The arithmetic is in our favour for the next election.' His friends were deceived. Brown was still manoeuvring for the succession. If Blair lost the vote on variable fees, he would be finished. Brown decided to show the limitations of his loyalty.

On Sunday, 25 January 2004, Brown volunteered to be interviewed on a breakfast programme. The key question he anticipated was whether Blair would still be prime minister at the next election. He prepared his answer precisely: 'Should he be? Yes. Will Tony Blair be? That's a matter for him.' He continued: 'Tony Blair has been a great prime minister for Britain and I think he has been a great leader of the Labour Party as well.' Those words were guaranteed to be endlessly analysed over the next twenty-four hours.

At 10 Downing Street, fearing defeat in the university fees vote, Blair's staff were franticly contacting dozens of dissident MPs. Next door, Brown's staff were completing their plans for a conference the following day at the Queen Elizabeth II Conference Centre, opposite parliament, called 'Advancing Enterprise – Britain in a Global Economy'. While Blair was fighting throughout Monday for survival, Brown was greeting Bill Gates and other international capitalists to listen to a succession of platitudinous lectures. Remarkably, after seven years there were no British tycoons, the products of Labour's 'popular capitalism', speaking. They did not exist. Gordon Brown's era had not produced a single outstanding entrepreneur – not one individual who epitomised 'Brownism'.

That failure matched the government's plight across Parliament Square. Brown knew that the government's majority was on a knife-edge. To avoid any blame, he had urged Nick Brown and the closest of his cabal to switch sides and support the government. His lobbying was conducted at high volume, so as to persuade Charles Clarke of his loyalty. To Clarke's irritation, some of Brown's alleged supporters rejected his entreaties, encouraging Brown's belief that Blair would be defeated. Indeed, until thirty minutes before the vote, Blair also feared defeat. In those last moments, two Labour MPs decided to support the government and three agreed to abstain. The government's majority on 27 January 2004 was wafer-thin – just five votes, but enough to defeat the latest threatened insurrection.

In the weeks following Tony Blair's survival, visitors to the Treasury remarked on Brown's happy demeanour. Many credited fatherhood. His confidants, though, credited Brown's conviction that Blair had finally committed himself. He would, Brown confided, resign eighteen months after the next election and support Brown's candidature for the leadership. Brown's enemies, however, told a different story. Blair, they said, intended to serve a full third term and resign during the fourth to allow the party to choose a leader, skipping a generation. Brown's cheerfulness suggested that he believed that his version was the accurate one.

TWELVE

Aftermath

'You'll never be prime minister,' Charles Clarke told Gordon Brown soon after Labour's election victory in 1997. Clarke, the most junior minister in the department of education, was unintimidated by a man whom he had disliked since the late 1980s.

Seven years later, in spring 2004, Clarke's judgement had not altered. Now secretary of state for education, he told his friends that Brown was not the automatic successor to Tony Blair. With little encouragement, Clarke volunteered that he would deploy all his efforts to prevent the chancellor becoming the next party leader and Britain's prime minister.

Unfortunately for Gordon Brown, Clarke's view attracted some sympathy. It was assumed that if a snap leadership election was held in early summer 2004, Brown would easily beat off a challenge from Clarke. But a majority of the cabinet and the parliamentary party still supported Tony Blair and, despite the erosion of public confidence in the prime minister, hoped that any question of the succession would be delayed for some years. They were not persuaded of any electoral advantage if Brown inherited the leadership before the next election. Blair might represent past aspirations, but Brown did not appeal to the majority of the party as the solution for the future. In the Blairites' opinion, the chancellor bore the aura of the twentieth rather than the twenty-first century. Deftly, Brown sought to change that impression while secretly undermining the incumbent.

The resistance to Brown coincided with the impression of him as a more self-assured person. He had shed his insecurity and, helped by deliberate silences, had adopted the status of a statesman. Some credited his frequent smiles to the hours he spent playing with his young son. Others explained his contentment by his assurance to close friends that 'It's all taken care of.' Blair's resignation, they understood, was certain by the end of 2005 – after a third election victory and a possible referendum on the European Union's constitution. Blair had, according to Brown, promised to endorse his candidacy for the succession, although he could not guarantee him the crown. A burst of praise for the chancellor from Blair appeared to confirm this. The prime minister's talent for saying what others wanted to hear rarely failed to seduce the credulous, and occasionally Brown ranked among their number.

He had little choice. Any trace of disloyalty which contributed to Blair's resignation would damage Brown's chance of succession. Although he discreetly encouraged his cabal to test Blair's strength and credibility, the chancellor feared the blame if his fingerprints were detected on any attempted coup. Since there was no evidence that, despite the prime minister's accumulated problems, Brown's popularity in Westminster had noticeably increased, he had no alternative but to accept Blair's truce until after the next election. He would ignore those who warned him of Cherie Blair's determination to prevent her husband's resignation. The 'first lady's' reasons were pertinent: she enjoyed the privileges of office, she was determined that her husband's legacy would not be besmirched by Iraq, and she hoped that an alternative to Gordon Brown would emerge. Others shared her prejudice.

Brown encountered one obstacle to his inheritance at
9.30 a.m. on 10 May 2004. The chancellor met Charles Clarke
near the Versace boutique on the second floor of Selfridges,
the central London department store, for a glitzy relaunch of
the government's 'Apprenticeships' scheme. Their audience
was 150 businessmen, civil servants and representatives of
various agencies. The expansion of the successful scheme vindicated Brown's campaign over the previous twenty years
to improve workers' skills. The presentation that morning
highlighted his dedication to improving society and his conviction of Labour's electoral invincibility. The Conservatives
would have been incapable of producing an equally slick commitment to education and industry. The comparison, quipped
one of the chancellor's friends, was 'the heavy mob versus the
local pickpockets'. The same might have been said of Brown
himself as opposed to Clarke.

The pair's philosophical disagreements had been highlighted the previous day. Five hundred miles north of London,
Gordon Brown had joined other Scottish politicians and the
Smith family to pay homage to John Smith on the tenth
anniversary of his death. In a service on the island of Iona,
the burial ground of Scottish kings in the Hebrides, the myth
was perpetuated that John Smith was the architect of Labour's
modernisation and the election victory in 1997. Privately,
Brown would have agreed with Clarke that Labour would
have risked losing the election if Smith had continued to lead
the party, although they would have disagreed about the
consequences of Smith's death. Clarke credited Tony Blair
with the vote-winning transformation of Labour, and disparaged Brown's contribution as irrelevant. He would have
endorsed the eulogy of the prime minister by the Reverend
Douglas Alexander, the warden of Iona and the father of
Gordon Brown's protégé, who spoke warmly of Blair's
achievements. Alexander's praise caused a frisson among the

congregation, some of whom, like John Reid, were Blairites if only to exclude Brown from the leadership. Others, like Lewis Moonie, the MP for Kirkcaldy who had been dismissed not long before as a junior defence minister, were declared Brownites.

Moonie's recent reaffirmation of his friendship to Brown served a purpose. In the reduction of Scottish seats at Westminster ordered by the Boundary Commission, Brown's constituency of Dunfermline East would disappear at the next election. The chancellor's search for a new seat focused on his home town after he heard that Moonie would be willing to retire in Brown's favour in return for a peerage. Brown's inheritance of Moonie's seat, however, had not been easy. Two other candidates with strong trade union support had seriously challenged his claim. Reflecting his position across Scotland, the chancellor's influence had weakened even in Kirkcaldy. The foundations of his power across Britain rested among the disgruntled rather than the optimistic.

At the end of the memorial service Brown had driven from Oban to Glasgow airport with John Prescott. Tony Blair's fate was being widely discussed in the media that weekend. The prime minister's U-turn to support a referendum on Britain's acceptance of the European constitution, his endorsement of Ken Livingstone as Labour's candidate in London's mayoral elections, the disarray of the government's immigration policy, and above all the continuing bad news from Iraq had prompted speculation about his resignation. Brown's position was enhanced, not least because he was masterminding Labour's election campaign for 2005.

Over the previous months the chancellor had carefully prepared the groundwork. He boasted about the government's expenditure, up from £322 billion in 1997 to an estimated £519 billion in 2005 to finance improved public services. He praised himself for creating the longest period of sustained

growth for two hundred years. Labour's heartlands were
reassured that the income of the poorest third of the population had increased by 12 to 15 per cent – about £1,000
annually – while the richest 10 per cent had lost 3.4 per cent
of their disposable income, or £1,600 per annum, in higher
taxes. So far there were few sustained complaints that taxation had risen from £261 billion in 1996 to £348 billion in
2002. Britain's economic boom, financed by £1 trillion of
private loans secured against the escalating value of homes,
had partially neutralised the middle classes' anger. Their general acceptance of the chancellor's repeated assertion about
Britain's most successful economy in a century remained
undisturbed by the reality that the leading shares in London's
stock exchange had fallen by 10 per cent in real terms since
1997, while Germany's Dax index had risen by 18.3 per cent
and New York's Dow Jones by 48.2 per cent. One of the
reasons for this stagnation, according to the World Economic
Forum, was the additional taxation and regulation introduced
since 1997, which had reduced Britain's global competitiveness ranking from fourth to fifteenth. Another was the
chancellor's excessive borrowing. In 2001 Brown had forecast
borrowing £30 billion over the following five years. In the
event he borrowed over £140 billion. That deterioration in
Britain's finances was camouflaged by the boom, which similarly concealed the cost of the country's unemployed.

Brown rightly claimed that the number of those employed,
28.35 million, was the highest in Britain's history – albeit that
37 per cent of them were employed by the public sector, a
record number over the past decade. Unemployment, based
on the number of benefit claimants despite Labour's former
criticism of the Tories' use of that measure, had fallen to a
historic low of 800,000. In reality, 1.4 million people were
looking for work. Even that number was a chimera. Only
74.9 per cent of the nation's potential workforce was

employed, the same as in 1990, and in poor areas like County Durham only 60 per cent were employed, while in London's East End the figure was just 54 per cent; 7.8 million adults were judged to be economically inactive, 250,000 more than in 1997. The unemployment statistics were also distorted by a threefold increase between 1990 and 2004 of those receiving incapacity benefits. Over one million unemployed in the old industrial areas had been diverted onto incapacity benefits – increasing the total to 2.7 million, a record, costing £16 billion every year.

Unemployment had fallen at the expense of the taxpayer, and not by an increase in the number of wealth creators. Compared to the 200,000 new jobs created in industry during Kenneth Clarke's chancellorship, 750,000 manufacturing jobs had been lost since 1997. In the three years since 2001, 160,000 jobs had been created in the public sector, all funded by increased taxation, compared to 98,000 new jobs in private business. Since 1997 an additional 500,000 people were employed by the public sector. Even Brown's crusade to improve productivity had failed. German workers were 16 per cent more productive than Britain's, and in France the figure was 32 per cent. One result was Britain's £33 billion trade gap in 2003–04, the biggest for two hundred years. The finance for that shortfall and the generator of economic growth was £1 trillion of private debt. The question of how that debt would be repaid when interest rates rose was ignored by the Treasury. In the late 1980s Brown condemned a similar situation, albeit amid high inflation, as 'boom and bust'.

The negative statistics, Brown knew, could remain shrouded from the public as long as his predictions were trusted, and his performance secured him that advantage. Although the Treasury had revised its forecasts four times since the budget in 2002, his own public reputation remained undented. Equally important was persuading the public of the government's success in having 'delivered' better health and education in return for the higher taxes. The method was professional. At a cabinet committee meeting on 4 March 2004 chaired by Tony Blair to discuss public service reform, Brown was presented with statistics compiled by the ONS showing that productivity in the public sector had fallen by 10 per cent since 1997. The fall in the health and education services was between 15 and 20 per cent. In other words, some of the extra billions of taxpayers' money raised by Brown was being wasted. The annual cost of the inefficiency, reported the ONS, was £20 billion. According to the minutes of the meeting, Blair directed the ONS to alter the presentation of those statistics to allow the government to present a more 'credible story'. As ordained, on 1 July the ONS officially announced that the NHS's efficiency, based on new data, had increased by 20 per cent rather than 10 per cent as previously estimated. The Statistics Commission criticised the revisions. The original revelation of waste mirrored a report of the Public Expenditure Committee which showed that the cost of government in 2003–04 had risen by 11 per cent to £21.3 billion, £1 billion more than estimated.

Labour, Brown knew, was vulnerable on waste. With some fanfare the Tories had commissioned the company doctor David James, to offer proposals aimed at saving between £60 and £80 billion from government expenditure during the next parliament. Brown suspected that in February the shadow chancellor Oliver Letwin would announce a grandiose plan to cut waste. Formulating cunning ruses to combat opposition policies was among Brown's specialities. But unfortunately for him, that year's budget meant that taxes could be neither raised nor reduced. Instead he would fight the Tories on their own ground. Soon after Letwin, as anticipated, pledged to save £35 billion a year by 2011, Brown delivered his retaliation, leaking a report by Sir Peter Gershon, the head of the government's efficiency review, that £15 billion a year could be saved by dismissing 80,000 civil servants. As a result the headlines reported that Labour would devote the savings to investment in the public services, while the Tory cuts would be used to reduce taxes for the rich. Letwin's critique was neutralised.

At first, few noticed the questionable substance of Gershon's report. He had criticised the large number of public service employees in human resources, the duplication of regulators, and the squandering of buying power among four hundred local authority purchasers. The unrealistic nature of his proposals was symbolised by his recommendation that the number of government purchasers be reduced to just four people to save £6 billion by 2008, a hallucinatory target. Throughout the eighteen years of Tory rule the only successful means of reducing the number of civil servants had not been to expect harder work by fewer employees, but to curtail the number of tasks undertaken by government. That option was rejected by Gordon Brown, who was steadily increasing Whitehall's involvement across the economy.

It required some audacity for Brown to propose cuts in government spending and dismissals of public employees when over 500,000 extra civil servants had been employed at his instigation since 1997, and to write his budget embracing Tory ideas. Nevertheless, with a flourish on 17 March 2004 he announced in the Commons that 40,000 public sector jobs would immediately be made redundant, and the £20 billion saved would be used on public services. His target, he said, was a 5 per cent cut in real terms in central government administrative costs over the next two years, reducing the cost of administration to proportionately less than in 1997. His ambition to save £20 billion each year by 2008 was described by the CBI as 'cosmetic' – a euphemism for unattainable – but Brown was beyond caring. He had achieved his aim, which was to inflict damage on the Conservatives' arguments.

In composing the details of his fourth Spending Review in July 2004, Brown was anticipating the next general election – possibly with himself as the party's leader. He would ignore his impetuous flourish to destabilise the Conservatives and return to his cardinal philosophy of increasing spending and state intervention to improve public services. Burying his original mantra in 1997 that Labour were 'wise spenders, not big spenders', he planned to increase government spending to £580 billion in 2007–08, a 42 per cent increase over a decade. Public spending as part of Britain's GDP would increase from 37.4 per cent in 1997 to 42.3 per cent. His somersault was complete. To finance that increase, he could not before the election raise basic taxes beyond the 13 per cent already imposed. Instead, he would promote himself as a waste-saver.

Brown, the author of many 'successful' programmes to save money and reduce staff, had already increased the number of civil servants by 500,000 since 1997, including more than 100,000 new employees over the previous twelve months. His headline target would be to dismiss 104,150 civil servants by 2007 and save £21.5 billion. Yet at the same time, he would recruit another 360,000 civil servants for 'front-line services' by 2006. The increase would be carefully minimised. Simultaneously, in an ultra-Thatcherite coup, he would announce the sale of state assets to raise £30 billion. All those savings – ill-defined and optimistic but pledged to save annually 2.5 per cent – were strikingly similar to Brown's pledge in 1998 to save 2.5 per cent annually by efficiency. Six years later, the Treasury admitted to MPs that meaningful measurements of the success of its new efficiency or savings had been impossible. In fact, every Treasury prediction since 1999 of lower administrative costs has proved to be inaccurate. Under Brown, costs have always increased, and the trend was unlikely to change. In writing the review in 2004, Brown was beyond caring about that inevitable history or the conse-

quence on judgement day in 2007. By then, he would hopefully be prime minister and perfectly capable of brushing aside
any criticism. His review would herald another step in winning a third landslide election victory. The only irritation was
Blair's insistence on fundamentally reforming the state institutions, especially the NHS and education, whose funding
Brown was massively increasing to £92 billion and £77 billion
respectively by 2007. Blair was again insisting on introducing
market forces into the state sector, using the catchword
'choice', both because he accepted Derek Wanless's recommendations and because the term would rob the Conservatives of an opportunity to counterattack. Brown could tolerate
'choice' so long as it was meaningless.

Accentuating the positive was hard for Brown. The compo-
sition of Labour's election manifesto had been entrusted by
Tony Blair to Stephen Byers and Alan Milburn. Both wanted
to offer new policies to deflect the criticism of Labour's failure
to deliver on its promises. Rather than defending past achievements, Byers spoke of 'a bold, ambitious manifesto of real
change', and proposed that the party should offer 'new,
radical' proposals for the future. While Byers repeated the
buzz word 'radical', Milburn emphasised the opportunity for
'choice'. Their coded assertion of Blairism was certain to
antagonise the traditionalists. John Prescott rejected the notion
that existing policies had been unsuccessful, although his entire
ten-year, £180 billion transport plan was to be abandoned,
while Brown dismissed the ideas as an affront to his agenda.

Experience had taught Brown that retaliation against the
Blairites was best achieved by using the same vocabulary,
albeit with different meanings. He would approvingly echo
Milburn's and Byers's mention of 'choice', 'change' and a
'reform agenda' in the NHS to undermine the Tory campaign,
but would insist that the manifesto would remain consistent
with 'traditional Labour values'. 'Choice' in Brown's political

lexicon was narrower than 'choice' in the Blairite free market. He would not tolerate any 'choice' which undermined the state's control of health. But within his financial constraints, he would encourage changes to increase value for money. The Blairites appeared powerless to overcome his veto.

Brown had so far avoided blame for the damage caused to the NHS, unlike the criticism he had attracted for damaging Britain's pensions and savings, for the costly chaos of tax credits, and for the expensive stagnation he had imposed on transport. In 1997 he had encouraged the wholesale jettison of Tory reforms, without considering the retention of any improvements. His tunnel vision had excluded original thought about the NHS other than the rejection of Tory reforms and the freezing of costs. Four shadow ministers of health in the four years before 1997 had failed to develop any policy other than opposing the Tories' changes. Derek Wanless had identified the cost of that failure in 2001.

The palliative in 2004 under Sir Nigel Crisp, the NHS's chief executive, was to restore some of the Conservative reforms but without relinquishing Whitehall's financial control. Crisp believed that by recruiting four highly paid 'business experts' and spending huge sums to develop new IT systems, one million NHS employees could become more efficient. He ignored Britain's failure to achieve that ambition in every nationalised industry since 1945. Brown also rejected that lesson of history. His belief that Britain's economy had entered a new era, breaking the historic mould with a permanent end to the risk of high interest rates and high inflation, was matched by a conviction that Britain's health service, unlike any other in the world, would flourish under centralised control. That remained, it appeared, the irreducible divide between himself and the Blairites. Yet even that difference, which he deliberately highlighted, appeared somewhat contrived.

In an article for the *Guardian* on 4 May 2004, Brown wrote under the headline 'Radical and Labour' that 'For Britain, this is a moment of great challenge.' The 'challenge' he described was identical to that he had outlined in 1997; and he repeated the same prescription for 'economic prosperity and social justice' he had outlined in 1994. The staleness was only relieved by his attack on Michael Howard for 'still trying to complete the unfinished business of the Thatcherite privatisation agenda'. Considering Brown's own privatisation of air traffic control, the partial privatisation of the London Underground and his proposal to privatise the Tote, it appeared that Brown's programme was quasi-Thatcherite, not least because of his support for wider home ownership, more competition, economic modernisation and denying the trade unions the restoration of their old rights. The confusion was deliberate. The chancellor wanted to retain the support of his old constituency while unobtrusively edging towards the Blairites.

The principal difference between Brown and Blair in 1997 had been the chancellor's devotion to spending billions of pounds on tax credits and his opposition to spending money on transport and the public services. Once that disparity had disappeared by 2001, with both being funded, Brown appeared to forge some differences between himself and Blair for effect rather than as a result of ideology. His status as the next leader depended upon presenting himself as an individual rather than merely a member of the team. To that end, while extolling 'teamwork' he constantly sought arguments with Blair, or provided an apparent refuge for the prime minister's critics. The dissatisfaction among Labour supporters with the government's conduct over Iraq stimulated Brown's popularity among the traditionalists although the chancellor, more Atlanticist than Blair and a declared friend of Israel, had supported the war. Ever the opportunist, in May 2004 Brown used the deteriorating situation in Iraq, especially the American attack on Muslim radicals in the western Iraqi town of Fallujah and the publication of photographs showing American soldiers abusing Iraqi prisoners in Baghdad's Abu Ghraib prison, to promote his own status at the expense of the Blairites.

The atmosphere was again feverish. Newspaper reports described Blair's 'loss of grip'. The legendary Downing Street news machine could not control an outburst of rumours that Iraq was Blair's Suez. The rising price of petrol, the rise in interest rates and wage rises of 5.2 per cent, substantially above the notional rate of inflation, evoked images of Blair's doom. Brownites were hollering about the pressure on Blair to resign. During the same week that Brown had paid homage to John Smith, Blair had told *Guardian* journalists that he would resign if he became a liability to his party and could not guarantee its re-election. The prime minister had gambled that by placing his future in play he would lance the boil and allow what he would one week later call 'the froth' to blow over.

The possibility of Blair's resignation was voluntarily raised by John Prescott in an interview with *The Times* on Saturday, 15 May. Prescott suggested that Blair might resign early, and that the race for the succession was under way: 'I think it's true that, when the plates appear to be moving, everyone positions themselves for it.' Ministers, confirmed Prescott, were repositioning themselves for the transformation. Considering his 'privileged discussions' with the prime minister, continued Prescott, he was sure that 'these decisions will look after themselves, they are very personalised'. Gordon Brown, Prescott concluded, would nevertheless not be blessed by an automatic coronation.

Prescott's candour inflamed the speculation the following day, 16 May. A Scottish Sunday newspaper reported that he and Brown had been seen in the deputy prime minister's car at the Loch Fyne restaurant during their return from Oban to Glasgow airport the previous week. Rather than mention that they had stopped to allow Prescott to buy kippers, the newspapers inferred that the two were plotting the succession. The combination of Prescott's interview with *The Times*, leaks that Rupert Murdoch had met the chancellor twice during that week, Brown's silence, encouraging the perception of a split, and Blair's own comments to the *Guardian* sparked a week of frenzied reports about a plot to remove the prime minister. Eventually, Blair said coolly, 'I think I should get on with the job. I enjoy doing it.'

Throughout those days Brown remained equally cool. Blair's discomfort was enjoyable and the speculation about a Brown premiership and his probable cabinet was reassuring. He expressed no opinion about the situation in Iraq, realising that the appearance of anything other than ultra-loyalty would be fatal. The seventy Labour MPs in marginal seats who might trigger a real leadership crisis in order to save their political lives were still not convinced that the English middle classes would support a Scottish redistributionist rather than Blair. Those who might have switched to Brown to save their careers were bewildered by his unpredictability. Part of a prime minister's skill is to forge and maintain a coalition of conflicting interests and personalities, but Brown's chancellorship was characterised by conflict. Unlike Blair, he did not proffer platitudes and compromises to those he disdained. Rather, he harboured grudges and gave vent to venomous outbursts. He had proved himself to be unclubbable unless the club was his own. The doubters found the intense loyalty of his cabal frightening. The obsessive secrecy – bordering on *omerta* – demanded by their chieftain was unattractive. The protection of Brown's privacy aroused suspicions. However much he smiled, the concealment of his emotions combined with an apparent incapacity for self-doubt were eerie to natural Blairites. Unlike the prime minister, Brown was instinctively unwilling to embrace foes and placate the outraged. He lacked the essential attributes of emollience and encouragement to gather a coalition of competitors to respect his leadership. Despite Blair's plight, Brown sensed the absence of any increase in his own support. On 17 May he called upon his supporters to dampen the speculation. He wanted to eschew any responsibility for a dirty campaign before the European and local elections on 10 June.

By coincidence, during those days Jonathan Powell, Blair's chief of staff, had encountered Boris Johnson, the Conservative MP, at traffic lights in central London. Unthinkingly, Powell replied to Johnson's question about whether Brown was likely to become prime minister with remarkable candour: 'It's a Shakespearean tragedy. Gordon Brown is like the guy who thinks he's going to be king and never gets it. He's never going to be prime minister.' Asked why not, Powell replied, 'Oh, you could never get a Scot as prime minister.' Inadvertently, Powell had expressed the reservations of the majority. The English middle classes who would determine Labour's chance for re-election were instinctively prejudiced against Brown.

Brown appeared powerless to overcome that hurdle. The party's poor results in the June local government elections, reflecting on Blair rather than himself, might have prompted the prime minister's resignation, but so long as the Tory challenge was weak, the chancellor was compelled to pledge his loyalty and to wait. Brown rewrote a speech for the Social Market Foundation to reaffirm that he and Blair were working on a programme of 'radical' reform of the public services that 'will go on and on'. His dilemma was how long Blair himself would go 'on and on'.

In June the tension once again became intolerable. While Brown had volunteered in an interview that Blair would probably remain prime minister for at least two more years,

he started again privately to mention the need for his departure before the election. The economic forecast, Brown knew,
was discouraging, and he feared the repercussions on his
reputation.

On 16 June, Mervyn King, the governor of the Bank of
England, publicly warned Brown – standing three places to his
right at the Mansion House dinner – about the government's
excessive spending and the danger of rising interest rates.
House prices, said King, were too high, and threatened to
destabilise the economy. Brown stared expressionless at the
governor while Ed Balls, certain of his nomination on 30 June
as the prospective parliamentary candidate for Normanton,
checked for messages on his mobile phone. The apparent nonchalance of both men belied their concern. King's warnings
were discomforting, but worse was the materialisation of yet
another sensitive milestone in the battle for the succession.

Brown had convinced himself five weeks earlier that Blair
might resign during July. Burdened by aggressive criticism,
especially over Iraq and a family crisis, Blair appeared to
Brown to be wilting. Physically and emotionally, the prime
minister seemed unusually detached. The chancellor persuaded himself that Blair had pencilled Friday, 9 July as a
possible date for his resignation. But as the days passed, Brown
noticed that key Blairites – the cabinet antagonists – were
urging the prime minister's importance to the party's election
victory. He suspected that they were encouraging Blair to
remain, undoubtedly keenly supported by Cherie. In that
atmosphere, any public indication of a Blairite move against
himself would be incendiary, and Charles Clarke would not
be shy to admit that he had visited Blair, 'because I very much
wanted him to stay . . . There was a rather frenetic atmosphere
and you never quite know how people react to those situations.' Brown remained quiet, but was irrepressible after the
next inflammatory revelation.

Derek Scott had submitted his memoirs to the cabinet office for approval. After six years of humiliation by Brown and Balls, parts of the manuscript not surprisingly reflected a torrid account of life in Downing Street. Based upon a diary and a collection of papers, Scott's book described the arguments between Blair and Brown about the euro, pensions and tax credits. Brown suspected that Scott's revenge – to be published during the party's annual conference in late September – had been encouraged by Blair's advisers. The public revelation of Scott's intentions on Sunday, 27 June, and the failure of Blair's spokesman quickly to affirm that the government would not sanction the breach of confidence, provoked from Brown that night an anguished scream of fear. 'This deliberate peddling of lies and distortions about Europe, tax and public spending and the management of public finances,' his spokesman announced, 'is deliberately designed and orchestrated to put the Treasury in a bad light and will not be tolerated.' Brown was convinced that 10 Downing Street was undertaking an 'orchestrated' campaign to smear his reputation. The aspirant's patience was being tested without any promise of early relief.

His allies would choose their moment, in early July, to whisper that Blair had considered resigning six weeks earlier. The destabilisation of Blair on the eve of the Butler Report into the conduct of Britain's intelligence agencies during the Iraq war, and of two by-elections, was intended to strengthen Brown's morale. Yet, despite the disappointments of Blair during that week, the conspirators failed. Although newspaper headlines described Butler's report as a semi-whitewash, and there was one by-election defeat, Blair resolutely decided to accept the wishes of the majority of the parliamentary party and remain its leader. He would stay in Downing Street, he assured his friends, for the foreseeable future. Brown was distraught. Years earlier, the Reverend John Brown had

extolled his congregation to emulate Churchill and Ernest
Bevin. 'Should not all of us,' he asked, 'like these two states-
men, have set objectives which we are determined to attain?'
Gordon Brown had still failed to achieve his Herculean task.

'There are only two alternatives in this world,' Napoleon said
after his disastrous retreat from Moscow in 1812: 'to command or to obey.' Gordon Brown has always wanted to command, but unlike Napoleon he lacks the aura of invincibility
that compels widespread adulation. His presence does not cast
the spell of an idol. Rather, his image is of a talented but
tarnished aspirant.

Under Brown's command, Labour has won plaudits for
economic competence. To some, that success seems a mirage,
but the majority believe his achievements are fundamental
and sustainable. Although his primary triumph – granting
independence to the Bank of England – was unveiled five
days after taking office, and no other major innovations have
followed, he has infused a new professionalism throughout
the Treasury and into Whitehall. The results are controversial
– profligate rather than prudent – but his imprimatur cannot
be denied. Contrary to forecasts, the debate for the new three-
year spending round was concluded in July 2004 without
bloodshed. By cajolery, he had taught a generation of Labour
politicians the painful lessons of the 1980s. In passing the
milestone on 16 June 2004 as the country's longest-serving
chancellor, Brown had acquired an unchallenged reputation
for personal competence. Whether that contemporary accol-
ade will be sustained by history remains debatable, but para-
doxically the milestone was an unwelcome achievement for
a man desperate to become prime minister.

Eventually Gordon Brown's opportunity for the premiership will arise, but in circumstances which remain frustrat-
ingly uncertain. Probably, and deservedly, his bid will be

successful. The power of the office might evoke hitherto
unseen qualities to silence the critics and cynics. Brown himself would certainly hope that having devoted his life to public
service and improved conditions for mankind, the fulfilment
of his ambitions would result in a government of unique
achievement, rated as a cornerstone of Britain's history alongside the premierships of Robert Peel, William Gladstone and
Margaret Thatcher, all politicians who broke the mould and
shaped the nation's destiny. That remains his challenge. Curi-
ously, even after he has spent seven years as chancellor, the
substance of a future Brown government remains an enigma,
reflecting the unresolved conflicts bedevilling the man himself.

ACKNOWLEDGEMENTS

Many people have generously given substantial help in the research of this book. Despite Gordon Brown's objections, over 150 of his friends and colleagues across Britain were interviewed. Most, for obvious reasons, asked to remain anonymous. Among those I would like to thank publicly are Jimmy Allison, Tim Ambler, Saul Billingsley, Robert Chote, Ken Clarke MP, Michael Crick, Tam Dalyell MP, Caroline Daniel, Frank Dobson MP, Vivo Doran, Derek Draper, John Edmonds, Richard Elson, Anne Evans, Dr Gillian Evans, Frank Field MP, Howard Flight MP, the late Paul Foot, John Forsythe, George Foulkes MP, George Galloway MP, Bryan Gould, Robert Harris, Roy Hattersley, Doug Henderson MP, Tim Holt, Will Hutton, Jim Keddie, Peter Kilfoyle MP, Neil Kinnock, Anne McElroy, Andy McSmith, Michael Meacher MP, Peter Morgan, Ken Munro, George Osborne MP, Michael Prescott, Charles Reiss, Paul Routledge, Mark Seddon, Barry Sherman MP, Jim Sillars, Chris Smith MP, Andrew Smithers, the late Geoffrey Tucker, David Ward, John Ware, Mike Watts, Martin Weale, David Willetts MP and Jonathan Wills.

Initially, Gordon Brown intimated that he would agree to be interviewed. In spite of several requests for a meeting, he failed to reply to my calls and letters. In a chance meeting outside Westminster Cathedral, his last words to me were, 'I'll get back to you.' He didn't. I have always been invigorated by the calculated snubs of the rich and powerful;

and the obstruction in this instance was as stimulating as ever.

In researching the book I was helped by three people. Mark Hollingsworth was particularly resourceful, leading me into areas and to people I had not considered, and was generous with his guidance. I am very grateful for his assistance. Barrie Penrose, an old friend, was as always brilliant in unearthing the unfindable and delivering gems. I am, as always, grateful to Oliver Figg who is a hard-working and loyal researcher, and who helped me avoid many pitfalls.

The legal work was done as usual by David Hooper. I am grateful to Michael Fishwick and Robert Lacey at Harper-Collins for their excellent editorial expertise. Thanks to Mike Shaw, my old agent, now retired, and Jonathan Lloyd at Curtis Brown for their help and friendship. As always, nothing could have been achieved without the support and love of my family.

SOURCE NOTES

Chapter One: Ghosts and Dreams

3   'My father was' Paul Routledge, *Gordon Brown* p.25
5   'Being brought up' *Evening Standard* 5 March 1993
6   'I don't think' *Telegraph Magazine* 18 November 1989
7   In successive weeks Paul Routledge, *Gordon Brown* p.32
8   'The inheritance of' ibid. p.36
11   'I felt such' *Daily Telegraph* 27 November 1997
15   'I don't know' Paul Routledge, *Gordon Brown* p.253
20   'It was quite' *The Times* 17 November 1988
20   'They forced me' Paul Routledge, *Gordon Brown* p.68
22   'I was almost' ibid. p.67
26   'The older people' ibid. p.71
27   'genuinely believed people' *Independent* 17 May 1994
30   'I never stopped' *Harpers & Queen* August 1992
37   The scoop, *The Times* 5 November 1982
37   'I am sure' Paul Routledge, *Gordon Brown* p.328
41   '80 per cent' ibid. p.124

Chapter Two: Metamorphosis

48   'would deter the' *Guardian* 5 October 1984
51   'I wasn't ready' Paul Routledge, *Gordon Brown* p.130
52   'A raid on' *Daily Telegraph* 16 May 1985
55   'put a cap' Paul Routledge, *Gordon Brown* p.140
61   'Britain is fast' *Daily Telegraph* 20 May 1988
61   'share option millionaires' *Guardian* 15 October 1987
63   Walking through the *Guardian* 27 October 1988

63   A few, aggressively *Daily Telegraph* 7 November 1988
64   'improved and becoming' *Mail on Sunday* 12 February 1989
64   'The government's real' House of Commons, 14 November 1988
64   'the most serious' *Daily Telegraph* 7 January 1989
65   His incandescence at *The Times* 31 January 1989
65   One day he *Independent* 4 January 1989
65   another day he *The Times* 28 April 1989
65   he trumpeted a *The Times* 20 March 1989
65   'this is the' *Guardian* 29 October 1986
66   'rising can turn' *The Times* 17 November 1988
67   John Smith sympathised *Guardian* 27 October 1989
70   There was nevertheless *Evening Standard* 5 November 1992
71   'I think most' *Telegraph Magazine* 18 November 1989
72   'single, reticent, good' ibid.
74   In crude terms *Observer* 28 October 1990
74   He failed to *Daily Telegraph* 31 January 1991
75   'markets [which] cannot' *The Times* 6 February 1990
79   His references to *Daily Telegraph* 2 October 1990
79   'vision for the' *Mail on Sunday* 14 April 1991
79   Those apparent conflicts *Tribune* 17 January 1992
80   his latest had *Financial Times* 1 July 1991
80   By spring 1991 *Sunday Express* 14 April 1991
81   'the causes of' Paul Routledge, *Gordon Brown* p.163
85   'Marriage is something' *Sunday Express Magazine* 29 September 1991
87   'strictly commercial lines' *The Times* 23 May 1990
87   'new agenda for' *Mail on Sunday* 5 January 1992

Chapter Three: Turbulence

93   Some observers wondered *Evening Standard* 28 July 1992
94   'to change our' Paul Routledge, *Gordon Brown* p.168
94   'a selfish, indeed' ibid. p.166
95   The state itself *Tribune* 17 July 1992

95   'The truth is' ibid.

96   'Labour,' warned Smith *Guardian* 24 August 1992,
       Evening Standard 27 August 1992

96   'There are those' *Sunday Express* 6 September 1992

97   In 1997 he Paul Routledge, *Gordon Brown* p.168

98   the 'current mess' *Tribune* 9 October 1992

100   'betraying Europe' *Evening Standard* 28 September 1992

100   'managed exchange rates' *The Times* 19 September
       1992, *Daily Telegraph* 29 September 1992

101   'harbouring dangerously revisionist' *Tribune* 1 January
       1993

102   'Labour rejects the' *Tribune* 25 September 1992

102   'a party of' *Independent on Sunday* 3 January 1993

103   'doing well out' *Evening Standard* 18 March 1992

104   'The Democrats' campaign' *Evening Standard* 8 January
       1993

104   Since 1988, Brown *Tribune* 1 January 1993

105   'We do not' *Evening Standard* 18 March 1993,
       17 February 1993

106   To improve those *Guardian* 17 February 1993 Brown
       article

106   'I see the' *Guardian* 13 March 1993

107   Smith supported large *Independent* 25 January 1993

107   'dishonest and incoherent' *Daily Mail* 7 January 1993

108   Even John Smith's *Daily Telegraph* 18 February 1993

108   Blair's insistence on *Guardian* 19 July 1993

112   'The Tory Party' *The Times* 1 May 1993

112   'public hammering' *Tribune* 25 May 1993

114   'invest and grow' *Guardian* 30 April 1994

114   With gusto, Brown *The Times* 29 July 1993, *Daily
       Telegraph* 18 August 1993

114   He would no *The Times* 19 September 1992

115   'Brown Demands Higher' *Daily Mirror* 27 September
       1993

116   Shedding Labour's traditional *Daily Mail* 28 September
       1993

118   'The Tories lied' *The Times* 14 January 1994

118   'They're incapable' *Daily Telegraph* 2 December 1993

118   'Unlike the Tories' *Sunday Mirror* 10 April 1994
119   'During prime minister's' *Independent on Sunday*
       2 March 1997
121   'Yes, for about' *Sunday Times* 23 December 2001
122   Smith repeated this *Sunday Telegraph* 1 December 2002

Chapter Four: Retreat

128   Inside the house John Rentoul, *Tony Blair* p.224
129   English socialists *Daily Mail* 13 May 1994
130   'I said Tony' James Naughtie, *The Rivals* p.62
132   'He's an iceman' *Evening Standard* 19 May 1994
134   'Because I'm not' *Evening Standard* 3 September 1996
138   a compromiser who *Independent on Sunday* 2 June 1994
141   'We always did' *Daily Telegraph* 27 February 1997
141   'a rare politician' *The Times* 29 April 1996

Chapter Five: Seduction

151   'What's going on' *Daily Mail* 30 June 1997
152   'I want the' *The Times* 28 June 1995
153   Failed industries *Financial Times* 3 October 1994
155   'the single most' Margaret Thatcher, *The Downing Street
       Years* p.421
156   'to use the' *Evening Standard* 12 July 1994
157   'I learned from' John Campbell, *Margaret Thatcher* p.85
157   'I want our' *Daily Mail* 30 April 1996
157   Among his confidants *Tribune* 7 October 1994
158   'no taxation without' *Daily Telegraph* May 1995
158   'The only tax' *Guardian* 29 September 1995
158   There were endless *Daily Telegraph* 14 February 1995,
       Daily Telegraph 4 October 1994, *Daily Mirror* 17 July
       1995
159   'Middle- and lower-' *The Times* 8 June 1995
159   'Once millions opt' *Guardian* 13 March 1993
162   'The fact that' *Daily Mail* 5 August 1995
164   He was judged Geoffrey Robinson, *The Unconventional
       Minister* p.82

168   'no massaging of' *Evening Standard* 2 October 1995,
       Daily Telegraph 3 October 1995

168   'Tough choices have' *Times* 2 October 1995

168   Brown pledged that *Daily Telegraph* 9 November 1995,
       22 November 1995

169   'reward hard work' *Guardian* 20 November 1995

169   'hugely expensive' *Daily Telegraph* 5 September 1996

169   'Gordon has done' *Daily Telegraph* 23 November 1995

169   means testing remained *Daily Telegraph* 24 November
       1995

170   'dangerous obstruction' *Evening Standard* 15 May 1996

171   'core idea' Paddy Ashdown, *The Ashdown Diaries* p.134

171   'there are no' *Daily Mail* 16 May 1996

171   'like scorpions in' Donald McIntyre, *Mandelson* p.332

171   An attempt by ibid. p.325

173   no one in *Sunday Times* 19 May 1996, *Sunday Express*
       16 June 1996

175   'I've never been' *Sunday Times* 23 December 2001

175   'absolutely necessary' ibid.

175   Stories appeared in *Sunday Times* 26 October 1997

175   'leadership by *diktat*' *Guardian* 14 May 1996

177   'a more effective' *Independent* 21 November 1997

178   'one of the small' *Evening Standard* 8 November 1996

178   'this is too' *Financial Times* 17 January 1997

178   Brown would later *New Statesman* May 1997, special
       issue

182   'one of his' *Daily Express* 13 March 1995

184   'ridiculous and untrue' *Evening Standard* 3 September
       1996

185   all of whom had *Sunday Times* 16 October 1994

186   In effect, he *Daily Telegraph* 26 November 2002

187   'We live in' *Times* 24 July 1996

187   'the importance of' *Guardian* 2 August 1996

188   he would make it *The Times* 24 July 1996

188   Government grants would *Guardian* 2 August 1996

188   'Work as the' *The Times* 27 February 1997

188   'where they create' Sam Brittan, *Financial Times*
       14 February 2003

189 'So it isn't' *Daily Mail* 30 January 1997
190 'generalised statements which' *Mail on Sunday*
     24 September 2000
190 The corollary was *Guardian* 26 July 1996
190 'vast black hole' *Independent* 24 March 1997
190 'Lies. It's the' *Daily Telegraph* 21 November 1996
190 'Our prudence and' *The Times* 11 October 1996
191 Labour would not *Evening Standard* 5 February 1997
191 'a complete waste' *Evening Standard* 11 February 1997
192 'demoted' *Independent* 11 March 1997
192 Policy, said Cook David Lipsey, *The Secret Treasury*
     p.193
192 snapped defiance after *The Times* 10 April 1997
192 'improve mutual understanding' *Independent* 20 June
     1998

     Chapter Six: 'Do You Want Me to Write a Thank-You Letter?'

200 'We've had a' *Daily Record* 23 May 1997
202 Strangely, Margaret Thatcher John Campbell, *Margaret
     Thatcher* p.22
203 'the repository of' Geoffrey Robinson, *The
     Unconventional Minister* p.183
204 Brown found it William Keegan, *The Prudence of Mr
     Gordon Brown* p.182
206 Five years later *Evening Standard* 26 June 2002
208 That was good William Keegan, *The Prudence of Mr
     Gordon Brown* p.183
217 Instead, he went *Evening Standard* 21 May 1997
217 'I'm pledging "honesty"' *Evening Standard* 30 June 1997
218 'There is widespread' *Financial Times* 26 May 1997,
     Mail on Sunday 29 June 1997
218 'reasonable' to assume *Evening Standard* 30 June 1997,
     Daily Mail 20 June 1997
218 'a series of unforced' Geoffrey Robinson, *The
     Unconventional Minister* p.56
219 'what had gone' ibid. p.57
219 'the Treasury's tendency' ibid. p.56

219   'clear and firm' ibid. p.54
220   'Gordon then looks' Scottish Television film
221   'I have nothing' *Evening Standard* 3 September 1996
222   Actuaries sent evidence *The Times* 31 March 1997
223   Privately, he urged *Mail on Sunday* 6 July 1997
223   He ignored them *Guardian* 16 April 2002
224   'If it were' *Daily Mirror* 3 April 1997
224   'Gordon fucks loads' *Daily Mail* 22 December 2001
224   'The handsome personification' *Guardian* 3 June 1997
228   'catastrophic collapse' *Tribune* 13 March 1992
228   100 per cent tax relief NAO Report on Film Council
229   'Gordon wants to' *Daily Mail* 30 July 1997
229   The manoeuvre reinforced *Daily Mail* 19 January 1998
230   'There is no' *Evening Standard* 9 May 2001

Chapter Seven: Fevered Honeymoon

240   'I was pleased' Geoffrey Robinson, *The Unconventional Minister* p.100
240   'official economic statistics' Nigel Lawson, *The View from Number 11* p.845
241   The resulting picture *Mail on Sunday* 30 November 1997
241   'to turn Britain' *Independent* 6 February 1998
245   Brown refused to *Guardian* 16 April 2002
245   'We've got a' *Sunday Telegraph* 6 July 1997
245   'There's no loose' *Daily Mirror* 24 November 1997
246   'Charlie Whelan's doing' *Daily Telegraph* 5 January 1999
246   'If you're not' *Sunday Times* 23 December 2001
248   Brown, it was *Financial Times* 27 September 1997
251   'an economic crossroad' *Evening Standard* 20 October 1997
252   'early in the' *Daily Mail* 29 April 1998
253   'A Labour chancellor' 30 June 1994, quoted in *Observer* 14 December 1997
261   'We'll get these' Andrew Rawnsley, *Servants of the People* p.114

Chapter Eight: Demons and Grudges

266 'This is not' *Daily Telegraph* 20 January 1998
267 'prevent them getting' *Sunday Times* 23 December 2001
267 Both knew that *The Times* 22 April 1999
267 'I have always' *Daily Telegraph* 15 January 1998
268 He intended to *Daily Telegraph* 12 June 1998
269 'The British economy' *The Times* 17 April 1998
270 'I do hope' *Daily Mail* 1 August 1998
272 By mid-1998 House of Commons, 14 July 1998
273 Those ministers who Brown speech to IFS, 27 May
      1999; Treasury press release 86/99
275 'local authority capital' *Daily Telegraph* 28 September
      1998
278 'A Modern Agenda' *Daily Mail* 10 March 1998
278 He wanted the *Independent* 25 May 1998
278 'I've always supported' *Daily Telegraph* 15 April 1998
278 to £100 billion *Daily Mail* 24 April 1998
278 £108 billion *Daily Telegraph* 15 July 1998
278 '23 per cent' House of Commons Committee on Public
      Accounts, IR Tax Credits, 14th Report 2003–04 HC89,
      Ev.p.2; *Daily Mail* 15 July 1998
280 'How on earth' *Independent* 10 June 1998
281 'And that's before' *Daily Mirror* 3 April 1998
282 'a fucking brilliant' Geoffrey Robinson, *The
      Unconventional Minister* p.185
288 Tax revenues were chancellor statement, 4 November
      1998
291 Smith departed, unsure *Mail on Sunday* 27 December
      1998
291 'I won't sack' *Mail on Sunday* 3 January 1999
291 'Charlie is entirely' *Sunday Times* 3 January 1999
292 'It angers me' *Daily Mail* 7 January 1999
292 As usual, the *Daily Mail* 6 January 1999
293 To confirm that *Guardian* 1 March 2000
293 and he quoted *Daily Mail* 12 February 1999
294 The tax credit *Financial Times* 3 April 1999
294 'There's a great' *Daily Mail* 7 April 1999

294   'Everyone's a winner' *Daily Mirror* 9 March 1999
296   'a seamless system' *Financial Times* 28 May 1999
297   But the chancellor *Evening Standard* 4 August 2000
297   'Britain will lead' *Daily Telegraph* 22 February 2000
298   With Alan Sugar *Daily Telegraph* 17 February 2000;
       Daily Mail 23 February 2000; *Sunday Times* 27 February
       2000
298   'a punt' House of Commons Committee of Public
       Accounts, 29 March 2004 p.25
299   wasted £10 billion NAO Report, December 2000
299   Brown cited predictions Wolmar, *Down the Tube* p.149
300   Livingstone favoured financing ibid. pp.144–5

Chapter Nine: Enjoying Antagonism

302   'Greater Britain' *New Statesman* February 2000
303   'I want to' *The Times* 10 January 2000
303   £100 billion more *Evening Standard* 18 July 2000
304   4.67 per cent *Daily Mail* 29 March 2000
304   his approval ratings *The Times* 18 March 2000
304   an independent economist Holly Sutherland, *Daily Mail*
       28 March 2000
305   'Britain in 1997' *News of the World* 7 May 2000
305   providing faulty statistics *Sunday Telegraph* 10 October
       1999
308   The leaking of *Daily Mail* 30 January 2001, *Independent*
       8 February 2001
309   approximately £1 billion House of Commons, HC544,
       Ev.14
313   'We need to' *Daily Mail* 27 July 1999
314   'When Europe and' *Daily Telegraph* 26 July 2001
315   a Mori poll *Evening Standard* 1 November 1999
317   Brown ignored him *Mail on Sunday* 2 July 2000
318   'Oh, I do' *Daily Mail* 1 August 1998
326   'fictional nonsense' *Daily Mail* 21 March 2001
326   Thereafter, they agreed *Sunday Times* 11 February 2001
326   'It is a' *Independent* 18 October 2000
327   'I won't be' *Guardian* 17 February 2001

327   'most popular chancellor' *Daily Telegraph* 10 March
      2001
327   'the master of' *Daily Mail* 7 March 2001
331   'We have set' *Daily Telegraph* 15 July 1998
332   the extra expenditure *Panorama*, 13 March 2000 and
      3 June 2001
332   'It's a long-term' *The Times* 3 February 2000, *Mail on
      Sunday* 23 January 2000
333   no more nurses *Evening Standard* 28 March 2000
334   NHS in Scotland CPS Report, 2003
335   Despite his assertion *The Times*, Brown, 'Let the People
      Look After Themselves'
337   Instead of stopping House of Commons, HC544, Ev.9
337   40 per cent *Daily Telegraph* 1 February 2001
337   'paying less tax' *Evening Standard* 28 March 2000
338   With the exception *Daily Mail* 17 April 2000
338   Tim Ambler's research Tim Ambler, London Business
      School
338   Brown's critics on *Daily Mail* 2 February 2001
339   Only 5,000 of *Financial Times* 23 June 2003
339   Britain's poorest had IFS 'Green Budget', January
      2003
339   'help families, particularly' *Daily Telegraph* 6 January
      2001
341   Independent experts IFS, *Financial Times* 9 April 2003
342   The growth of *Daily Telegraph* 4 May 2001, Adam
      Smith Institute
342   Brown predicted that *Independent* 30 April 2001
343   His pride was *Guardian* 21 July 2003
344   'civic renewal' *Independent on Sunday* 13 May 2001
344   quangos and initiatives *Evening Standard* 9 November
      2000, *Daily Telegraph* 3 June 2000
345   The proof of *The Times*, Brown, 'Let the People Look
      After Themselves'
346   'In the 1980s' *Daily Mail* 19 June 2001
347   His own agenda *Financial Times* 5 April 1999
349   'Impossible' was the *Daily Mail* 18 November 2001,
      Independent 19 November 2001

Chapter Ten: Turmoil and Tragedy

365 'This is a' House of Commons HC544, Ev.4,
4 November 2002

368 explosion of fraud *Daily Telegraph* 11 December 2001

369 51 per cent *Daily Telegraph* 17 September 2002

369 extra £24 billion *Daily Mail* 12 April 2002

369 £35.8 million *Prospect* magazine

369 '1.2 million fewer' HM Treasury, 'Tackling Child
Poverty, December 2001, para 9, p.vi

369 Revenue's computer systems NAO report

370 officials had failed *Daily Telegraph* 19 June 2003,
15 May 2003

370 between £510 million NAO Report, *Financial Times*
20 November 2003

371 'an exemplar of' PAC 14th Report, May 2004

371 'serious questions about' House of Commons Treasury
Committee, 'Inland Revenue Matters', 10th Report of
Session 2002–03, HC834; *Sunday Telegraph* 26 January
2003

372 'nothing short of' *Financial Times* 22 April 2004

372 The running costs *Guardian* 17 September 2003

372 'letters of comfort' House of Commons Treasury
Committee, 'Inland Revenue Matters', 10th Report of
Session 2002–03, HC834, p.6; Paul Foot, *Private Eye*
special report

373 To the anger *Sunday Times* 10 March 2002, 7 April
2002

373 sanctions against Jersey *Daily Telegraph* 17 April 2002

374 'very hurtful' *Evening Standard* 26 June 2003, *Observer*
16 February 2003

374 'an unfortunate coincidence' Paul Foot, *Private Eye*
special report; Andrew Rawnsley, *Servants of the People*

375 'typographical error' *Independent* 10 July 2001

377 Frank Field called *Daily Telegraph* 19 November 2001

379 'The test now' *Daily Record* 23 May 1997

382 'On a day like' *Evening Standard* 27 November 2001

386 Investment in the *Observer* 27 January 2002

387   The recent discovery KPMG studies
390   To bury the *Daily Telegraph* 23 December 2002
391   'Today in Britain' *Mail on Sunday* 14 June 2002
392   from 2.4 per cent Amicus, *Financial Times*
       25 September 2003
392   1.5 per cent *Daily Telegraph* 28 March 2003
393   £93 billion over *Daily Telegraph* 19 July 2002
394   'He never says' *Daily Telegraph* 31 January 2003
394   'He has made' *Mail on Sunday* 21 April 2002
395   Alan Greenspan *Daily Telegraph* 26 September 2002

Chapter Eleven: Revolt

402   'Economics can never' *Daily Mail* 4 January 2002
402   'If you enter' *Daily Telegraph* 26 February 2002; *Daily
       Mail* 26 February 2002
402   by £10 billion *Daily Telegraph* 12 February 2002
403   reinforced Brown's credibility *Evening Standard*
       27 December 2002, *Daily Telegraph* 29 June 2002,
       Financial Times 23 October 2002
404   'Markets can't work' *Mail on Sunday* 1 December 2002
404   'duel to the death' *Daily Mail* 3 December 2002
404   arrogant non-team player *Times* 27 November 2002
404   'so difficult for Tony' *Daily Mail* 10 February 2003
405   'I started out' Jon Sopel, *Tony Blair: The Moderniser*
405   'Ever since this' *Daily Mail* 30 January 2003
406   3,000 new regulations BCC, February 2003
407   'Thanks. I've got' CBI, 6 March 2003
408   'I do not accept' *Daily Telegraph* 26 November 2002
408   He scoffed at *Financial Times* 30 January 2003; Carl
       Emmerson, IFS
409   His approval rating *Guardian*-ICM poll 18 February
       2003
410   Colman's report criticised *Sunday Telegraph* 16 June
       2002
410   25 per cent PAC Review, *The Times* 26 September
       2002, *Sunday Times* 17 November 2002, Labour
       Research Department

410   'strong evidence that' NAO Report, *Financial Times*
       5 February 2003
411   'grossly inefficient and' *Financial Times* 27 April 2003,
       House of Commons Transport Select Committee
412   'extremely reluctant' Winsor evidence, Transport Select
       Committee, HC239-ll, question 765
412   further £14 billion *Sunday Telegraph* 26 January 2003
418   'How I'll Start' *The Times* 15 October 2003
418   'Business Should Thrive' *The Times* 4 December 2003
419   from 35.6 per cent *Daily Telegraph* 28 July 2003
420   2 per cent less *Daily Telegraph* 17 April 2003, ONS
423   'the mistake is' Fabian Society
424   'a lot of lies' *Daily Telegraph* 19 May 2003
427   the euro referendum *Guardian* 12 June 2003

Chapter Twelve: Aftermath

443   the poorest third IFS survey
443   London's stock exchange CPS, 30 April 2004
443   Only 74.9 per cent *Guardian* 17 May 2004
444   7.8 million adults *Daily Telegraph* 28 June 2004
444   Over one million Centre for Regional Economic and
       Social Research, Sheffield Hallam University, *Guardian*
       22 May 2004
444   an additional 500,000 ONS, *Daily Telegraph* 27 May
       2004
444   German workers were National Institute of Social and
       Economic Research, *Financial Times* 30 April 2004
445   'credible story' *Sunday Times* 25 April 2004
445   £21.3 billion *Financial Times* 20 April 2004.
451   The rising price *Guardian* 13 May 2004
453   'It's a Shakespearean' *Spectator* 5 June 2004

INDEX